TIME TEAM'S Dig Village

"To Katie, Elliot, Olivia and Zoe — the next generation, and in memory of my dear friend, Mick Aston"

and to Faye and Alex my Swiss family.

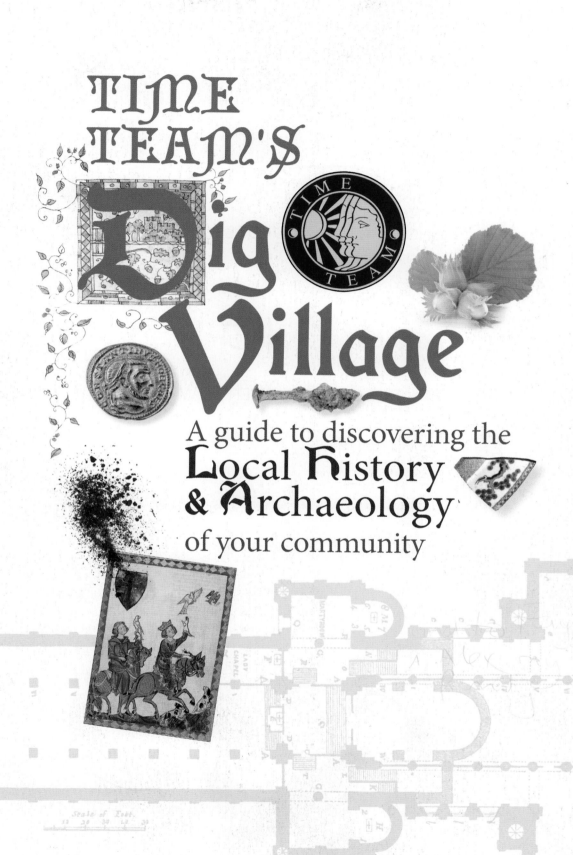

TIME TEAM'S Dig Village

A guide to discovering the Local History & Archaeology of your community

CONTENTS

II. Key Buildings

III. Documents & Resources

IV. Historic Background

V. Life Within the Settlement

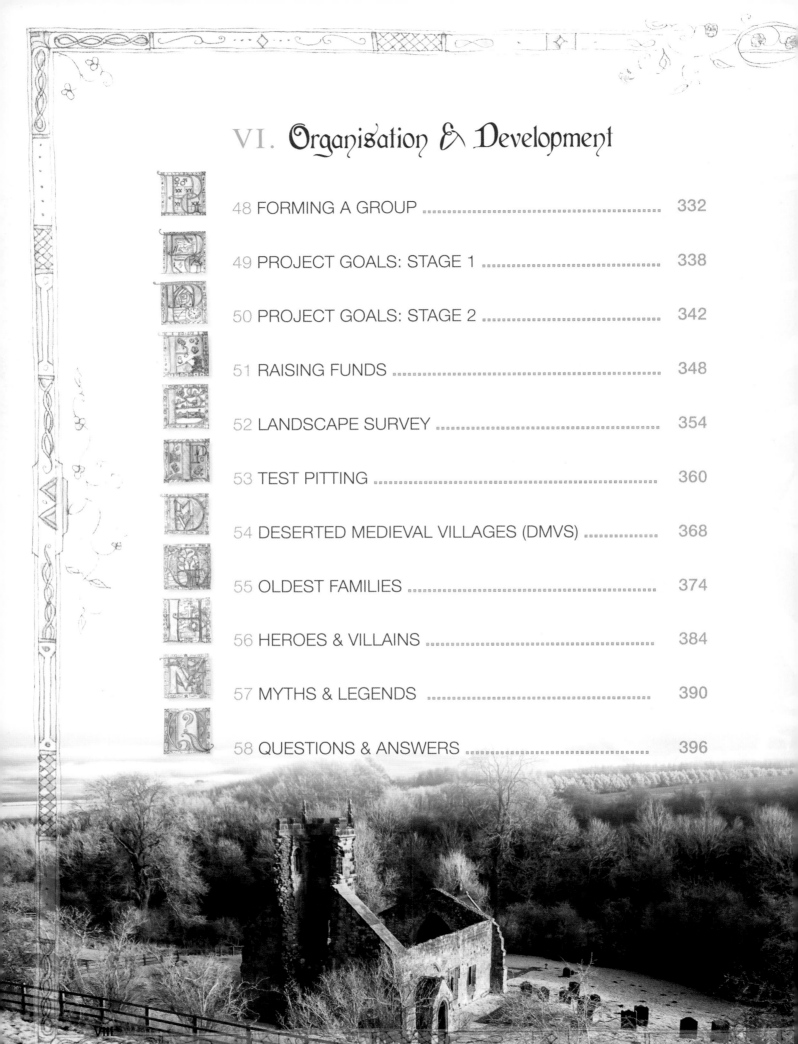

VI. Organisation & Development

VII. Outreach & Presentation

Reconstructions bring history to life

INTRODUCTION

Welcome to **Time Team's Dig Village**, the place where you can explore, discover and learn about the fascinating worlds of local history, archaeology and heritage. And it's all on your doorstep!

Your local villages and towns contain a wealth of fascinating information. Our goal is to help provide the tools and expertise needed to unlock their secrets, and then share them with a wider community. As you will discover, Dig Village is not simply a book. It's a comprehensive project, bringing together a host of resources, including a digital platform and online community, to build a better understanding of your local history and archaeology.

We hope you will enjoy reading this book, but also be encouraged to get out and about in your local community. We see this guide as a 'call to action': a practical 'how-to' manual, providing historic context, useful hints and professional insights to aid and stimulate your own active research.

We encourage you to engage your local community in the project, and then share your finds and insights with other enthusiasts on our social media channels. Together

we can build a fascinating and unique record of our villages and small towns. Simply put, Dig Village is a local history project on a national scale.

Decades of experience

The project draws upon wide-ranging skills and experience accumulated across 25 years of Time Team. We have gathered together the expert knowledge of many regular Time Team contributors, including the decades of experience that Professor Mick Aston accrued and shared with us. Sadly Mick is no longer with us, but his huge influence lives on. His work in the Somerset villages of Shapwick and Winscombe involved testing and refining many of the various approaches to the subject.

Over the following pages, we will pass these insights on in the form of basic skills and tips that will kick-start your journey towards becoming a local history and archaeology expert!

A village visit with Mick

One of the earliest memories I have of Mick, some 27 years ago, involved us exploring a small village near the site of the Roadford Reservoir in Devon. We were poking around in the back garden of an ancient cottage. The soil in the vegetable patch was black and crumbly and amongst the rather splendid vegetables we found small fragments of pottery. Mick lifted a mud covered fragment, gave it a clean and looked at it with all the interest of an explorer uncovering a Roman amphora. He had an ability to turn such an ordinary object into the starting point for a whole story about the life of people who had once occupied the house hundreds of years ago. Walking around the village, he talked about the street plan that was essentially Medieval and the layout of the houses that clustered around the church, which might represent the earliest centre of the settlement.

Mick Aston

The magic of artefacts

Although not exactly 'great' finds, the discoveries we made that day still delivered the magic that comes when, from a pile of soil, an artefact emerges that unlocks the past. It's a visceral process that delights all the senses. The smell of the soil, the rough surface of the pot, the small glittering pieces of quartz that caught the eye; these factors combine to make it just as

exciting to the local archaeologist as some exotic piece of decorated fine-ware from a foreign shore. The detective story of the origins of the village provides similar excitement, and both can set in motion a lifelong journey of discovery.

Our visit took place at the start of a series called Time Signs, the first step in the Time Team story and my first meeting with Mick and fellow archaeologist Phil Harding. That village exploration with Mick stayed in my mind. After many years of working with him and observing his enthusiasm and excitement for local archaeology, it seemed the right time to put these ideas together in a guide to help the ordinary amateur enthusiast get to grips with the subject.

Your own back yard

There is a famous classical quotation that says something to the effect that no piece of land is as dear to us as the acre or two that lies just outside our own backdoor. I think the same may be said of the discoveries that can be made there. Given the current interest in local values, the awareness of our carbon footprint and the contribution to wellness that local activities can promote, what you are hopefully about to undertake has many positive attributes.

Why it's important

The information you might uncover is important because the small towns and villages of Britain are the places where, as a nation, we have

LEFT *A dig taking place at Reeves Restaurant in Dunster*

ABOVE *Tim Taylor, author and creator of Time Team's Dig Village*

evolved. The shape of the landscape, the buildings, the churches, the community interactions that we have inherited began in small clusters of houses and farms that were the start of village life. The legacy of this is hidden beneath our modern villages and small towns, an archaeological and historic wealth of information waiting to tell its story.

In a way, Dig Village is about rediscovery. Often we have become so familiar with our local surroundings that we don't really see them at all! Yet once you know where to look and exactly what to look for, an individual story begins to emerge. Through unearthing this story, each and every village can illustrate an element of the key aspects of the way British settlements have developed.

How did your village begin?

A village or small town is essentially the coming together of a group of people to share resources and other advantages of a location because it benefits them to do so.

We know that in the Mesolithic period, sites tended to develop where there was a seasonal occupation of a spring or river site where animal carcasses could be processed.

On the coast we find the build up of shell middens (rubbish heaps), implying regular visits to that location. The form of shelter appears to be temporary and as yet there seems to be no commitment to a single site.

In prehistory the urge to settle, not to hunt and gather, must have been influenced by the events surrounding the start of farming. To plant a crop and wait for it to be harvested, to store the resulting grain with a view to replanting in the spring on land that has been cleared, implies a more settled existence. In the same way, a group of animals that are becoming domesticated have to be protected from predators and be cared for when the next generation is born.

In the late Bronze Age and early Iron Age, we begin to see the development of clearer boundaries that mark out territorial areas and the presence of settlements where a group of roundhouses mark a more permanent settlement. The Dartmoor Reaves have shown how early this sense of territorial space has been established as solid features in the landscape. Could our first 'villages' be said to date from this period? There is also the aspect of defensive safety here and the division of the landscape into areas that have a specific purpose. The location of Bronze Age barrows on sites that can often be seen from the settlement fits into this pattern.

The hillforts of the Iron Age provide the first examples of an enclosed space with ditches and other earthworks and settlement concentrated in a single location. When you are looking at your site it may be worth looking for Iron Age evidence. Faint glimpses of this can be found in many areas. It may be that the names of your rivers, for example, originate from this period.

Looking at the topography of your site (the shape of the landscape), what natural advantages would have appealed to the first settlers? A good supply of water from

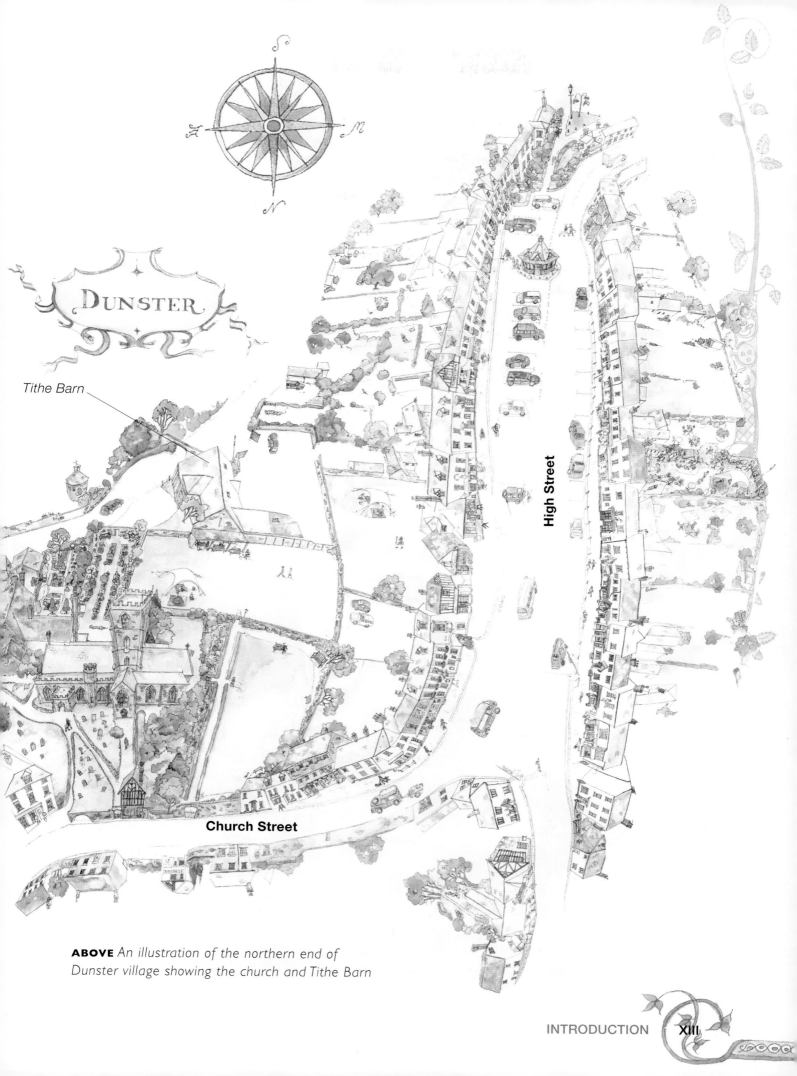

DUNSTER

Tithe Barn

High Street

Church Street

ABOVE *An illustration of the northern end of Dunster village showing the church and Tithe Barn*

rivers and in particular springs; an area of raised ground to provide a dry and secure base; and some fertile, south-facing slopes for planting crops have always had advantages from the prehistoric past to the present day. Even a relatively modern village may have had ancient origins and its secrets will be waiting in the archaeological record for you to discover.

Landscape archaeology and the community

As many Time Team fans will know, Mick was firmly committed to community archaeology projects and spent over ten years looking at two small villages in Somerset, Shapwick and Winscombe. Having new community projects developed by Dig Village members would make a contribution to our store of knowledge, but it can take many years of dedicated effort. Some idea of the amount of work entailed can be seen in *Interpreting the English Village*. This wonderful book written by Mick with Chris Gerrard gives a marvellous, detailed summary of the working methods and results of their efforts. It should be on everyone's bookshelf!

Although Shapwick was a fascinating case study, it wasn't chosen as a typical, picture-box, ancient village, so you don't have to feel that your village needs to be either. It can often be fascinating to see what is hidden beneath a rather unpromising exterior! On Time Team we carried out a number of Dig Village type projects, in villages including St Osyth, Bitterly, Nether Poppleton, Plympton amongst others. Many of these programmes can still be seen on More 4. While they were relatively ordinary villages, each produced a magical story.

The other element of Time Team's approach to archaeology very close to Mick's heart was the emphasis on seeing archaeology in its wider landscape. Mick was a landscape archaeologist, and in this respect he followed in the footsteps of some of the great heroes of the subject. W.G. Hoskins, Henderson, Beresford and others found their excitement in exploring the villages and towns in Britain. (See the bibliography for further details.)

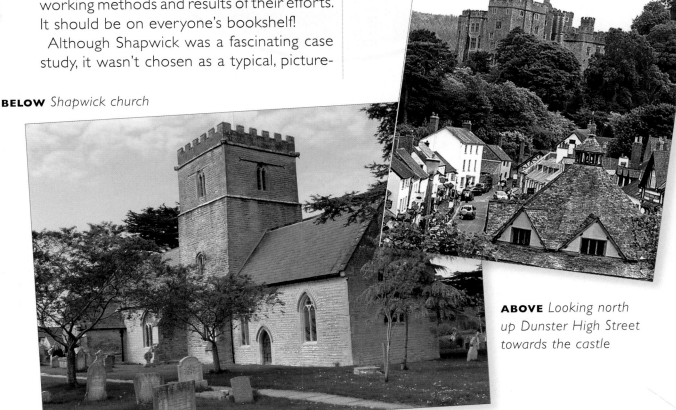

BELOW *Shapwick church*

ABOVE *Looking north up Dunster High Street towards the castle*

ABOVE *Residents of Dunster including children from the local school getting involved with Dig Village*

Currently we are lucky to have the engaging works of Richard Muir, who has a special understanding and affection for this kind of archaeology. He has often pointed out how research into a village is good for the community, the environment and the individuals involved.

Dunster: years of research

Since 2012, we have been working with the good people of Dunster in Somerset, putting many of the lessons we've learned on Time Team to good purpose. Dunster became the trial site for many of the ideas and methods you will find in this book. Although, as you'll discover, strictly a town, we have labelled Dunster our 'Ambassador Village'. You might be surprised at just how many of the discoveries and real-life examples from Dunster apply to your own village or town.

We have tried to deliver an idea of the excitement and also the responsibility involved in conducting such work. Importantly, we have had first hand experience of every element you are about to read in what follows.

Even if you have one of those wonderful local people known as the 'font of all knowledge', first try to look at your village with an open mind. In the case of Dunster, we had a place where a huge amount of history was already known. Its historic castle, high street and main houses had

already attracted considerable interest. But within a short period, we became aware that relatively little archaeology had been carried out. For instance, none of the major Medieval houses had been dendro-dated. In many cases, we were to find out that they were over 400 years older than had first been thought. The town would eventually yield up pottery that took its history back to the Romans and prehistory! So, remember, however much has been done there is always a fascinating secret waiting to be unlocked. Perhaps your project's efforts might help to 'rewrite' your area's history.

How to make a start

Before you get started, let's take an imaginary journey to a village, St Keverne, in the far west of Cornwall, to give you a sense of how it might be approached as a potential local archaeologist and historian.

RIGHT *Maps will play an important role in your journey of discovery*

Initial preparation

Before you head out, take a look at the village on the OS map and see if you can work out its basic structure. Do the roads and other routes radiate out from a central hub? Or is it more linear? Draw a sketch of the basic village plan showing all the routes including public footpaths. Mick used to say that using a pencil was "the best way of looking", so make a sketch of what you can see in your notebook. The habit of using this, noting down observations and questions, will be invaluable.

What you see above to the left is my sketch of St Keverne. You can see how the routes converge and how the footpaths, which may be indicators of much older routes, all head for the main square, which is conveniently occupied by two pubs. In Medieval times, the square may have been the site of a marketplace, and one of your first questions may be to find out if there was a license to hold a market. You will see how to do this later in the book.

ABOVE *St Keverne church, West Cornwall and Tim's sketch showing the main routes in and out of the village*

You will have to think like an explorer, visiting a place for the first time! We have put together a local archaeologist kit bag, with some of the key things you will need. (See page XXII.) A 1:25000 Ordnance Survey (OS) map is essential, and the current OS Explorer series comes with a download for your phone. We have included a notebook, pens and pencils, a scale to place in photographs, binoculars, a compass, and a tape measure. On an iPad or similar tablet it's useful to have an aerial picture preloaded from Google Earth, a download from the Historic Environment Record and a parish boundary map. Not all of this is essential, but may inform the way you record your observations and provide a fresh perspective on the scene.

Getting out and about

So, let's imagine you are on your first visit to this new village with your Dig Village hat on. Try to see it with a new eye and use all of your senses. Notice where people seem to congregate. This may be the village shop, the local pub, the church or

at a weekly farmer's market. The nature of village life essentially means that it's a location where people are going to interact in one way or another.

Ask yourself: is this where the earliest village might have begun? It's always useful to take photographs of any key features as you go and, in particular, note any houses that appear to be larger and older than others. Of course, remember that a modern bit of DIY or render might be hiding something more ancient.

It's a good idea on this first visit to go into the church which, if ancient, will have played a major role in the village's history. It always amazes me to think that these buildings had once been alive with the activities of village life, but are now often rather gloomy, under-heated and usually empty! Keep your eye open for the church booklet, which can be invariably obtained by depositing a few coins in a box. I've got a small collection of these often informative documents. They are typically the result of the dedication of a local vicar, church member or historian, for whom a study of the historic events of their church and village must have represented an exciting evening's work.

As you walk back into the village, notice any unusual place and road names which can provide clues to the local history. On the OS map for this area you will see many place names with 'Lann', which often indicates an early monastic site. In this case, I would be interested to know where the original Lann was, assuming it wasn't underneath the church itself, and the booklet helpfully tells me it was at a site called Tregonning. It's never too early to start a list of potential sites for further research and even some archaeological work. In Wales, these sites are to referred to as 'Llans'.

Having survived your first explorative foray, it's a good time to return to the pub or teashop for refreshment, and to make a few notes on your general impressions, perhaps adding the key buildings and any other features to your sketch map. There is

BELOW *Church pamphlets can be a great source of information*

BEHIND *A sketch of Dunster High Street*

eyeglass

notebook and pencils

ABOVE & RIGHT *Drawing of a side elevation of an old Dunster house plus a notebook, pencils and an eyeglass for close viewing*

no substitute for this sort of gentle wander around your chosen site, making a note of your first impressions.

Sharing an ethos and respecting the evidence

Dig Village has at its heart a shared ethos based on respect for the evidence that lies hidden in your particular village or town. Making the most use of that evidence requires a structure that satisfactorily records what is found and secondly makes it available to the wider community. As W.G. Hoskins pointed out, work that produces archaeological or historical evidence without being recorded and communicated is a form of vandalism. In addition, all your work should be looked at in the wider context of the relationship with the local archaeological community in your area. In 2019, after four years' work we produced our interim report on Dunster, *Unearthing Dunster*. See the Dig Village website for more details on obtaining a copy.

When it comes to physical evidence you will be reliant upon archaeological experts to identify material and to help guide the process of field walking and potential test pitting once the initial research stage has been completed. This should not be undertaken without professional archaeological supervision. Piles of random finds produced by over-eager project members will be useless unless recorded and identified correctly. What's more, their unsupervised collection can unwittingly damage the very evidence we are seeking to find! In addition, such activities will swiftly lose you the support of your key allies – the local archaeologists and other professional experts you depend upon.

Needless to say, it's also important to respect private property and personal privacy, obtaining the permission of landowners before embarking on your investigations.

A lot can be learnt by closely studying the older buildings in your village or town

How to use this guide: a framework and methodology

By following our guidelines, you will be supported by the best possible experts. Dig Village's range of technical support will help to ensure that the evidence you discover becomes a valuable and long-lasting contribution to the historical record.

OPPOSITE *A drone image of the priory garden at Dunster before we did a test pit*

Many of us will have had experience of groups that begin with great enthusiasm only to lose their way and gradually decline. With our support, based on over 25 years of experience, we hope to steer you around the pitfalls and help to create something that will really make a difference to your community.

So where should you start? When I have talked to villagers about the subject I often ask the question "how many different elements do you think would form a useful checklist for the work you are about to do?" People usually suggest up to ten possibilities, a dozen maybe. But here in this book we have been able to suggest 66! These can be worked through from the start, one by one, or simply by selecting the specific aspects that interest you.

Indeed, depending on the focus of your research, you may not necessarily wish to read the book in chronological order, from category to category. We have designed it to be a handy reference book that you can dip in and out of, to find what you're looking for, with references to other categories throughout for easy navigation.

However, for a basic project overview, we advise that you read the categories covered in Sections VI and VII (dealing with organisation, development, outreach and presentation) at the beginning of your journey. Wherever your research takes you, there are some important pointers and provisos to pin down early in the project!

RIGHT *Tim and Stewart Ainsworth with Dunster's Interim Report, 'Unearthing Dunster'*

Why your project matters

Today, we all perhaps live more alienated lives than in the past; neighbour may not even know neighbour, and yet in the Medieval period for instance, the great events of village life, the ploughing, sowing, and the harvest, brought the whole village together.

We might wonder what might have been lost when the process of working in the common fields and the shared tasks of village life became a thing of the past. I'd like to think a Dig Village project could become the stimulus for such a gathering. It will hopefully harvest knowledge and understanding, uncover wonderful finds and information and along the way provide much excitement and pleasure.

I wish you luck and much joy in the process!

BELOW *A farmer working a plough and horses; a traditional method used for centuries before modern mechanised practices*

Home | Digs | Shop | Membership | Team | FAQs | Masterclasses | Contact | News

0 Item

Tags: Dig Village, Time Team, What is Dig Village, Tim Taylor, Mick Aston, history, archaeology

TIME TEAM'S

Dig Village

Dig Village is the new project of Prof. Tim Taylor, creator and series producer of Time Team. It is an investigation of the **history** and **archaeology** of Britain's most amazing villages, starting with **Dunster, Somerset.**

The Dig Village crew visited Dunster for a **Dig Weekend** at the end of last year. The strategy was mainly based on landscape analysis and test pits, with experts Rob Wilson-North, Stewart Ainsworth, Danni Wootton and Paul Blinkhorn. The Dunster Dig Weekend was filmed and is currently being released episodically on Youtube.

Facebook Activity

Be the first of your friends to like this

On Instagram

DIG VILLAGE:
NOT JUST A BOOK

There is so much more to Dig Village than this book alone! Visit the official Dig Village website for news, extra resources and useful links. For example, you'll notice throughout the book that many key terms are highlighted in bold. Visit our website for the accompanying online glossary.

We also encourage you to share your discoveries and insights with other Dig Village enthusiasts on our social media pages.

www.digvillage.co.uk

THE DIG VILLAGE EXPLORER'S KIT BAG AND CONTENTS

All the essentials you'll need to kick-start your Dig Village adventure...

back pack

notepad, pen and pencils

mini compass

compass

hat

tablet

maps

eyeglass

sample bags
*refer to the Countryside
Code and obtain the
landowner's permission*

trowel & case
for use on supervised digs

binoculars

**magnifying
glass**

**gloves for
handling
items**

identifier books

**tape
measures
and 1m rule**

The Priory Church of St George, Dunster

I.
The Basics

This first section is all about familiarising yourself with the key basics that will lay the foundations for your research. Over the following pages, we address some of the main themes that we return to throughout the book. You may find yourself referring back to this section throughout your research.

1 VILLAGE MAPS

We are very lucky in Britain to have the marvellous Ordnance Survey maps, which contain so much useful information. Starting with the most widely available, the Explorer series has a scale of 1:25,000, which means that every centimetre on the map is equal to 250 metres. Look at your village and see just how much the map can tell you. Look for unusual names, strange road patterns and how the houses relate to the church. Look at the contours that give you the height and shape of hills, valleys and other features. Can you see where the areas of flat, south-facing land are, which would have been favourable for growing crops?

A good first exercise is to lay a sheet of tracing paper over the map and with a soft pencil draw in the main roads, rivers and bridges, as well as the main or oldest church. When you take it away, what sort of shape are you looking at? Is your village or town linear or do the roads appear to converge at a crossing or village green? Are there places where the most obvious straight route has been blocked or detoured? Is it possible to see where the traffic enters and exits your village and does this look as if it is the obvious route? Do the main areas of houses seem to converge around the church or have they spread out into other areas? Keep this first trace map safe. It is the skeleton of your site and will be a useful place to keep a note of more information as it arrives.

BEHIND *An historical map of Chagford (circa 1880)*

Your journey starts with a map

As Mick often said, "every village project should always begin with a decent map."

The next step in your map work is to get together all the maps, both modern and historic, that relate to your village. Not only is the Ordnance Survey (OS) an excellent and very reliable source for detailed mapping, it also produces maps in a wide range of scales. In order to help your search you will need to look for the scale on each map, which affects the level of detail you can see. Visit the OS website for details on the range of maps available, including historical maps from different periods that will prove invaluable in your research.

OS began producing publicly available maps around the 1840s and even these early maps have a superb level of features, including scale drawn buildings and lanes and individual marked trees. If possible, try to get both an early edition map of your village as well as a more recent 1990s or 2000s edition. They can be purchased from high street bookshops and stationers or online.

For Dunster, the first edition (1890) and second edition (1904) maps are available, as well as more recent editions from the 1970s and 2000s. Having access to these scaled drawn maps will provide the basis for your work with other historic maps and your later work in the field.

Aside from OS maps, other historic estate maps are some of the most important resources for any village project. A lack of early maps will make the task of researching your village extremely difficult. It was quite common for large estates to privately commission a map of their land and if you can find them, they are invaluable.

The county records office should be your first port of call when searching for historical maps, but it is worth noting that there are also a number of key online resources where you can also obtain these. Some websites that provide historical mapping are:

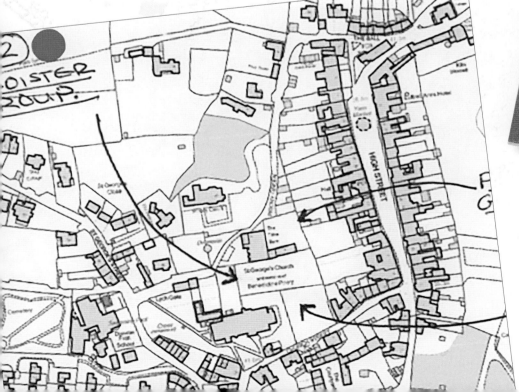

LEFT *A recent OS-based map of Dunster*

Old Maps (**www.old-maps.co.uk**), Digimap (**www.edina.ac.uk/digimap.ac.uk**) and The National Library of Scotland (**maps.nls.uk**). From time to time, valuable historical resources turn up in private collections, so remember to ask your neighbours to have a poke about in dusty attics and cellars.

When an estate or farm was put up for sale it was relatively common for a map to be drawn of the land, so this may be another source of information. There is an element of detective work and persistence needed here, but tracking down a 'lost' estate map can give you a great sense of satisfaction and contribute another layer of fascinating detail to the picture of your location.

The earliest and most useful map for many parishes will be the **tithe map**. These were compiled around 1842 and were originally used to assess the value of land for tax purposes. A typical tithe map provides us with the land use, tenants, owner, value, field name and acreage for each plot, making it a fantastic historical resource and benchmark for any project. We look at tithe maps more closely in Category 17.

Occasionally you might be lucky enough to find a large-scale map earlier than the tithe map. In Dunster, there is a map of 1792, showing details of the town, including the names of some of the householders. This was part of the castle document collection and, as we have noted, you may find a large manor house or a castle with a considerable estate where the owners decided to record their land holdings. Even when the family has disappeared from the area the records can end up in the county records office.

Map regression

Once you have gathered all the available maps, the next step is a to carry out a **map regression** exercise. The idea behind a map regression is to clearly identify the changes that have taken place to field boundaries, roads and buildings. It is only when comparing one map closely with another that such subtle changes can be picked out.

BELOW *Tithe map of Dunster and detail of No 68* **BEHIND** *An historic map of Chagford*

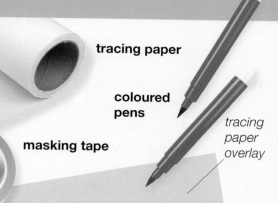

tracing paper

coloured pens

masking tape

tracing paper overlay

HOW TO: CREATE A MAP REGRESSION

An example of map analysis from Dunster. The red line on the tracing paper is a modern road that is on the modern map labelled '1' but is not on the Dunster town map from 1842. When the tracing of the 1842 map is placed on top of the modern map the later road, 'Priory Row', can be seen as missing.

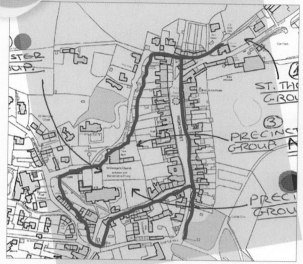

1. Take a modern map of your town or village, in this example Dunster, and trace the main modern routes on a piece of tracing paper.

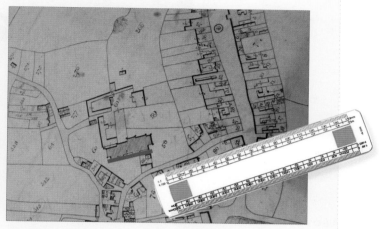

2. Take an earlier map, in this case the tithe map from 1842. Using a computer or copier, scale the earlier map to match the modern map. In this case, we use the length of Dunster church as size guide.

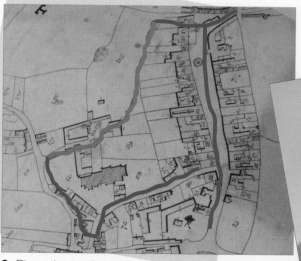

3. Place the tracing paper over the 1842 map, and you will see that the road we have coloured green is not on this map. This shows that it must have been built after 1842 and is now called Priory Green.

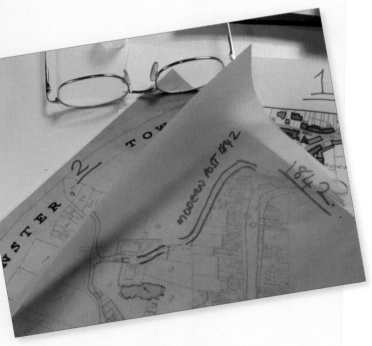

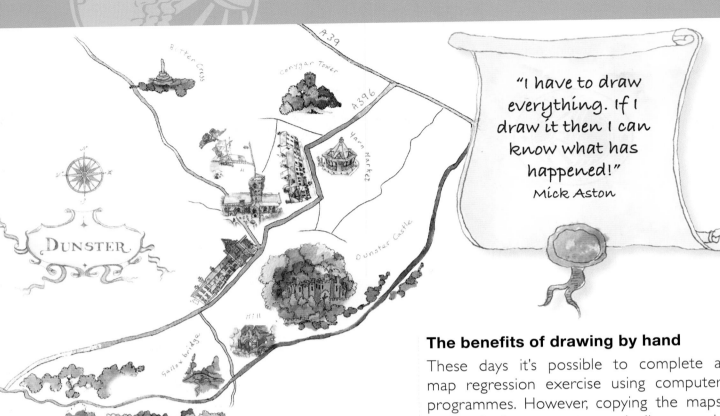

Map labels: A39, Butter Cross, Conygar Tower, A396, Yarn Market, Dunster Castle, DUNSTER, Mill, Gallox bridge, Gallox Hill Settlement

ABOVE *A watercolour map of Dunster showing the general layout*

The exercise will only work with maps that have the same scales, so you may need to re-draw some of the earlier maps or use a computer and scanner to match the scales. This can be done using a scale ruler (available in high street stationers) and simply re-measuring all the lines and re-drawing them to the same scale as a 1:10,000 OS map.

> "A map regression analysis involves looking at patterns on maps and seeing if they're traceable to the present day."
> Stewart Ainsworth

> "I have to draw everything. If I draw it then I can know what has happened!"
> Mick Aston

The benefits of drawing by hand

These days it's possible to complete a map regression exercise using computer programmes. However, copying the maps by hand allows you to gradually appreciate the changes in landscape, enabling the smaller details to be understood.

As Mick said during one of our master-class sessions, "I have to draw everything. If I draw it then I can know what has happened. The analogy is that if you see a view and take a photograph of it then you haven't really looked at it; but if you sit and paint the same view, you have looked at it. Doing it by hand forces you to look at every single bit of the landscape. Even if a field is not depicted entirely accurately, you can often see what was intended. It's as if we can get inside the surveyor's head and appreciate the landscape as they would have seen it!"

We also now have Google Earth, which can provide a useful overview of the village and allows you to highlight certain details. However, there is no real substitute for getting out your pencils and tracing paper and spending an evening watching the plan of your village through time appear. Mick described the ideal combination for an entertaining evening as a good set of maps and "two glasses of Sauvignon!"

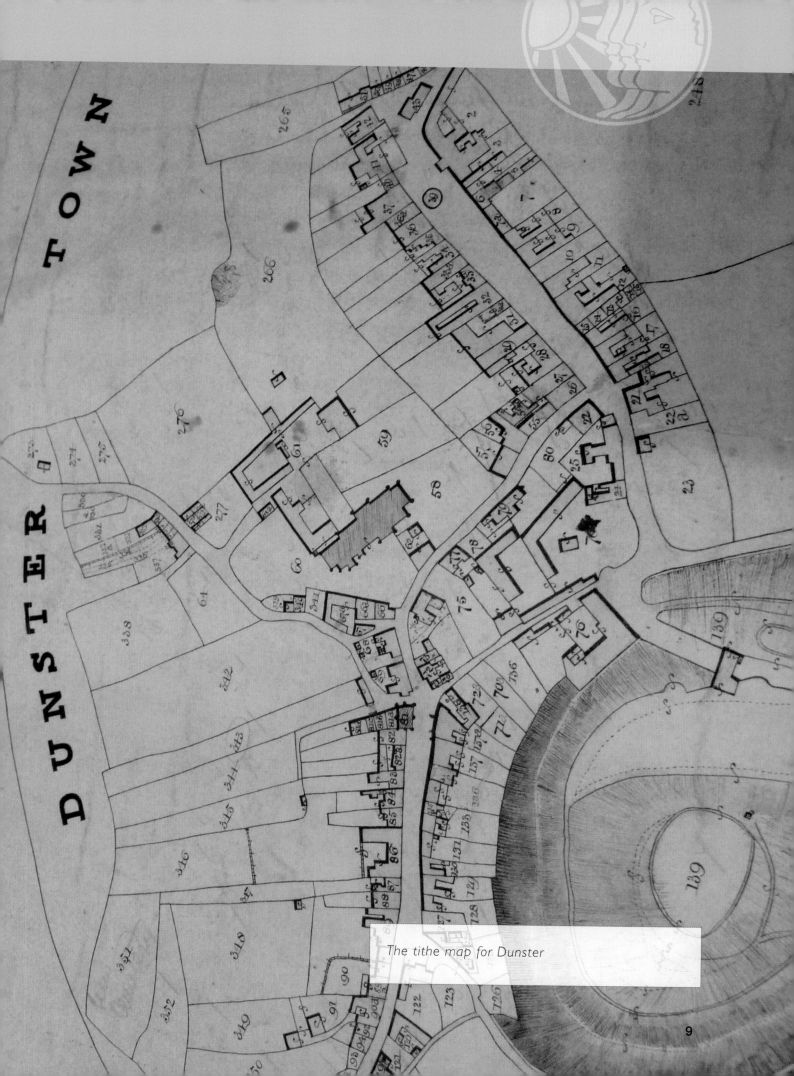

The tithe map for Dunster

9

2 ROADS, PATHS & BRIDGES

When we first arrived in Dunster at the start of the Dig Village project, we took the chance to wander around the town and get an idea of its layout. It made us ask the question: what historical, social and economic forces made the roads and paths the shape they are? We noticed how the main road, called, appropriately enough, High Street, was orientated on the entrance to the castle, running approximately north-south. On High Street is the famous Yarn Market and it's likely that this wide street would have been occupied by a considerable market in Medieval times.

BELOW *Dunster High Street with its distinct Yarn Market*

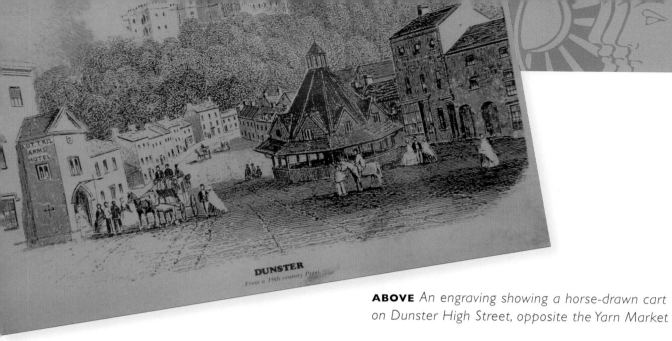

DUNSTER
From a 19th century Print

ABOVE *An engraving showing a horse-drawn cart on Dunster High Street, opposite the Yarn Market*

In order to make your way out of the town heading west you have to take a sharp right turn and travel down, at some risk to life and limb, the narrow Church Street with its small or non-existent pavement, before it broadens out to West Street. Today this route is managed by traffic lights. When such a difficult route has been created it suggests that some new or imposed plan has evolved, cutting across the gently curved route that carts pulled by oxen or horses would have followed in earlier centuries.

A new high street

As we did more research, we found that the High Street, with its set of **burgage plots** (Category 19), had been created by the lord of Dunster in the twelfth century. He was looking to make money from his estate by letting out land, at the cost of 1 shilling a year, on which properties could be built and by setting up a market to attract trade. He wanted to exit his castle gates and look down on his new development, so imposed a new dominant north-south route, doubtless looking forward to all the rents he would soon receive from the citizens of Dunster.

We are perhaps more aware of the idea of new planned towns like Milton Keynes than we are of the massive growth of towns that began, like Dunster, from the twelfth century onwards. If you live in a town with a castle it may well have been created at a

date as early as this. Try to find out when it was given a market and look for the date of early burgage plots.

Looking for the main road

The pattern of roads and other routes in your area may have been created and affected by events that occurred centuries ago. Finding their origins can be a fruitful and enjoyable piece of research. Ask yourself a few basic questions: What was the first main road in your village? Do the routes respect a particular building like a church, or market place? Can you see roads with a specific purpose of, say, bringing goods from a port, delivering salt or pottery to the village, providing links to a coaching inn (Category 39), or returning the harvest to the tithe barn (Category 17)? There may be paths to the local church or heading out to a place of pilgrimage (Category 46).

Getting started

When you first approach the task of looking at the streets and roads that pass through your town or village it will be useful to have a simple map of the main elements traced from the corresponding OS map, as shown in Category 1. Eventually, you will create a route-based version of a map regression analysis.

Once you have drawn out a simplified plan, look for some basic patterns and see if there are any unexplained interruptions to the most obvious route. Odd deviations or unnatural constrictions may have been caused by buildings or planning schemes lost in the mists of time.

Historic maps

Compare historic maps from various time periods to see if you can work out how and roughly when new roads have been added over time. Use different colours to indicate rough date divisions.

In the case of Dunster, a west-east detour was created around the town to respect the grounds of the twelfth century priory. You can see how this appears in the rough plan (right), labelled Castle Street.

You can create several plans as you begin to eliminate the more modern roads. It's worth remembering that in several places in Britain a modern road, such as the A10, is actually imposed on top of a Roman street! However, this mainly applies to major routes. Finding the earliest roads in your village will be part of your search for its origins, providing valuable groundwork for later research. Of course, archaeology can provide clues and you should keep an eye on trenches dug up the main street for utilities, or areas where older layers are exposed, for extensions or developments.

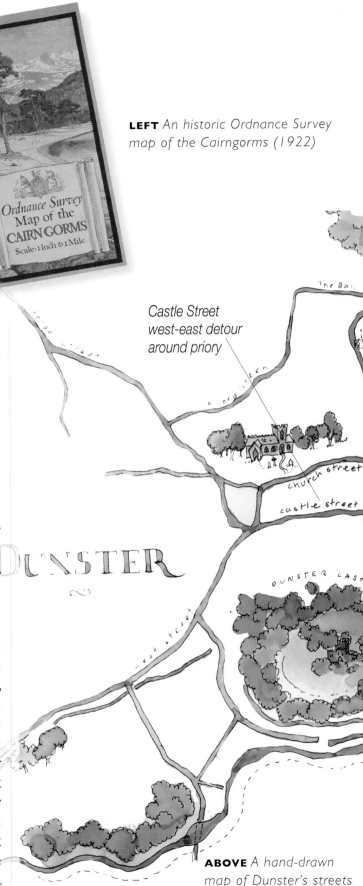

LEFT *An historic Ordnance Survey map of the Cairngorms (1922)*

Castle Street west-east detour around priory

ABOVE *A hand-drawn map of Dunster's streets*

new roads in red

old roads in green

ABOVE *A map of Chagford circa 1908*
RIGHT *A map of Chagford circa 1800*

A visit to your local history library will give you details of recent excavations that may be relevant.

State of the roads

For much of your village's life the main roads would have been very far from the smooth tarmacked surface with pavements seen today. With no county or parish council to take responsibility for repairs, roads in winter quickly became impassable. Farmers would move their stock through the village, and carts would cut deep ruts in the ground. The streets were convenient places to dump rubbish and sewage. Villagers would have to make their way across improvised plank or brush walkways.

BELOW *Historically, wheels would have been wooden rather than the tyres here, cutting deep ruts in the roads*

The Medieval 'patten', a wooden shoe strapped over normal shoes to provide extra height and protection, was designed to keep the owner, usually unsuccessfully, out of the mire. The number of streets given the name 'Shite Row' or similar variations is just one recognition of the conditions!

In some towns today you can still see the remains of street drainage systems using water from local rivers and streams to flush out the contents of the local ditches. Truro, in Cornwall, has a very well built system of carved granite drains running throughout the town. In Dunster, the picturesque houses just before Gallox Bridge have small streams running in front of them and these may be remnants of a much earlier drainage system.

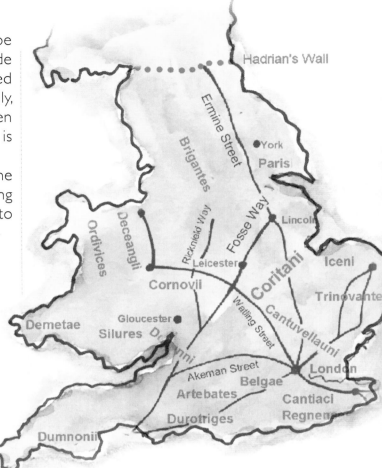

ABOVE *A map showing major Roman roads around Britain, many of which have been incorporated into modern routes in use today*

RIGHT *The 'patten' shoe was worn over normal shoes to keep the owner out of the mire (detail from 'The Arnolfini Portrait' painted by Jan van Eyck, 1434)*

RIGHT AND BELOW *Small streams running near cottages by Gallox Bridge, Dunster*

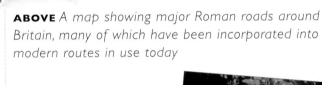

Roman roads

The Romans gave us, among many things, a wonderful system of roads. In some cases, these were based on earlier routes. It has been estimated that over 15,000 kilometres of roads were created in Britain for the fast movement of soldiers and supplies. These formed a road system that can still be found in parts of the country today. Roads including the Fosse Way, Ermine Street and Watling Street radiate across the country, once linking Roman towns and forts.

The OS produces an excellent map of the main Roman routes and it's a good idea to locate the one nearest to your village. There are some wonderful examples of these constructions, with their distinctive 'aggers' or ditches, and some still retain parts of the stone surface (as illustrated below).

On Time Team, we spent a few fruitless programmes trying to find them and even when we knew we were on a route we came across relatively little evidence. As a source of stone and hardcore they were obviously too tempting for local builders.

In 1994, we visited Lambeth Palace in search of the Roman road into London. One of the fascinating skills that emerged was watching the reconstruction of Roman methods for laying out a straight line across miles of country.

BELOW *Cross-section illustration of a Roman road*

large stones

ditch on either side for water

slabs of stones

layer of clay

crushed stones and pebbles

An aerial view of Dere Street Roman road, today incorporated into the B6275, County Durham

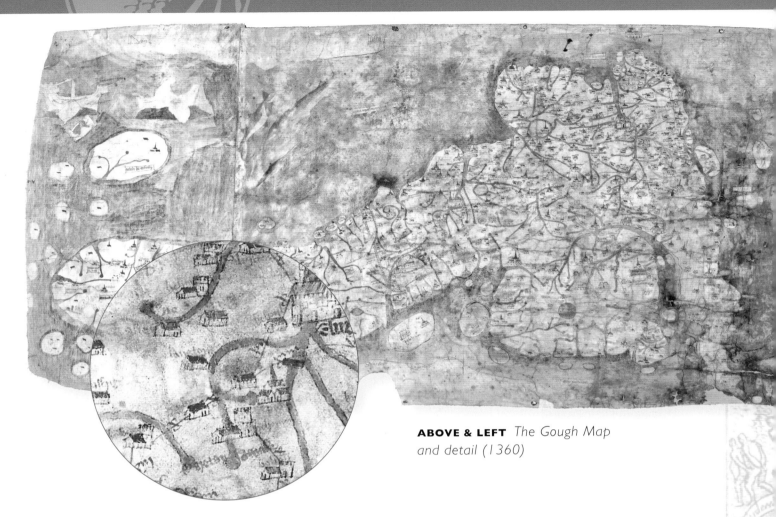

ABOVE & LEFT *The Gough Map and detail (1360)*

Links to a wider world

Once you have a good idea of the streets and roads in your immediate locale, it's useful to see how your village was linked to the wider countryside and cities.

Early examples like the Gough Map of 1360 (above) show the sophistication of the wider network by the fourteenth century.

As we reach the Tudor period, we begin to see the development of postal routes and the first forms of public transport, with the main cities being connected by coach and horses. The Tudor postal system aimed to deliver mail throughout the country, from towns like Falmouth in the far southwest to Carlisle in the north.

Teams of horses and riders were part of the system, with inns providing linking points for fresh horses and overnight stops. Difficult sections were covered by post boys on foot. In the seventeenth century, it could take up to two days in fair conditions to deliver post from Bristol to London. Under the new mail coach system introduced in the late eighteenth century, the journey time was shaved down to a mere 16 hours!

These roads often passed through areas of relatively wild country and highwaymen and other robbers were a real threat. Certain areas on major routes, such Hounslow Heath, were the territory of notorious bandits like the eighteenth century's Dick Turpin. As a result, many stage coaches carried an armed guard.

One of the interesting things about these wider routes is how they reflect the historic cities and major areas of settlement. Regions such as the West Midlands were relatively unpopulated until the Industrial Revolution (Category 32), so didn't get connections until much later.

ABOVE *The Luttrell Arms, Dunster showing a coach and horses arriving where they would probably have stayed overnight*

LEFT *The Luttrell Arms today*

Coaching inns

Did your village have a coaching inn? There are hundreds of pubs across Britain called 'The Coach and Horses' or something similar (Category 39). Many were built with distinctive arches to allow coaches to drive into the courtyard, with stabling for horses. Over time, many have been converted, but traces of the archways often remain (as seen in Dunster's Luttrell Arms, above).

All villages and towns recognised the advantages of a good road. It enabled people to visit the market, thus enhancing trade and commerce. Your research should find out if, and how early, your community received a market charter (Category 19).

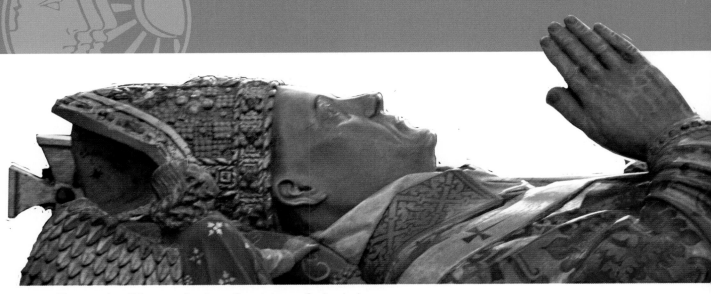

ABOVE *The tomb of Thomas Becket, Canterbury Cathedral*

Pilgrim and other routes

It's worth remembering that one set of routes across the wider country was created by pilgrims visiting shrines. In the Medieval period, famous shrines like Hailles, which claimed to have the blood of Christ, and Thomas Becket's tomb at Canterbury were the focus for a network of pathways across the country (Category 46).

At certain times of year, people would have set out like those described in Chaucer's *Canterbury Tales* (circa 1400), and headed towards their favoured shrine. Was your village anywhere near one of these paths? Pubs' names can again be an indication and the routes to a holy site like Canterbury had well-defined directions, passing through key villages which would have provided rest and refreshment.

In the Anglo-Saxon period, many villages were connected by a system of **herepaths** that helped communication and defence. The **Burghal Hidage** document provides an invaluable list of key fixed points in a network of fortified sites (Category 25).

Ancient roads, bridges and highways can be uncovered, like a hidden web lying beneath the surface of your area. As you make each discovery, place it on your basic map and see if it suggests links to historic features still yet to be discovered.

Bridges

Helping to make these routes effective were the bridges that crossed the many rivers spread throughout Britain. Fording a river in winter can be a dangerous business, and, where a ford existed, place names

BELOW *The pilgrimage route from London to Canterbury Cathedral*

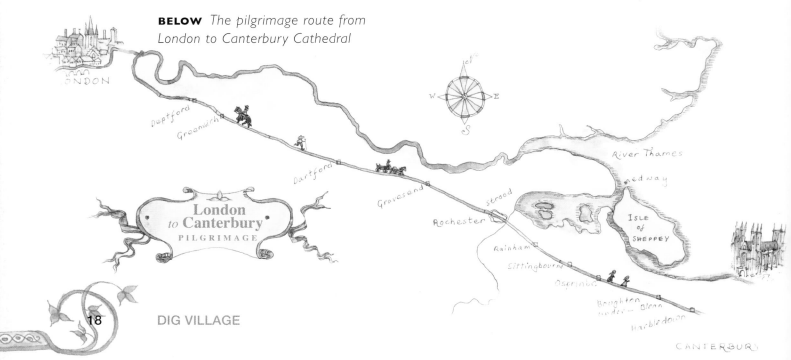

helped to guide travellers to the spot. We are reminded of this today in locations such as Hungerford, Oxford and Guildford. The term 'ford' comes from the Old English, itself derived from the same proto-Germanic root of the Norwegian word, *fjord*.

Before local or national government took responsibility for funding bridges, their construction and maintenance was dependent upon the local lord, the Church or, in the case of the capital cities, the Crown. The Church could use **indulgences** to fund construction. These were payments made by parishioners to receive forgiveness for their sins and often local records exist of such examples.

Over a tiny stream in Cornwall called Polwheveral Creek, there is a beautifully crafted little bridge with abutments and a single arch. Thanks to Charles Henderson, one of the country's first great local historians, we have a record of how it was built using indulgences (see the Bibliography).

Bridges are often wonderful examples of the stonemason's craft and often employed features seen in early church architecture. In Dunster, we have a wonderful Medieval packhorse bridge over the river Avill. Built in the fifteenth century, Gallox Bridge is still in use and would, with the ford, have been a link to the ancient route to Carhampton.

Exmoor is home to the prehistoric stone-slab **clapper bridge**, Tarr Steps, reminding us that river crossings have been important from the earliest settlements.

The construction and upkeep of larger bridges necessitated a considerable degree of community participation, with individual spans often built by different parties. This usually left useful information in the local archives. Piercebridge over the Tees is a wonderful example, with an almost cathedral-like construction. Incidentally, it lies close to the site of an excavated Roman bridge that once crossed the river.

Bridges were extremely important to communities. Many, built in wood, have been lost, but thankfully we still retain a remarkable number. 'Collecting' bridges from your area is a very worthwhile piece of research.

Footpaths

Once you have mapped the local routes and the wider systems linking to distant towns, it is good to return to one of the simplest route ways – the public footpaths as they are now called. As you find them, draw them on your basic map as dotted green lines and see if they appear to suggest a focus or purpose. Some of them will be ancient in origin. You may be looking at the path that originally took the villagers out to their fields and then returned the harvest to the tithe barn. There may be paths to the local church or heading out to a place of pilgrimage.

RIGHT *Gallox Bridge, Dunster*

Tarr Steps, Exmoor, a wonderfully preserved prehistoric stone-slab bridge

3 THE OLDEST BUILDINGS

When visiting a village, Mick was fond of pointing out the tendency for us to alter the appearance of our houses by adding new windows, garages or extensions, but that somewhere underneath the surface a whole history could be hidden. This is particularly the case if, in the roof and foundations, elements from the original structure can be seen. Doing a thorough survey of your village's older buildings is an important element of getting to grips with your local history. Even some of the most unprepossessing buildings can be of great interest. We say "don't judge a book by its cover". Well, it's even more true to say "don't judge a building by its exterior." Beginning research in this area can open up a fascinating line of enquiry, involving a whole range of subjects from building construction to dendrochronology.

Dunster High Street is a patchwork of historic buildings from different eras, which have been altered over time

Getting started

A good question to start with is: which buildings are the oldest?

Begin by looking at the buildings nearest to the church. If the church if it has Medieval origins then the village's early core is likely to have grown up around it.

If you are lucky there maybe some buildings with structural elements that hint at an early date. Exposed timber beams, for example, may be part of the original structure. However, beware of the later tendency to gentrify buildings with faux Tudor black and white embellishments, which could be Victorian or even later in date. Dunster Museum has a wonderful set of timber frames, but these were added in the nineteenth century. By careful observation you should be able to differentiate between the structural and the decorative.

Don't neglect the smaller structures. Buildings that acted as over-night lock-ups or places to house straying animals can have early origins. Toll houses on the edge of towns are worth exploring. In your initial survey, take numerous photographs and see if, as a group, you can select one or two targets.

ABOVE *The lodge near Dunster church with Tudor timbers showing on the exterior*

Once these are chosen you will have to be brave and approach the owner to see if they might be interested. This is not always a given! If they are, you may be invited to look inside and they may have information in their deeds that you can research.

BELOW *An artist's impression of Dunster High Street*

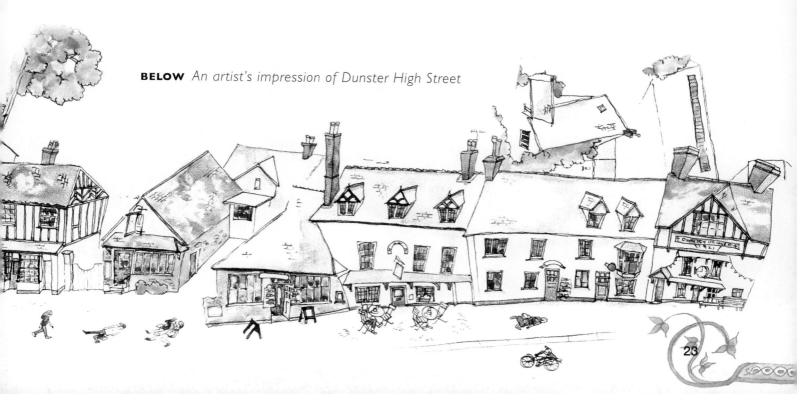

Access to the roof

One of your main goals is to get access to the roof. This has to be handled delicately. Most of us dump our household junk in the attic and would be reluctant to open it up to strangers. In addition there is the possibility of putting your foot through the ceiling, so caution is needed! This is, however, where some great discoveries can be made. In Dunster, we were able to explore houses that had been dismissed as eighteenth or even nineteenth century and found wonderful roof timbers dating back to the fourteenth century! We will look at how to undertake a more intensive survey later in this section.

House names

While doing your initial, general survey keep an eye open for interesting names. Court House, Manor Cottage, Priory Lodge and The Nunnery could all be the result of some owner's desire to give their house historic kudos, but if the origins of the name are early, more research may be

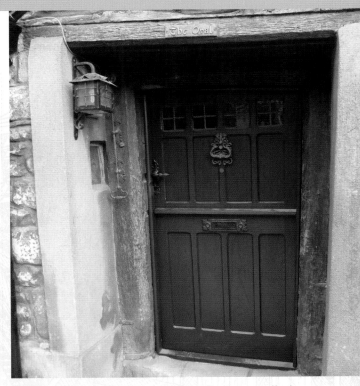

ABOVE Doorway to a house in Dunster called 'The Oval', once known as 'the Hovel'

BELOW A ceiling showing the beautiful rafters in The Luttrell Arms, Dunster

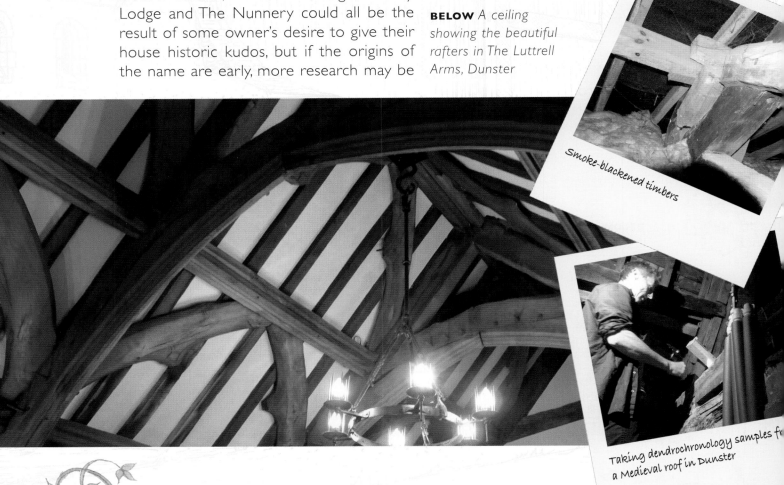

Smoke-blackened timbers

Taking dendrochronology samples fr a Medieval roof in Dunster warranted. One of the houses in Dunster is called 'The Oval'. However, originally it was referred to as 'the Hovel'!

Names can be traced back in various local records. Land Tax (1780-1832) gives details of landowners and occupiers in a parish; manorial and estate records can record specific houses if your property was part of a larger estate; there will also be tithe maps, which include the locations of boundaries and buildings. If you know your property was a public house then the licensing records might hold useful information. You can also use census and electoral registers to trace a property and details of previous occupants.

Local allies

Useful allies in your research can be the local builders, painters and decorators. Once the word gets out that you are researching buildings, a quiet suggestion of an interesting timber here or old looking beam there can be the first clue to an undiscovered gem. Most house owners love to know more about their property and if you can hold out the possibility of giving them a document detailing your findings or, in special cases, a reconstruction drawing or perhaps even a 'dendro' date — not to be undertaken lightly — most people will be only too glad to co-operate.

Dendrochronology is a fascinating scientific technique for dating timber, which we return to in detail later.

BELOW *An examination of a roof in Dunster revealed some exciting discoveries about the building's age and method of construction*

The top of the collar beam above the modern ceiling

An exposed cruck beam in the bedroom of the house

BEHIND *Richard Parker's detailed reconstruction of a Medieval abbey refectory*

The apex of the cruck truss and its 'saddle'

"The fabric of a building reveals many things about its development."
Richard Parker

23/10/16 - Today, we're surveying what could be one of the oldest house in Dunster – a residential property made of local stone...

HOW TO: COMPLETE A BUILDING SURVEY

PART 1: The initial assessment of the building involves the recording of basic information and taking photographs of the exterior.

1. For each individual building, create a record including its address, current use (for example, residential, industrial, agricultural), the direction the front door faces, what it's made of, and any datable features (such as a plaque over the door, drain pipes or chimney stack).

23/10/16 - Chimney stack east facing and wooden windows; local stone walls

23/10/16 - Cottage roof tiles are terracotta. Wooden window frames and local stone walls

2. Next, conduct a photographic survey. This involves taking photos from different angles of the various walls and features. Take as many as you can! Note down the key details of each photo, for example, which feature is in shot, the direction it's facing (for example, north facing), the date and time. Make a quick annotated sketch of any particularly interesting features.

23/10/16 - The east-facing exterior elevation of the house

3. Finally, record the type of roof, how many windows and doorways there are (and what material the frames are made of), the number of storeys, the way the building is linked to its neighbours and any extensions.

chimney stack

RIGHT & ABOVE
One of the oldest known houses in Dunster, which we dated back to 1307. Next door, a Dig Village test pit!

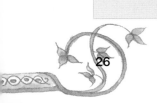

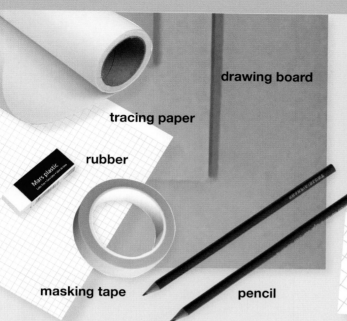

drawing board

tracing paper

rubber

masking tape

pencil

PART 2: The next stage is to make more detailed scale drawings, such as a floorplan and elevations. These will allow you to go into a greater level of detail, perhaps helping to identify and illustrate how the building has evolved over time.

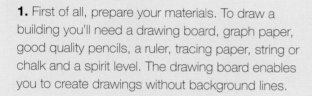

1. First of all, prepare your materials. To draw a building you'll need a drawing board, graph paper, good quality pencils, a ruler, tracing paper, string or chalk and a spirit level. The drawing board enables you to create drawings without background lines.

2. Prepare your drawing board by covering an A3-sized board in graph paper. Secure the graph paper to the board using tape or staples. Once the board has been made, you can reuse it over and over again.

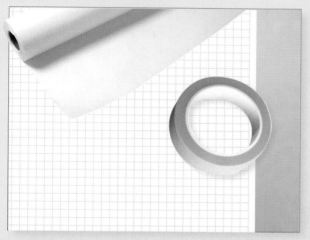

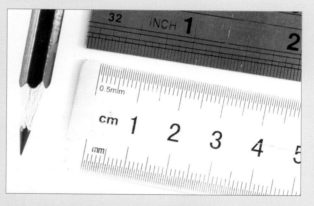

3. To prepare for each new drawing, secure some tracing paper onto the board using masking tape. Use the squares that show through from the graph paper as a guide for your measurements.

4. Before you start, choose a scale depending on the size of the area you're planning to draw. A smaller feature will use a larger scale to provide more detail, whilst a large piece of wall will naturally need a small scale to fit it all in. For an entire wall, try 1:20 (every 20cm of wall will be 1cm on your drawing).

To survey any building you will, of course, need the owner's permission. This provides a useful opportunity to enquire about any knowledge, plans or old photographs relating to their home. It is equally important to be observant and open-minded when drawing, as different buildings will need to be drawn and measured in different ways. This could mean throwing this guide out of the window and following your intuition!

ruler

tape measure

eraser

pencil

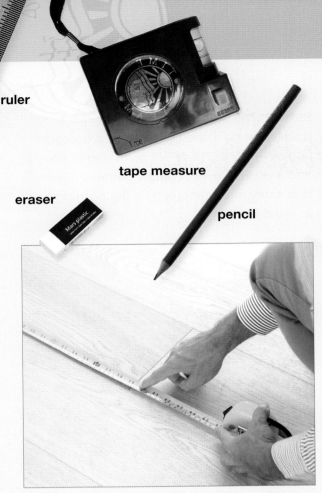

PART 2 *(continued)*: When drawing the interior of a building, the best practice is to conduct a 'running' survey, where measurements for each room on a single floor are linked by a single tapeline that runs the length of the house. This is similar to the baseline used in an earthwork survey.

1. Lay one long tape through interconnecting rooms or along a single linking corridor. The aim is to make a measured, sketch floorplan of each room, with all vertical internal surfaces.

2. Measure the length of each wall and the position of all the windows and doorways. Also measure the diagonals across the room, and the depth of any recesses or fireplaces.

a line level

HOW TO: DRAW AN ELEVATION

Now, we look at drawing an 'elevation', the vertical parts of the building, both inside and out. You will need two people for this exercise: one to measure the wall using the datum line as a guide and the other to mark these measurements on the drawing board.

1. The first step is to set up a 'datum line' on the wall you plan to draw. This is simply a fixed line from which you will take all of your measurements. If the wall isn't very high, you can use the ground as your datum, as long as it is level. Otherwise, run a piece of string across the wall or feature, ideally roughly halfway between the ground and the top. Use a line level (which attaches to the string with hooks) to ensure the line is exactly level. Either fix the string in place with nails or mark the wall with chalk, to show where the line has been.

string

chalk

The exterior of 'The Nunnery', Dunster

HOW TO: DRAW AN ELEVATION
(continued)

2. Using very light strokes (that can be rubbed out later), draw a straight line across the middle of your tracing paper. This represents the datum line that you have pegged onto the wall.

3. Measure on the wall the height of the ground level and the top of your wall. Starting at one end of your datum line, measure to the ground and let the first person mark a corresponding point on your drawing board.

4. Measure to the top of the wall and make another point on your drawing board. Repeat this process every 10, 20 or 50 cm along the datum line, depending on your chosen scale.

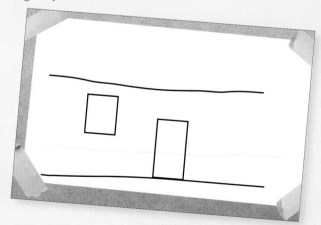

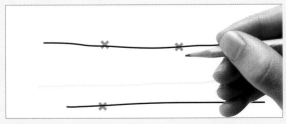

5. When you reach the end of your datum line you should have a series of dots representing ground level and the top of your wall. You can now connect these dots together.

6. Now measure in all the features, such as doorframes, windows, carvings and areas of damage, again using the datum line. You can draw in all the bricks and stonework. However, a simpler solution is to draw a sample around the door or windows.

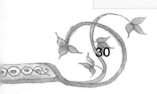

Many groups across the country specialise in buildings research. Although we encourage you to make your own initial observations, these experts may be able to provide further advice and assistance. They can be particularly helpful in dating specific joints and structures, as well as providing an overview of general trends in **vernacular building style** over the centuries.

Like many aspects of this project, discovering a 'lost' ancient house using your own initiative and tenacity will feel much more rewarding than starting with someone else's discovery. In Dunster, we were able to add a group of entirely new discoveries to the historical record, which was very satisfying.

As the project progressed, we kept in touch with the Somerset Vernacular Buildings Group (SVBG) and they were always helpful and pleased to hear about our discoveries. There are just too many vernacular buildings – ordinary houses of the ordinary people – for the existing groups to research comprehensively, and a new initiative in a village or town will be welcomed.

Building surveys

Completing a building survey of your village can be a great tool to explore how your village's appearance has changed over time, as well as making a record of how it looks today. Mick described buildings as "the first layer of archaeology." A building survey should not solely focus on the oldest or the most impressive structures but instead cover a range of buildings from all periods.

An extensive survey covers a wider area and is useful in presenting an overview of the village, whereas an intensive survey drills down into greater detail of a specific area, such as a particular building.

You may be able to draw every building within your village. However, if your timescale doesn't afford you that luxury, try to conduct an intensive survey on a variety of interesting buildings, from the humble labourer's cottage to the grand manor house and include the rest within an extensive survey.

BELOW *Richard Parker's detailed reconstruction of a Medieval abbey refectory*

ABOVE *An exposed barn roof, laying bare its beautiful oak-framed construction*

As with our map analysis in Category 1, the best way to understand a building is to draw it. You may wonder what is the point of drawing a building when it is much simpler and quicker to photograph it. The process of drawing helps you to look closely at the finer details and potentially notice bits that may be missed if you just point and click. That being said, it is always worth taking photos to support any drawing you do. Completing an intensive survey on a building involves making a detailed, measured plan of the interior and exterior.

You need to think carefully about which building you wish to draw, bearing in mind that drawing in this manner can take a long time, so it's a good idea to pick out a particularly interesting building that is related to your project.

Architectural features

When drawing internal elevations remember to include all the architectural features, such as: doors, windows, mullions, fireplaces, lintels, beams, posts and rafters. Annotate any important details or observations like missing peg holes or hidden joints. Roof spaces should also be included within your intensive survey. These can be particularly valuable as they often contain early timbers.

It is very important that you label your plan. Note down the date, your name and the names of anyone who may have helped, the name of the building and wall being illustrated, for example 'east elevation'. Finally, all of your plans should be drawn up in ink or scanned into the computer as soon as possible.

ABOVE *Look out for dates carved into masonry or mounted on plaques, but remember these may denote an extension rather than the original build*

ABOVE *An historic window in Dunster reveals much about the time of the building's construction*

Whilst completing your building's survey, think about how old each building is and how it might have changed over time. This is when drawing, rather than photographing, a wall is especially useful, as it will help you to notice the smaller details. The most obvious clue, of course, is a date engraved on the building. To find a date, check above the front door, the top of drainpipes, or the corners of the building. However, don't let an engraved date fool you. In some cases, it may refer to the year the house was extended rather than built.

You can also look at the building itself. Does is have a symmetrical Georgian or a Gothic Victorian style? How big are the windows? Do the doorways have arches over them? What are the walls made from?

An incredibly useful book for dating architectural features inside and out is Linda

RIGHT *An illustration comparing window styles, which can help date a building to a specific period*

23/10/16 - A beautiful example of detailing in a corner of a fireplace. This may help date an interior renovation

Georgian window   **Victorian window**

Hall's *Period House Fixtures and Fittings 1300-1900*. Trevor Yorke has also written a range of invaluable reference guides. These are worthwhile investments for any project that includes buildings. Whilst dating the original building is important, you should also look for clues as to how the building has changed. Of course, the older the building you're studying, the more alterations and additions it will have undergone.

If the glass panes are smaller in one part of the building, it is likely this area is earlier than the rest. Perhaps a window has been inserted or a doorway has been bricked up. Even a break in the surface of a straight wall may allude to an original wall that once stood there. Note down any clues on your drawings. Then, using books, the Internet or the help of a buildings expert, you can interpret these clues.

Dendrochronology

Finally, there is the option to date some of the timbers within your building using dendrochronology. This scientific technique dates timber by analysing the tree rings, also known as growth rings. Each year most trees grow a layer of new wood under their bark. The thickness of that layer depends on various factors, including the environment, the soil type, the genetic make-up of the tree and the climate. Therefore, examining tree rings may not only reveal the age of the wood but also the fluctuating climatic conditions during the tree's lifetime.

This method of dating is often very accurate and precise. In some cases, the tree rings can be dated to the exact calendar year in which they were formed. However, there are a few drawbacks. Firstly, the technique is only able to date the rings present within the sample. This is not necessarily the same

BELOW *A dendrochronologist studying samples taken from the beams of a house in Dunster*

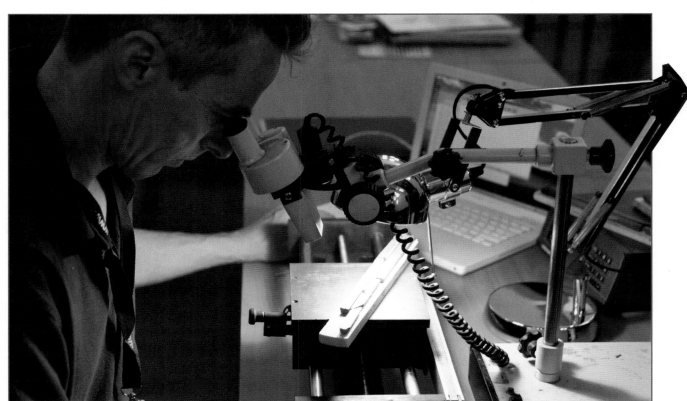

ABOVE *Dendrochronology samples taken from important beams*

RIGHT *Cross-section of a yew tree showing its rings used by dendrochronologists for aging buildings*

as the date when the timber was felled. If the bark is present, the date of the last measured ring will be the year in which the tree was felled, and so a very precise date can be established. Without bark, the date of felling will be less precise. Secondly, a dendrochronologist can be fairly expensive. So, if you wish to use the technique it is a good idea to focus on a key building that's likely to provide the most benefit to the aims of your project.

BELOW *A special drill bit used to take dendrochronology samples*

new growth

bark

dendrochronology samples

4 GEOLOGY & TOPOGRAPHY

Where do you start when searching for geology in your area? Good places to look are the walls of local houses, the church and other key buildings, as well as boundary walls. Moving stone around is a difficult and expensive business, particularly during the times in our history when there were no tarmacked roads and little in the way of modern transport. A local exposed outcrop of stone or a small quarry would be the best place to obtain this essential building material. Stone was sometimes imported, but this would usually be to embellish a basic structure built in material that was most easily available locally. Many villages would have, hidden in the woods and fields, deep pits or quarries cut to expose and exploit the local geological formations. There is something about the process of exploring the local geology that connects you to a very basic and important element in your area's story. It often defined the nature of soils and created resources not just for building but also mineral deposits on which many towns and villages built their prosperity.

Natural granite outcrops at Dartmoor's Hound Tor, a material used in many local buildings

Underlying geology

Geology can be difficult to research locally but a good starting point are the maps created by the British Geological Survey. These show the basic underlying material and offer an insight into how threads of minerals or ridges of a particular stone radiate across the country.

Let's take three geological features with which you will be familiar: the chalk headlands that make up the iconic White Cliffs of Dover; the granite uplands that we usually associate with the high moors like Dartmoor and Bodmin Moor; and the slates and shales of the areas bordering the Bristol Channel, which make up the bedrock of the Dunster area. We can look at how each was created from a basic geological material.

Chalk

The **sedimentary** chalk deposits of Britain's south east coast were created in warm seas about 100 million years ago. Chalk is formed from the remains of marine plants and animals, the fossils of which can often be found in the rock.

Granite

Areas of granite are **igneous**, formed 250 to 350 million years ago by molten magma from the Earth's core erupting to the surface. Granite regions are often rich in metals and minerals, and so typically have formed the basis of local settlement based on mining.

Slate and shale

The sediments of the Dunster area were formed in shallow seas from layers of mud and

LEFT *A piece of raw chalk*
RIGHT *White Cliffs of Dover*

silt almost 200 million years ago, during the period known as the **Jurassic**. Slate is a form of **metamorphic** rock, which has transformed under pressure from shale sedimentary rock.

As you can see, when you deal with geology, you are taking an amazing trip back in time. The buckling and faulting of the Earth's surface can lead to the lower levels of rock being exposed, giving you a snapshot of what lies beneath.

Exploitation of minerals

Geology helps us to identify various mineral deposits that became the focus for mining and other industrial activity. Regional deposits are pinpointed on free, downloadable maps from the British Geological Survey (**www.bgs.ac.uk**). Particularly in Cornwall, you can trace the igneous veins containing tin and copper deposits and see how the mining towns follow them across the county. The Romans had a keen eye for mineral deposits. Lead and silver from the Mendips and the Derbyshire Peak District were quickly exploited. Mendip lead even made its way back to Pompeii!

Towns and villages across Britain have sprung up to exploit the local deposits of coal, iron ore and, in the West Country, tin. A key ingredient in bronze, tin has been exploited from prehistoric times. As the industry expanded, small towns in Devon and Cornwall became centres for the trade and, eventually, **stannary towns** responsible for assaying the tin (Category 38). It may be that your village or town owes its origins to such deposits. Yet with the decline

RIGHT *'Devil's toenails' fossils often found in coastal areas*

ABOVE *Cornwall's Botallack tin and copper mines*

of industrial activity, much awareness of the underlying geology has been lost, except perhaps for the odd pub called 'The Miners Arms'.

When you think of areas of the country once dominated by coal mining, the effect of its decline on hundreds of small village communities can be imagined. The Welsh coal fields were created over 300 million years ago in a period known as the **Carboniferous** from the remains of the plants and trees of swamps and estuaries.

Fossils

A surprising number of regions in Britain have rocks containing fossils from the ancient past. I remember field-walks in Devon where we collected numbers of hard, stone fossils referred to by the locals as 'Devil's toenails'! The scientific name is *Gryphaea* and they were formed in seas 300 to 500 million years ago. They turn up in many places, including areas of Warwickshire and the Vale of Belvoir.

HOW TO: IDENTIFY ROCK USED IN BUILDING YOUR VILLAGE

Collecting samples of bedrock from the ground beneath the surface is a useful first step. Look for rocky outcrops or exposed hillsides. Always check you have the landowner's permission.

eye glass

4/7/19 – Visited Chagford church to examine the type of stone used in building its walls. Several photos taken.

notebook

marble
metamorphic

granite
igneous

slate
metamorphic

1. Locate an interesting stone wall in your village.

A close-up of the stone used to build the walls of Chagford church

2. Use an eye glass to look closely at a face of the stone, then make notes and perhaps a small drawing. If you have a camera with a macro lens take a close-up of the stone.

3. See which kind of rock your stone matches most closely to. Does it appear to be igneous, sedimentary, or metamorphic?

4. Look for possible local sources of this material. Is there a quarry, pit or riverbank that matches this geology? Locate the sites on a map and consult the BGS map.

Safety warning: Quarries and similar sites can be dangerous places. Always check if you need permission to enter. No geological samples from private sites should be taken without the owner's permission.

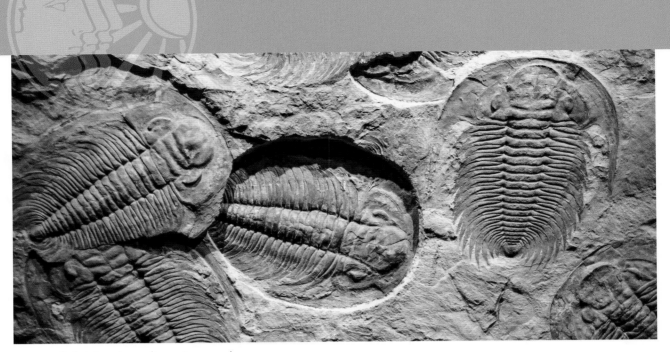

ABOVE *Trilobites in sedimentary rock*

Dorset and East Devon's Jurassic Coast is justifiably famous, but smaller areas of fossil rich rocks are scattered all over the country, particularly where there are beds of limestone. Local quarries can be useful sources of information.

Near the town of Dudley in the West Midlands is a fascinating outcrop of stone from an ancient seabed over 400 million years old. Wren's Nest is a Site of Special Scientific Interest (SSSI) and a nationally important nature reserve. Over 700 different types of fossil have been discovered there.

I remember this area well, as my geography teacher offered us sixpence for every trilobite we could find on a field trip to Dudley! Trilobites were so common in the area that they were referred to as the 'Dudley Bug'!

Distinguishing between rocks

Many of us find it difficult to tell one rock from another. As we touched upon in the introduction, a good starting point is to distinguish between sedimentary rocks, usually in the form of layers of compressed seabed deposits, and igneous rocks like granite, originating in the heat and eruptions of early volcanic activity.

What's more, a third broad class, metamorphic rocks, arises when sedimentary rocks are changed by heat and pressure to become a much harder and denser material. Metamorphic rocks include quartzite, marble and slate.

Sedimentary rocks include shales and chalk. We now associate shale with the practise of fracking and it's the cracks between the sedimentary layers that provides a place for the gas and oil to collect.

BELOW *Cornish stone wall made from slate, a metamorphic rock*

View of Chagford from Meldon hill as it is now.

ABOVE *A basic topographical sketch with buildings removed to show the key features of the landscape*

Although metamorphic, slate retains its layered property. Rock that fractures into layers can provide a useful building and hedging material. Slate seams have provided a living for many a Welsh and Cornish village. The wonderful dry stonewalls of the Derbyshire Peak District and the Cotswolds give you a chance to see the basic geology used above ground.

By and large, igneous rocks are harder and contain the deposits of minerals and metals. A typical widespread example is the granite that we associate with the high moors. Huge quarries operated in Cornwall, sending massive blocks of granite building stone across the country. Tower Bridge and many other London monuments were built from Cornish stone quarried by quarrymen living in small villages scattered throughout the countryside.

Topography

It's also useful to look at the key elements of the **topography**: the hills, valleys, rivers and floodplains. You have to imagine your site with all the buildings and other modern features removed – to see the landscape that first greeted the eyes of your prehistoric predecessors. Begin to notice which pieces of land face south and therefore are warmer and more sheltered. Which areas are protected from the prevailing wind and which hills could afford a place of protection if attacked?

How easily could the first settlers get access to water, either from a spring or river? It is likely that water was one of the most important considerations when people were looking for a site to settle.

The advantages of high land

Any high land can provide a useful strategic advantage. Dunster's massive tor would have always been a defendable place in times of conflict. In the flatter country like parts of Norfolk and Somerset it's amazing how relatively small differences in height can attract settlement. Just being a few feet above floodable land could have helped your village to survive.

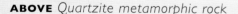

ABOVE *Quartzite metamorphic rock*

BELOW *The Goring Gap, west of London*

ABOVE *A LiDAR scan of the Avill valley, showing hypothetical flood levels around Dunster Castle*

ABOVE *Stewart Ainsworth conducting a land survey*

It was not always an advantage to be seen from the sea, as raids from Vikings and other sea raiders were a common threat throughout history. Some settlements grew up to take advantage of low land crossing routes through a line of hills. The Goring Gap, west of London, has played a significant role in our history, allowing the easy transit of supplies and armies towards the north.

A useful exercise is to complete a simple survey of your village, noting the various levels. See Category 52 for more information on land surveys.

> "Topography is a key element of the landscape and essential to your survey."
> Stewart Ainsworth

As always, looking carefully can produce some surprising insights. In Dunster, we knew the monks had landscaped the area around the farm and the tithe barn, but it was only after we had surveyed the heights that we realised that in some cases they had terraced down through levels that were 3 to 4 metres above the present ground level.

Maps and scans

Your basic OS map will be a valuable guide to the simple topographic features. It's a useful skill to be able to draw a section of a feature, like a hill or valley, using the plan and contour lines on the OS map. The OS produces a number of guides showing how to do this.

We now have **LiDAR** scanning technology available through organisations including the Environment Agency. LiDAR stands for 'light detection and ranging', and essentially it sees through all surface features to reveal the shape of the land beneath. The data covers large areas of the country for various purposes and, with luck, there may be scans of your area.

In Dunster, we were interested in seeing how the effects of small rises in sea levels had affected the area around the tor. In the past, the sea level has changed due to drainage and reclamation. Historic documents have been interpreted as indicating that seawater may have lapped at the base of the feature. Landscape archaeologist Stewart Ainsworth was able to manipulate the LiDAR model to show a sea level rise, and how far the water would have come up the valley of the River Avill (see LiDAR model opposite). It seems likely that a relatively small increase in sea level would have allowed ships in the thirteenth century to come nearer to the castle, possibly using a port in the area that today is called Marsh, but it seems unlikely the sea reached the castle. This has led our research in the direction of looking for a potential harbour in a location nearer to the sea.

Changes to the historical landscape

Research into the details of historical landscape changes near the coast is a complex matter, but it seems to be the case that today's coastal valleys and flood-plains have been inundated by storms in the past. This continues to be a highly volatile environment, now more than ever affected by climate change. On Series 19 of Time Team, we visited Dunwich, Suffolk, the site of a lost Medieval coastal town, reclaimed by the sea from the late thirteenth century onwards. This is a useful illustration of how geological changes influenced by the climate can affect the landscape.

There is some evidence that the sea may have once reached the base of Dunster Castle

5 WATER, SPRINGS, RIVERS & WELLS

If you have ever lived on an island with a limited water supply, relying on a rainwater cistern that gradually diminishes as the summer progresses, you will appreciate the miracle of Britain's modern water supply system. To just turn on a tap and get 'potable' drinking water is amazing. The fact that, in addition, we flush two gallons of high quality water down the loo every time we use it seems bizarre! Water supplies are one of the most important factors when it comes to settlement. The small well or stream that you take for granted may once have been vital to your village's survival. Without a plumbing system, taps and other modern conveniences, how did your predecessors get the water they needed?

An ancient 'clapper' bridge over Walla Brook on Dartmoor, near Scorhill

ABOVE *Sulis, the water goddess, at Bath*

Vital to life

Water is vital to life. As is well known, you can live a long time without food but not without water. The magic of pure water welling up from the ground has always proved an attraction. A spring site during the prehistoric period was often a place where animals were butchered prior to carrying the joints of meat back to the main camp. There are a number of sites on South Dartmoor with a spring, around which are scattered handfuls of Mesolithic flint. Often near them are the remnants of later Neolithic settlements – the first farmers. Are these the places where early settlement began – groups coalescing around a source of water?

Water has always had both a practical and spiritual element. All the major spring sites in the Iron Age and Roman Britain were considered to be sacred to ancient deities. The Romano-British goddess of water, Sulis, and her veneration represented the impor-tance of some of the springs and sources of rivers to the people. One of the most interesting Time Team finds was at a Roman villa that we excavated in Series 2. Until we discovered it, a beautifully carved water spout that would have probably emptied into a sacred pool had lain unnoticed as a garden feature.

As Britain became Christianised, the act of baptism and the importance of water in monastic establishments meant that many small towns and villages were located on the basis of an adequate supply of water. The spring in Dunster, which is Medieval in origin, was eventually channelled down the aptly-named 'Conduit Lane' straight to the priory.

Sources of water

Rivers are more problematic as water sources because you never know what your neighbours are dumping in the water upstream! In 1492, three Dunster locals were punished for polluting the lord's water source, with dye from clothing manufacture.

BELOW *The spring at Dunster, protected behind a wooden door and Medieval stonework*

For the lord in his castle, a water supply was crucial to survive wars and sieges. Exeter Castle was thought to be impregnable until its water supply ran dry and it fell within two weeks. Tremendous efforts were made to provide castles with a water supply that could not be poisoned by attackers. Beeston Castle in Cheshire has Britain's deepest well at 117 metres.

An interesting question to ask yourself is: what was the villagers' source of water and how did they distribute it to their homes? Anyone who has carried a bucket of water any distance knows it is back-breaking work. In Medieval illustrations, we see a two-handled yoke used to carry buckets of water. The sophistication of lead pipes introduced by the Romans, and later copied in Medieval times, was something the average peasant could only dream of. Each day must have included a regular journey to and from the spring or stream. Cooking, washing, cleaning and flushing out the drains all required water.

ABOVE *Hands Well in Tissington, known for its annual well dressing ceremony*

Water and health

Early village water supplies were in many cases unhealthy. The large amount of ale and beer consumed may have been partly due to the necessity of drinking fluid that had been boiled first. The best advice for a Medieval peasant was not to drink any water, although there were some springs that were regarded as pure. The range of bacteria, faecal matter and other pathogens in the average supply was a great danger to health. Diseases like

LEFT *Woman carrying buckets of water with a two-handled yoke*

cholera and typhoid frequently killed off many in village and town communities. It's not so long ago that the only toilet facilities working class communities had were 'outhouses'. Many examples still exist, often storing the lawn mower. Collecting outhouses could make an interesting research project!

During the plague outbreaks in Derbyshire, a number of villages were said to have been less affected as the water coming from certain springs was of greater purity due to it passing over limestone. All the local well dressing ceremonies in the Derbyshire Peak District are a memory of how important this resource was to their lives. It would be rather nice to re-instate some of these ceremonies at every village's well.

Lucky, or wealthier, households could have

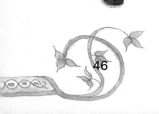

had access to their own wells and digging these was a specialist job that involved a couple of villagers digging down to depths often of over 22 metres. Air supply at the lowest point was an issue and parallel holes were dug to allow air to circulate.

Wells existed in the Neolithic period and the Roman engineer Vitruvius gave precise instructions as to how a well should be dug. Many houses had wells and it would be good to carry out a survey in your local area. There are some interesting articles about chance discoveries of wells, including a couple from Plymouth who uncovered a 33-foot sixteenth century well after noticing a 'slight bump' under the carpet!

Holy wells

All over Britain there are holy wells, some associated with early Christian sites. They often have healing properties in local folklore and some like the Chalice Well at Glastonbury are still venerated today. A search for any such well near you would be a worthwhile piece of research.

ABOVE *The Chalice Well at Glastonbury*

Water systems

In some places, systems were put in place to drain water and waste from the village or town. London had a conduit of lead pipes built in the thirteenth century. Deep sewers were dug under some Medieval towns and local benefactors constructed long distance channels, including aqueducts to bring fresh water into the towns. We've noted Truro's remains of handsomely carved granite channels. In Dunster, there

BELOW *Pontcysyllte Aqueduct in Wales*

HOW TO: CREATE A MAP OF WATER SOURCES SUPPLYING YOUR VILLAGE

tracing paper

A useful exercise is to track down all the water sources in your area. These can be then recorded on your OS traced map. Look for places where streams have been channelled under ground and rivers diverted. Many rivers became vital sources of power for driving mills. In Dunster, up to seven mills have been in operation at various times taking their power from leats that date back to the Medieval period.

tracing paper overlay

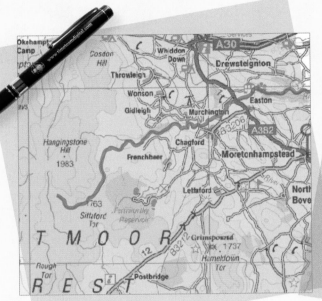

1. Look for rivers and streams, then trace them on your map in a colour (here they are blue).

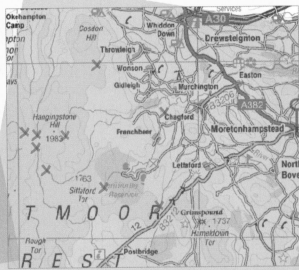

2. Look for any springs or wells, then mark them on your map (shown here as crosses).

3. Next, add and bridges or other crossings, such as fords (shown as circles). Are they strategically important for your village, perhaps connecting a major route through your village?

4. Look for any mills and the leats that supplied them. Has your local river been diverted to create a power supply in the form of a leat? These may be referred to in Domesday, the tithe map or appear on the OS map.

are small streams running in front of the cottages on Park Street. They would have made a very convenient dumping place for household waste in the Middle Ages.

If there was an abbey or priory in your village or town, it is very likely that a piped water system was created to supply the generous amounts used in these establishments. A key part of the monastic water supply was a **lavabo** or washing area for the monks to purify their hands before prayer or meals.

Proper water systems didn't appear until late Elizabethan times and mains sewers much later in the eighteenth century. As late as the nineteenth century large numbers of people died from cholera and typhoid. The first public water system was created in Nottingham by a pioneer called Thomas Hawkesly in 1831. The innovation he devised was to deliver water along pipes at high pressure thus avoiding outside contamination seeping in. There should be, one hopes, a rather grand statue of him somewhere!

ABOVE *A 'lavabo' used by monks to purify their hands before prayer and meals*

RIGHT *A leat running through the nearby fields in Dunster*

6 FARMS & FIELDS

The fields that surround your village or town, perhaps now hidden under new estates or other buildings, were once the places that kept your predecessors alive. Each community was a microcosm of self sufficiency, but if the crops failed the village starved. The majority of the village worked in activities connected in some way to agriculture. It was the heart of everyone's life. Most of the Medieval life of your village or town, up to the late nineteenth century, would have been dominated by farming. Virtually every villager would have played some role in caring for the crops and the animals. At harvest time, a communal response was needed to bring in the crops. The threat of starvation if a harvest failed was ever present. There were failures in the early fourteenth century due to a deterioration of the weather and millions died across Northern Europe. The average lifespan during this time was under 28 years of age.

Raking hay to dry before baling

The strip field system

In many Medieval villages, the surrounding land consisted of two or three large fields, divided into strips. Part of the idea behind the **strip field system** was to share out both the good and bad land fairly. It meant that a person might have a number of strips scattered across fields, but it also enforced a communal effort at the time of ploughing and during the harvest.

In some areas, these fields are known as 'champion fields', from the Latin, *campus*, meaning field or plain, and the strips have a number of different names, including a furlong and a yard.

Whilst researching Dunster's agricultural land, we came across a reference to the existence of two possible strip fields. These had been found by a familiar archaeological researcher – one Mick Aston!

The distinctive reverse 'S' shaped fields can still be seen across the landscape today. Laxton, Nottinghamshire, is home to some wonderful examples, and the village still preserves the court held to administer the strips. What's more, we can also look up the names of individual owners going back to the late Medieval period. Other examples include Braunton in Devon, and Forrabury in north Cornwall.

BELOW *A plan of the open fields at Laxton, which still preserves the Medieval strip field system today*

51

ABOVE *The Tithe Barn at Dunster*

Managing the system

With villagers often only having one team of oxen or cattle to plough, the co-ordination of the process of tilling the earth and planting seed was critical and needed careful management. People in the village would be keenly aware of where their particular strips had existed since time immemorial.

The process of harvest would again bring the village together with a huge communal effort needed to get in the grain that would prevent the likelihood of starvation through the coming winter. In many countries in Europe, up until fairly recently, the whole village, including school children, would be given the day off to help with the harvest.

During the feudal system (Category 26), and throughout much of the Middle Ages, the land, the fields and the people on them were the property of the lord. Not only could he command the villagers to work in his field and do all the hard labour, but he'd take his portion from each crop. A **villein**, a peasant who was not free of his obligations to the lord, had to set aside two or three days each week, and more, if the lord demanded it. In the case of a community like Dunster with a priory or abbey, the Church also took its tithe (Category 17) of the produce and could demand free labour.

The manorial system employed individuals such as the **reeve**, who kept a close eye on proceedings. There were strict rules about when carts could be moved around the village at harvest time and when fields with ripe crops could be entered, in order to stop the harvest being stolen. The tithe barn acted as the collecting point for all crops and enabled the reeve to keep a close eye on the lord's share.

Crop rotation

Effective agricultural practice involved ancient systems of crop rotation and a range of attempts to fertilise the soil. Gradually, farmers began to realise it was unwise to keep planting the same crop in the same ground, and that manuring the soil was worth the effort. By at least 6000 BC, farmers in the Middle East were employing a form of primitive crop rotation on alternate years. The Old Testament also advocated a fallow year every seventh year, to allow the land to recover.

BEHIND *The reeve organising the tithes*

These practices made their way across Europe, with Medieval farmers eventually transitioning from a two-field to a three-field system. In some cases, a crop like wheat would be grown in one field or a set of strips one year and then left fallow (from the Old English *fealgian* meaning 'to break up land for sowing'), for the next three or four years.

Certain grains would have been dominant in your village, depending on where in the country it is: wheat in the warmer southerly regions, barley and oats in the north. It's interesting to note that only a few people today would be able to tell the difference between, say, wheat and barley. The big advantage of modern wheat, as opposed to 'emmer' wheat of the Iron Age, is the ease with which the outer husk can be separated from the inner kernel. The process of threshing the crop, taking place in barns set aside for the purpose, and then 'winnowing', to separate out the chaff, usually using assistance from the wind, involved many of the village people.

Every year, some of the seed would have to be carefully collected and stored for the next sowing. Prior to threshing, the hay would be stored in 'ricks', usually standing on **staddle stones**, to reduce the effects of vermin and damp. Building and caring for a rick required skill.

BELOW *An old fashioned rick to dry the hay*

oats

ears of wheat

wheat kernels

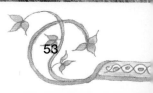

ABOVE *One of Bruegel's stunning paintings depicting the rural lives of Dutch farming folk (1565)*

The farming year

Illustrations like the fourteenth century Luttrell Psalter (commissioned by a separate branch of the Luttrell family to those who occupied Dunster Castle) show many marvellous cameos of the farming year (see page 58). Each season had its distinctive agricultural activities, and people's lives played out to the rhythm of the seasons. There is a sense of this to be seen in Pieter Bruegel the Elder's sixteenth century paintings of Dutch country folk.

W.G. Hoskins remains one of the best sources for advice on local history. His *Local History in England* refers to a number of sources of information about farms. The tithe map highlights the fields that existed in the mid-nineteenth century, and field names may give a clue as to their use. The appearance of the word **close** indicates a change in landscape, where strip fields were gathered together to form fields set aside for a specific purpose like grazing animals. Probate inventories, the record of someone's property at their death, provide details about which land the farmer used for arable, animals or orchards.

In a large estate, the lord would require his bailiff or reeve to keep the accounts. In Dunster, these are kept in the castle records. Large estate holders, such as monasteries, would also keep records of what was being grown on their land.

BELOW *Castle records showing field names around Dunster*

54   DIG VILLAGE

HOW TO: CREATE A MAP OF HISTORIC FARMS

tracing
paper

At the start of your research, it's useful to record existing farms and to look at their land and boundaries. Establishing a good relationship with local farmers is essential. Footpaths and rights of way should be respected and access carefully negotiated. Farms often contain a wide variety of historic and archaeological features and finding out more about them requires getting the owners on your side from the start. It may turn out that a deserted part of the original village lies under your local fields!

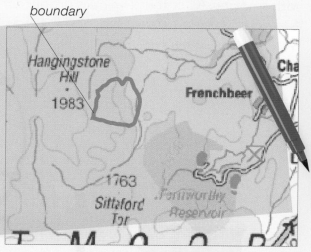

1. Starting with your OS map, identify local farms. Searching on Google Maps may also help.

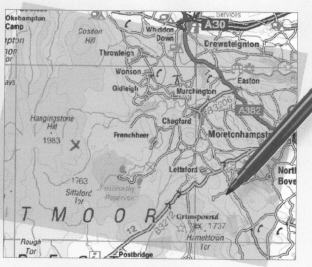

2. Mark the farmhouses on your traced version with a red cross.

boundary

3. Using a different coloured pen, mark the boundaries of the existing farm. Complete a map regression, using historic maps, to see how boundaries have changed.

4. Finally, pay a visit to the site, in this case, the ruins of Teignhead Farm on Dartmoor.

ABOVE *Cattle are one of the 'trinity' of farm animals alongside sheep and pigs*

Farmers in Suffolk refer to the 'trinity' of farm animals – cattle, sheep and pigs – and for most of your village's life they would have been the key animals, along with chickens. It has been estimated that at one stage in the fourteenth century there were over 10 million sheep in Britain!

Diet

We find large amounts of animal bone in excavations and can therefore make a list of species that ended up in the average diet. Large amounts of pig teeth are common, as well as the remains of bones that have been cut to extract the marrow – a valuable and nutritious food supply for which we have lost the taste. In areas close to moorland or forest like Dunster we find the remains of red deer. If they could afford it, many families

bone marrow

would keep a pig. They are the supreme converters of virtually anything into food, and the Medieval autumn calendar regularly featured the pig being slaughtered and then salted to provide food for winter. Salt was the main means of food preservation along with smoking. All of these animals produced a variety of by-products and nothing was wasted (see Categories 42 and 43).

wheel that rolls along the ground —————

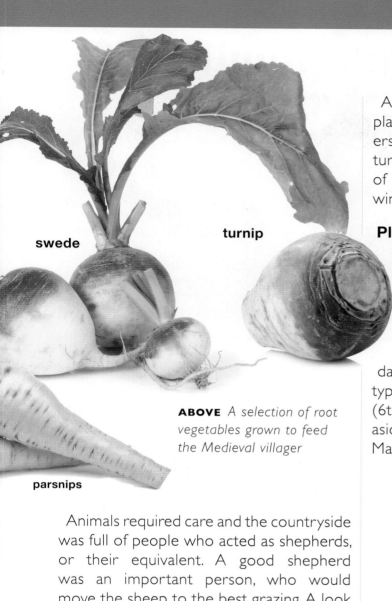

swede

turnip

parsnips

ABOVE *A selection of root vegetables grown to feed the Medieval villager*

A range of vegetables would have been planted to provide food for both villagers and livestock. Root crops like swedes, turnips and parsnips formed a staple set of vegetables that could be stored over winter.

Ploughing

With the completion of harvest, the field would then be ploughed– usually from January to March. The nature of ploughing has always been an important part of the village's life. It was given its own day in the ecclesiastical calendar, 'Plough Sunday' or 'Plough Monday', typically the first of these after Epiphany (6th January). This was originally the day set aside to celebrate Christ's visitation by the Magi or 'wise men'.

Animals required care and the countryside was full of people who acted as shepherds, or their equivalent. A good shepherd was an important person, who would move the sheep to the best grazing. A look across your fields in the Medieval period would have revealed a range of breeds, some of which we have lost today. A visit to a rare breeds farm is an enlightening bit of research.

handles to push the plough

the cutting blade to turn the soil

LEFT *An historic plough*

ABOVE *An illustration from the fourteenth century Luttrell Psalter depicting the start of the farming year*

The plough was such an iconic object in the villager's life that it would often be brought into the church to be blessed and be part of celebrations when it was ceremoniously pulled around the village.

The harvest festival hymn, 'We Plough the Fields and Scatter' recalls activities that go back to distant history. Pubs with variants on 'The Ploughman' are numerous – we still visit them today to eat a ploughman's lunch!

Ploughs were originally single pieces of timber with a pointed ard dragged through the soil by hand. Gradually the strength of animals was used, with oxen and then horses playing their part. But in poorer areas of the countryside, ploughs had a long history of being dragged by hand by the men and women of the village.

The ability to drag a straight furrow has been part of our history for generations. Folklore, folksong and the manor records all refer to the key importance of this skill.

The first iron ploughs arrived with the Romans, a simple metal blade being added to the wooden plough. The vertical cutting blades, the share and coulter (from the Latin, *culter*, meaning 'knife' or 'cutter') were its essential parts, and are referred to by these terms in Anglo-Saxon documents.

On a number of Time Team Anglo-Saxon excavations, we found the signs of primitive ploughs without a coulter. The evidence, marks scratched across the ground, was created by an 'ard' – a simple predecessor to the metal plough.

BELOW *A modern tractor ploughing the soil*

Mechanisation

The first mechanised ploughs, driven by steam, arrived around 1850, with tractors following over the next half-century. By the late nineteenth century, work in the fields had become increasingly mechanised. This reduced the need for labour and for the involvement of the whole village in a process like the harvest. Doubtless this was a relief to many but it also reduced the sense of community cohesion. From our own time on some Roman sites, we have found evidence of the damage done to mosaics by modern deep ploughs.

Celebrating the harvest

Throughout the Medieval period and later centuries, the harvest home supper was one of the great events of the year. The lord or squire would be expected to provide the food and the ale, and it was the celebration of a success that meant the village could survive the winter. There are some wonderful, authentic scenes of a harvest festival supper in the film *Far From the Madding Crowd*, based on the book by Thomas Hardy. The film also gives you an idea of the roles played by the squire, farmers and shepherds in the West Country in the late nineteenth century.

BELOW *An illustration inspired by The Luttrell Psalter, showing preparation for a harvest feast*

7 HEDGEROWS & PLANTS

Hedges are one of those things we take for granted. We drive past endless miles of them on our car journeys and mostly regard them as a living fence to keep in the livestock. In fact, some of the hedges in the vicinity of your village or town may be the oldest features in the landscape! There are hedges on the Lizard Peninsula, Cornwall that date back to the Bronze Age.

In one of his final interviews with us, Mick discussed his delight in being able to date hedges as part of his Shapwick project. A farmer had wanted to insert a gateway into a hedge line, which meant that the base could be excavated. Mick's team were thrilled to discover early Medieval pottery, highlighting just how old some hedges really are!

It's worth remembering that hedges are not only boundaries but, over the centuries, have acted as habitats for wildlife including pollinators, and sources of medicine, shelter and food.

The desire to demarcate our territory is a very primitive human instinct. We like to know what is our property and what is our neighbour's. It speaks to our sense of security and it also helps us to keep our animals penned in, stopping them from straying into other people's properties. Medieval court records contain many references to people being fined for letting their pigs, sheep or cattle stray. If you've ever experienced the damage a young bull or hungry goat can do to your garden you will appreciate the value of a good hedge!

Stone 'hedges' or walls on Dartmoor, where the soil is thin, with green hedges in the surrounding the lower fields

The divided land

Recent discoveries have identified evidence of prehistoric land division. The pioneering work of archaeologists on Dartmoor, for example, has resulted in the mapping of miles of prehistoric boundaries called **reaves**. Now often no more than raised ridges, they show that the concept of land ownership has been with us for many thousands of years.

We get the word 'hedge' from the Old English, *hegg*, and it may derive from an even older Indo-European word, *kadj*. Depending on local custom, a hedge is usually taken to be a field boundary made up of plants, trees and shrubs, but there are also a wide range of other boundaries, including stone walls, dykes and earthen banks.

Hedges have not always been considered the benign feature we regard them as today. During the Medieval period, the landscape made the transition from large open fields shared by the community, to areas acquired by the wealthier villagers and surrounded by new hedges. This was resented by some in society and the 'Diggers' movement, which arose out of the English Civil War, regarded hedges as a symbol of a new grab for land by private owners. We discuss enclosure of land in greater depth in Category 30.

Making a start

So where to start? Using your OS map or Google Earth alongside the tithe map, if you have one, look at the local field boundaries and target a few possible hedge-lines for research. As a rule of thumb, the squarer, more angular lines are probably more recent than the rounded, curved variety. However, there is no substitute for getting out and walking a length of field hedge. Safety considerations are important – don't choose a busy roadside and make sure you have permission if you want to enter a field.

Identifying trees

Before you venture out, a useful skill to acquire is the ability to identify species of trees and woody shrubs. You may think you know very few but it's surprising what we carry hidden in the recesses of our brains. A helpful field guide is provided by the National Trust. It is good to take photos of particularly fine examples. Children enjoy tracing fallen leaves and making crayon impressions of different bark.

BELOW *Laying hedges by hand using traditional methods*

holly leaves
with berries

oak

holm oak

ash

hazel leaves
with nuts

beech leaves with nuts

We're going to assume that you are heading out sometime in the late spring to late summer, as leaves are obviously going to be a key indicator. If we start with the main species, most people will instantly be able to identify holly from its prickly evergreen leaves and wonderful berries in winter. A holy tree to some pre-Roman civilisations, it was considered to be bad luck to fell one. They were used to mark out strip divisions in fields and the wood is hard and dense.

Most of us will know the oak, one of the most important trees of our countryside that supplies wood for buildings and ships. The wood contains high levels of tannin which helps preserve it. It is also useful to recognise another species of oak, the holm oak, which is evergreen and has smaller leathery leaves.

Added to the holly and the oak, we have the ash, with its black pointed twig tip. It is a hard wood useful for tool handles. We look at more folklore and uses of trees in Category 8, but two sayings unite these two trees: "oak before ash, we're in for a splash, ash before oak we're in for a soak!" and "oak for a king, ash for a queen". This second adage refers to the type of timber appropriate to burn dependent upon one's status. Ash burns with a white flame and can be burnt without seasoning.

Hazel is a common hedgerow tree and you may find signs of it being coppiced to create long slender branches of new growth useful for making walking sticks and hurdles, a kind of woven fence. Some coppice hazels are very ancient. The hazel also produces delicious nuts, if you can get to them before the squirrels!

Beeches have traditionally been important hedgerow trees and Britain's longest and tallest hedge is thought to be the Meikleour Beech Hedge in Scotland, which runs for 530 metres and is 30 metres high, planted in 1745.

horse chestnut flowers and chestnuts or conkers

sweet chestnuts

blackthorn blossom with sloes

sloes

hawthorn blossom and berries

elderberry flowers and berries

Two chestnuts will probably make an appearance: horse chestnuts, which produce the distinctive conkers, and sweet chestnut, which produces excellent wood and tasty nuts covered in splendidly spiked covers.

Two spikey trees are important: blackthorn and hawthorn. They are the 'green barbed wire' of the hedge, as you will know if you've ever got a blackthorn spike in your finger! These put on a wonderful display of white blossom in the spring, usually referred to as May blossom. The blackthorn produces sloes used for sloe gin, and hawthorn berries can be used to make a hard jelly jam. While talking about blossom, the British hedge-lines also have wild cherry, *prunus avium*, and wild pear.

Finally in this overview there is the elderberry, which you will recognise from its great bunches of white spring flowers that make an excellent drink, and the beautiful rowan, also known as mountain ash, supposedly planted outside houses to discourage evil spirits.

A species count

So why do we want you to get familiar with these tree species – to become an amateur botanist? The short answer is **Hooper's Law**, devised in 1974 by Dr Max Hooper, who suggested that a hedgerow could be dated by counting the number of tree and woody shrub species in a 30-metre (approximately 100-foot) length

elderberry flowers

A hedgerow along an English country lane, containing some of the typical species

HOW TO: CONDUCT A HEDGE-HUNTING FIELD WALK

On your first 'hedge-hunting' field walk, select a large, broad section of hedge that perhaps appears on the tithe map, and after measuring out a thirty metre length begin to count the species.

It's a good idea to divide up into a couple of teams so that you can cross check the results. As we have said, this isn't an exact science but once you have the species number (not the number of trees of that species), multiply by Dr Hooper's 110 and see what you get. There are more pernickety calculations such as multiplying by 99 and subtracting 16, and so on, but I don't see why we shouldn't let Dr Hooper and his original theory get the credit!

1. Locate the specific hedge that you have already identified on an historic map.

2. Measure out a 30-metre section of the hedge to investigate, then mark this out.

3. Begin the survey, splitting into groups in order to cross-check your results.

4. Use a checklist to identify different species. Once complete, use Hooper's Law to find its age.

and multiplying it by 110. This produces a very approximate idea of age. That said, as Mick was fond of pointing out, many hedges have been purposely planted with multiple species, and so are not necessarily ancient. He had one at his bungalow with 25 species that only dated from the 1980s! However, if you don't regard the results as scientifically accurate, a species count will give you a rough idea of date and spur you onto further research.

Hunting for ancient hedges

Hedge hunting expeditions can be great fun and you may begin to trace the route of some really ancient hedges, which can perhaps be matched with parish boundaries or, even better, Anglo-Saxon boundaries (Category 25). The enclosure movement, agricultural 'improvements' and the subsequent removal of ancient curved hedges created hedges with fewer species, mainly with hawthorn and blackthorn predominat-

ing. Hopefully, you will soon have a hedge map of your area and see how the hedges change through the seasons. In winter, for instance, you will be able to see the different kinds of bark more clearly.

There is an important point to hedge dating, because if a hedge is successfully proved to be ancient then it can be protected under the planning laws. It is illegal to root out an old hedge without permission. See the planning regulations online.

A hedge-hunt can also be combined with a wildflower study. There is a whole range of useful books on wildflower identification, but a good place to start is to identify the many species in the average hedge that have acted like a medicine cabinet for generations of villagers. Wild garlic, nettles, fennel, borage, wild mint, dandelion, ground elder are just a few. Yarrow was used to help coughs and ribwort plantain made a poultice that could help bruises.

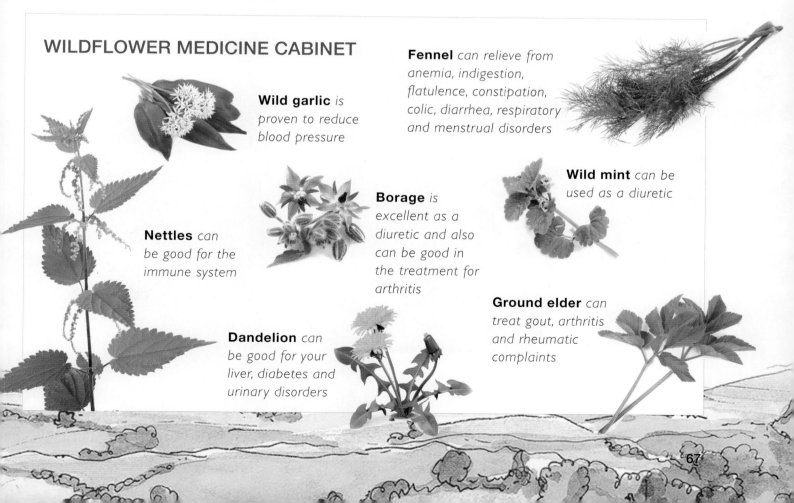

WILDFLOWER MEDICINE CABINET

Wild garlic is proven to reduce blood pressure

Fennel can relieve from anemia, indigestion, flatulence, constipation, colic, diarrhea, respiratory and menstrual disorders

Nettles can be good for the immune system

Borage is excellent as a diuretic and also can be good in the treatment for arthritis

Wild mint can be used as a diuretic

Dandelion can be good for your liver, diabetes and urinary disorders

Ground elder can treat gout, arthritis and rheumatic complaints

A hedgerow full of flowers in the spring

Some plants are also indicators of previous activity. For example, large amounts of nettles imply high phosphates, perhaps as a result of waste from human habitation. Bluebells can be an indication of historic charcoal burning. Meanwhile, presence of wood anemone implies that the woodland may be ancient, as the species takes so long to spread and establish.

Any excuse for a wander in the British countryside is worthwhile in its own right. Hedges are often the only remaining strips of wild land surviving in a landscape where species have been removed by centuries of intensive agriculture. The hedge is a haven for wildlife, so you will also find traces of badger, fox, rabbit, hare, field mice and voles, if you are lucky.

If you discover an ancient hedge it will be a great achievement for your village or town group. Make sure you record it on a map and look for other references on older documents like the tithe map or historic estate maps. Take plenty of photographs and see what connects this hedge with the rest of the village's history. Remember, it could be the oldest structure you'll find!

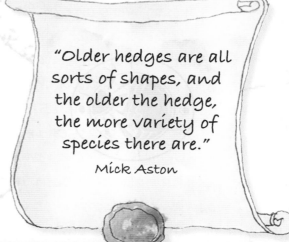

Hedges dividing up the countryside

Typical hedges in the fields surrounding Dunster

"Older hedges are all sorts of shapes, and the older the hedge, the more variety of species there are."

Mick Aston

BELOW *Bluebells may indicate historic charcoal burning, while wood anemones suggest ancient woodland*

8 FORESTS & WOODLAND

The forests were one of the major resources of a Medieval village. Timber for multiple uses, grazing for animals, cover for deer and other wild animals all made it an area jealously guarded by the lord and the monarch. For the villager, the forests were the lord's domain. Some of the most severe laws applied to those who trespassed in the woodland, poached game or removed timber.

The forest has always been a rich source of myth and legend. The wild wood, where fugitives and villains hid and magical events might occur, became part of the Medieval imagination. To regard the removal of much of our native woodland as a fairly modern event is a mistake. Large tracts were cut down by our Neolithic and Bronze Age ancestors. In Time Signs, the series that preceded Time Team, I invited Phil to show us how a Neolithic polished flint axe could be used to fell a tree. Apart from a few initial mishaps when the axe head fell out of the haft – "Oh bu**er!" said Phil – it proved to be a remarkably effective tool.

ABOVE *Timber has long been an essential building material as these roof beams in a Medieval house in Dunster highlight*

Britain's forests

The Medieval period had a voracious appetite for timber. Huge numbers of trees were felled for the construction of houses and ships, the internal supports for cathedrals and a myriad of household items. The vast roof of Westminster Hall that I visited when Time Team was excavating at Westminster Abbey took nearly 500 prime oaks in its construction – that's almost 600 tons of oak! But, as we discovered in Dunster, even the humble three-bay peasant's cottage required a substantial number of mature oaks to create its cruck frame structure (Category 3).

It has been estimated that by the sixteenth century only around 8% of Britain retained its forests, as opposed to the 30% that was covered in the sixth century. There was little understanding of sustainability and many of the felled trees had been growing for over 400 years. The First World War led to thousands of trees being felled and much of the subsequent replanting left us a legacy of tracts of monotonous pine forest.

Dunster Castle is still surrounded by the remains of a deer park and standing in splendid isolation are some ancient oaks, like ships stranded on a deserted beach. They are over 400 years old and are the remnants of a forest that once covered the upper slopes of the valley, extending up to Exmoor, which was once a royal forest. Even in the centre of the village a large oak remains, not from the great forest perhaps, but one that was spared.

RIGHT *An engraving of a small doe sheltering beneath an old oak tree*

Even if your village or town has lost its connection with the woods, a careful search of documents, estate records, place names and maps combined with field-walks may uncover the evidence of this major feature of our ancestors' lives.

Ice Age regeneration

After the Ice Age, the woodland regenerated and species including oak, ash and hazel began to grow. During the Neolithic period, woodland was cleared to plant crops and the arrival of bronze axes increased the speed of deforestation. There was a regrowth of woodland after the Roman period. In the decades following the Norman

bronze axe head

invasion, with many new towns being created, an increase in population prompted a growing need for timber. Between 1300 and 1600, much ancient woodland disappeared. In some areas across the country, only the narrow strips preserved between cultivated land retained some of the ancient trees. Small leaved lime and spindle, a wood used to create the spindles in making wool thread, are indicators of an ancient forest. A search of hedge banks for surviving oaks and other trees, as discussed in Category 7, is a valuable piece of research.

Royal forests

What did help the forests to prosper was their connection to the royal obsession with hunting, or 'the chase'. Although hunting didn't just include forest, the woodland provided an important place for the deer, the main quarry of the hunt, to find cover. The Crown's interest in the hunt made forests a carefully managed and protected resource (Category 47).

spindle tree

ABOVE Spindles with wool
LEFT A spindle tree

In the late twelfth and early thirteenth centuries, over 30% of southern England was set aside as royal forest. Other locations include Exmoor, Kinver, Sherwood, Allerdale, and one of the largest, the New Forest, where William the Conqueror's third son, William 'Rufus', met his death. Windsor Great Park has an ancient history and here you can still see deer grazing amongst some ancient trees in the grounds of a distant Medieval castle. This royal hunting ground was part of a vast area called Windsor Forest, the outline of which can still be traced today by reference to ancient maps.

BELOW *A map showing royal forests of England in the thirteenth century, from Margaret L. Bazeley, 'The extent of the English forest in the thirteenth century', Transactions of the Royal Historical Society, 4th Series, 4 (1921)*

ABOVE *The Charter of the Forest (1225) lists many royal forests*

The Charter of the Forest, enacted in 1225 by King Henry III, carried heavy penalties for illegal entry, poaching, and theft of timber. Although later fourteenth century legislation passed by Edward III was loosened to allow peasants to graze their pigs and other animals, a right known as **pannage**, and to take small amounts of wood for fuel, the forests and woodlands were still the Crown and lords' domain. The Charter of the Forest is a useful document as it lists many of the royal forests. These were vast areas and point to the existence of woodland in some areas that today may seem surprising. Sutton Coldfield in the West Midlands, for instance, had a large forest called 'Sutton'.

KEY

Royal Forests

The productive forest

The strict definition of 'ancient' woodland refers to woodland that is over 600 years old. Large estates often had maps that allow you to recreate the original size. Another useful reference for woodland in some regions is Domesday (Category 16). The entry for Lancarffe in Cornwall, for instance, records 30 acres of woodland amongst its assets.

The forest was a valuable resource for fuel and this meant that many trades relying on the need for copious fuel found a place there. Charcoal burning was very common, as was small scale iron-working, glass making and potash production. Potash, a by-product of wood ash, was an important ingredient of many useful materials, including gunpowder and 'lye' for making glass.

There were also itinerant 'bodgers' — chair makers and tool handle turners working in the woods.

Many forests must have been busy places and in areas like the Forest of Dean, where woodland and mineral and metal resources were found together, small scale industrial production thrived. In times of war, the forest was instrumental in the production of arrows and crossbow bolts. Surnames

ABOVE & RIGHT
Boletus edulis mushroom and fruits growing in the forest

like 'Fletcher' and 'Arrowsmith' hint at this activity, and can provide clues in the local registers for the number of people involved.

In the autumn, acorns would provide grazing for pigs and the mushrooms and forest fruits a valuable addition to the diet. Villagers in some areas were allowed to capture wild birds and, of course, the poacher was always busy (Category 47).

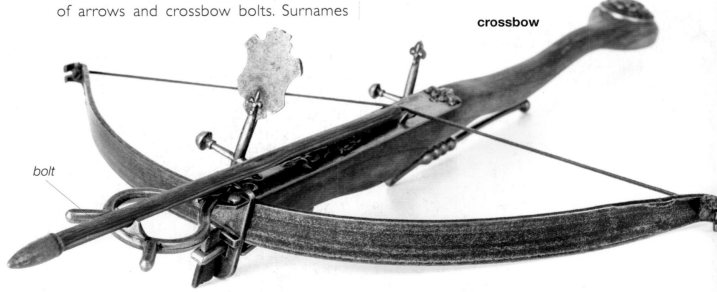

crossbow

bolt

HOW TO: DATE A TREE BY MEASURING ITS CIRCUMFERENCE

1. Ancient trees are worth recording and treasuring. A rough rule of thumb is to first decide if you have a slow growing species like oak or a fast growing species like pine or spruce. Using oak as an example, measure the circumference 1.5m above ground, then divide it by the growth rate (oak: 1.88 per year; pine: 3'13 a year). (Figures from the Hungerford virtual museum website)

2. There are some fancy tree diameter tapes that do it for you but a bit of calculation never hurt anyone! Above, you can see friends from Dunster measuring one of the oaks in the park. It turned out to be 480 years old!

long soft tape measure

a pair of light and dark rings showing a year

3. Keep an eye out for any trees that have been felled after storms or just decayed from old age and see if you can persuade the local saw mill or woodsman to cut you out a nice slice showing the tree rings. Its fun to use these like a timeline: counting back the rings (a pair of light and dark rings for each year), place labels marking some key historic events.

4. The forest is a wonderful educational resource and many trips can be made to record the height and date of trees, make bark tracings, look for woodland plants and record the wildlife.

The forest of myth

The forest has always played a fertile role in our imaginations, from Robin Hood's Sherwood Forest to the Forest of Arden where Shakespeare set *A Midsummer Night's Dream*.

The image of the 'green man', a mythical forest creature, part-human, part-tree, is part of village folklore and carvings can be found occasionally on church pews and stonemasonry. Up until the seventeenth century, wolves and wild pigs were still present in British woods. The last wolf was claimed to have been killed in 1680 in Scotland. Some ancient maps still carry the legend "wolves be here"!

Coppicing

As touched upon in Category 7, two important forest skills were coppicing and pollarding. Both involved cutting trees down to their base to force new growth of multiple branches. Hazel, lime and ash were the main species used and some coppiced trees have vast 'stools', the remains of the central stump, of considerable age.

ABOVE *An illustration of the 'green man', as celebrated on May Day, traditionally 1st May*

Westonbirt Arboretum has a small leaved lime with a large stool that is claimed to be over 1,000 years old!

Your research into forests begins with the maps and Domesday. Place names can provide clues ; for instance the Old English word 'leah' refers to land cleared in a wood, and words like 'lodge' may refer to a hunting area. A good task is to discover whether a royal or manorial forest once existed in your area – look out for the name 'Kingswood' on maps, denoting a royal forest. You may be lucky to uncover traces of deer banks, which kept deer from escaping the park, as we discuss in Category 47.

BELOW *'Stools' left after coppicing*

coppiced wood stump

Ancient stunted oaks growing out of boulders at
Wistman's Wood, Dartmoor

9 PLACE NAMES

If you decide to go for a walk in an unfamiliar area, you'll probably identify outstanding features along your route, in order to retrace your steps – 'the crooked rocks', 'the old pine', 'the deep valley', and so on. However, if you know who owns a particular field or hill, you may call it by their name – Smith's field or Jones' meadow, for example. These are the two primary ways of naming a particular feature. In the case of Dunster, we have a combination of both: a personal name, 'Dunna', probably an Iron Age chief, combined with the Old English for a hill, 'torre', giving us 'Dunna's Torre', or Dunster! Names can be invaluable clues in revealing something about the origins of the feature you are researching.

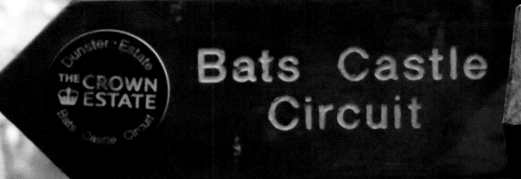

Language and its significance

When you consider the huge range of people who have occupied Britain over the centuries, each with a different language and culture, it won't be surprising to realise how diverse our range of place names, personal names, and names for other features can be. You are going to have to become a bit of a linguist!

The study of place names is a fascinating and informative adventure into the past. A good background book on the origins of language, Sir Colin Renfrew's *Archaeology & Language* provides an idea of just what a complex and worthwhile subject it is.

One of the earliest languages that may have been used in Europe was **Proto-Indo-European (PIE)**, possibly in use around 4500 to 2500 BC. Researchers have looked at all the various languages in Europe and tried to find an original basis for some of the most common words we use. Words like 'ox', 'water', 'mother', 'father', 'sea', and so on. This has enabled them to conjecture that there was some kind of original mother tongue. It's intriguing that linguists have identified some of our oldest river names

BELOW *Place names can reveal invaluable insights about a location and its origins*

as having derived from this language. The Ouse near York may have a name which originates from the PIE word for water, *wed*, the Thames from the PIE word *tamas*, meaning dark. The Avon and Dunster's own river, Avill, may have equally ancient roots.

Some important reoccurring names around settlements are a veritable trip around ancient languages! These include the old English 'tun' which also appears as

BELOW *The River Avill that passes through Dunster may get its name from the ancient language, Proto-Indo-European*

'-ton' at the end of towns like Crediton and Northampton. The suffix '-by', usually preceded by a personal name, has a Viking root, as in Whitby and Saxby. Places with the name Wearlas, Wollar or Wellar possibly originate from an Iron Age or Roman term for areas lived in by the ancient British. Burgh and Ham are old English words for a settlement and, in places like Wales and Cornwall, 'Llan' (or 'Lann') and 'Eglos' relate to early Christian settlement. 'Eglos' is the Cornish for 'church', taken from the same root as the French, *eglise*, and the word ecclesiastic. Hoskins, in his book *The Making of the English Landscape*, points out the possible importance of words like 'summer' and 'winter', as in Summerbourne and Winterbourne to indicate a settlement that moves between two locations to benefit from better grazing, or a supply of seafood from the coast. He also suggests looking at any place names that have '-black' in them, as this can indicate an ancient origin to a piece of land where use over many centuries has darkened the soil.

LEFT *The name 'Hangar Close' in Dunster derives from the area used to hang clothes to dry*

There are numerous books and websites devoted to the origins of names. W.G. Hoskins' *Field Work in Local History* has an excellent chapter on the subject, and he recommends Ekwall's *Dictionary of English Place Names*, as 'the bible' on the subject. If you find yourself becoming obsessed by the subject, the English Place Name Society has a huge database that can be easily accessed.

Key elements of place names

A broad overview of the different categories of names should include the following key elements:

1. Place, street and road names:
These may reflect their use or describe an individual feature of that site.

2. Topographical feature names: Those for fields, rivers, valleys, hills, and so on.

3. Field names: These might relate to the kind of crop or the animals farmed in that location.

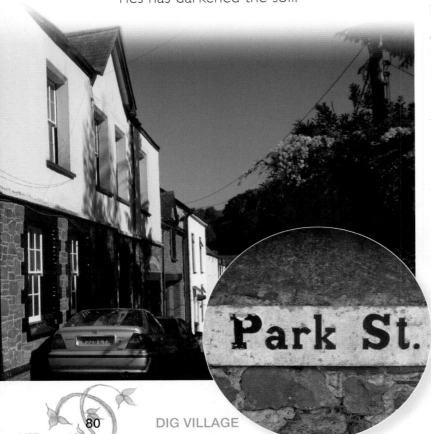

LEFT & DETAIL *Dunster's Park Street used to be called Gallox Street, after the nearby gallows*

4. Personal names: These are based on places of origin, such as John from Sutton, William of Malmesbury, and are usually referred to as 'locative'.

5. Occupational names: These include Smith, Barber, Fletcher, and so on, and may be both a personal name and also a location where this occupation took place.

Examples from the Dunster area

During our work at Dunster, we have come across many examples that broadly fit into these categories. One of the main roads that eventually crosses the river is called Gallox Street, which led to the site of the gallows. This derives from a thirteenth century Middle English word, *gealga*, related to the Old Norse, *galgi*, meaning a wooden pole. Near to Dunster is the headquarters of the Exmoor National Park at Dulverton, originally 'Dieglaford-tun' – a culmination of 'diegla' and 'ford', a hidden crossing; and 'tun' meaning a settlement.

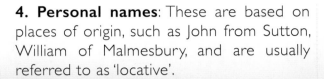

Conygar Tower, Dunster, suggesting the site of an historic rabbit warren

DUNSTER

RIGHT *Dunster, or 'Dunna's Torre'*
as it was originally known

Within Dunster, there are two fields with names that suggest their use. Firstly, Hangar Close refers to the place where the cloth was hung out to dry as part of the textile industry. This may originate from a seventeenth century French word, *hangar*, meaning 'a place of shelter.' At the edge of the village is Conygar Field. This is a combination of two Medieval words: 'coney' meaning a rabbit, from the Anglo-French, *conis*, and Latin, *cuniclus*; and 'gar' which appears as 'garth' in some records and is related to the Middle English, *garth*, and derives from the Old Norse, *gartha*, meaning a garden. The same root gives us in Old English *geard*, from where we get our word 'yard'.

Navigating between languages and place names is not always helped by the fact that some letters appear differently in different languages. In Welsh for instance, Caernarv-on in English is spelt with a 'v' but in Welsh an 'f' and pronounced the same, and *araf*, which means slow, is pronounced as 'arav'. This provides interesting problems for name researchers wandering throughout the valleys in Wales!

Continuing our survey of Dunster, the nearby port of Watchet derives its name from a Celtic word, *waesc*, which means 'a land flooded by water', possibly a useful warning to the early settlements.

Names don't always stay the same

Mick often noted how place names tend to change over time because they no longer suit modern tastes. Our ancestors had an earthy sense of humour. Many settlements

BELOW *A view of Dunster Castle over the village from Conygar Field*

HOW TO: HUNT FOR PLACE NAMES AND DISCOVER THEIR ORIGINS

What are the origins of the place names in and around your village? Remember that occupations, geographical features and personal names often played a part. Look at the examples below – can you find similar examples near you?

1. Functional name: 'Butts' or more commonly, 'Butts Lane' denotes an area historically used for mandatory archery practice. Other examples include Hangar Close and Mill Road.

2. Geographical feature: Marsh Lane has a clear link with the local geology. Other examples include the suffix 'Tor' to describe a dominant hill (often found in locations like Dartmoor), or 'ford' near a river.

3. Occupational name: Like functional names, these describe the location of a specific activity. Examples include Tanner Street, Fletchers Crescent, Baker Street and Butchers Row.

4. Personal name: Often a street or location is named after a specific person or family, typically connected to the area, such as Downing Street, Albert Road, Denmans Close and Killigrew Street.

have names that identify locations where some of the more illicit and unpleasant aspects of village life found a home. These occasionally get sanitised. Lovers Lane may appear on modern maps, but in some cases it might have originally been called Whambottom Lane, as in Lancashire! As you can imagine, this can be a colourful area of research. On our journeys around the West Country, we came across the unambiguous Shitterton in Dorset, and it is to the credit of the villagers that they have never changed it!

Surnames, geography and trade

A surprising number of surnames come from quite geographically specific locations, in some cases a single farm. All the people with that name can trace their ancestry back to a common root. Amongst our friends at Dunster was a Stinchcombe, which may mean a gnat or bird infested valley! A small village in Gloucestershire called by that name has a lot of Stinchcombes in the graveyard. This type of surname is known as **toponymic**.

Amongst our DigVillage helpers, we have a Webber, the occupational name for weaver, and a Bender, possibly relating to the Old English for a bow maker, or for the German for a cooper or barrelmaker known as Fassbender.

Where to start

A good starting point in your village is to note down as many names as you can, ordered into the five categories we suggested above. Personal names will be provided by the records of the poll tax, the tithe map and the burial records for the church. Look out for unusual names that may have earlier languages or occupations built into them. It's a useful is to research the trades in your area to see if any of the names relate (Category 37). Finding one particular name and hunting down its origins is a good task to undertake (Category 55).

Google, *The Dictionary of British Place Names* by A.D. Mills, *The Oxford Dictionary of English Surnames* and, in the West Country, Oliver Padel's *Cornish Place-Name Elements*, will be useful companions along the way.

BELOW *Searchable online tithe maps showing registered names of the landowners*

Names like 'Shitterton' and 'Love Lane' provide colourful clues to the locations' original uses

Dunster High Street looking towards
the castle

II.
Key Buildings

In this section, we take a look at some of the key buildings that will have informed village life and the development of the settlement throughout its history – the physical structures that reinforced the social order.

10 CHURCH & GRAVEYARD

One of my earliest memories of Mick on Time Team is of our visit to the church at Dorchester on Thames at the start of the pilot programme. He pointed out all the features that would enable us to read the history of the building. He had a great eye for the small details that previous alterations had left in the outside walls. As an aside, he noted that a church should be circled in a specific way – clockwise – or you would, by going in the opposite direction to the natural route of the sun, be in a state of 'widdershins' which was not good! For most of your Medieval predecessors, the Church was essential to their existence. It gave them God's blessing on the most important events of their lives. It crucially pardoned their sins and allowed them to say prayers for themselves, their

The Priory Church of St George towers over the rooftops of Dunster

deceased friends and family that would reduce the pain of Purgatory. As many church wall paintings and other illustrations in bibles and illuminated books confirm, Purgatory and the ever-present threat from the Devil were only too real for the Medieval villager. They would have believed that the little village church and its priest were their only protection and salvation.

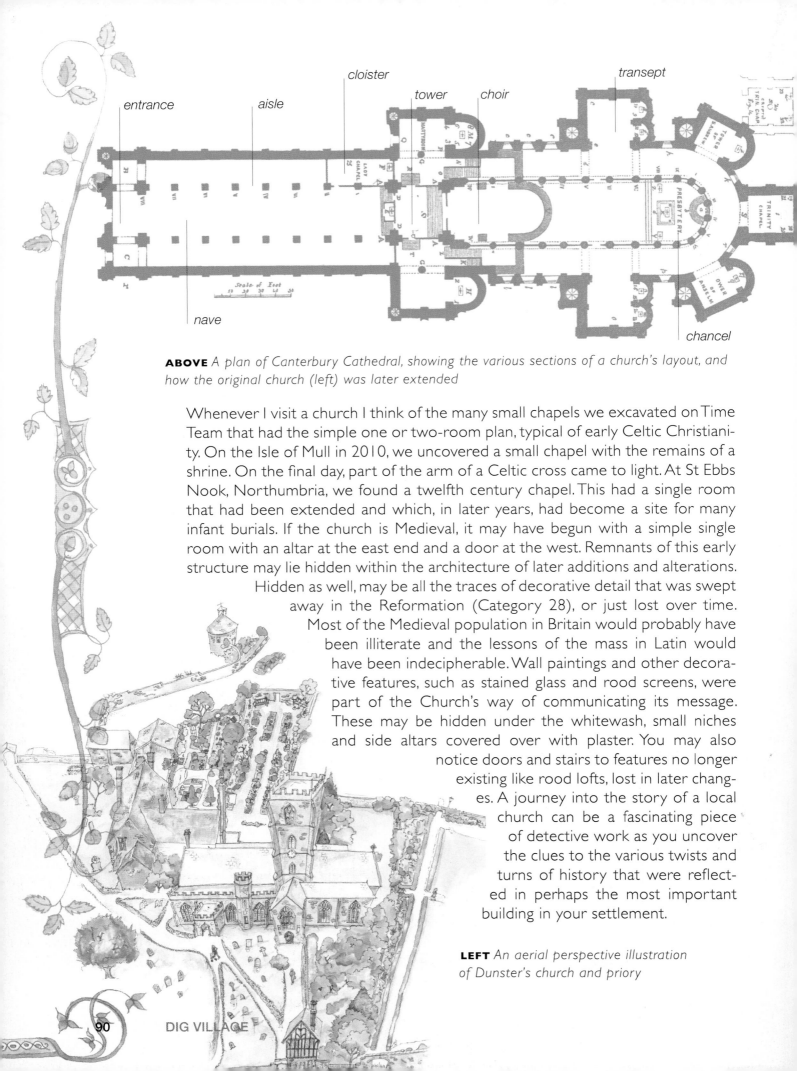

entrance   aisle   cloister   tower   choir   transept   chancel

nave

ABOVE *A plan of Canterbury Cathedral, showing the various sections of a church's layout, and how the original church (left) was later extended*

Whenever I visit a church I think of the many small chapels we excavated on Time Team that had the simple one or two-room plan, typical of early Celtic Christianity. On the Isle of Mull in 2010, we uncovered a small chapel with the remains of a shrine. On the final day, part of the arm of a Celtic cross came to light. At St Ebbs Nook, Northumbria, we found a twelfth century chapel. This had a single room that had been extended and which, in later years, had become a site for many infant burials. If the church is Medieval, it may have begun with a simple single room with an altar at the east end and a door at the west. Remnants of this early structure may lie hidden within the architecture of later additions and alterations. Hidden as well, may be all the traces of decorative detail that was swept away in the Reformation (Category 28), or just lost over time. Most of the Medieval population in Britain would probably have been illiterate and the lessons of the mass in Latin would have been indecipherable. Wall paintings and other decorative features, such as stained glass and rood screens, were part of the Church's way of communicating its message. These may be hidden under the whitewash, small niches and side altars covered over with plaster. You may also notice doors and stairs to features no longer existing like rood lofts, lost in later changes. A journey into the story of a local church can be a fascinating piece of detective work as you uncover the clues to the various twists and turns of history that were reflected in perhaps the most important building in your settlement.

LEFT *An aerial perspective illustration of Dunster's church and priory*

The plan of the church

At the centre of most English villages you will find a church. Many of these spectacular buildings are over 700 years old and each one has its own unique history to tell. Learning how to spot the clues behind the local church is key to unravelling the history of your village. As we have said, the first thing to realise is that the building you see today is likely to be completely different from the original church building.

A good starting point is to familiarise yourself with some of the names used for each part of the church. Many of us know these words but are uncertain of their origins and meaning.

As you enter the door of most churches you will be standing in a large space, which since the fifteenth or sixteenth century has been filled with pews. This is called the **nave**, a word with its origins in the idea that the church was a kind of boat carrying Christian souls towards God. The word 'navigation' has the same root, the Latin, *navis*, meaning ship. For much of the past, the congregation would have stood in this space. Chairs for the wealthy and later pews, from the Dutch word *puye*, meaning a 'stone ledge', were a later addition. The old and infirm could lean on the wall for support. This may have been the basis for sayings like "the weakest go to the wall."

BELOW *Leighton Buzzard church, with the transepts extending from the centre*

transept

A stained glass window at St Michael's
Mount chapel, Cornwall

The congregation face the end of the church with the altar and this area is called the **chancel**, coming from the Latin, *cancelli*, meaning crossbars. In churches of the Greek Orthodox faith and others this area is screened off by an elaborate panel to acknowledge the mystery and holiness of this area. The chancel or the area immediately in front of it can be extended to the left and right which creates the traditional cruciform shape. These extensions are called **transepts**, from the Latin, *trans*, meaning across and *septum*, meaning a division or fence.

ABOVE *A small Saxon window in St Bueno's Church, Culbone, Somerset*

Orientation of your church

You will have no need for a compass when you are near a church because the building is almost always set out with the altar to the east and the transepts aligned north-south. The reason for this orientation is obscure but may have originated in the fact that early Jewish communities faced towards Jerusalem to pray and this for the majority meant facing east, and also this was the expected location for Christ's resurrection.

As churches were expanded over time, space was added to the right and left of the nave and these are the aisles. Between the nave and the aisles are usually a series of arches and this structure is called the **arcade**. It may contain remnants of the earlier church wall. It's worth comparing the style of the arcade with the exterior wall of the aisle as this will usually be later. The Victorians however, who did a lot of church 'improvement', sometimes re-used the older windows in the newer exterior. Don't forget to look at the floor beneath your feet. Grave slabs and decorative tiles can tell a unique story.

Corners and windows

While you are exploring the recesses, have a look at the corners of the nave. The nave walls were often knocked through when a church was extended, however its original corners may remain intact. If they are high shouldered with tall narrow proportions it is possible that this part of the building may date from either the Norman or Saxon period.

See if you can spot any tiny windows in this part of the building. Most early English Medieval churches had small windows, partly because glass was very expensive at the time but also because a building was much more secure from attack without large windows.

If you are lucky, you may have some splendid stained glass windows, usually at the east end. These can include fragments of earlier glass and you can usually distinguish between glass that has the deep colour of Medieval craftsmanship and the later glass, which tends to have colour and etchings painted on the surface.

RIGHT *Steep pitches on the roof of Dunster's church*

93

In the Priory Church of St George in Dunster, there is a small fragment of Medieval glass. With any window, it's worth looking at the shape of the upper part as this can be stylistically dated and be a useful clue for dating.

ABOVE *Dunster's St George's Church at night*

The roof and tower

Any church roof is worth a good look. They often require replacing, at a considerable investment of money and skill. The roof may also provide clues as to the age and development of your church.

The earliest roof is likely to be situated over the chancel or nave. Steep pitched roofs tend to be older, whilst shallow pitched roofs are often newer. Although this is the general rule of thumb, it is not foolproof. The Victorians, for example, often used steep roofs as part of a revival of older architecture.

The final key piece of your basic church plan will be the tower that often contains the church bells. These were complex and difficult constructions, prone to collapse. They may be supported by massive arches and in some churches they are built at the west end. Again they require a considerable investment and details of costs and the craftsmen who built it and the parishioners who donated funds can be found in church records. Dunster's church has a central tower, which was built in 1443 and required considerable arches to support its weight.

This is probably a good time to take a detailed look at the exterior, paying particular attention to those places where the nave meets the chancel and the transepts have been added. The remains of additions or doors can leave traces and a good set of photographs will be useful. Take them in a good low-raking light, so that variations in the surface will stand out.

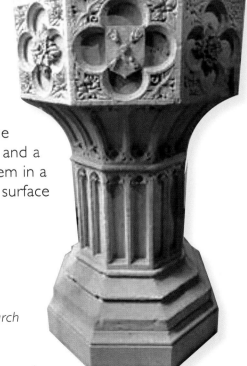

RIGHT *The font at Dunster church*

Church furniture

Having created a basic plan of the main features both inside and out, you now need to work your way through some of the key elements of what is sometimes called church 'furniture'. Many books provide a good guide on this subject, but we have selected a few key points to look out for.

Firstly, have a look at your church's **font**, the basin that holds the water used during baptisms. Old fonts were often retained as a symbol of status; therefore the font you see today may, if you are lucky, be very early.

The origin of the word comes from the Latin, *fons*, meaning a 'spring' or 'fountain'. Baptism is such an important part of Christianity that this feature can be a highly valued part of the church, enhanced with beautiful carvings and inscriptions.

In the later Medieval period, the font was embellished with an elaborate hood or canopy. This was a way of protecting the sacred, blessed water from those who wanted to use it for non-benign purposes.

Many fonts in English village churches even date back to the Saxon and Norman period. Norman fonts were generally made from stone, although a few were made from lead. In some Cornish churches, the stone used for the font was imported from France. To begin a record of as many of your local fonts as possible, particularly if they are ancient, would be a useful piece of research.

Fonts can be in a variety of shapes and styles and are generally beautifully carved. Examining your font is a useful starting point because if your church has a very old looking font, it's a fairly safe assumption that your original church building is of a similar age.

You may be lucky and find that your church has preserved its **rood screen**. This divides the chancel from the nave and may reflect an earlier division between a more sacred space at the east end and a community space in the nave. Rood screens can be some of the most beautiful features in British churches (see below). Although many were vandalised during the Reformation, some still survive and in areas like Norfolk still retain traces of their original paintings.

BELOW *The intricately carved rood screen at Dunster church*

The ancient floor tiles at Dunster church

The word 'rood' comes from an Old English root meaning 'rod' or 'pole', relating to the crucifix that was placed on top of the screen. It was Church law that every church had to have a representation of the crucifixion at the east end. The rood loft allowed access and along the rood beam candles would be lit. Dunster church has one of the longest rood screens in the country, at over 40 foot.

Keep an eye open for your parish chest that many churches have hidden away. This can be of considerable age and was where the priest kept the church funds. They were strongly constructed with iron bands and a number of different locks to improve security. Some may date back to the thirteenth century.

Finally, architectural features such as doorways, tombs and brasses and other details can provide brilliant clues as to the age of your original church and all of its various additions.

To find out more, have a read of *Historic English Churches: A Guide to Their Construction, Design and Features*, by Geoffrey R. Sharpe. Whilst these features can provide great clues, there are two important points to bear in mind. Firstly, if a later feature such as a Georgian window has been inserted into a Medieval wall, then there is no obvious way of telling if the wall is Georgian or Medieval. Secondly, various features like fonts, doorways and windows were often regarded as special and so may have been reused during later extensions. This often happened during the Middle Ages, particularly with Norman doorways. This is because history was a way of proving the authority of the church. If an old door was inserted into a new part of the building, it could make the extension look as old and important as the rest of the church.

HOW TO: CONDUCT A GRAVEYARD SURVEY

Having investigated the main church structure, you can then look at the graveyard. Graveyard surveys can be a fascinating route into your village's past. When you think of the literally hundreds of burials that an ancient churchyard contains it is an astonishing place where the villagers of the past who created your village have left their mortal remains. These bodies and the soil brought in to create an extra level of space can result in graveyards that are raised well above the surrounding street level.

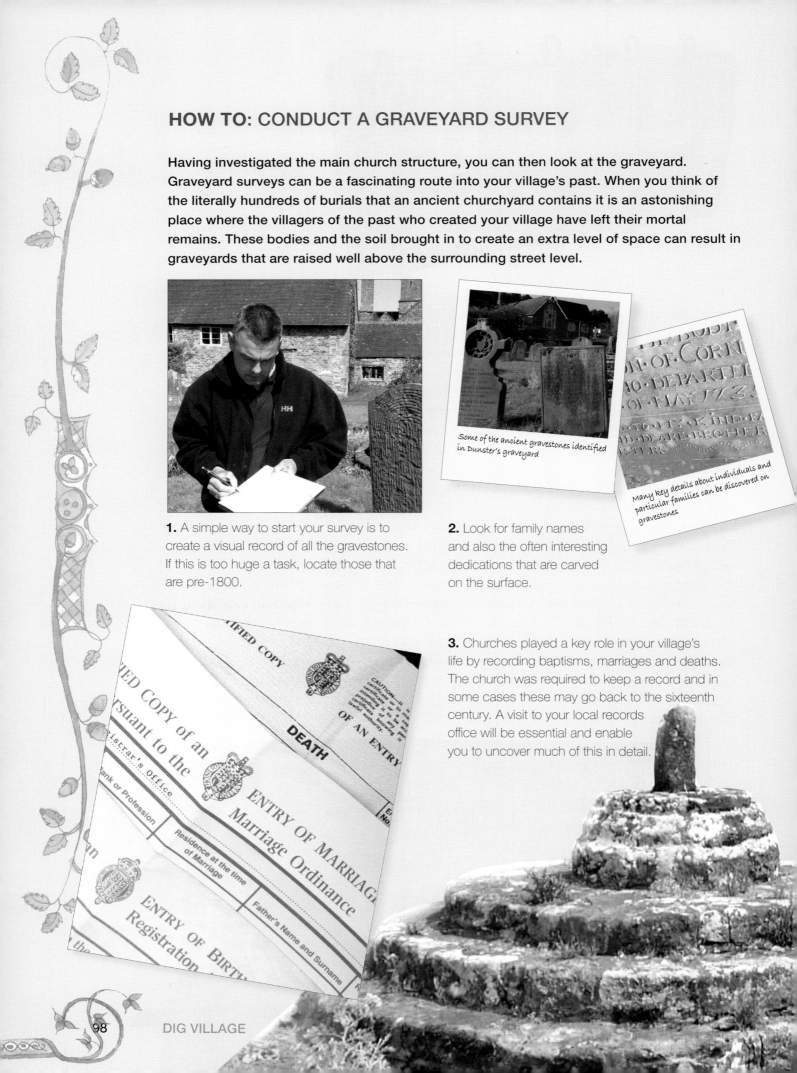

Some of the ancient gravestones identified in Dunster's graveyard

Many key details about individuals and particular families can be discovered on gravestones

1. A simple way to start your survey is to create a visual record of all the gravestones. If this is too huge a task, locate those that are pre-1800.

2. Look for family names and also the often interesting dedications that are carved on the surface.

3. Churches played a key role in your village's life by recording baptisms, marriages and deaths. The church was required to keep a record and in some cases these may go back to the sixteenth century. A visit to your local records office will be essential and enable you to uncover much of this in detail.

Learning how to interpret the clues in your church that have been discussed above is an important archaeological skill that can be transferred to a range of buildings. These clues, of course, also help you to identify the age of your church, as well as understand how it has changed over time and the reasons behind its development.

Church boundary

Take time to look at the boundary of your church. Many churches were founded on more ancient sites and a round boundary may indicate that the site's origins can be found in prehistory. Standing stones from the Early Bronze Age, cross bases from the early Medieval period and remnants of Roman carvings have all turned up in the graveyards of British churches. Also look at the relationship between the position of the church and the village or town.

ABOVE *St Peter's, Llanbedr Y Cennin, Wales*

Is it in a central position or does it seem to be located on the outskirts?

As we have said, there are many books on examining churches and these will give you useful information. But, at first, there is no substitute for a good detailed study with your own eyes. However, one series of books requires a special mention. Mick regarded Nikolaus Pevsner's guides to British churches as the Bible for this kind of research.

If your church is covered by a Pevsner guide, you will have an ideal starting point for your research, after you have had an initial look for yourself.

Although many of us may not attend a church regularly or at all, they deserve huge respect and attention as they are unique records of your settlement's history and represent one of the most important elements of your village's life throughout history.

We've focussed on the early Catholic Church, due to its direct impact on the development of villages. However, it's worth noting that many synagogues across Britain also have ancient origins. The gradual relaxation of religious freedoms led to a greater diversity of faiths allowed to worship openly. There's a wonderful variety of beautiful houses of worship from many denominations across the country, including Methodist chapels, synagogues, temples and mosques. These have fascinating histories and regional variations, and would have been integral to the development of communities in more recent generations.

"I always think of the church as a little microcosm of the village. The church is a reflection of the interest, the spare money, and the attention of the local community and the local lords."
Mick Aston

LEFT *The base of a possible churchyard cross in Dunster's graveyard*

11 FORTS & CASTLES

We have a rather romantic set of images associated with castles – knights in armour, jousts, the lords, ladies, and a chivalrous code of honour. But for most English settlements, the arrival of a Norman castle was anything but romantic. It would have been a threatening, alien structure, occupied in the main by a French lord and his knights. The latter were a fighting force on horseback, who were often paid mercenaries. Any threat of rebellion, failure to pay the lord's taxes, or a refusal to carry out the unpaid service demanded by the lord would be met by an armed response. Castles have appeared throughout our history, but it was the Normans who turned them into a projection of the invaders' power.

Forts of prehistory

There is evidence that some towns and villages across Britain have developed out of settlements rooted in the Iron Age and earlier. A notable clue is the presence, or at least the remains, of a hillfort. These prominent features, still often visible in the landscape that surrounds our communities, were crucial to Iron Age chieftains in defending a particular territory and asserting their power.

These forts took advantage of natural high points to provide a commanding view of the surrounding landscape and a physical advantage over attackers. The defendability was enhanced further by the construction of multiple vast ditches that were extremely difficult to attack. One of the most famous examples is Maiden Castle on the outskirts of Dorchester in Dorset. This impressive structure was occupied in the Neolithic period, during the fourth millennium BC, and later reoccupied in the Iron Age, with one of the largest hillforts in Europe.

On the hills surrounding Dunster, there are a number of Iron Age features, including several hillforts. It's likely that there would have been some Iron Age activity on the huge tor on which the current castle sits. However, the significant alteration of the site by the construction of the Medieval castle has probably obscured any evidence. We take a closer look at ancients hillforts and ways to identify signs of Iron Age activity in Category 23.

Anglo-Saxon forts

Not far from Dunster is the port of Watchet, the site of what is today known as Daw's Castle. Although itself probably of Iron Age origin, the fortification was enhanced under the Anglo-Saxons, and became an important Burghal Hidage fort to protect the coast from Viking attack (Category 25). A number of Somerset coastal towns were raided by the Vikings, and so Alfred and his successors devised a system of forts for defence. The *Anglo-Saxon Chronicle* reports an attack in this area by "thirty-five ships at Carhampton and great slaughter was made there and the Danish had possession of the place of slaughter." Many of these fortified Burghal Hidage towns also became the site of mints and, eventually, expanded to become larger settlements such as Lydford, Shaftesbury, Hastings and Chichester.

BEHIND *Dunster Castle as seen from the deer park*

ABOVE *The surviving gatehouse of Whittington Castle, Shropshire, built circa 1138 on the site of a Norman motte and bailey*

The Normans

From their first years as conquerors, the Normans built castles to shore up their power (Category 26). One of the first was built at Hastings, close to the site of their victory over the final Anglo-Saxon king, Harold Godwinson. Often these fortifications began as a 'motte and bailey', with a large mound, the **motte**, surrounded by a deep earthwork ditch, often with a wooden palisade, the **bailey**. The Bayeux Tapestry contains some rather nice illustrations of these. On the motte was built a **keep**, initially in wood and later in stone. These structures could be built at an amazing speed. It has been estimated that a group of Norman soldiers and a workforce of slaves could create a large motte and bailey castle in four to nine months – considerably faster than the years it could take to build a stone keep.

In a hostile country, with the ever-present threat of rebellion, William the Conqueror looked to these castles as a primary means of asserting his power. William was careful to create a ring of castles around London and to protect certain strategic points of the kingdom. The famous white tower that we now call the Tower of London was a typically Norman design, guarding the access to London via the river. Windsor Castle was another part of this early strategic building programme and is one of the oldest castles in the world that is still occupied. Dunster Castle was built by William de Mohun in the late eleventh century, with a stone gateway added in 1216.

As the Normans tightened their grip on the country, many hundreds of new towns were created, often just outside the castle walls. At Dunster, you can see how the newly laid out town high street is commanded by the castle.

The development of castles

Gradually, the wooden structures were replaced by stone and their design adapted to face the threats that confronted them. Moats and drawbridges were added, and a curtain wall created to provide a platform for archers. In 2007, while excavating the moat of Codnor Castle, Derbyshire, with Time Team, we found one of our most memorable artefacts – a gold coin from the reign of Henry IV, which must have fallen from the purse of a careless knight crossing the drawbridge on his horse.

Before the arrival of cannons and gunpowder, castles were virtually impregnable. The only really effective attack was to dig mines under the walls or attempt to starve the defenders by preventing access to food and water. In 1138, during the civil war between Stephen and Matilda, Dunster Castle was besieged and survived for months before eventually running out of food and being forced to surrender. The siege of Kenilworth Castle in 1266 lasted over six agonising months. In an effort to deny a castle its resources, one method of attack involved laying waste to the surrounding countryside, and in many cases the local villages and towns became innocent victims of the conflict.

Throughout the Medieval period, the great barons, lords and clergy looked to castles as important strategic hubs, both in war and peace. Castles including Warwick, which began as a motte and bailey in 1068, subsequently became vast establishments that often dominated the region.

BELOW *With parts dating from the Conquest, Windsor Castle is one of the oldest occupied castles in the world*

ABOVE *Edward III after the Battle of Crecy (circa 1410)*

The art and science of castle construction had become refined by the reign of Edward I, in the late thirteenth century. Edward built a number of castles in Wales in response to rebellion, and these included some of the magnificent structures we can see today: Harlech, Caernarfon, Conwy and Beaumaris, which represent the peak of castle design. It would take an advance in cannon technology to finally threaten the castle's dominance.

The age of chivalry

By the time of Edward III, in the fourteenth century, we begin to see the appearance of elements of chivalry and romanticism that subsequently became associated with castles. His intentional glamorisation of the role of knights, in attempt to improve the image of the court after the corrupt reign of Edward II, led to a reconstruction of the chivalrous aspects of knighthood that became part of the popular image. At Windsor, he created a vast circular room for his version of the round table, and during Time Team's Big Royal Dig in 2006, we were able to find the traces of this structure, thanks to John Gater's geophysics.

Throughout our history, castles have been built, improved and destroyed, and there are thousands of examples to discover. Dunster was 'slighted' after the English Civil War, but enough remains to imagine what it would have been like in its heyday. If there is one near your village or town, it would certainly have played a central role in its history. We are lucky to have some of the Medieval records for Dunster, in which we can find wonderful details of the lords' lifestyle. These include long lists of exotic foods and descriptions of the finery purchased for all the lords and ladies so that they could enjoy Christmas celebrations. It's these kinds of records that bring day-to-day activity of the lord and his castle to life.

The castle archives

Castle collections and archives are invaluable resources for the researcher, brimming with unique historic documents, diplomatic correspondence, one-of-a-kind maps and rare

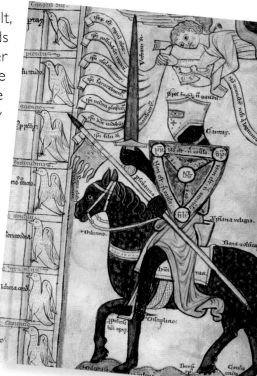

ABOVE *A thirteenth century depiction of a knight preparing for battle*

books, sometimes dating back hundreds of years. Throughout history, lords and landowners kept a tight grasp on the running of their estates and so would have commissioned all manner of documents, accounts and inventories that might aid your research. As well as old estate maps (Category 1), there may also be more recent records of previous digs and conservation reports. Enlightening finds frequently turn up in castle archives, having sat there collecting dust for centuries. Windsor Castle was once said to contain scandalous letters from Queen Victoria. Likewise 'lost' masterpieces by Rembrandt and Rubens, among others, are occasionally identified, having hung above a castle staircase for years, hiding in plain sight! These are extreme examples, but with access to the castle records, a lot of patience and a healthy dose of luck, who knows what you might unearth?

ABOVE *Rothesay Castle on the Isle of Bute, Scotland*

Identifying evidence of 'lost' fortifications

But what about ancient sites that have been lost in the mists of time? It's surprising how often you can find a fortified site somewhere nearby. Usually the best place to start is the topography – hilltops with a good strategic viewpoint overlooking rivers or road junctions. See if any hilltops have the appearance of ditches or walls around them. OS maps occasionally have 'earthworks' or a 'motte and bailey' located on them. A helpful guide is *Castle: A History of the Buildings that Shaped Medieval Britain*, by Marc Morris, who worked with us on Time Team.

Building a fortified structure would have been a significant investment, typically involving the whole community. It would therefore leave a considerable presence in the ground to be discovered by archaeologists. However, bear in mind that not every mound surrounding your village will be ancient. During the English Civil War, large mounds known as **siege castles** were often created for the purpose of attacking an enemy's castle; often leaving visible earthworks.

THINGS TO DO

- Research known historic records of local fortifications.
- Look for strategic positions to build a fortification, such as a good vantage point or feature that would have needed defending, like an important road crossing.
- Look for signs of manmade aspects of the landscape, for example unnatural or uniform ditches or mounds.
- Visit the local castle and see if you can access the archives for historic estate maps and other, perhaps more recent documents.
- Log your discoveries and plot the key dates on your timeline.

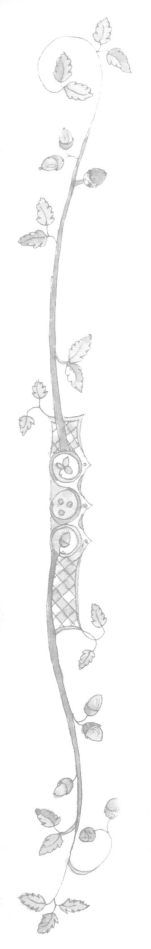

12 ABBEY & PRIORY

You may be surprised to know that, whatever part of the country you live in, prior to the Reformation which began around 1535, vast areas of land would have been owned by the Church. It has been estimated that over 1,000 religious institutions, like abbeys and the smaller priories, were created to manage this land and to provide the administrative and spiritual focus for the power of the Church.

In Dunster, we have evidence from early documents of a priory, occupied by a prior and five monks, being created by the lord of the manor in the twelfth century. For the lord, there would have been spiritual advantage to be gained by such a foundation. For the villagers, it imposed an additional burden as they would be expected to support this establishment, sharing their church, through paying tithes, and with the added obligation to carry out any work the prior demanded. This was not something that Dunster's new merchant classes were prepared to accept and, as you will see, they took a rather direct form of action in protest!

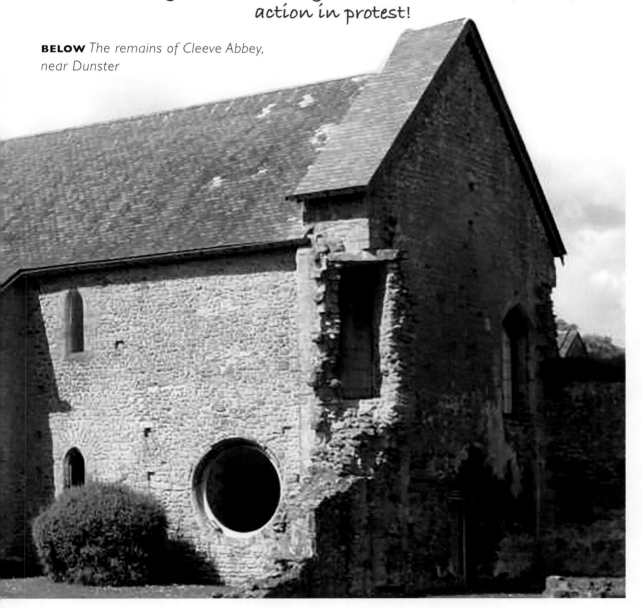

BELOW *The remains of Cleeve Abbey, near Dunster*

Church hierarchy

Many local parish churches had an allegiance to a **mother church**, and the mother church might belong to an **abbey** or a **priory**. In general, abbeys tended to be larger establishments than priories, and were usually considered to be superior, although this wasn't always the case.

Dunster Priory came under the control of Glastonbury Abbey, a vast establishment controlling huge expanses of land. The ruling order for the monks in Dunster were the **Benedictines**, introduced to Britain by the Normans. They followed the strict rules laid down by St Benedict, who decreed that each abbey, priory or monastery should be self contained, supplying everything that the monks required. This avoided the need to be in contact with the 'sinful' world, as they saw it, outside the monastery walls.

Where the monks did engage with the general population was inside the church. This was divided into two areas, with the monks occupying the area around the high altar.

Saintonge ware

The ruins of Glastonbury Abbey, a significant establishment at the height of its power

108

ABOVE *The possible site of Dunster's priory, near the church*

Church wealth

Before the Reformation, the Church acquired vast sums of money through tithes, the selling of indulgences and gifts of land. The highest levels of clergy lived like princes, with their own armies and courts, answerable to no one but the pope.

The **prior** would have been a wealthy man of high standing in the village. In our test pits near the site of the cloister in Dunster, we found pieces of **Saintonge ware**, high status French pottery used to contain wine, which gives some sense of the prior's social standing.

The big advantage the Church had was a supply of labour and the habit of noble families to donate land. The land that abbeys and priories were given was often poor and of relatively little agricultural value, but with the arrival of sheep farming, became a huge source of profit. Wool became the basis for many ecclesiastical fortunes. Institutions such as Fountains Abbey in Yorkshire took advantage of this and, with a monastic system that encouraged efficient management and a supply of free labour from the monks, created an estate that was large enough to rival those of lords and princes. The importance of wool to the Medieval economy is symbolised by the woolsack on which the Lord Speaker still sits today in the the House of Lords.

RIGHT *The Lord Speaker sitting on the traditional woolsack in the House of Lords*

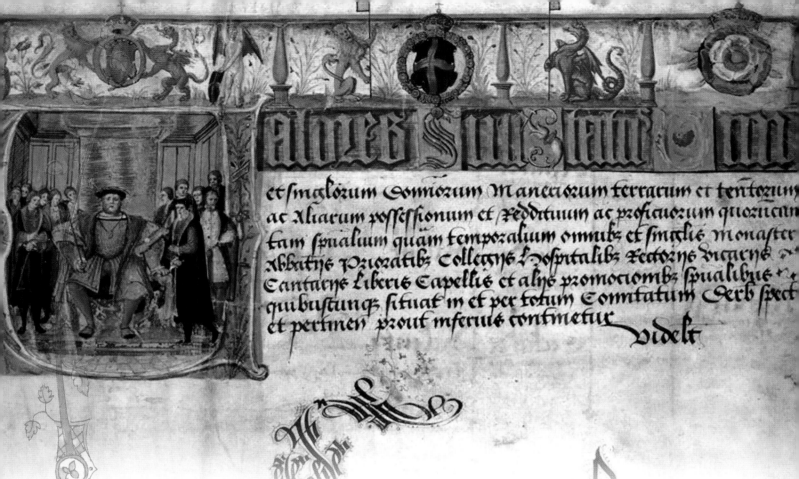

ABOVE *The Valor Ecclesiasticus, the survey of the lands and wealth of England's monasteries prepared for Henry VIII (1535)*

The most important social change that this created was that on many ecclesiastical and secular estates it became more profitable to farm sheep than operate an arable system that required many workers. In consequence a large number of settlements were forcibly deserted and abandoned, resulting in widespread rural unemployment. It was said at the time that the sheep was the greatest enemy of the ordinary man.

With the Reformation, the power of the great abbeys and priories was lost, land was sold off to the aristocracy and the new merchant classes, and the influence of the Church decreased.

Church dissent in Dunster

In 1497, Dunster's villagers took matters into their own hands, when a group angered by the tithes needed to support a group of monks and the priory decided to take direct action and remove the bell ropes from the church tower. These bells controlled the regular timing of monastic prayers and were at the heart of the priory's life. Understandably annoyed, the prior took the villagers to the Church court in Glastonbury, where an equitable arrangement somewhat in favour of the townspeople was concluded. Perhaps the citizens of Dunster had become aware that a change was in the air!

At the start of Henry VIII's Reformation in 1535, Henry had drawn up a list of all monastic property, with a view to confiscating its wealth. Known as the *Valor Ecclesiasticus*, it identifies over 800 properties and estates, detailing the assets of each establishment. Not only might this record be useful in locating sites within your area, it also provides specific information on the organisation's wealth and holdings, giving a real sense of its size, scale, power and outreach.

From the high point of Church power in the twelfth and thirteenth centuries, to the decline and destruction of the Reformation, the Church's great wealth created some of our most beautiful monuments and buildings. The great cathedrals and the works of art, sculpture and painting, sadly destroyed in the Reformation, were at the time the high point of European religious art.

BELOW *Dunster's Priory Church of St George and the site of the monastic buildings*

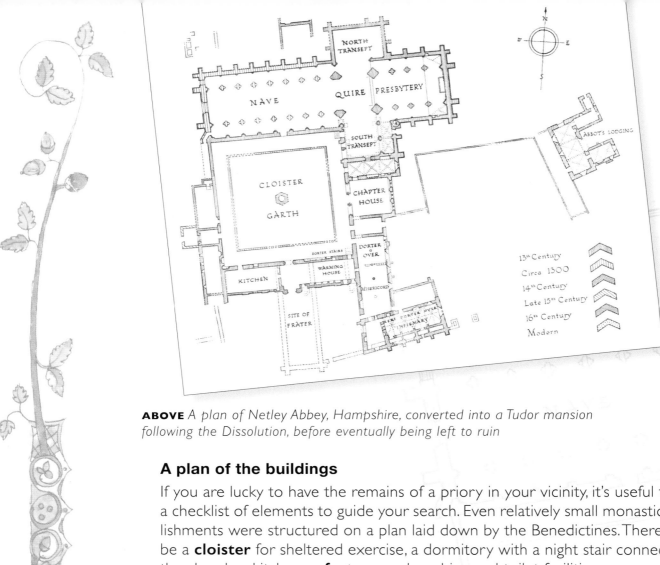

ABOVE *A plan of Netley Abbey, Hampshire, converted into a Tudor mansion following the Dissolution, before eventually being left to ruin*

A plan of the buildings

If you are lucky to have the remains of a priory in your vicinity, it's useful to have a checklist of elements to guide your search. Even relatively small monastic establishments were structured on a plan laid down by the Benedictines. There would be a **cloister** for sheltered exercise, a dormitory with a night stair connecting to the church, a kitchen, **refectory**, and washing and toilet facilities.

Conducting your own search

If you have a priory near to you in your village or town, see if you can find the mother abbey that controlled it. One of the best places to search for information about the land surrounding you will be in the local records office under the heading of the priory or abbey that once controlled the land in your area.

THINGS TO DO

- Combine field and desk research to find the nearest abbey or priory to your town or village.
- Next, find the mother abbey that controlled it. Often, this was a considerable distance from the satellite church, maybe even in another part of the country altogether or even abroad.
- Find out how much land the priory or abbey owned. TIP: Visit your local records office for more information. The *Valor Ecclesiasticus*, a record of all the land owned by ecclesiastical organisations may help.
- Log your discoveries and plot the key dates on your timeline.

ABOVE *A piece of church floor tile found in Dunster*

HOW TO: TRACE A LOCAL ABBEY OR PRIORY

So, where do you start with your own investigations? Unless you're already aware of a former monastic site, then why not begin with our tried-and-tested street name method (Category 9). Let's take, for instance, Abbey Road in North West London, which today is familiar to many as the location of the iconic recording studio where The Beatles recorded.

1. Clues in local addresses: This street has become so iconic and imbued with new associations that we don't stop to consider what the name tells us. But more clues are hidden nearby: Priory Road and Hermit Place. Perhaps you're so familiar with your own Abbots Close or Abbeyfields that its significance no longer registers. Check historic maps for old names and features that have disappeared.

2. Desk research: A quick online search reveals a link to Kilburn Priory, supposedly sited at what is now 134A Abbey Road. Wikipedia provides a comprehensive list of monastic houses, divided by county. It's not foolproof, but as a starter for research it's a fantastic resource. If lucky, there might be details on the specific order, patrons, parent houses, and dates of founding, transfer and dissolution.

3. A picture emerges: It seems Kilburn Priory was in fact a nunnery, with its own Abbey Farm, founded around 1130 (initially Benedictine, later Augustinian). We even have a 1722 sketch. These are just clues, so next, visit your local records office and search under the parent abbey (in this case, Westminster Abbey), as well as existing excavation reports, building records, and even the *Valor Ecclesiasticus*.

4. Physical remains: Of course, nothing beats returning to the field to explore the landscape. Amazingly, even in this heavily populated and densely developed corner of London, enthusiasts have discovered masonry work and a well that probably originate from the priory. So, even if the building or ruins have long since disappeared, tangible evidence might be waiting to be discovered.

13 MANOR HOUSE & ESTATE

Many villages and towns will once have had a large house in their vicinity, which may originally have been the manor house. This would have been the home of the lord or the most important person in that settlement. It would have consisted of a great hall, a kitchen, rooms for the servants and a storage area. Some of the buildings also had what is known as a 'solar' or a private space for the lord and his family. Many of these buildings still exist today and, in former centuries, they would have been the centre of an important estate that managed the agricultural life of the village or town.

BELOW *Lytes Cary, a manor house in Somerset with parts dating back to the fourteenth century*

ABOVE *A carved wood relief of a lord being served in his manor*

The origins of the manor

The word **manor** comes from the Anglo-Norman French, *maner*, meaning 'dwelling'. This, in turn, came from the Latin, *manere*, 'to remain', suggesting the place where someone of importance was based. In the eastern and northern parts of Britain, manor houses are sometimes referred to as 'halls'.

The lord would have built the manor house to live in, in order to manage the agricultural land of the village or town, and it was originally a description of the largest house in the village. The term is also used more generally to describe the wider estate owned by the local lord.

In their heyday, manor houses would have been at the centre of an important estate, typically of 1200 to 1800 acres. They also occasionally became the location of temporary law courts. Much like the parish church, the manor house itself was a physical symbol of status and wealth, demonstrating the lord's social superiority and dominance over his tenants and serfs.

ABOVE *The grand staircase of Knole, a manor house at Sevenoaks, Kent*

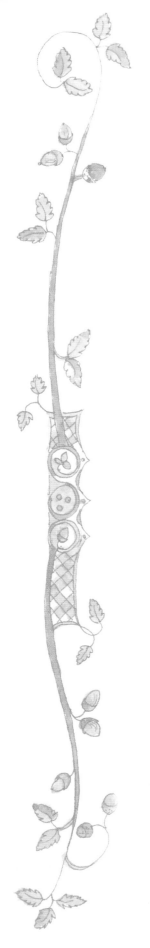

The manorial system was already established before the Normans arrived, with many existing estates of Anglo-Saxon origin. Indeed, some writers believe that the area they denote may actually derive from ancient land holdings, possibly even Roman in origin. But manor houses themselves became more common after the twelfth century. Most Medieval villages and towns would have had one, and it's estimated that there were around 40,000 to 50,000 manor houses across the British Isles in the period.

Thousands of these grand structures still stand and are often some of the most attractive buildings in Britain, the precursor to the large stately homes that appeared in later centuries. There are some particularly nice examples in Somerset, including Lytes Cary, which was built in the mid-fifteenth century, and Cothay Manor, built around 1480. Interestingly, because of the castle that dominates the town and that once served as its administrative centre, Dunster doesn't have a manor house in its centre.

Locating the original manor

For those that are still standing, a manor house's size and prominence in the village would make it fairly easy to identify today. If, however, you are interested in looking for signs of an earlier manor, one clue may be the existence of a large building plot with the remnants of a moat. In Hoskins' *Field Work in Local History*,

BELOW *Cothay Manor in Somerset, dating from the late fifteenth century*

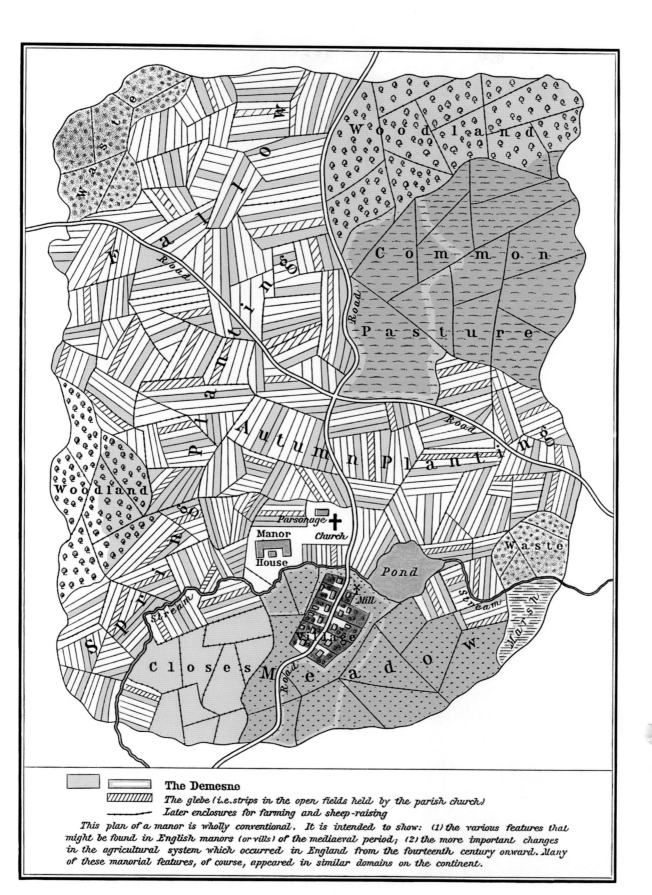

The Demesne

The glebe (i.e. strips in the open fields held by the parish church)

Later enclosures for farming and sheep-raising

This plan of a manor is wholly conventional. It is intended to show: (1) the various features that might be found in English manors (or vills) of the mediaeval period; (2) the more important changes in the agricultural system which occurred in England from the fourteenth century onward. Many of these manorial features, of course, appeared in similar domains on the continent.

ABOVE *A plan of a hypothetical Medieval manor, showing the demesne land*

ABOVE *A Medieval illustration of a reeve from Chaucer's 'Canterbury Tales'*

he refers to a study by F.V. Emery, 'Moated Settlements in England', in which over 3,500 sites were located. Bear in mind, though, that not all manor houses had moats, so a careful look at earthworks, or an Ordnance Survey map, may give you a starting point.

The lord of the manor, who occupied these estates, received his land directly from the king and, in return, would have been expected to provide knights and soldiers to fight the king's battles (Category 26). You may be able to find your local lord of the manor by looking in the *Liber Feodorum*, or 'Book of Fees', a compilation collected circa AD 1302 of local landholding records from the late twelfth to the late thirteenth centuries. Modern transcripts of this text can be found or ordered online.

Manors often acquired a large amount of paperwork and maps and can prove to be a useful source of this material for your village. Look out for 'Barton' place names. The word 'barton' derives from the same root as beer and barley, and may indicate a connection with the lord's land.

LEFT *Evidence of a moat, like this example at Hever Castle in Kent, might suggest the location of a former manor house*

The lord's land

The land of the estate was often divided in two. The land retained by the lord himself for his private use was known as the **demesne land**, which is where our modern term 'domain' comes from. The remainder of land was let out to tenant farmers, referred to as 'land holders'. Villages often retain a reference to this, with a local farm being referred to as the 'demesne' or 'domain farm', which could originally trace its ownership back to the lord.

From the late fourteenth century onwards, England was devastated by periodic waves of the plague, or 'Black Death', which decimated large parts of the population (Category 27). With the resulting difficulty of obtaining labour, many lords turned the domain land into tenanted land during this time.

Much later, in the eighteenth and nineteenth centuries, the demesne land was sometimes referred to as the 'home farm', so keep a look out for references to this term in more recent maps and documents.

The administrative centre

As the local centre of administration, manors also employed some of the key people in the village. The reeve, for example, was the person who recorded and made sure that the lord's tithes were paid. In this official post, elected either by the lord or the peasants of the shire, the reeve held a significant measure of influence in the region. It is from 'shire reeve' that we get the term 'sheriff'. It was the reeve's task to make sure that the lord's work was completed by the villages, and this involved an intimate knowledge of all those who lived in the village. If you can find out who was the reeve of your village at any given time, you will have located a very important person in its history. Returning to Dunster, the reeve occupied one of the largest houses outside the village, and when you look up Dunster Manor you will see it is referred to as his home.

THINGS TO DO

- Look for signs of a manor house. If it is still standing, it's likely to be one of the oldest, largest and most prominent buildings in the village. Otherwise, look for signs of a moat, and search the historical records for references. TIP: look for physical signs of earthworks, or an Ordnance Survey map for references.
- Search maps for 'Barton' and 'home farm' place names, or references to 'demesne' land, which may indicate a connection with the lord's land.
- Look in the *Liber Feodorum* ('Book of Fees') to find information about your manor, including the name of the lord who presided at that time.
- Log your discoveries and plot the key dates on your timeline.

14 MILLS

In Medieval times, the mill would have been one of the key buildings at the centre of village life. However, it's unlikely that the average miller was particularly popular. Chaucer's portrayal of a miller in 'The Canterbury Tales' refers to him as a "stout and evil churl fond of wrestling" and someone who was always eager to cheat his customers! It was illegal for villagers to grind their own grain, or even to own a handmill. This meant that, as well as paying a tithe to the lord (a tax of a tenth of their income), villagers also had to pay another duty to the miller in return for his services. The first mills in the village would most probably have been the property of the lord, and the only place to grind corn.

A watermill on the River Eye, Gloucestershire

ABOVE *The restored watermill at Dunster*

There were around 8,000 mills registered in the Domesday Book. If your village was recorded in the survey, look for references to a mill (Category 16). Of course, many mills were constructed throughout Britain in later centuries too, so a search through more recent public records may provide some interesting results. Historic mills could take various forms. By nature, they were large structures, typically housing relatively sophisticated machinery, including adjustable systems of wooden or metals gears, as well as cogs and pulleys for lifting loads.

The machinery itself might have been powered by horses or other animals, wind or water – or sometimes a combination of these.

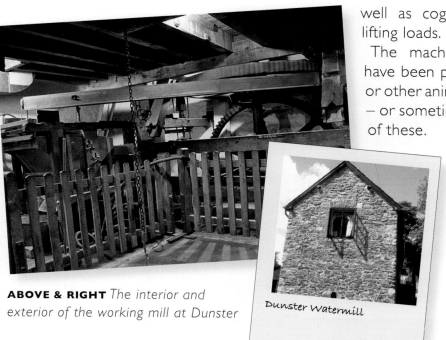

ABOVE & RIGHT *The interior and exterior of the working mill at Dunster*

Dunster Watermill

ABOVE *Peeling bark for tanning (circa 1850)*

Types of mills

There are many different types of mills, each using the power it generates to fulfill a specific function.

A **gristmill**, for instance, was dedicated to grinding grain, and these would also have contained a pair of large circular millstones. However, mills have been employed in various industrial processes aside from producing flour, from pumping water to cotton spinning.

In the process of producing cloth, there were **fulling mills**, cotton mills and woollen mills, as well as **stamping mills** to soften cloth. Bark mills, or **catskill mills** were used to produce tanbark, an important material used to tan leather, made by milling bark or branches into a fine powder. Gunpowder mills played an important part in military history, as well as in the mining industry. There are a number still preserved today, such as the Royal Gunpowder Mill at Waltham Abbey, which was originally used by the monks as a fulling mill, then later converted to produce gunpowder in 1665.

ABOVE *A machine for cutting bark*

Location

As with other features we've looked at, clues to a mill's original location can often be found in building or street names. At last count, there were 1,318 Mill Roads spread across the country, giving some sense of the prevalence and importance of mills in bygone years. 'Millbrook' is also a fairly common place name, in reference to a stream or brook where a mill was once situated.

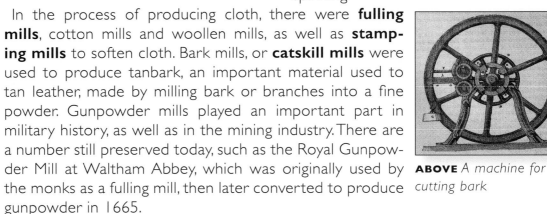

Powder Mill Pottery & Cafe on Dartmoor takes its name from the derelict gunpowder mill on site

ABOVE *A waterwheel at Combe House Hotel in Holford, Somerset, originally used to grind oak bark for the tannery*

If the building still stands in your village, it may have since been converted into a private home or commercial space. As a result, the machinery has probably been removed and its original function may not be immediately obvious. However, often architectural clues remain that reveal its former use. These might include remnants of cogs and shafts, doors or hatches at a high level (for unloading flour), or perhaps an old millstone set into the grounds and repurposed as a garden feature.

Watermills

Watermills, the most prevalent type of mill, are recognisable by the large wheels typically set on the outside of the building, over a watercourse. However, the wheels are not always visible or may have been removed. If not situated directly above a natural river, another important clue to look out for is the presence of a **leat**. These artificial watercourses were often dug into the ground, using gravity to channel the water towards the wheels to power the mill. A leat might cross over or run beside a river, and some had stone linings, which may still be in situ long after the mill's closure.

A variation of watermills are tide (or sea) mills, and there are many wonderful historic examples to be found on estuaries across Britain, often with early origins.

ABOVE *An old millstone repurposed as a garden feature*

Mills in Dunster

direction of mill wheel

water

buckets

One of several mills in Dunster, the watermill dates from the late eighteenth century and stands on the site of a mill mentioned in the Domesday survey. The mill is now managed by the National Trust, and is once again producing flour following its restoration in 1979. It has twin 'overshot' waterwheels, which means that the water flows over the top of the wheels. This is in contrast to 'undershot' water-wheels, where the water flows from under the wheel. As well as the example in Dunster, a few other restored watermills are open to the public across the country.

Windmills

paddles

TOP *Overshot wheel*
BOTTOM *Undershot wheel*

Windmills have also been used by people for thousands of years. They were typically favoured in areas where water power was less effective, includ-ing the flat landscape of Norfolk or colder regions where water was likely to freeze in winter. Large sails, which could be adjusted with gears and cogs, turned in the wind to operate the machinery inside. Several beautiful windmills still stand in Norfolk, and other examples can be found across Britain in various states of repair. Bursledon Windmill in Hampshire, for instance, was built in 1814 and has been restored for the public to enjoy and experience.

If you can find a fully-functioning mill near you, whether powered by water, wind or other means, it's well worth a visit to witness the machinery in action and get a sense of the scale of these impressive struc-tures. You might also be able to buy some flour produced the traditional way!

THINGS TO DO

- Look for references to local mills in the Domesday record and more recent public archives.
- Try to locate the mill in your village, looking for signs such as leats, waterwheels, remains of machinery or millstones.
- Discover if there are any old families still living in the village with the surname Miller.
- Visit a restored watermill or windmill.
- Log your discoveries and plot the key dates on your timeline.

A leat in Dunster leading to the Old Mill

Cley Windmill is one of many windmills in Norfolk, where the land is relatively flat, making watermills less efficient

15 THE VILLAGE HALL & CHURCH HOUSE

A theme we've returned to throughout the book is that the Church was central to life in Medieval Britain. As an institution, it brought the village community together, with the church building itself providing a physical meeting place and focal point. Today, we're not used to the idea of church buildings having such a secular function. In the Medieval period, as well as the spiritual aspect and role in upholding social order, church buildings served as a hub for various recreational and administrative activities.

Historically, the churchyard was a popular place for socialising and the playing of sports, particularly as villagers spilled out of the church on a Sunday. Not all of this activity was endorsed by the authorities, however. There are many accounts of priests complaining about all manner of nefarious happenings in the churchyard!

ABOVE *Fornham All Saints village hall, a wonderful social space in Suffolk*

A secular space

Traditionally, villagers needed somewhere to meet and carry out more civilised secular matters relating to the community. Sometimes, especially in earlier centuries, the church nave would have been used for this purpose. Yet as pews were increasingly introduced, a designated space became necessary. Hence many villages would have built a separate designated building within the church grounds, known as the **church house**. More modest and functional in its design in comparison to the church itself, the church house accommodated various activities. It may have been where the church ales festivities were held, with games, plays and ale that was brewed and sold, in order to raise money for the upkeep of the church building.

OPPOSITE *The historic grade II listed Village Hall beside the River Eye at Lower Slaughter, Gloucestershire*

ABOVE *South Tawton's church house*

There is a beautiful example of a fifteenth century granite and thatch church house in South Tawton, Dartmoor, which is still a thriving community space today. The church house provided a space for activities that would not be allowed in the church. Many of them later became almshouses, schools and inns.

Community space

In turn, the village hall that we typically see across the country may have evolved from the church house. For many communities, the space continues to be a crucial establishment, hosting everything from parish council meetings and village fetes through to children's parties, local amateur dramatic performances and wedding receptions. Indeed, it may even become the headquarters for your local Dig Village project!

Brueghel the Younger's 'Wedding Dance in a Barn' (1620)

St Margaret's Village Hall in Alderwasley, Derbyshire a contender for oldest village hall

The oldest village hall

A number of villages have traced the history of their halls back to the thirteenth century, although the building itself may not have started life as a village hall. St Margaret's Village Hall in Alderwasley, Derbyshire, for example, lays claim to being the oldest village hall building in the country. However, it was originally a chapel and served this purpose into the twentieth century, before its more recent conversion.

Dunster's community space is its Tithe Barn (Category 17), which dates from the sixteenth century or earlier. Villagers believe it may originally have been connected to the local Benedictine priory, which thrived before the Reformation. It has recently been restored into the community centre, which is used for various events, including Dig Village meetings, and is available to hire.

RIGHT *Dunster's Tithe Barn*

ABOVE *The village hall in Little Downham, near Ely, Cambridgeshire*

St Jude's Community Centre

Christ Church Community Centre, Bebbington

Purpose-built village halls

Purpose-built secular village halls (as opposed to traditional church houses) are a fairly modern conception, typically only appearing within the last 150 to 200 years. Nowadays, village halls are governed by legislation and the village hall constitution. Unfortunately, newer village developments built today very rarely include a designated community hall. Yet with some villages also losing their local pubs and shops, communities are showing a greater appreciation for those that do exist, finding new ways to use them and help secure their future.

ABOVE *Dunster Memorial Hall*

Your village hall

Find out what you can about your local village hall or community space, if one exists. It should be relatively easy to establish whether it was built specifically for this purpose or converted from a chapel or other building. Vintage photographs might reveal how it has changed over the years, perhaps from a former use. Equally, modern building work often uncovers hidden treasures, such as evidence that the building is older than initially expected.

Local village and parish records can be useful in determining when a building was built, repaired or converted for its current use, or where it was originally located. In particular, **glebe terriers** (an inventory or survey commissioned by the Church to list its properties and lands), tithe maps and churchwarden accounts should prove valuable.

Many village halls owe their existence to a local wealthy patron associated with the village – perhaps a prominent family that has already cropped up in your research. Likewise, halls are often dedicated to a specific cause, such as the many memorial halls built to honour the fallen following the World Wars, a fitting tribute that continues to serve the local community.

THINGS TO DO

- Many written archives can help you to discover more about your church house or village hall. Look for references in the glebe terriers, tithe maps, and churchwarden accounts, which might contain details on the building's maintenance.
- Look for vintage photography and visit your village hall to find out more about the building's history and evolution.
- Some church houses may since have been converted for other uses, whether as a communal space, a commercial operation or a private home. Look at historic buildings surrounding the church grounds for signs that they might have once been a church house.
- Log your discoveries and plot the key dates on your timeline.

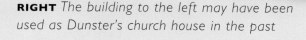

RIGHT *The building to the left may have been used as Dunster's church house in the past*

Dunster's Yarn Market and High Street

III.
Documents & Resources

Having identified the key buildings and investigated them further, it's time to return indoors for more desk research to follow up all the leads you've discovered. In this section, we go through some of the key documents and resources — both historic and secondary — that will be pivotal to your research. If you can locate and harness these records for your specific village or town, you'll be well on your way to making some useful discoveries.

16 DOMESDAY

Mick used to say that looking at history through the perspective of the Domesday Book was like peering back in time under the influence of two glasses of Southern Comfort! This was his way of pointing out the difficulties of interpreting this text, but this shouldn't distract us from appreciating what an extraordinary document it is. Nothing would be created of similar detail until the census returns of the nineteenth century. Written in AD 1086, William the Conqueror's great survey of all the land and goods he had acquired by conquest gives us a unique picture of life at the time of transition from the Anglo-Saxons to Norman rule. Because the king's commissioners recorded every detail, the survey was likened to a survey at Judgement Day or Domesday – 'Doom' being the name given to the painting of the Last Judgement that often appeared on church walls.

RIGHT *A 900-year commemorative stamp*

If you are lucky enough to live in a village or small town that has an entry in Domesday, that is quite something! It is evidence of a community in existence nearly 500 years before Shakespeare started writing his first plays, and just under 600 years before the first American colonies were settled. It also takes you back to the Anglo-Saxon community that was in place before the Normans arrived.

Reasons for Domesday's creation

Domesday was an attempt by William to understand the value of everything he owned post-Conquest, down to the last field, forest, hen and pig. Commissioners were sent throughout the country and local juries of both Normans and Saxons were created to record all the local holdings of land and property. Over 13,400 places were recorded. In some cases, juries from outside a specific area were sent in to check the original findings. Any errors were rigorously punished and reported to the king's senior commissioners. It has been estimated that 7 to 8,000 people were involved!

William's main motivation was to raise money. He still had battles to fight and needed funds for both French and English wars. In particular, he had always paid large numbers of mercenaries to fight for him and their upkeep was high. The need for money meant that the commissioners always wanted to know how much more a landholding could pay and, in many cases, William increased this amount, up to three times the original figure.

The information in each entry follows a set pattern in answer to six main questions: Who holds the land? Who held it before? How much land is there? What is its worth in terms of tax? What other assets are there (such as mills or woodland)? Who occupies the land? Finally, what might it be worth now, and in the future?

BELOW & BEHIND *An extract from Domesday, showing entries for Bedfordshire*

Dunster's Domesday record

If we look at the entry for Dunster, we can see the process that was followed. The record tells us:

"William de Mohun holds Dunster and his castle is there. Aelfric held it at the time of Edward the Confessor and it paid geld for half a hide. There is land for one plough. There are two mills rendering ten shillings and fifteen bordars and five acres of meadow and thirty acres of pasture. It was formerly worth five shillings, now fifteen shillings."

We have in this short entry a number of useful pieces of information. We know it was held by William de Mohun for the king. This was just one of the many manors he held, both locally and throughout Somerset. Altogether, by searching under his name in the Domesday index, we can find three or more large manors and over 56 in Somerset alone! Aelfric is named as the Anglo-Saxon chief or **thegn** who originally held it, before being displaced following the Conquest. Edward the Confessor is referred to as king and this was a deliberate attempt by the Conqueror to remove mention of Harold, whose claim on the kingship William regarded as illegitimate.

Geld is a form of Anglo-Saxon taxation on land. The land itself was calculated in units known as **hides**, approximately equal to 120 acres, although the figure could vary. This was the amount needed to support a family. The reference to 'one plough' is the amount of land that could be ploughed by a team of eight

RIGHT *'Writing the Domesday Book',*
Joseph Martin Kronheim (1868)
BELOW *The twelfth century cover of*
the Winchester Domesday Book

HOW TO: SEARCH YOUR VILLAGE'S RECORD ONLINE USING OPEN DOMESDAY

As Mick probably had in mind, not every village or small town as we know it today was recorded in Domesday. To complicate matters further, many villages were recorded under an archaic name that's no longer in use. It takes some careful interpretation, but it's well worth the perseverance. Thankfully, several sites have already done the legwork. So, what will Domesday reveal about your village?

1. Log on to the online Domesday Book, which has been compiled using data from J.J.N. Palmer and the team at the University of Hull: *opendomesday.org*

2. Searching by place name brings up the record in modern English. It also provides an image of the original Medieval manuscript. You can search for individual people too.

The entry for Dunster gives an idea of a typical Domesday entry.

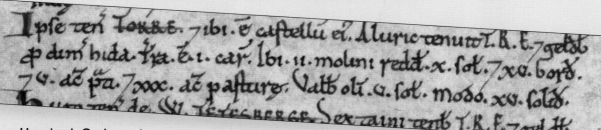

- Hundred: Carhampton
- County: Somerset
- Total population: 15 households (medium)
- Total tax assessed: 0.5 geld units (very small)
- Taxable units: Taxable value 0.5 geld units
- Value: Value to lord in 1086 £0.8. Value to lord c. 1070 £0.3
- Households: 15 smallholders
- Ploughland: 1 ploughland (land for)
- Other resources: Meadow 5 acres. Pasture 30 acres. 2 mills, value 0.5
- Lord in 1066: Aelfric
- Lord in 1086: William of Mohun
- Tenant-in-chief in 1086: William of Mohun
- Phillimore reference: 25,2

http://opendomesday.org

oxen. We have a reference to two mills, probably for grinding grain, which should be seen in the context of the other land that William de Mohun held. The **bordar** describes someone at the lower end of the social scale who had enough land for a small dwelling and was required to give service to the lord.

You will also come across references to **cottars**, who had even less land, and villeins, who may have up to 30 acres, but were not free. There are often 'slaves' mentioned, who were the least favoured members of a Medieval manor. The increase from 5 to 15 shillings mentioned at the end of the entry probably reflects the growing economy of the area associated with the building of the castle. If we look at the Exon Domesday, the more detailed version for the West Country, held at Exeter Cathedral, there is some additional information including the name of 'Torre' for the site where the castle stands today.

Dunster's entry is not untypical and it's possible to appreciate that with such information for every land holding in the country, King William would have had control over what he regarded as his lands. At the beginning of each of the main counties of Domesday, the first land holdings are the kings and then those he is giving to his followers to 'hold' in return for service. In the case of William de

BELOW *Exeter Cathedral holds the Exon Domesday, a more detailed version of entries for the West Country*

138

Mohun, who would later style himself the Earl of Somerset, he had to provide 40 knights' fees – that is areas of landholding that would support a knight who would then be available to support the king in battle. Essentially, this was the birth of the Normal feudal system in operation in England (Category 26).

The results of Domesday were presented with great fanfare by William at Salisbury in 1086. Thousands of his followers, his barons, lords, knights, members of the royal family and the senior clergy were present. The people who were not there were the Anglo-Saxons. Domesday was the ultimate stamp of the Conqueror's victory at Hastings. By this stage, the land held by those who had been conquered was minimal. The king now knew who administered every piece of land and what they owed him in return. Any rebellion or dissent could be crushed and the perpetrators' assets seized. It gave William ultimate control. Almost a quarter of the country was owned by barons, close French supporters of the king.

Domesday is an extraordinary document. On creation, it was known as *The Book of Winchester*, where it was originally kept at the royal court. Today, the original documents are held at the National Archives, Kew, in more recent binding. A thousand years on, its contents still provide valuable evidence of who has the right to own what land. Three other copies were made in the Medieval period and, in addition, there are the smaller more detailed books including the Exon copy, which can be seen in the cathedral library. Permission has to be obtained beforehand, but it is certainly worth the effort!

THINGS TO DO

- Find the Domesday entry for your village, if one exists.
  TIP: Look out for alternative spellings or names for the village (Dunster is recorded in Domesday as 'Torre', in reference to the hill that gives the town its name)
- Determine what Domesday tells you about your village, in terms of its size and importance at this time.
  TIP: You might need a glossary to help with interpreting terms.
- Look for evidence of a mill site for your village, to get a sense of its size.
- Log your discoveries and plot the key dates on your timeline.

Mill wheel at Dunster's Mill

USEFUL WEBSITES

There are several useful open source online versions of Domesday which can help you in your searches:

opendomesday.org
www.domesdaybook.co.uk

17 THE TITHE MAP

Most of our meetings in Dunster are held in the magnificent Tithe Barn. We dated some of the timbers to the sixteenth century, but its origins are probably a lot earlier. I always like to imagine what the barn would have been like during the harvest, when all of the town's people brought their produce to the barn. The reeve would then carefully note and set aside the tenth owed to the Church and the lord. Crammed all around the sides would have been sheaves of wheat, as well as fruit, vegetables and even chickens and eggs.

An aerial view of the Tithe Barn, Dunster

ABOVE *Dunster's Tithe Barn has a long history and is still an important community space today*

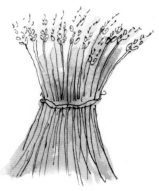

These were impressive buildings at the heart of the local economy. They had to be big enough to store huge amounts of produce. If you pay a visit to one of the marvellous examples, such as in Bradford-on-Avon, Wiltshire, you'll see they have the air of a secular cathedral. The tithes paid to the head of the local church were supposed to be used to care for its upkeep. During the Reformation, Henry VIII saw this as a good source of money and sold off the tithe rights to the highest bidder. In turn, this created even more bad feeling about its payment within the community. You had to feel a lot of love and care for your local church and vicar to feel happy about paying your tithes!

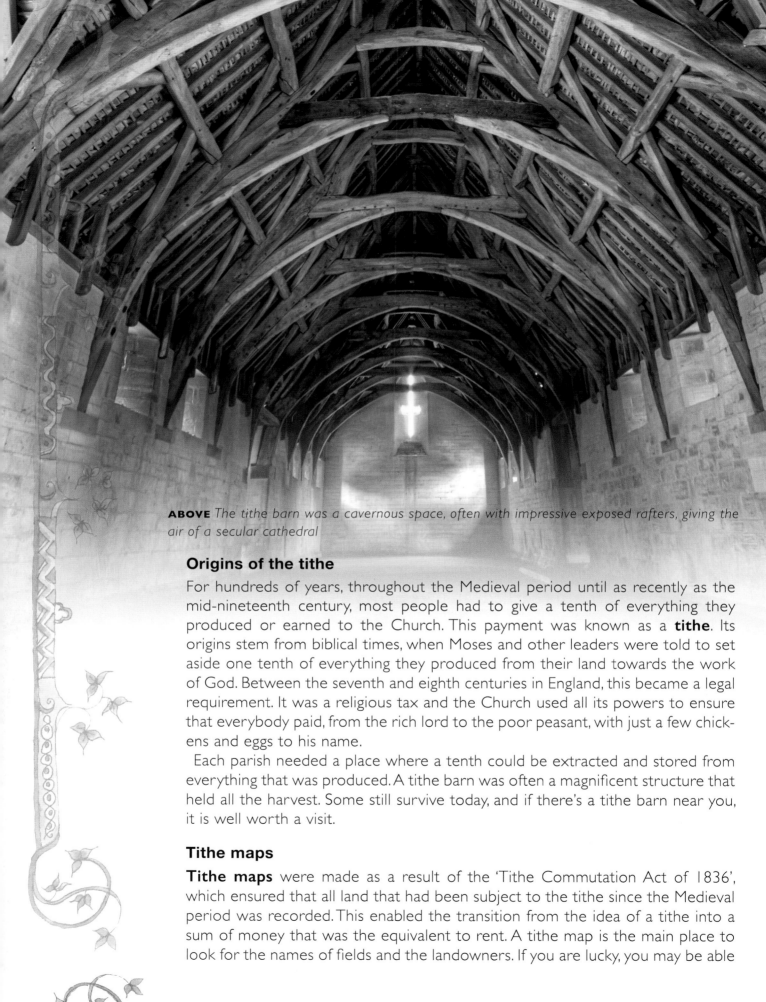

ABOVE *The tithe barn was a cavernous space, often with impressive exposed rafters, giving the air of a secular cathedral*

Origins of the tithe

For hundreds of years, throughout the Medieval period until as recently as the mid-nineteenth century, most people had to give a tenth of everything they produced or earned to the Church. This payment was known as a **tithe**. Its origins stem from biblical times, when Moses and other leaders were told to set aside one tenth of everything they produced from their land towards the work of God. Between the seventh and eighth centuries in England, this became a legal requirement. It was a religious tax and the Church used all its powers to ensure that everybody paid, from the rich lord to the poor peasant, with just a few chickens and eggs to his name.

Each parish needed a place where a tenth could be extracted and stored from everything that was produced. A tithe barn was often a magnificent structure that held all the harvest. Some still survive today, and if there's a tithe barn near you, it is well worth a visit.

Tithe maps

Tithe maps were made as a result of the 'Tithe Commutation Act of 1836', which ensured that all land that had been subject to the tithe since the Medieval period was recorded. This enabled the transition from the idea of a tithe into a sum of money that was the equivalent to rent. A tithe map is the main place to look for the names of fields and the landowners. If you are lucky, you may be able to locate the name of the specific field or person that you are researching. The document shows the size and usually the use of the land and the payment made in lieu of tithe.

These tithe maps, like Domesday, provide a wonderful picture of a moment in time, when some of the elements of modern life we take for granted had yet to make an appearance. Agriculture was still reliant on animal power and the landscape of fields retained some of the details of the Medieval period.

Tithe maps were usually drawn to a large scale, so that field divisions and other details can easily be seen. The map was accompanied by the **apportionment**, which included the names of fields, the owners and tenants. This was one of the first accurate surveys of parishes including a record of each farm's acreage and, in some cases, the use of the land. In the case of Dunster, there is a wonderful tithe map (a section of which is reproduced over the page), which includes the layout of the fields.

Regional variation

The enclosure process (Category 30) was often accompanied by the removal of the tithe, and so the existence of a tithe map is useful for demonstrating those areas that were still not enclosed by 1840. The evidence for early enclosure in the West Country, for example, is more limited than further east in England. However, there is much   evidence of enclo-

BELOW *The tithe barn at Bradford-on-Avon*

sure of commons in areas including Cornwall, East Devon, the Peak District and Lake District in the late eighteenth and early nineteenth century, as a result of the boom in mining and consequent population increase. *The Tithe Maps of England and Wales*, by Roger Kain and Richard Oliver, is an excellent resource, which will show you if there is a map for your area. The National Library of Wales had digitised over 300,000 tithe maps and their apportionments (***www.library.wales***).

You may also wish to research the Tithe Redemption Commission in London, which was set up at the time to administer the process. A copy of your tithe map should be held in the local records office and occasionally there is a copy in the local church. Arguably, the tithe map is one of the three most important documents relating to your village. The others are Domesday (Category 16) and, if you have one for your area, the Victoria County History (Category 21).

BELOW *A section of Dunster's tithe map showing field boundaries*

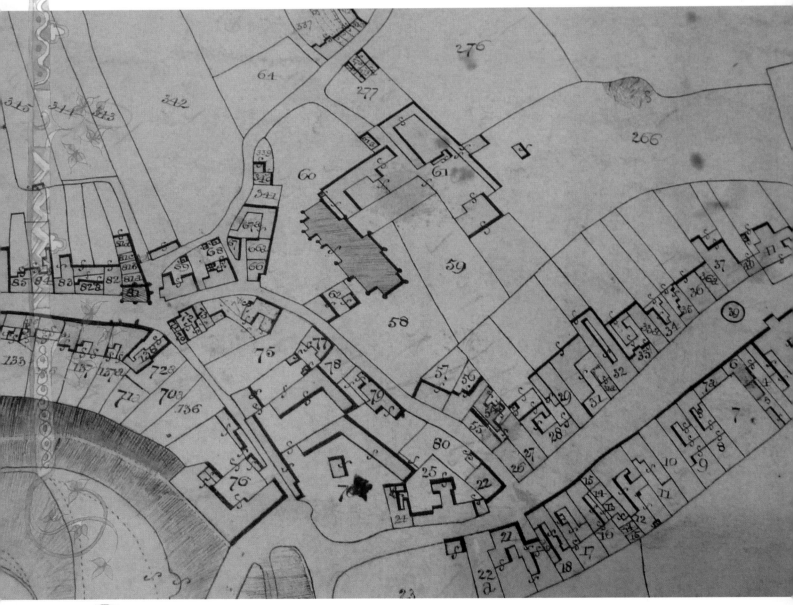

ABOVE *Breughel's 'The Payment of the Tithes (The Country Lawyer)'*

Today; locate the village's tithe map in the records office and look for fields associated with the key families highlighted in our research...

THINGS TO DO

• See if there is a local tithe barn still standing that you can visit. If not, maybe you can find out where it once stood.

• Contact your local records office to see if they hold a copy of a local tithe map. This will help you answer the following questions:

• How much or how little has the area changed since the map was made?

• Have any new roads or buildings been named after some of the old field names or people mentioned in the tithe map and apportionment?

• What information can you find out about the various occupations people had?

• What was the land being used for (for example, orchards, pasture, crops)?

• Log your discoveries and plot the key dates on your timeline.

18 PARISH BOUNDARIES

A parish, as a boundary and land area, can often date back to the Anglo-Saxons. If your church has a 'minster' name connected with it, this is a good indication that the boundary might originate from this period. A parish was the smallest ecclesiastical area used by the Church to divide up the land into governable units. Documents related to the parish were kept in the parish chest and occasionally survive, usually now held in the local records office. Another good starting point is a 1:25,000 OS map, which should show the parish boundary. Sometimes these boundaries have been altered in more modern times, so you may need to do a bit of research to go back to the earliest historical version.

Ancient standing stones were often repurposed as Medieval boundary markers

ABOVE *Beating the bounds in the parish of the University Church of St Mary the Virgin, Oriel*

Beating the bounds

It's a wonderful bit of fieldwork to try to follow the route of the parish boundary on the ground. Walking around the boundary is known as a **perambulation**. This boundary often has very ancient origins, stretching back to Medieval times, when parishes carefully and jealously monitored the distinction between themselves and the **parish** next door. Each parish had financial responsibility for the welfare of its own parishioners, demarcated by its boundary.

An important church service was created called **Rogation Sunday**, during which all of the villagers would assemble to 'beat the bounds'. This may have origins in a pre-Christian ritual that involved a rite of passage for the young men of the area. Some sources refer to a ritual where they would be symbolically beaten at significant places around the boundary to help them retain a memory of where their local boundary was marked! Around the country, references can be found to objects such as willow sticks being carried during the rogation tide ceremony. Throughout Europe, there are references to customs involving walking the land to ward off crop diseases and to help fertility.

ABOVE *Carfury Menhir, an ancient standing stone in West Cornwall*

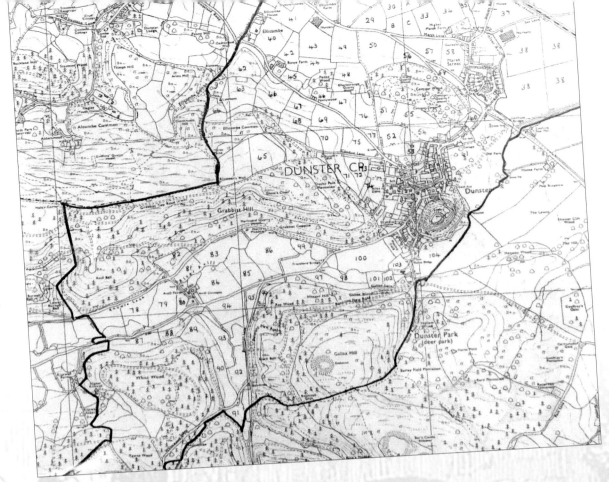

ABOVE *An historic map showing Dunster's boundary*

Beating the bounds had a serious purpose in ensuring that neighbouring parishes hadn't encroached on each other's land or removed markers such as boundary stones. In the early Christian period, these often focussed on one or two key places such as a prominent oak tree where people would gather. Place names like 'Gospel Oak' or 'Amen Corner' might relate to this tradition.

Like many rituals with a pagan origin, the beating of the bounds declined after the Reformation, possibly due to its associations with superstition.

In Tudor times, as the power of the manor declined, parishes became a way of managing local administration. They governed themselves and were answerable to the Church of England.

"...theare the parysh were accostomed to have drynkyng"

BEHIND *An engraving of the gathering of beating the bounds*

Beating the bounds in Dunster

In Dunster, we have a rather wonderful seventeenth century record of beating the bounds that details the various landmarks, the names of streams, roads and particular boundary stones. In some cases, these specific markers can still be found. It also records the tradition that these events were accompanied by much drinking, with the villagers stopping off at regular intervals to quench their thirst. Dunster historian, Sir Maxwell Lyte, quotes part of the perambulation for the reign of James I, 'The perambulacon of processyon in the weeke caulyd Processyon weeke', from the Luttrell Collection, held in the Somerset Records Office:

"From thence backwarde downe by the water to Yllycombe to Pyne's howse and theare a gospell and theare the parysh were accostomed to have drynkyng, and from thence to Dene Lane and so to Dunster church."

(Source: p. 347, *A History of Dunster and the Families of Mohun & Luttrell*, by Lyte (1909), quoting from a memorandum from the Luttrell Collection, in the Somerset Record Office.)

ABOVE *The starting point for beating the bounds in Crowborough, East Sussex*

Researching the boundary

Ipplepen in Devon is one of several British villages that still regularly holds its beating of the bounds. In 2015, hundreds of parishioners walked the parish boundary, covering a distance of around 13.5 miles.

The route of the parish boundary was often written down. Ask at your local county records office if they hold any documents referring to it.

Once you have a copy, it is good fun to see if you can walk the old boundary of your parish. If you are lucky, you might still be able to find the old oak tree, stream or lane mentioned in the perambulation.

If you are able to match your boundary with an Anglo-Saxon boundary, you are in possession of a vital piece of landscape history. Its rediscovery would clearly be a wonderful thing. Beating the bounds could be reintroduced as part of the village social calendar. If the local church is sympathetic, reinstating Rogation Sunday would be very worthwhile.

ABOVE *Beating the bounds in Devon*

THINGS TO DO

- Visit your local county records office to find documents referring to the perambulation of your parish.
- See if you can link the parish boundary to that of an earlier Anglo-Saxon boundary. TIP: Read Robertson for further advice.
- Have a go at walking the parish boundary and look out for landmarks referenced in the original text such as trees and boundary stones.
- Find an early OS map that includes the parish boundary and see how it compares.
- Log your discoveries and plot the key dates on your timeline.

Anglo-Saxon boundaries

As mentioned, these perambulations were often based on earlier Anglo-Saxon boundaries. To give you an idea of how you might look for these, you could start with a book like *Anglo-Saxon Charters*, by the esteemed A.J. Robertson. In his book, Robertson refers to a grant of land by King Offa (AD 757 to 796) to Aldred of Worcester. The land grant contains a description of the route of the land boundary. This goes from the old dyke (or in Anglo-Saxon 'Ealen dyke') and from Sege's pond (Seges mere) and includes references to a bridge called 'baka brycge', finally ending up at the river Teme, referred to in the original document as 'Temede stream'.

Mick used to recommend studying these documents as a nice activity on a winter evening with a large glass of wine! This is an interesting activity as, in addition, you will begin to recognise the origins of our present-day language in the Anglo-Saxon.

RIGHT *A ninth century extract from the Anglo-Saxon Chronicle*

BELOW *An Anglo-Saxon boundary marked by a line of recent trees at Frith Common, Lindridge, Worcestershire*

151

19 TOWN & MARKET CHARTERS

Whenever we visit Dunster, the local people are very fond of reminding us that Dunster is not a village but a town! A vast number of English towns were created between the Norman Conquest and the Black Death (from the late eleventh to the late fourteenth century). They were deliberately set out as commercial settlements aimed at creating income for the lord. It has been suggested by some historians that the dominant aspect of their economy was that it was not purely agricultural. As in the case of Dunster, a series of adjoining plots of land (known as 'burgage plots') would be laid out, with the land let out to freemen (known as 'burgesses'). In other words, they didn't owe a right of duty to the lord, but instead would pay a yearly rent for the privilege of trading. A town became a borough when the king confirmed its rights by a royal charter. One piece of research that you can carry out is to look for the royal charter, which first included the rights of the burgesses who would become some of the most important people of the town.

RIGHT *A single burgage plot*

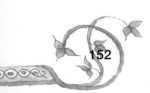

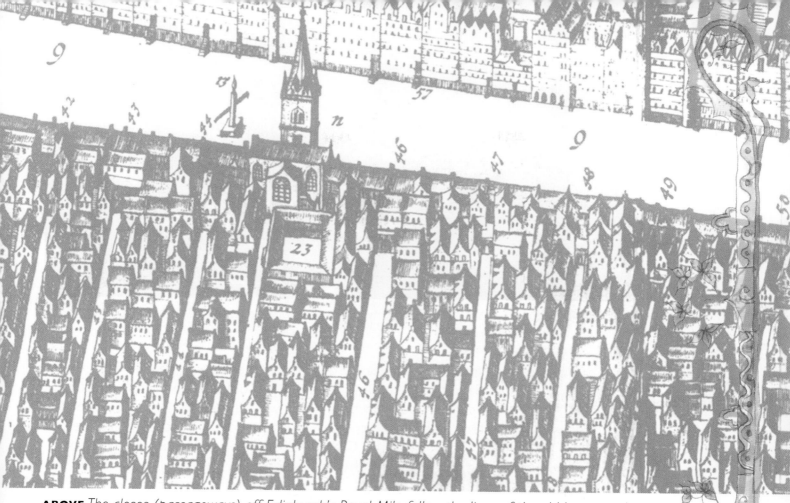

ABOVE *The closes (passageways) off Edinburgh's Royal Mile follow the lines of the old burgage plots*

Many towns in Britain have ancient origins. When the Roman army set up forts, towns often gradually grew up around them. So many of our towns and cities had their origins around 2,000 years ago! It may still be possible to trace the original site of the fort, or parts of it. For example, at Exeter we know that the military bathhouse was situated where the cathedral stands today. You may also be lucky enough to find remnants of the Roman walls, again at Exeter and also York, where the remains survive within the later walls surrounding the cities.

Clues in names

As we discuss in Category 9, the names of towns, or features within them, can provide useful clues to the era when they were established or their original function. For example, you may be able to trace the original defended entrances to the towns, which often have name with a '-gate' ending such as 'Northgate' or 'Southgate'. This might also help you to work out where Roman roads led out of the town into the countryside, linking with other settlements beyond.

ABOVE *Remains of Roman walls in Exeter city centre*

ABOVE *Totnes, an Anglo-Saxon burh town, with its motte and bailey castle, added later by the Normans*

During the ninth and tenth centuries, due to the increase in attacks from the Vikings, the Anglo-Saxons re-used and repaired the old Roman fortified settlements. Again, clues can be found in the names we still use today. For example, places with a '-caster', '-cester' or '-chester' ending (such as Lancaster, Gloucester and Manchester) stem from the Old English, *ceaster*, itself derived from the Latin, *castra*, meaning 'fort'. So, from the name alone, we can conclude that these settlements were named by the Anglo-Saxons to describe an ancient walled or fortified town, often of Roman, or sometimes even pre-Roman, origin.

The Anglo-Saxons also established new towns, known as **burhs**, which again were fortified. Many towns such as Barnstaple, Totnes and Plympton in Devon, where Time Team has excavated, began life as an Anglo-Saxon burh. It is from this Old English word to describe a defended site that we get many others in our vocabulary, including burgage, borough and burgess.

The Burghal Hidage

A notable set of documents known as the *Burghal Hidage*, probably produced after AD 914 in the reign of Edward the Elder, names over 30 burhs in Wessex, created as a defensive network by his father, King Alfred (AD 871 to 899). Places such as Wallingford in Oxfordshire and Lydford in Devon still retain some of the original street plan and fortifications. The Anglo-Saxons also created 'ports', which were market or harbour towns.

RIGHT *Anglo-Saxon burhs across Wessex, as listed in the Burghal Hidage*

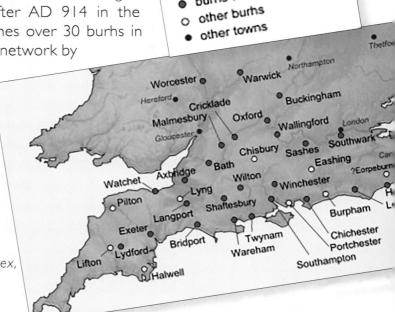

Planned commercial centres

As touched upon in the introduction, many new deliberately-planned commercial towns emerged during the Medieval period. These were often centred around a motte and bailey or, later, a castle with streets laid out in a grid pattern. Keen to encourage trade, and so generate revenue, local lords established markets to bring in traders from the surrounding areas. First, however, the lord needed to be granted a **royal charter** by the king, in order to formally set up a **borough** for trading. There is an early charter for the creation of Dunster. If you get the chance to locate and view charter for your town, you'll see they are often beautifully illustrated documents, containing a wealth of valuable information to aid your research, including the date of issue and the names of key individuals.

Burgage plots are an important feature of Medieval towns. The local lord would rent out these plots of land with houses, built along busy streets. Long strips of garden would run from the back of each house, providing just enough land for each family to keep a few animals and grow some vegetables. In the case of

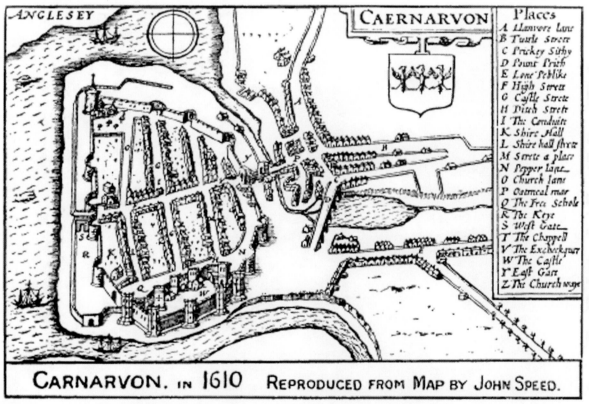

RIGHT *Examples of historic royal charters*
BELOW *A typical Medieval town, deliberately planned around a castle*

Dunster in the late fourteenth century, new burgage plots were rented out at a shilling per year. The **burgesses** who rented these plots were freemen, exempt from the onerous duties that could be imposed by the lord. They were allowed to practise a trade and vote for members of the town's council.

Identifying burgage plots

It is well worth seeing if you can find evidence of burgage plots in your area. The original plots are often recognisable today because they were created using the old measurement of a **perch**, which was eventually standardised at 16.5 feet (5.03 metres). Over time, the plots may have been divided into two, or even doubled or tripled. However, Stewart Ainsworth was able to work out that there were over 70 burgage plots throughout Dunster. He did this by measuring out the width of the houses along the street frontage and calculating original plot boundaries based on divisions or multiples of a perch. As always, studying historic maps can help to identify signs of conscious town planning and the presence of burgage plots.

RIGHT *Dunster's tithe map showing burgage plots on the High Street*

A drone image of Dunster's High Street clearly shows the long, thin burgage plots at the back of the houses

ABOVE *Houses and shop frontages on Dunster High Street, planned as a commercial centre*

Eager to maximise their rental income, lords would often create even more burgage plots. Thus, towns started to grow and develop new 'suburbs'. Mick noted that this is evident at Dunster, where we can see the original burgage plots close to the castle, and then later Medieval suburbs laid out further away at Gallox Bridge. Historic documents quoted by Lyte reveal that there were in fact 176 and a half burgage plots in Dunster in 1266, considerably more than the 70 examples identified by Stewart. So the question remains, what happened to the rest of them? Perhaps many have since been lost by new development within the town.

THINGS TO DO

- Research the origin of your town's name – an ending such as '-caster', '-chester' or '-burgh' might help to indicate the era it was established.
- Have a look at historic maps to see if you can trace the old street patterns. Do any of the old streets leading into and out of the town still exist?
- Look for references to '-gate' in street names or local areas, which may signify one of the original gate ways in the walls leading out of the town.
- Conduct a survey of the shop frontages in your nearest town – do any of the buildings and divisions appear to be divisions of perches (16.5 feet)? This may indicate evidence of the buildings being laid out in burgage plots.
- If you live in a town, try to find the original royal charter which will have details of the burgage plots being offered. In the case of Dunster, we actually have the names of some of the original burgesses.
- Log your discoveries and plot the key dates on your timeline.

Today: Look for evidence of burgage plots in the town High Street, compared against the tithe map...

20 AERIAL PHOTOGRAPHY & SURVEYS

One of Mick's great delights on Day Three of Time Team was to look at the site from the helicopter. Once commandeered, he would direct the pilot's route off into the surrounding countryside, looking for ecclesiastical remains, a personal obsession! Often, these had little to do with the site we were filming, but every flight produced fascinating results! Aerial imagery is particularly valuable if produced under the guidance of skilled archaeologists. On many occasions, both Mick and Stewart would join together to discuss exactly what was appearing and get the pilot to fly specific angles so that the picture of the site would be enhanced. Now, of course, we have Google Earth and the possibilities afforded by drones to get fantastic coverage. But nothing beats having an archaeologist and skilled pilot working together.

ABOVE *An aerial view of Old Sarum, Salisbury*

Aerial photography and satellite images can be incredibly useful in helping you to spot subtle clues that may indicate archaeological features. Aerial photos can either be taken from a vertical angle (straight down) or at a low, oblique angle. Vertical photographs provide a great overview plan of the site, whilst oblique photos are much better at revealing the contours of the land. Low walls or earthworks, which might not be immediately visible from the ground, can cast long shadows, especially during the early morning or late afternoon, making them very easy to see from the air.

A satellite image of the British Isles

ABOVE *An aerial view of a Roman site near Tetbury, Gloucestershire*

Soil and crop marks are often only visible from the air. Soil marks occur due to differences in soil moisture or texture. In a newly ploughed field, a flattened burial mound will be a different colour to the surrounding area. Crop marks occur due to variations in the height, health or type of vegetation growing within a field, caused by buried features. For example, over a buried ditch, soil tends to be richer in moisture and phosphates. Therefore, the plants growing above the ditch will be taller and denser than the surrounding areas. Conversely, over a buried wall or stone feature, soil will be thinner and drier, resulting in plants that are stunted, sparser or otherwise different. During very dry summers, parch marks will be created in areas with a shallow depth, over what may be hidden archaeological remains, close to the surface.

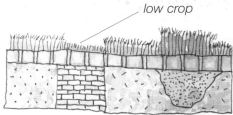

low crop

ABOVE *Features hidden below ground can affect the growth of crops above ground*

Dunster from the air

ABOVE *Modern drones make it much easier to take aerial photos*

Many Time Team sites began with an aerial photograph sent in to us, and it was often a matter of chance that a particular set of weather and crop conditions met up with the flight overhead by an interested archaeologist or farmer with a suitable camera. Often the same site when visited at a later period would reveal nothing.

RAF reconnaissance

The RAF took a huge amount of aerial reconnaissance photography in the 1940s and 1950s, and much of this can now be accessed through various websites. 'Britain from Above' is a wonderful archive of almost 100,000 historic images (***www.britainfromabove.org.uk***). Historic England, meanwhile, has a collection of over 4 million aerial photographs in its Swindon archive, including many that have not yet been digitised.

This category gives us a chance to refer to one of our heroes in this area, O.G.S. Crawford, who flew with the Royal Flying Corp in World War I. Crawford was the man responsible for the archaeological content that appears in Ordnance Survey maps. His 1929 book, *Air Photography for Archaeologists*, is a classic. Many of the photographs he took provide a unique record of features in the landscape.

RIGHT *Aerial photography pioneer, O.G.S. Crawford*
BELOW *An aerial reconnaissance photo of RAF Wrexham (1941)*

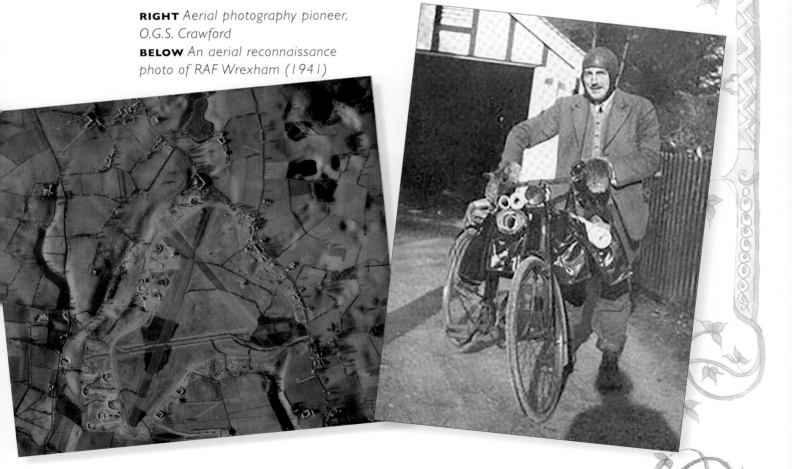

ABOVE *Aerial photography helps to identify hidden patterns and features in fields that may otherwise remain undetected*

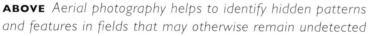

With the advent of modern technology, aerial and satellite images are abundant and usually free. Google Earth has a historical feature enabling users to flick through older satellite imagery. These older images are often taken during different times of the year, so it is worth checking as some features, such as crop marks, might be more visible. See if you can pick out any archaeological features in your village. For example, long narrow gardens off a high street may have once been burgage plots, and round marks in fields might be prehistoric earthworks.

While helicopters are out of the reach of the many, drones are readily available. Perhaps a local enthusiast has one that could be used for the project. Alternatively, you might be able to club together to purchase a drone specifically for use of the group. They can be extremely useful tools for today's archaeologists. Needless to say, though, their use should be carried out within accordance of the law, respecting local restrictions and the privacy of private landowners, and avoiding flightpaths!

RIGHT *A drone fitted with a camera for taking aerial imagery*

THINGS TO DO

- Search the archives for historic and more recent aerial photography. As with maps from different periods, you can compare the same area to see how it has evolved over time.
- Search the online collection of Britain from Above: *www.britainfromabove.org.uk*
- Use Google Earth's historical feature to compare periods and identify features in the landscape.
- If appropriate (and with the necessary permissions), use a drone to take contemporary imagery or film of features you have identified.
- Log your discoveries and plot the key dates on your timeline.

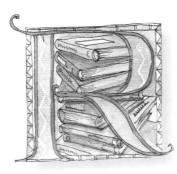

21 KEY RESOURCES

One of the most useful resources throughout our research in Dunster has been the online Victoria County History (VCH). It gave us a great start and we were able to look at material that had not yet been published in print. It helped to answer a number of questions at the beginning of our research. This is one of several key collections that you'll likely return to as your project progresses.

Historic Environment Record

When researching your village or town, the first step is to have a look at your local Historic Environment Record (HER). The HER contains lots of useful information such as known archaeological sites, historic landscapes, historic buildings, and details of excavations and finds. This information is stored on a database and linked to a digital mapping system.

HERs are maintained and regularly updated by various authorities such as county councils, unitary authorities, and national parks. The information they contain is used to consult for planning and development and to inform the management of important areas, sites, or buildings. However, these public records are also a very useful research tool as they can provide lots of information about the area to help get you started.

Many HERs are now online, so you can easily look up information on their websites. If your local HER is not online, it is possible to contact your local authority and ask them to send you details, or to make an appointment with them to visit the offices to consult the database.

LEFT *The Historic Environment Record is an invaluable resource*

Heritage Gateway

Another good place to start is the Heritage Gateway website, maintained by Historic England. This website brings together information from local HERs and also other local and national records such as Parks and Gardens UK and Images of England. A search on the Heritage Gateway website (searching on the 'WHERE' button> 'Dunster, Somerset > 'within '1km') revealed 597 results gathered from nine different resources, including the Somerset HER, the Historic Milestone Society database, and the National Trust database.

You can then click on the individual results to view particular records. It is possible to further refine your search by choosing additional options, selecting the 'WHAT', 'WHEN', 'WHO' buttons and then choosing from the drop-down menus. *www.heritagegateway.org.uk*

ABOVE *The Heritage Gateway homepage*

The Victoria County History

The next step is to have a look at the Victoria County History (VCH). These are fantastic encyclopaedic publications written by historians, which gather together a wide range of documents and research about your county. They are one of the best sources for general information. This research project began in 1899 and has been based at the Institute of Historical Research at the University of London since 1933.

To find out if there is a VCH for your county, visit the website. If one has been published in your county, then there should be a copy at your local library or you will be able to purchase a copy of it online. *www.victoriacountyhistory.ac.uk*

The Portable Antiquities Scheme

The Portable Antiquities Scheme (PAS) database holds information about archae-ological artefacts (often referred to as 'small finds' or 'portable antiquities'). It is possible to search the PAS database to see what finds have been discovered and recorded in your area. To get started, you could try a simple search, such as looking at your parish to see what has been recorded in the area. Alternatively, you may like to try searching on a particular period, such as Roman or Medieval, or a particular artefact such as coin, jug or shoe. Please note, only general, not exact, find spots are given on the database, as many finds are found on private land, for example. Contact your local Finds Liaison Officer, who will be able to advise you on how to use the database (Category 60).

www.finds.org

ABOVE *An English sixpence of Philip of Spain and Mary Tudor, recorded via the Portable Antiquities Scheme*

THINGS TO DO

- Search the various databases and plot any finds you discover on your timeline.
- Contact your local Finds Liaison Officer for help in using the Portable Antiquities Scheme database.

RIGHT *A sherd of Roman pottery*

A typical selection of finds from a Dunster test pit, prior to being processed

Dunster High Street

IV.
Historic Background

While settlements evolve gradually, certain milestones will have left a greater impact on your village's story, for better or worse. This section highlights some key historic periods and events that will have shaped the development of your village. Some developments may have directly sparked the creation of new villages, or helped existing ones to prosper. Others may have spurred their decline. If lucky, through your own research, you may identify features, landmarks, artefacts or documents that correspond to each time frame, essentially tracking your village's evolution from its earliest incarnation to the present day.

22 PREHISTORIC EVIDENCE

Trying to find evidence of the prehistoric in your area can seem like a daunting task. Many of us will be familiar with sites like Avebury, Stonehenge and Maiden Castle, but how would the prehistoric period leave evidence in your village or town? Local museums are probably a good starting point and many will contain small collections of flints and other implements found nearby. It is also possible to search your local area for some of the larger prehistoric monuments. One of the key prehistoric moments is the transition from hunter-gatherer to settled farmer. This makes any Neolithic evidence, usually in the form of flint artefacts, very important to the origins of settlement. A favourite location in the prehistoric period may well have had advantages that would prove attractive to later generations.

Arbor Low, a Neolithic stone circle in Derbyshire

ABOVE *Cornwall's Lizard Peninsula is home to field systems dating back to the Bronze Age*

The origins of settled communities

Mesolithic communities consisted of hunter-gatherers who moved around the landscape depending on the season, to hunt and forage. **Neolithic** farmers, however, began to cultivate and grow grains such as wheat and barley. The need to tend to these crops year upon year, and then store the grain, effectively tied people to a specific piece of land, bringing about a more stable and settled way of life. In essence, this was the birth of localised 'village' communities. With some searching, prehistoric field systems can be discovered, and may even form the basis of those still in use today. Some field systems on the Lizard Peninsula and West Penwith in Cornwall, for example, date back to the Bronze Age. Aside from the iconic sites and smaller monuments, there are other, less immediate clues to prehistory in the countryside around us, which, if you're lucky, can be discovered with a bit of research and field detective work.

Barrows and burial grounds

Burial mounds, or **barrows**, from prehistory seem to have enjoyed resurgence during the Iron and Bronze Ages. Much older burial mounds were reused in this period and new burial mounds were also constructed. In later periods, some of these mounds were re-purposed as boundary markers for parish boundaries and rabbit warrens (Categories 18 and 47).

Prehistoric settlements

Remnants of prehistoric settlements have been found in the recent past, and sometimes it takes a bit of luck. The Iron Age Carn Euny in West Penwith, and the Neolithic site of Skara Brae on the Orkney Islands, for example, were both discovered in the nineteenth century. Skara Brae only came to light by chance, following a violent storm which exposed some of the buildings.

Some prehistoric structures can cover a considerable area. It's only recently, for instance, that we have recognised the importance of the Dartmoor Reaves. A **reave** is a long, straight boundary wall constructed of stone. Modern research has dated them back to the Bronze Age, and they cover a region of almost 40 square miles.

Prehistoric Dunster

There are many signs of prehistoric activity in Dunster and the surrounding area. Most notable are the Iron Age hillforts of Bats Castle and Black Ball Camp on the hills overlooking Dunster itself. Slightly further afield, in wider Somerset, there are Bronze Age sites such as Brent Knoll Hillfort at Burnham on Sea, Small Down Knoll at Shepton Mallet and Neolithic sites including Stanton Drew near Bristol. Somerset's best-known prehistoric site is probably Cheddar Gorge. We visited the caves in Series 6 of Time Team, which have evidence of both **Palaeolithic** and Mesolithic activity.

Skara Brae on the Orkney Islands

ABOVE *Prehistoric evidence discovered at Cheddar Gorge during a Time Team dig*

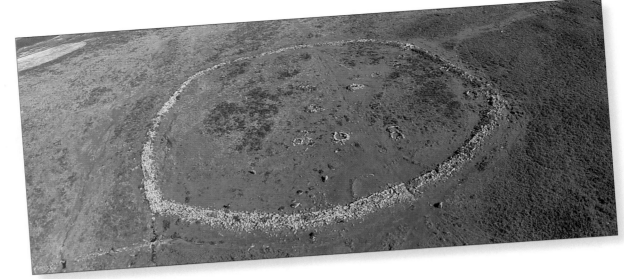

ABOVE *Grimspound, a Bronze Age settlement on Dartmoor*

Identifying prehistoric activity

So, what can you do to discover signs of prehistoric settlement in your area? Firstly, look up the Historic Environment Record (sometimes referred to as the 'Sites and Monuments Record') for your region to identify known sites (Category 21). You might also find reports from previous excavations. Prehistoric activity is sometimes enshrined in folklore, and it may be that ancient monuments gave rise to local legends, such as the 'Hurlers' and 'Merry Maidens' in Cornwall (Category 57). However, if there aren't any known sites already documented locally, you can look for clues in the landscape yourself.

Today's prevalence of drones and the advent of Google Earth make aerial and satellite photography much more accessible than in previous years (Category 20). These tools can reveal ancient field lines or even evidence of roundhouses, which began to be introduced in the Bronze Age, replacing the earlier rectangular housing of the Neolithic. Equally, simply walking the countryside can throw up some unexpected evidence that you hadn't realised was there.

Look out for any unexplained ridges or bumps that might hint at activity. Prehistoric field systems were typically brick shaped, often with soil mounds used as borders. Some Medieval churches, including St Edward's in the Cornish village of Mawnan Smith, were built upon existing prehistoric ritual sites. If your local church has a large round circular enclosure, this may well date back to the Iron Age.

LEFT & BELOW *A drone, and a low-flying drone photo showing roundhouse foundations*

ABOVE *The twelfth century church at Knowlton, Dorset, built in the centre of a prehistoric henge*

Sources of raw material

Each age in prehistory brought about new developments in the evolution of tools. This may have encouraged settlement near the sources of raw materials: flint, bronze, copper, iron and tin were important hubs in a network of production and exchange (Category 38). The copper mines in Great Orme in Wales and Cornish tin mines are good examples. Sometimes, a well-known industrial site from more recent history will in fact have prehistoric origins. Poldark Mine, for example, is the site of the eighteenth century tin mine, Wheal Roots, yet has a mining heritage that dates back to the Bronze Age.

Likewise, routes of exchange and communication were important, as tools made in one region, such as flint from the Norfolk area, have appeared all over Britain. Many established routes across the country are regarded as prehistoric highways. Icknield Way, for example, which stretches 170 miles from Norfolk to Wiltshire, is perhaps one of the oldest 'roads' in Britain. So, although there may not be a large monument nearby, your village could be near an important location for raw materials or a route used for trading.

ABOVE *Pieces of flint made into tools*

THINGS TO DO

- Find the local Historic Environment Record (or 'Sites and Monuments Record') for your region to identify known sites, then search the PAS database.
- Search the local records for reports of previous archaeological excavations.
- Try to determine if modern industrial sites in fact have ancient origins.
  - Use Google Earth and existing aerial photography to find clues in the landscape, such as brick-shaped field lines, signs of roundhouses, or other prehistoric activity.
  - Log your discoveries and plot the key dates on your timeline.

copper piece

23 IRON AGE HILLFORTS

Today, we tend to take large buildings and structures for granted. Diggers and bulldozers make light work of shifting tonnes of earth and moving heavy building materials. However, it's amazing to consider some of the impressive prehistoric earthworks across the country, constructed without the help of modern machinery. In 2012, Time Team visited Caerau Hillfort in south Wales, one of the largest Iron Age earthworks in Britain. One can only imagine the impact these huge hillforts that dominated the landscape would have had on visitors of the time. There is some evidence that hillforts like these could become the focus of later settlement.

Maiden Castle, Dorset

The period in history that we know as the Iron Age, which began in Britain in approximately 700 BC, is notable for the growth of what we term hillforts. There are some excellent examples of these left today, such as Maiden Castle in Dorset (pictured below) and Old Oswestry in Shropshire.

Although we call them forts, they were really enclosed settlements, with the inhabitants living in roundhouses within the boundaries. These wooden or stone structures had floors made of compressed sand or clay, with a fire for cooking and to provide heat and light. Were these the first villages?

Roundhouses

Some roundhouses were also used for storing cooking utensils, food and tools. While the example illustrated over the page is constructed of granite, they were often made of wood, so the timbers will have long-since rotted away. However, the foundation holes sometimes still remain, enabling archaeologists to work out their original size. Other physical remains have been found, such as pottery and carbonised food left in the fires, as well as beads, tools, weapons and decorative objects.

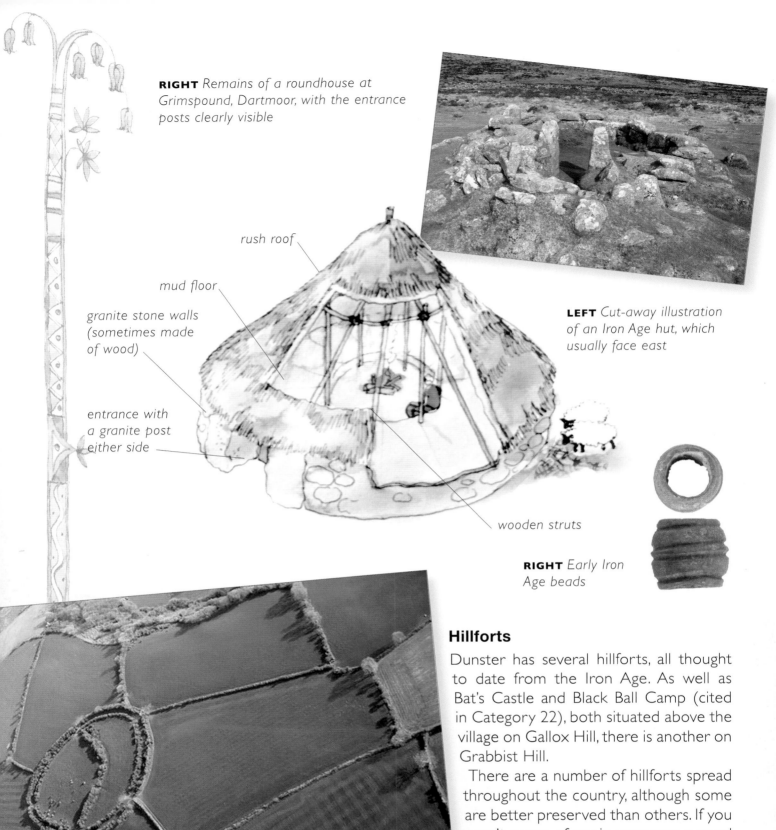

RIGHT Remains of a roundhouse at Grimspound, Dartmoor, with the entrance posts clearly visible

rush roof

mud floor

granite stone walls (sometimes made of wood)

entrance with a granite post either side

wooden struts

LEFT Cut-away illustration of an Iron Age hut, which usually face east

RIGHT Early Iron Age beads

Hillforts

Dunster has several hillforts, all thought to date from the Iron Age. As well as Bat's Castle and Black Ball Camp (cited in Category 22), both situated above the village on Gallox Hill, there is another on Grabbist Hill.

There are a number of hillforts spread throughout the country, although some are better preserved than others. If you aren't aware of any in your area, a good starting point is to look at local aerial

LEFT An aerial view of Castell Mawr, Pembrokeshire

photography (Category 20). Images of the same site taken at different times of the year and in different daylight conditions can be particularly useful. Very often the sun will create shadows on some features that might not otherwise be clear. Ask at your local records office if they hold aerial photos. Take a walk and look at the hills, searching for any ridges or features that don't seem natural. Again, both old and new maps can include references to ancient hillforts.

THINGS TO DO

- Look at aerial photography taken in different seasons for unusual or clearly manmade features in the topography that might be evidence of a hillfort.
- Walk the local area, looking for unusual features in the landscape. See Category 11 for more on identifying an Iron Age hillfort.
- Log your discoveries and plot the key dates on your timeline.

RIGHT *An autumnal aerial view of British Camp, Malvern Hills*

British Camp, taken from a different angle – see how the fort's shape and artificial enhancements are more pronounced in the aerial image (above)

179

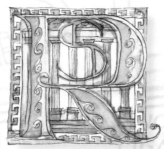

24 ROMAN SETTLEMENT

Archaeologists and amateur detectorists frequently make exciting new discoveries across Britain that reveal tantalising glimpses of the country's Roman past. In recent years, these have included intricate floor mosaics from villas and richly adorned jewellery, reminding us of the elegance and refinement of the Romans. We often visited Roman sites on Time Team, such as the villa at Dinnington, Somerset, and Cirencester. However, it was the Roman desire to build towns that provided the origin of some of our largest cities. The Roman road system linked strategic centres of settlement, and many had major buildings like bath houses, villas, amphitheatres and marketplaces. This was the beginning of town life.

The iconic Roman bath house in Bath, with later additions above ground

BEHIND *Roman city layout of Colchester*

ABOVE *Stane Street, Billingshurst*
LEFT *An historic map showing the Roman Fosse Way marked in red, crossing Watling street*

Roman Britain

Britain was part of the Roman Empire for over 350 years until the late fifth century, which had a significant impact on the way people lived. The Romans encouraged the growth of towns, believing that this orderly system was the only civilised way to live. Streets were laid out in a grid formation with a **forum**, or public square, at the centre. Some Roman street systems survive today, while some of our modern roads still follow these lines, such as Stane Street, linking London to Chichester, and Watling Street, which runs from Wroxeter in Shropshire to the Kent coast. There are plenty of visible Roman town remains, including the prominent examples in Bath and Wroxeter, and many more can be found across the country.

ABOVE *Remains of the baths at Wroxeter*

ABOVE & RIGHT *Fishbourne Palace's mosaic floor and a reconstruction give a sense of grandeur*

High status officials lived in great villas and it is well worth paying a visit to Fishbourne Roman Palace in West Sussex, which dates to around AD 75. Here you get a sense of the huge scale and sophistication of these grand buildings. Fishbourne's footprint is larger than that of Buckingham Palace, and it is home to a beautifully preserved mosaic floor.

Roman Dunster

Roman coins and pottery have been found in and around Dunster, most notably in 1983, when a small hoard of coins dating from 102 BC to AD 350 was discovered in the ramparts of Bat's Castle. A recent geophysical survey by a team including members of the Dunster Museum Archaeological Group has identified a potential Roman settlement. Elsewhere in Somerset, in August 2018, an amateur metal detectorist discovered an ornate gold ring, believed to date from AD 200 to 300, near Crewkerne. The elaborately carved 24-carat gold ring, which includes an engraving of the Roman god, Victory, is one of many finds in the area and must have been owned by someone of high status.

ABOVE *Gold and silver Roman coins*

ABOVE
Illustration of a Roman ring found in Somerset. Finds like these should be recorded in the HER record for your area

Local connections

Are there any known Roman connections in your area? Search local archaeological records and news archives for relevant finds. Field names can give clues to previous uses, and those that contain the word 'black' and 'stony', for instance, may be associated with Roman sites. It's believed that this is a reference to industrial activity in the area, which supposedly changed the soil colour. As we highlight in Category 19, the suffixes 'chester', 'caster' and 'cester' in location names are also indications of Roman connections. Note that both Exeter and Wroxeter are corruptions of this rule. As always, historic maps are a useful reference point for further investigation.

THINGS TO DO

- Search the local archives, in particular the HER and Portable Antiquities Scheme database for evidence of Roman activity in your area, including finds of coins or pottery.
- Look at historic maps for references to 'chester' variations of place names and field names containing the word 'black'.
- Determine the nearest Roman roads and settlements.
  TIP: See Ordnance Survey's Roman Britain map.
- Log your discoveries and plot the key dates on your timeline.

BELOW *The beautifully preserved Balkerne Gate in Colchester, part of the Roman town walls of Camulodunum, contender for the oldest town in Britain*

183

25 THE ANGLO-SAXONS

When we began to work on Time Signs, the precursor to Time Team, the archaeological work was initiated by the discovery that, beneath many Medieval farm and village sites, there was evidence of earlier Anglo-Saxon occupation. However, trying to find Anglo-Saxon remains can be challenging work. Many artefacts from this period were made of organic materials, which rot over time. In some parts of the country there was very little pottery in use, and many buildings were made of wood rather than longer lasting materials such as stone.

On Time Team, we've often had a fruitless search for Anglo-Saxon building remains. They can appear as sites near to Anglo-Saxon burial grounds, which are typically easier to find than the ordinary buildings. However, it has been estimated that thousands of new villages were created around the ninth century. So, clearly some element of Anglo-Saxon life must have helped to shape the development of our current settlements, and it may be that many of today's villages grew up from a collection of scattered Anglo-Saxon farms.

Of all the historic periods, it's perhaps the Anglo-Saxon pre-Viking culture that is nearest to that mythical land, 'the Shire', beloved of Tolkien and others.

ABOVE *Remains of the stunning Anglo-Saxon helmet discovered at Sutton Hoo*

The birth of England

The gradual decline of the Roman period by the middle fifth century created the ideal opportunity for a new set of migrants to enter Britain from Northern Europe. From the fifth century onwards, Germanic tribes including the Jutes, Saxons and Angles settled in England. The cities, roads and typical villas of Roman life, which had introduced many of the advantages of a civilised life, were abandoned. The incomers were Pagan, and would remain so until the seventh century. The ancient Britons were eventually driven westwards, and Wales and areas like Cornwall and Devon, originally referred to as Western Wales, became the refuge of what were broadly a Celtic people. Towns declined and early settlements were made up of largely wooden structures that, as we have said, left little archaeological trace (see the photo over the page). At the centre of the largest Anglo-Saxon settlements was often the great hall, one of which we helped to uncover on Time Team in 2010 at Drayton, Oxfordshire.

By the eighth century, they had become established into four main kingdoms: Northumbria (covering most of Northern Britain), Mercia (including much of the Midlands), East Anglia and Wessex. The gradual development of large Anglo-Saxon settlements produced a culture rich in material wealth, as seen in the remarkable finds of Sutton Hoo.

Anglo-Saxon literature

The conversion of much of the country to Christianity, around 700, generated great works of ecclesiastical history and sacred literature. The first history of England, *The Ecclesiastical History of the English People*, completed in 731 by the Benedictine monk, Bede, in the monastery at Jarrow, is a remarkable document. The beautifully illustrated *Lindisfarne Gospels*, produced in the early eighth century, also highlight the sophistication of Anglo-Saxon writing by this stage.

This new interest in the written word was encouraged by monarchs like Alfred the Great and his grandson Aethelstan, who laid the foundations for a unified England. It is the *Anglo-Saxon Chronicle* to which we owe a lot of our information about this period.

LEFT *The eighth century monk, Bede, writing the first history of the English*

BELOW *As this reconstruction of a typical seventh century village at West Stow highlights, the Anglo-Saxons built predominantly out of wood and thatch, leaving few physical remains behind*

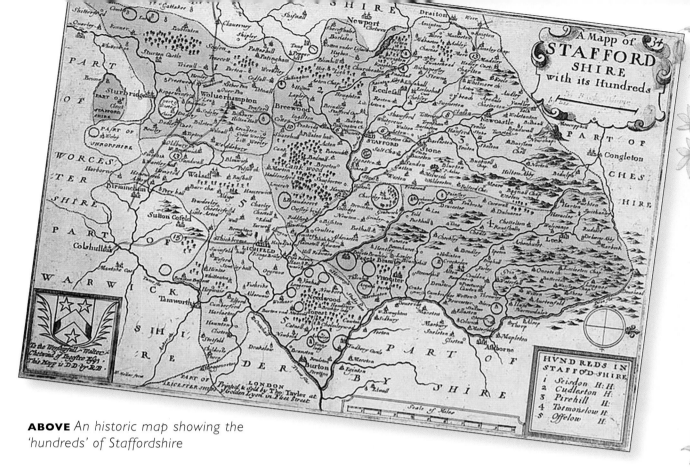

ABOVE *An historic map showing the 'hundreds' of Staffordshire*

Administration and organisation

How can you find evidence of Anglo-Saxon activity in your region? You are probably going to have to use alternative methods to finding dateable artefacts. A good place to start is by finding out if your area was part of a **hundred**. These were Anglo-Saxon land divisions made up of 100 hides. As we note in Category 16, a **hide** was the amount of land needed to provide for an extended 'free' family. Typically the average hide was around 120 acres, but could extend up to 180 acres or more.

In some cases, there are Anglo-Saxon records referring to these units of land, which can still be traced in the landscape today. Near Dunster, the nearest reference we have is to the Carhampton Hundred. If lucky, you might find an historic map showing the hundreds for your county, like the example for Staffordshire illustrated above.

Around the country, hundreds can have different names. For instance, in the North East, they were known as **Wapentakes** — a reference to a place that can provide a certain number of weapons.

The creation of these land divisions began to organise the way the country was ruled. In small

RIGHT *An illumination from the Lindisfarne Gospels, highlighting the Saxons' exquisite and intricate calligraphy*

ABOVE *A rare example of an Anglo-Saxon church in Bradford on Avon*

villages and settlements, the king's laws, the organisation of people into tithings of twelve (to be responsible for administering justice and a system of government via **moots**, or motes – communal gatherings), created a society that, although still ruled by powerful local thegns, gave ordinary people a degree of representation and justice.

The Burghal Hidage

The coming of the Vikings in the late eighth century would have a destructive effect on much of Anglo-Saxon culture, and forced the Anglo-Saxons into areas like Wessex, where under Alfred they eventually defeated the Danes and established a northern boundary, the **Danelaw**, that kept the invaders at bay.

Another line of research is to determine whether your village is near a **Burghal Hidage** fort, created as part of the Anglo-Saxon defence system against Viking attacks (Category 19). Lists of 'burhs' are easily available online, with a simple search. Watchet, not far from Dunster, is today a small port, but it was once an important defensive fort in this network.

Domesday

Of course, the greatest challenge to Anglo-Saxon dominance was the Norman Conquest, and the Domesday Book is an invaluable source in documenting this change. Entries often mention the Anglo-Saxon landowner pre-Conquest, providing a snapshot of the period when the early village began (Category 16). As we have seen, Dunster had a landowner named Aelfric, while Carhampton has a reference to Dunn – both names being Anglo-Saxon in origin.

RIGHT *The Alfred Jewel, believed to have been owned by Alfred the Great*

Anglo-Saxon churches

While they built their homes out of wood, the Saxons built some churches in stone. However, many of these were rebuilt by the Normans, partially as a way of asserting their dominance. As Mick once noted in one of our masterclasses, Medieval communities had no concept of heritage in the way that we do now and would happily tear down an historic building to make way for a new one. That said, examples do exist, including St Laurence's Church in Bradford on Avon. If you know what you're looking for, you might find evidence of Saxon building work, perhaps tucked away in a supposedly Norman church – see, for example, the Saxon window at Culbone highlighted in Category 10.

Boundaries and trackways

ABOVE *A buckle found at Sutton Hoo*

If you are lucky, parts of your parish boundary may correspond to an earlier Anglo-Saxon boundary (Category 18). These land divisions were important because they represented an organisation of the landscape with collections of family units at their centre.

Ancient trackways and other routes led to traditional meeting places and these occasionally became part of the origins of a settlement or village. Another Anglo-Saxon name often found in the landscape is **herepath**, a trackway used by the 'here' or 'army'.

Royal mints

Finally, search historic records and maps for references to an Anglo-Saxon coin mint in the area. There was an important mint at Lydford in Devon, for example, although most traces of Anglo-Saxon activity in the area have since vanished.

Anglo-Saxon coin

THINGS TO DO

- Look at the Domesday record for your village or town to find the name of an Anglo-Saxon lord before the Normans arrived in 1066 (Category 16).
- Try to discover if your area was part of an Anglo-Saxon hundred. Again, this information might be found in Domesday.
- Look for signs of an Anglo-Saxon Burghal Hidage fort (Category 19).
- Identify locations in or near your village with variations of the words 'moot' (or 'mote') or 'herepath', which have Anglo-Saxon origin.
- Keep an eye out for references to an Anglo-Saxon coin mint on maps.
- Log your discoveries and plot the key dates on your timeline.

26 THE NORMANS & FEUDAL SYSTEM

Imagine that you are living under the feudal system today. You are at the lower end of the system, a serf, which appropriately comes from the Latin 'servir' meaning a slave. To begin with, you are owned by the lord and can be sold to any other person he designates. You are obliged to work at least two days a week on the lord's land with no payment. He can also ask you to do a wide range of additional tasks, ironically called 'boon work'. Your daughter cannot be married without the lord's permission and it is forbidden for you to leave the village or live elsewhere. You cannot grind your own corn, brew beer, hunt for game in the forest, kill a pigeon that is eating your grain, or collect waste wood. All of these are punishable by severe fines, mutilation or even death. The courts are administered and run by the lord, so you have no legal redress. In the event of a war,

LEFT *A late sixteenth century depiction of William the Conqueror*

ABOVE *An extract from the Bayeaux Tapestry showing Harold swearing an oath on holy relics*

you will first be expected to pay extra taxation and then, if called upon, fight for your lord in battle. Everything you produce from the sweat of your own labour will be taxed and a tenth collected by the lord's reeve. You will also pay a tenth to the local church and clergy. To add insult to injury, when you die, your best beast – a cow or oxen – will go to the lord as a death tax. Welcome to life under the feudal system!

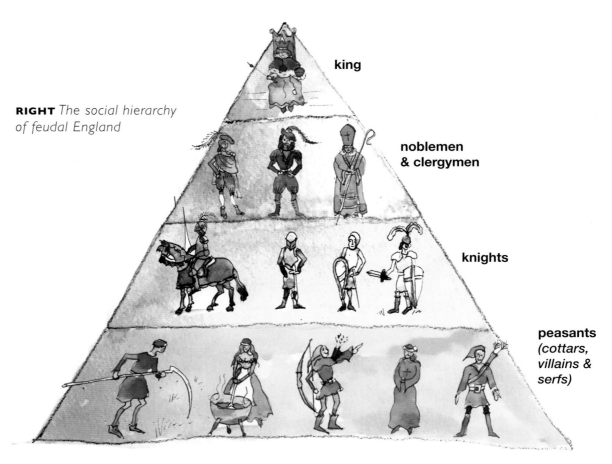

RIGHT *The social hierarchy of feudal England*

king

noblemen & clergymen

knights

peasants *(cottars, villains & serfs)*

Origins

Understanding the way that the **feudal system** worked is important because if your settlement existed in the Medieval period, your predecessors would have lived under its strict laws, which influenced every area of life.

Typically, we associate the arrival of feudalism in England with the Norman Conquest of 1066. However, many historians, including the Victorian historian F.W. Maitland, have taken the view that some elements of the feudal system were already in place in the early-Medieval period prior to the Conquest. Essentially this related to how land was given in return for service. At its upper levels, this may have required a local lord or chief to provide the monarch with armed forces in the time of war. At the lower level, the services included labouring without pay. The term 'feudal' derives from *fife*, an area of land or an estate.

Enforcing the system

With the Conquest, the feudal system became more onerous and pronounced, reinforced by a victorious invading army keen to repress rebellion and backed up by military might. This included numerous castles, which multiplied into the thousands during the early Norman period.

As far as William the Conqueror was concerned, the land was his and he parcelled it up and gave it to his supporters in return for rent, service and loyalty. Vast amounts of land became controlled by French allies of William.

In the case of Dunster, we known that William de Mohun received large areas of Somerset. Like many Norman lords, he began to build a castle as a centre of administration and as a point from which to defend his territory.

HOW TO: FIND SIGNS OF THE FEUDAL SYSTEM

As we've highlighted, the arrival of Norman feudalism would have had a significant impact on village life and there are ways to get a sense of out how it might have affected your own village. Applying some of the key themes and research tools we suggest throughout the book will open up some interesting avenues of research.

1. Domesday: Beginning with Domesday is always a logical place to start, following the example given in Category 16. This might tell you if your village was part of a new estate established under one of William's barons, or of earlier Anglo-Saxon origin. Looking at Domesday in conjunction with later Medieval records will help to illustrate how the system developed and formalised over a period of time.

2. Key characters: County history books should identify lords and landowners who held sway over local villages. Look for older copies at the local records office. Remember that fortunes could shift, and the dominant family might have changed over the centuries. In Dunster, for example, the de Mohuns made way for the Luttrells. Pubs and landmarks might suggest local influence (the Luttrell Arms).

3. Find the manor: The manor was the lord's local centre of administration. Many manor houses still stand, but hundreds more once dotted the countryside. Archaeological reports and historic maps might help to identify the original location of a 'lost' manor. Maps are particularly useful for identifying old boundaries created under the feudal system, and field or road names no longer in use.

4. Social effects: Research the impact that feudalism had on lives from a social perspective. Much of law and order in the Medieval period centred upon upholding the social hierarchy (Category 36). Contemporary written accounts and court rolls reveal fascinating insights into this in practice, including the injustices often inflicted on the lower ranks of society, and clues about wealth and status.

ABOVE *A postage stamp commemorating Domesday*

The castle occupied by French lords and knights must have represented a frightening prospect to the average villager. In the centuries that directly followed the Conquest, the dominant language of the rulers was Medieval French and their authority was imposed by the army, the courts and the Church. It was the advantage of a victorious invasion that allowed William and his followers to apply this feudal system with such severity. At its centre was the idea of a manor (Category 13).

The court records throughout the Medieval period contain evidence of stringent justice to those who failed to conform. At regular court sessions, usually supervised by the lord or his representatives, villagers were fined or suffered some severe punishment (Category 36).

Resistance to feudalism

This system was so onerous that it's perhaps not surprising that resentment built up. Gradually those at the receiving end began to fight back. One aspect that tipped the scale slightly in their favour was the loss of labour caused by the Black Death (Category 27). The lords had land, but without workers it could not be farmed. Eventually the more limited number of agricultural labourers meant that lords had to pay more to gain their service or at least reduce the servile elements of their service. Workers became more mobile and moved to those places that offered better conditions.

Despite some improvement, the lot of the average peasant was still poor. When unrest began to appear in the fourteenth century, the feudal system was threatened by its first revolutionary resistance. In 1381, the Peasants' Revolt broke out, stirred into action by a poll tax repeatedly raised to produce money for wars against the French. Given the repressive power of the system, it's amazing

that so many people had the courage and tenacity to join the rebellion. Led by men including Wat Tyler, the revolt got as far as London and forced a meeting with the king. Shortly after offering to abolish serfdom, the king (the 14-year-old Richard II) had the ringleaders rounded up and hanged. The revolt, although ultimately unsuccessful, did begin to bring some of the legitimate demands of the labouring classes to the fore.

Another change in many settlements came about with the development of small towns (Category 19). This happened in Dunster, where the lord saw money to be made from renting out plots of land either side of the main street. This created a new class of people, the burgesses, who were free men, meaning they did not have to provide service to the lord. This was, in a way, the beginnings of a middle class of merchants and craftsmen who had the money to buy land and also gain justice through the courts.

It is an interesting thought that there has always been an importance related to land ownership in Britain. To be free and own your own land represented a level of independence that few in the feudal system could achieve. But it was a status that many must have aspired to, and maybe our contemporary desire for ownership had some of its origins in the late Medieval period.

The social hierarchy

Many terms are used to refer to those at the bottom of the feudal system, and it's useful to clarify some of them. A 'serf' was on the lowest rung. Along with the 'cottars' who received a small amount of space to occupy in return for labour, the 'villains' (or villeins) were slightly better off, as they were considered to be part of the estate and therefore not liable to be bought or sold. Typically, all of the agricultural labouring classes tend to be referred to as peasants, but in the Medieval period 'serf' and 'villain' were the most common terms.

THINGS TO DO

- Find the Domesday entry for your village, if one exists (Category 16).
  This should give you the name of the lord who owned the land.

Norman lord

- Search the local archives for information, such as archaeological reports including potential sites of the castle or manor house occupied by your Norman lord.
- Look through historic maps for changes in the boundaries and ancient names.
- Search court records for examples of the feudal system in action.
- Log your discoveries and plot the key dates on your timeline.

27 THE BLACK DEATH

The Black Death caused widespread devastation on a scale that was hard to fathom. It quickly spread everywhere, and was especially rapid in the more densely populated villages and towns. It was as deadly as it was quick, with physical symptoms that were truly horrific. In its first bout, roughly a third of England's four million inhabitants were killed by the disease, leaving some villages completely decimated.

Unlike the poor, who were bound to the manor, the rich were free to move around the country in hope of escaping its clutches. Henry VIII, for example, raised his son Edward away from the city at Hampton Court to avoid contact. Ultimately, however, the plague favoured no particular class over another and took the lives of millions from all walks of life.

RIGHT *Rats are traditionally associated with the plague although some recent research challenges this theory*
BEHIND *The Grim Reaper descending upon his victims*

ABOVE *A fifteenth century painting illustrating the horrific physical symptoms of the plague*

Arrival from the continent

In 1348, the **Black Death** arrived on England's shores. An epidemic that we now know as the **plague** was first reported in Italy in January and swept across the continent, before arriving in southern Britain by the summer. It spread quickly, reaching Scotland, Ireland and Wales in 1349, and reappeared several times throughout the century.

Medieval doctors didn't know the causes of the plague and had no idea how to cure it. As with most unexplained catastrophes of the era, many viewed it as an act of God. Rats have traditionally been identified as the carriers responsible for transmitting the disease to humans. However, more recent research has led to new theories that challenge this notion. What is clear is the havoc it wreaked. Once it took hold, life expectancy was no more than three days.

Unexpected consequences

With such a large proportion of the population wiped out, many communities struggled to keep their crops and animals alive. Food became more expensive and people had to move to avoid starvation. Under the feudal system, peasants had to seek the lord's permission to leave their villages and once they left they were not allowed to return again without the lord's permission. However, ironically, the resulting shortage of manual labour helped to redress the balance of power. To an extent, it improved the lives of the peasants who survived. They now had greater bargaining power and could be more selective in their choices of who to work for, and the compensation that they would receive.

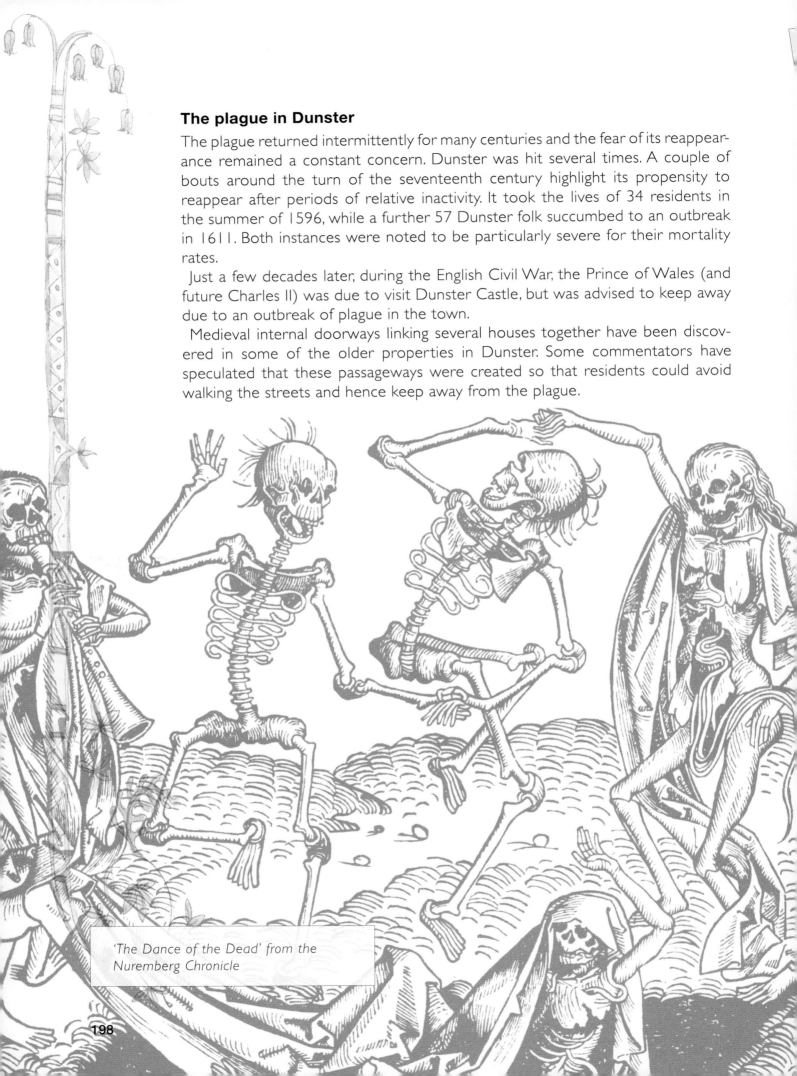

The plague in Dunster

The plague returned intermittently for many centuries and the fear of its reappearance remained a constant concern. Dunster was hit several times. A couple of bouts around the turn of the seventeenth century highlight its propensity to reappear after periods of relative inactivity. It took the lives of 34 residents in the summer of 1596, while a further 57 Dunster folk succumbed to an outbreak in 1611. Both instances were noted to be particularly severe for their mortality rates.

Just a few decades later, during the English Civil War, the Prince of Wales (and future Charles II) was due to visit Dunster Castle, but was advised to keep away due to an outbreak of plague in the town.

Medieval internal doorways linking several houses together have been discovered in some of the older properties in Dunster. Some commentators have speculated that these passageways were created so that residents could avoid walking the streets and hence keep away from the plague.

'The Dance of the Dead' from the Nuremberg Chronicle

ABOVE *Known plague pits scattered across London*
RIGHT *A man wearing a death mask and protective clothing to deal with plague victims*

Deserted Medieval villages

Traces of abandoned settlements, known as **deserted Medieval villages (DMVs)**, can occasionally be seen on the ground (Category 54). In some cases, these may be examples of villages that were devastated by the Black Death.

Perhaps you have noticed unusual earthworks while walking around your village. Visible hints of **ridge and furrow systems**, or the footprints of former buildings, may show up at certain times of the year. Advances in aerial archaeology and satellite photography can help the search for these villages, and a look at Google Earth may throw up some interesting results.

However, while it makes a great headline, there is a danger of falsely attributing a village's desertion to the plague. There were, of course, many other reasons that could be responsible for people leaving an area, including both natural causes and changes in the use of land, as we discuss throughout the book (see Categories 30 and 34).

That said, if the dates match, it's not unreasonable to suggest that an outbreak of the plague – or more likely a succession of bouts over a number of years – was at least a contributing factor.

Plague pits

Occasionally, construction workers or archaeologists stumble across Medieval plague pits – large burial sites containing victims who fell to the plague. In 2015, up to 30 plague victims were discovered by Crossrail in a pit in central London, while building a new train line. In 2016, archaeologists discovered a mass grave containing 48 men, women and children from the fourteenth century at the site of Thornton Abbey, Lincolnshire.

Check the local archaeological records and newspaper archives for evidence of similar pits known to be in your area, highlighting the scale of devastation that could be inflicted upon a community.

Influence on Church decoration

The Black Death left other physical evidence behind, particularly in its influence on Church adornments, furniture and architecture. In the immediate aftermath of its initial arrival in the mid-fourteenth century, a more austere style was adopted in some cathedrals and churches then in construction. Simple straight lines reflected both the sombre times and the more practical issue of a lack of skilled labour.

Another phenomenon was an increasing fixation with mortality and graphic visual representations of death, which increasingly seeped into the paintings, carvings and other architectural embellishments of many churches.

BELOW *The tomb of John FitzAlan, Earl of Arundel, highlights a mid-fifteenth century fashion for explicit displays of mortality inspired by the Black Death*

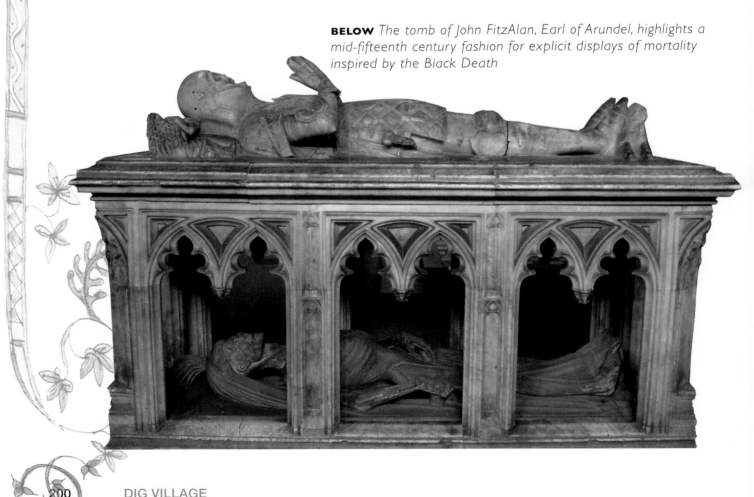

The mid-fifteenth century onwards, for instance, marked a fashion for **cadaver tombs**. These intricately carved monuments found in some churches are often characterised by a stone effigy of the deceased in all their splendour, contrasted with another underneath it of the decaying corpse — a stark reminder to the populace that death comes to us all, regardless of social status. Wonderful examples include the tomb of Alice Chaucer, Duchess of Suffolk, at St Mary's Church in Ewelme, Oxfordshire, and that of John FitzAlan, Earl of Arundel, in the chapel of Arundel Castle.

If your church is Medieval in origin, it's worth taking a closer look at the decorations and carvings throughout to search for clues. These could be anything from representations of the 'Grim Reaper' and plague victims to inscriptions on tombs or gravestones that shed light on causes of death.

While many walls were whitewashed and carvings defaced during the Reformation (Category 28), if you're lucky you might make some surprising discoveries. One astonishing find is the fourteenth century Latin graffiti carved into the walls of St Mary's Church, Ashwell, in Hertfordshire, which reads:

*"1350 Miserable, wild distracted 1350;
the dregs of the mob alone survive to witness"*

This inscription refers to a notably intense outbreak that is known to have swept through the region in that year. The fact it's written in Latin suggests it was probably the work of a monk. Such explicit epitaphs are rare, but if you look closely enough in your own village church, you may just spot some evidence of the Black Death's wider impact on the local community.

RIGHT *A fourteenth century Latin inscription on a church wall that vividly records a severe bout of the plague*

THINGS TO DO

- Search the local records for references to 'deserted Medieval villages', DMVs (Category 54).
- Use Google Earth or look for signs in the landscape that might hint of earlier settlements that have been deserted.
- Search the archives for records of known plague pits in the area.
- Visit your local church and look for architectural details or tombs that may have been influenced by the Black Death, such as visual representations of mortality or written inscriptions.
- Log your discoveries and plot the key dates on your timeline.

28 THE ENGLISH REFORMATION

The Reformation, beginning in 1535, was one of the biggest changes to affect villages and towns in Medieval England. For centuries, the whole fabric of life and death was woven around the rituals and observances of the Church, with life's major events – christenings, marriage and funerals – bound up in its doctrine. Religion was the one opportunity to lessen the pain of Purgatory. Regular attendance at church was obligatory and the social meeting after services was an important part of village life. The interior of your local church would have looked very different from today, with richly coloured wall paintings and decorated altars and rood screens. Following the Reformation, these rich interiors were stripped away and the small links that connected daily life with the local church were broken. Walls were whitewashed, rood screens vandalised and beautiful altars reduced to plain tables. It became a crime to say public prayers for the dead or to openly follow elements of the 'old' religion. It was a form of cultural devastation.

Fountains Abbey, Yorkshire

The English Reformation came about because of Henry VIII's wish to control Church power. In 1534 an Act of Supremacy was passed, effectively making Henry the head of the Church of England. The Pope had refused to grant Henry a divorce from Katherine of Aragon, as he had already granted Henry a special dispensation to marry Katherine, his brother's widow, in 1509. Henry wished to marry Anne Boleyn, who he hoped would provide male heirs. By making himself head of the Church of England he no longer needed the Pope's permission. The Church of England became the supreme religious power, rather than the Church of Rome.

Wealth and control

The actions that affected the lives of so many were driven by the self-interest of relatively few. Various individuals and factions in court took advantage of Henry's desire for control to promote their own personal, political or religious agendas. It paved the way for Protestantism in England with the Dissolution of the Monasteries, the first published Bible in English, and the outlawing of many Catholic trappings. As well as greater authority, breaking up the old Church gave Henry access to its considerable wealth – a point that wasn't lost on those whose religious interest it served.

RIGHT *The beginning of the Gospel of John in a copy of John Wycliffe's translation of the Bible*

Young Holbien's portrait of Henry VIII

Valuation of property

In 1535, Henry commissioned the *Valor Ecclesiasticus*, a valuation of all Church property, detailing the value of each religious complex in wealth and property. From 1536 to 1540, two thirds of the Church's land was sold, with its wealth used by the crown to fund coastal defences and weapons, amongst other things. This was followed by the destruction of many beautiful buildings. Together, these developments had a major impact on the surrounding villages that benefitted from their closeness to a monastery.

Of course, the Church and monastic complexes were sometimes unpopular, and no doubt elements of reform would have been welcomed by some. The priest, prior and abbot were senior figures in village life and had to be paid a tithe from agricultural produce (Category 17). This could breed resentment, with some clergymen abusing their positions to gain wealth and property. However, the religious orders helped local communities too, often providing alms and help for the sick (Category 41).

The Reformation in Dunster

Medieval Dunster had a Benedictine priory, a daughter cell of Bath Priory. Following the Reformation, it passed over to the crown, with its buildings and lands leased and then later sold off. As was often the case across the country, the land initially passed into the hands of the local ruling elite, the Luttrell family – a name still familiar in Dunster today with the Luttrell Arms public house. This breaking up of ecclesiastical assets had an impact on the town's development. The building known as the 'Nunnery', for example, was sold off and eighteenth century records show that it was later used as a malthouse.

RIGHT *The 'Nunnery' in Dunster*

ABOVE *The original beautiful vaulted cellarium at Mottisfont hints at its former use*

Wider impact

The wider impact of the Reformation can't be understated, and its repercussions are still felt today. Hundreds of people lost their lives because of their religious beliefs, and the 'fall out' led to decades of troubled monarchy. To this day, as head of the Anglican Church, a British monarch cannot be Catholic – a law that still regularly comes up for discussion.

A bit of investigation can help to reveal some of the effects that the Reformation had in your area. Maybe your village is close to the site of a known monastery or priory. Once riches were taken from the site of an abbey or priory, local people were often allowed to use the remaining bricks for themselves. Perhaps older buildings in your village have signs of masonry that has been repurposed. Sometimes, the abbey itself was remodelled as a grand home for the local lord, such as Mottisfont Abbey in Hampshire, which still reveals fascinating insights into its original function, including a beautiful vaulted cellarium.

Mottisfont in Hampshire is a grand country house built on the site of a former abbey, whose vaulted cellarium still stands today

ABOVE *A sixteenth century depiction of the destruction of a church by reformers*

Clues in your church

Have a look at the outside, inside and history of your local church for clues to how it has evolved. Church buildings were used by rich villagers to express their piety and aid their passage to heaven by providing for new chapels or additions. Societies of men and women would form around a particular chapel in order to fund its care and provide for the candles, known as lights, that were an important part of worship. There may be indications of how chapels and other features have developed or been altered over the years, both prior to and following the Reformation. Some churches still have evidence of vandalism to statues or carvings, such as decapitation or defacing (see above). There may also be local stories of people who suffered from religious persecution.

THINGS TO DO

- Check the *Valor Ecclesiasticus* and see if you have any sites near you.
- Search for local place names or buildings including the name 'Abbey', suggesting a former use. TIP: See Category 12 for more on abbeys and priories.
- Visit your local church to find evidence of destruction as a result of the Reformation.
- Log your discoveries and plot the key dates on your timeline.

29 THE ENGLISH CIVIL WAR

The English Civil War (from 1642 to 1651) was a period of huge upheaval, with brothers often fighting against brothers and fathers fighting against sons. The growing distrust of King Charles I by Parliament led to a bloody period in English history, which left many dead and the country torn apart. Villages were divided and destroyed, with armies stealing both crops and animals to feed themselves, leaving little for the villagers. This landmark event would change the country forever. Ultimately, it led to the king's execution and the founding of a republic. Although the monarchy was later restored, all future kings and queens of England (and later Britain) would have significantly limited powers as a direct result.

ABOVE *Postage stamps commemorating the English Civil War*

ABOVE *An engraving of Charles I, who clashed with Parliament*

Causes of the conflict

There were many causes for the English Civil War but one of the main factors was Charles I's belief in the 'Divine Right of Kings'. In his view, Parliament was simply there to do his bidding and, as God's representative on Earth, the king could never be wrong. As a result, Charles had several clashes with Parliament over money and when members didn't do as he wished, he simply locked them out and shut Parliament down for 11 years.

In 1635, Charles tried to order everyone in the country to pay Ship Money, a tax historically paid by those who lived near the sea to help for the upkeep of the navy. Many people refused to pay this tax and Charles had no choice but to recall Parliament to get access to the funds he needed for war. When his request was denied, Charles tried to arrest certain members of Parliament. However, they had been pre-warned and fled. This action led to a complete breakdown in communication between Charles I and Parliament and consequently to civil war.

Years of bloodshed followed, with thousands of people unwittingly drawn into the conflict. Loyalties were split between the Royalists (or Cavaliers) and Parliamentarians (or Roundheads). However, a variety of factors influenced people's decisions to take sides, from religion and class, to regional loyalties and simple opportunism. The conflict eventually culminated in Charles' execution in January 1649 with Oliver Cromwell becoming Lord Protector.

Dunster's siege

Dunster played a significant part in the Civil War, a fact that is still commemorated every year at a Civil War Weekend held at Dunster Castle. The Royalists established a garrison at the castle under the command of Colonel Francis Wyndham, from 1643. The castle came under siege in September 1645, until it finally surrendered in April 1646. The Parliamentarians were led by Colonel Robert Blake, who based himself at the Ship Inn in the village (now the Luttrell Arms). If you visit the Yarn Market in the town centre, there is a large hole through one of the inside struts, supposedly made by a cannon ball fired during this period.

ABOVE *Oliver Cromwell, a key Parliamentarian and first Lord Protector*

The aftermath

The scars of the Civil War can still be seen across the country. One of the reasons that there are so many castle ruins across England is that they were razed to the ground during this period. Many were damaged or destroyed in sieges, while others were **slighted** – intentionally demolished to prevent them from falling into the hands of the enemy. Corfe Castle in Dorset, which, like Dunster, stands on a large hill above the town, is a notable example.

Clues to Civil War associations can sometimes be found in local place names. The parish of Oliver's Battery on the outskirts of Winchester, for example, is named after Cromwell's forces, who camped in the

LEFT *Dunster's Yarn Market, which was supposedly damaged by a stray cannon ball during the conflict*

ABOVE *Distinctive helmets gave the Roundheads their nickname*

area shortly before the Parliamentarian siege of Winchester in 1645. Civil War armies often built earthworks when conducting a siege, which might still be visible near a castle (see Category 11).

See if records exist of local allegiances during the Civil War. Your village or town may have been a Royalist or Parliamentarian stronghold, or perhaps loyalties were divided. There are many examples of individuals who switched sides, depending on which side held greater influence at the time. It wasn't unusual for friends or family to come face to face on opposing sides on the battlefield. Comprehensive lists of Civil War battles can easily be found online – see if any notable battles, skirmishes or sieges took place nearby.

THINGS TO DO

- Find a list of Civil War battles and sieges to identify those that happened closest to your area. It's possible that smaller skirmishes occurred in or around your village.
- If there is a castle nearby, find out if it was a Royalist or Parliamentarian stronghold during the war and whether it was involved in a siege. In some cases, a castle may have changed hands throughout the course of the war.
- Revisit Category 11 to find out how to spot Civil War 'siege castles'.
- Log your discoveries and plot the key dates on your timeline.

Corfe Castle in Dorset was slighted by Parliamentarian forces

Charles I's death warrant, including the signatures and seals of the regicides

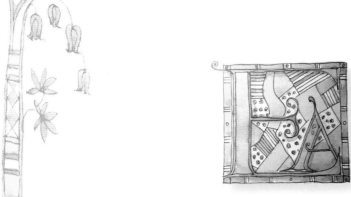

30 THE ENCLOSURE ACTS

For millennia, communities of people have worked the land and harnessed its natural resources, initially for shelter and hunting, then later for pasture and the growing of crops. In ancient times, this 'common land' would have been seen as a gift to all. Yet with the passing of time, increasingly more land became privatised for the benefit of the privileged and powerful. The creation of vast hunting parks and forests, for example, had a huge impact on Medieval village communities, as hundreds of acres of land were fenced off, with severe penalties including death for those who fell foul of its laws.

Another considerable land grab, which drastically affected the livelihoods of many, was the practice of enclosing land for lucrative sheep farming. Enclosure was a gradual process over generations, affecting areas at different times. Illegal enclosure in Norfolk, for instance, led to Kett's Rebellion of 1549. But the issue became increasingly pronounced during the eighteenth century, with the process officially enshrined in law.

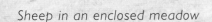

Sheep in an enclosed meadow

ABOVE *Common land historically provided for all, before the process of enclosure began, as landowners increasingly fenced in land for their own use*

The introduction of the Enclosure Acts in the 1700s had a significant impact on the countryside and its communities. The Enclosure Acts removed all the rights of local people to rural land that they had worked, sometimes for many generations. This legislation enabled rich landowners to close off large areas of common land for themselves. The poor were simply left to decide whether to stay as tenants, working for significantly lower wages, or leave the area and try their luck in the towns. In many parts of the local landscape, the ancient curved and winding field boundaries were replaced by more regular, squared off enclosures.

Potential benefits of enclosure

Despite the significant social repercussions, one perceived benefit of the Enclosure Acts was improved agricultural productivity, through bringing more land into effective use. Many landowners across the country used the acts to introduce more profitable farming methods, such as sheep farming for the production of wool. Grazing sheep also required less manpower, typically just a shepherd and perhaps a boy, rather than the team of labourers needed for ploughing, sowing and harvesting crops. This practice coincided with the onset of the Industrial Revolution (Category 32). Together, these developments often had a knock-on effect, for better or worse, as in the case of Dunster.

ABOVE *The Yarn Market in Dunster*

Dunster's wool trade

For generations, Dunster's main trade had been wool production, which provided an income for many of the town's inhabitants. The historic Yarn Market in the centre of the town was built for its trade and can still be visited today. From the mid-eighteenth century onwards, the process of turning wool into cloth was becoming increasingly mechanised nationwide, which meant that regular supplies of raw wool were needed for production. The greater efficiency brought about by enclosure enabled farmers across the country to meet this demand for increased wool production, resulting in greater competition from elsewhere.

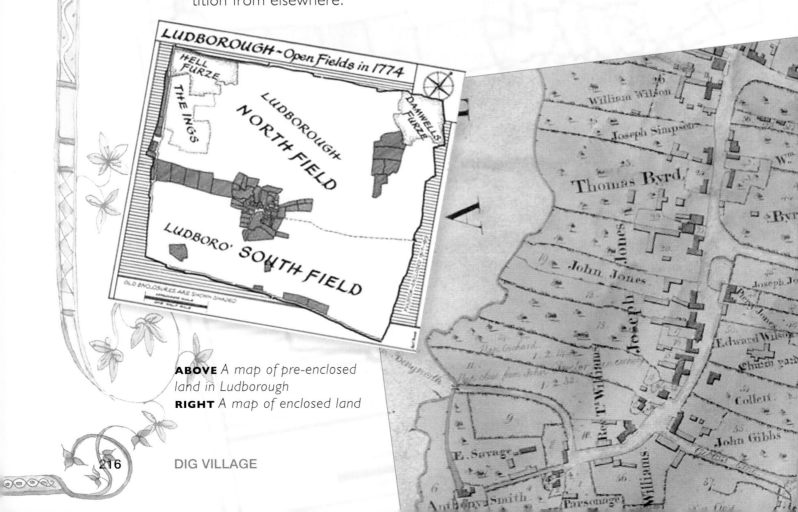

ABOVE *A map of pre-enclosed land in Ludborough*
RIGHT *A map of enclosed land*

Pre-enclosure land

Post-enclosure land

Local enclosure

In some regions, the commons and areas of rough grazing were taken into cultivation as smallholdings with cottages. In Cornwall, for example, hundreds of these were created in the late eighteenth and early nineteenth centuries.

Your local archives may have records of what happened during and after the Enclosure Acts. Comparing boundaries of several historic maps from this period might reveal how the local land was redistributed. Try to establish if the acts had a negative impact on a local trade such as wool production. One way to judge the impact, for instance, is to discover whether new mills were created during this time to meet the demand. It's likely that this would have damaged the local cottage industry, which may have struggled to compete with more efficient modern production.

Another approach is to study local records in order to find out whether people were moving out of the area in significant numbers around the same time as local enclosure legislation. If so, you may be able to determine if there was a link between the two events.

Alternatively, enclosure may have improved conditions in the area by bringing in greater productivity of crops. What's more, some tenants positively welcomed enclosure due to the compensation they were granted, enabling them to start new lives elsewhere.

THINGS TO DO

- Compare maps created before and after the eighteenth century Enclosure Acts for notable boundary changes as a result. However, also note that enclosure may have already begun long before the acts.
- Look for evidence of mills opening or closing around this time.
- Search the local newspaper archives for stories relating to enclosure in your area.
- Log your discoveries and plot the key dates on your timeline.

31 AGRICULTURAL ADVANCES

We are so used to the idea of modern scientific farming, we forget that for much of the lifetime of local farms, agriculture was based on age-old methods that had barely changed for hundreds of years. Farms and agriculture have been a major feature of British landscapes for millennia. The introduction of farming from around 4500 BC and the gradual evolution of field systems have created many elements of the landscape we know today.

Each crop variation and farming technique has had a bearing on how the land has been managed and, crucially, how many people were required as agricultural labour. For most of your predecessors this would have been their main occupation until what might be called an agricultural revolution occurred in the eighteenth and nineteenth centuries. It was often the case that advances in farming and an increased ability to feed a growing population came at the price of rural unemployment!

Somerset fields growing different types of crops on rotation

LEFT *The seed drill*

Inventions and innovations

Farming has seen many innovations over the centuries. The concept of crop rotation to improve harvests was a crucial discovery. Planting the same crop of, say, wheat on the same piece of land year after year would inevitably lead to lower yields. Farmers discovered that allowing the land to lie fallow would help its fertility and then planting a crop like clover would increase levels of nitrogen in the soil. Different crops were tried and, over time, wheat and barley replaced grains like rye.

New inventions helped to mechanise many aspects of farming life. The seed drill, popularised in England by Jethro Tull in the early eighteenth century, was one of many innovations that heralded the Agricultural Revolution. Meanwhile, the Industrial Revolution had created a move towards cities and a growing population that needed to be fed (Category 32). Improvements in agriculture meant an acre of land that in the twelfth century produced eight bushels of wheat was producing over 26 bushels by the eighteenth century.

ABOVE *Jethro Tull, who popularised the seed drill*

The measurement of a **bushel** was introduced by the Normans, and the term itself
comes from the Old French, *boissiel*,
meaning 'small box'. Historically, it was
defined as eight dry gallons.

It has been estimated that only 22% of
the British work force were still working in
agriculture by the mid-nineteenth century, a
significant decline compared to earlier centuries. Today, that figure is around 1.5%! Innovations like a threshing machine drawn by horses
vastly improved the efficiency of the harvest and
reduced the number needed for manual labour.

ABOVE *A brass imperial bushel
standard measure from 1878*

Incidentally it also increased the number of accidents occurring on farms and
there are some fairly gruesome records of men losing hands in the new machines.

In the first half of the eighteenth century, Viscount Townshend promoted the
Norfolk four-course system. Rather than allowing a fallow year, followers of this
system alternately grew wheat, turnips, barley and clover. The planting of turnips
provided extra fodder for cattle when the weather was at its worst. The Viscount
was given the nickname 'Turnip Townshend' for his troubles!

Selective breeding

The other scientific advances in agriculture came with the selective breeding
of animals to improve both their size and ability to produce meat for food and
improved wool in the case of sheep (see also Category 43). Robert Bakewell
created a breed of sheep that combined many improvements and led to the
English Leicester. This breed, which was exported across the Empire, is sadly now
on the endangered list.

RIGHT *An
engraving of a
Leicester ram,
now on the
endangered list*

LEICESTER RAM.

Bakewell also worked on improving cattle breeds with the result that, by the late 1700s, their weight had almost doubled. The main technique involved the farmer choosing those animals with the features he most wanted to encourage, such as size, muscle definition or high lactation. It's an interesting historical note that when applied to horses, it produced the massive shire horses and battle horses of the late Middle Ages. In comparison, Roman horses would have looked like ponies!

Vegetables underwent scientific improvements, too. Carrots, for example, were originally grown as animal fodder and generally yellow or purple in colour, before being improved by Dutch farmers who created the sweeter orange carrot with which we are familiar today.

ABOVE *Different varieties of carrot*
RIGHT *A vintage, pre-computerised tractor*

We can get useful information on our ancestors' diet from an unexpected source – the tithe records. In Yorkshire, in the seventeenth century for instance, we find references to carrots, turnips, artichokes and other vegetables being tithed.

With the advent of the Enclosure Acts, larger fields became more common and this made it easier for mechanised farming to operate. When researching your local farms, it's a good idea to see which show a clear evidence of enclosure (Category 30). Through your research, you may be able to locate some of the oldest farms that still retain the curved, irregular boundaries of the pre-closure time. One of the big changes in your village or town would have been the transition from horsepower to motorised tractors.

LEFT *Shire horses at a local agricultural show*
BELOW *Horseshoes as made by a blacksmith (smithy)*

Many small settlements still have a building called the smithy, and one of its most common activities in the past generations would have been the making of horseshoes.

It's still possible to find farmers with memories of a pre-motorised age, and they will often be glad to talk about their memories of the past. In Cornwall, there are still memories of the excitement and alarm created by the appearance of steel ploughs and other modern advances! These agricultural developments typically resulted in greater efficiencies and economies of scale, but there was a cost to rural communities. The social nature of the village coming together to share in the process of ploughing, sowing and harvesting represented a degree of communal interaction that was sadly lost as agriculture advanced into the modern age.

THINGS TO DO

- Try to locate the oldest known farm in the area. See what the farmers can reveal about advances in agricultural technology. Perhaps the farm changed hands during the Agricultural Revolution, due to the changing circumstances.
- Search local collections and archives for historic photographs of farming in and around the village. Sometimes you'll find a few gems in private collections as well as the walls of local pubs.
- Look for signs in the landscape of historic farming. TIP: See Category 22 for identifying prehistoric field systems.
- Log your discoveries and plot the key dates on your timeline.

Vintage farm wheel from Scotland

Farm labourers using traditional, non-mechanised methods

32 THE INDUSTRIAL REVOLUTION

The Industrial Revolution (from around 1760 onwards) was essentially the birth of the modern age as we know it today: people living in large metropolises connected by efficient transport links, with easy access to cheap, mass-produced goods made in factories. On Time Team, we often witnessed the Industrial Revolution's influence, highlighting the huge scale of manufacturing and impressive advances in technology that came about over the period. In Series 13, we visited Manchester's very first cotton mill, built by Richard Arkwright, one of the forefathers of the factory system. We also investigated old furnaces and forges in a County Durham forest in Series 18, taking us back to the time when new industrial practices were just beginning to take root. In 2004, we visited Sheffield for a Time Team Special, to find out about the Steel City's rich industrial heritage. Of course, there were considerable downsides to this revolution, not least the poor working conditions imposed on workers, smoggy environments and frequent outbreaks of disease. What's more, the rise of the cities and modern industry would have a sharp knock-on effect on rural village life too.

ABOVE *Old steelworks in Sheffield*

Technological advances

The Industrial Revolution was a period of great advances in agriculture, industry and transport, which led to wholesale change in society. Agriculture was particularly affected (Category 31). As more mechanised methods of working were introduced in industry, hordes of people left the countryside for the cities, where work was more readily available. In 1750, only about 15% of people lived in towns, compared to 85% by 1900 – a complete cultural reversal in the space of 150 years.

The shift from agriculture to industry left villages with fewer people to handle food production, whilst towns and cities became overcrowded and disease ridden. The introduction of mechanised methods of farming, however, aided recovery and increased output, which enabled the growing population to be fed.

ABOVE & BEHIND *Mechanised looms inside a cotton mill*
RIGHT *One of Manchester's earliest cotton mills*

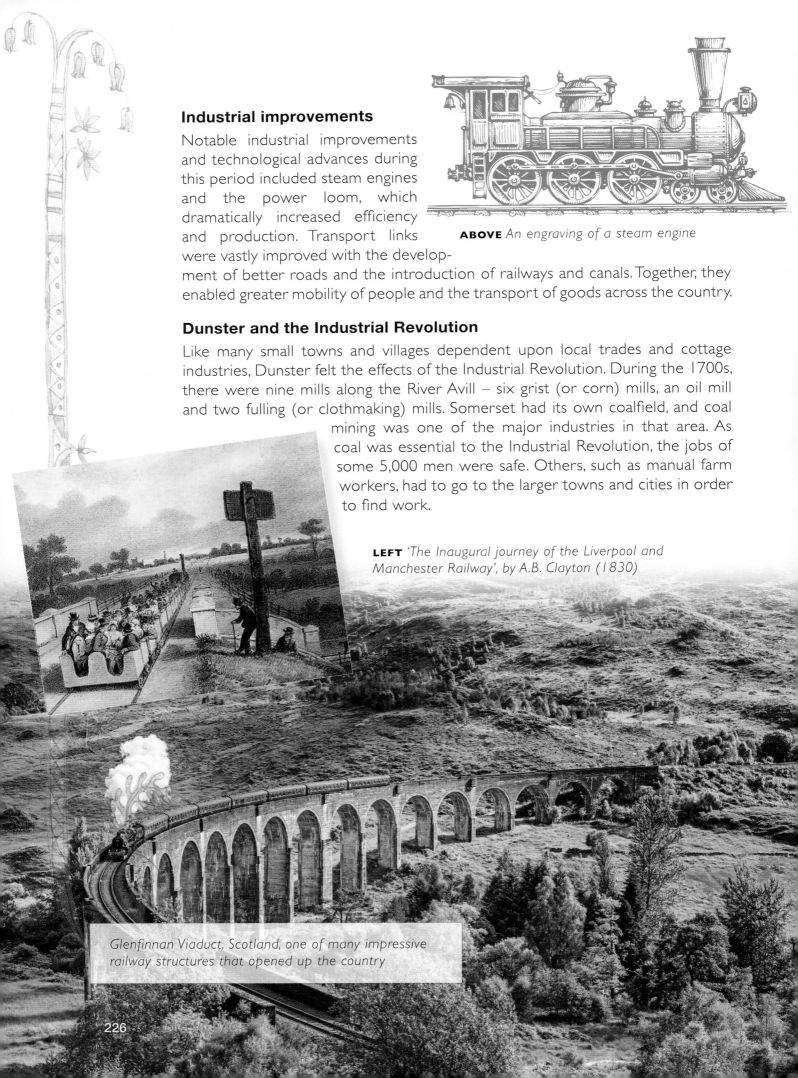

Industrial improvements

Notable industrial improvements and technological advances during this period included steam engines and the power loom, which dramatically increased efficiency and production. Transport links were vastly improved with the development of better roads and the introduction of railways and canals. Together, they enabled greater mobility of people and the transport of goods across the country.

ABOVE *An engraving of a steam engine*

Dunster and the Industrial Revolution

Like many small towns and villages dependent upon local trades and cottage industries, Dunster felt the effects of the Industrial Revolution. During the 1700s, there were nine mills along the River Avill – six grist (or corn) mills, an oil mill and two fulling (or clothmaking) mills. Somerset had its own coalfield, and coal mining was one of the major industries in that area. As coal was essential to the Industrial Revolution, the jobs of some 5,000 men were safe. Others, such as manual farm workers, had to go to the larger towns and cities in order to find work.

LEFT *'The Inaugural journey of the Liverpool and Manchester Railway', by A.B. Clayton (1830)*

Glenfinnan Viaduct, Scotland, one of many impressive railway structures that opened up the country

ABOVE *The site of an old coal mine in Radstock, Somerset*
RIGHT *A map of coal mines in Somerset*

Dunster was known for its wool trade (see Category 31), but by the mid-1800s people were struggling to find their rents. Some of the more unfortunate people ended up in the workhouse, leaving properties to fall into disrepair, with some being demolished. During this period, the tourist industry was beginning to form and Dunster started to provide shops and places to stay in the village, thus evolving into the Dunster we know today.

The local impact

How did the Industrial Revolution impact upon your area? A good starting point is to look at local trades that had traditionally prospered to find out if any suffered as a result of rising competition from elsewhere. You might be able to find records of traditional trades closing down, such as the village blacksmith. Clues to former use might appear in addresses that exist today, such as 'The Old Smithy', 'The Forge', 'The Workshop', or even just 'Shop'. The hamlet Box's Shop in north Cornwall gets its name from a local blacksmith who once plied his trade there. Look in newspaper archives for evidence of unrest as a result of new technology or factories. On the other hand, workers may have welcomed the opening of a new factory or mill nearby, for providing much needed work. Research whether agriculture or the size of your village were affected by changes during that period, such as migration to the big cities.

New railways and canals

Maybe the arrival of a railway impacted on the village, or perhaps the railway bypassed your village entirely causing a negative impact on the area. Micheldever Station, for example, is a new village, just a couple of miles from the much older village of Micheldever, which sprang up around a new railway line linking the South East to London. Neighbouring village, Sutton Scotney, also benefitted from its own railway on a separate line that is now no longer in use, a fact that may have impacted on its fortunes. Villages such as these are often characterised by distinctive rows of 'railway cottages' that date from the time of the station's arrival. Search the local archives for references to a station and look out for clues in location names, such as Station Road.

BELOW *Micheldever Station is a relatively modern village that developed with the arrival of a new railway line*

RIGHT *An old, disused railway line, highlighting that not every line that emerged would continue to prosper*
BEHIND *An historic railway map*

DIG VILLAGE

ABOVE *The Grand Union Canal, spanning the country from London to Manchester*

During the Industrial Revolution, a huge network of canals was created across the country. Online databases can help you discover whether a route once passed near your village. Equally, historic maps might help you to identify both canals and railway lines that have since disappeared and been lost in new development. It's amazing how quickly physical traces of once dominant structures can disappear from first sight! However, once you know what you're looking for, signs can be found in the landscape relatively easily. Look for evidence of manmade ditches, banks and even disused rails and sleepers.

Your village's geographic location would have shaped how it was affected by industrialisation. For example, the Midlands and the North were characterised by the rise of big cities, such as Birmingham, Manchester and Sheffield, which became home to many new factories. Coastal areas were dominated by shipbuilding and ports, bringing trade from overseas. Mineral rich areas such as the North East, Cornwall and Wales were centres of mining. Focussing your research in these localised industries might produce some key answers.

THINGS TO DO

- Try to locate any old mills – look for buildings or street names with 'mill' in them. Find out when the mill was built in relation to the onset of the Industrial Revolution.
- There may be old railways or canals no longer in use. Sometimes this is reflected in road names such as Station Road, or there might be clues in old maps.
- Search newspaper archives for the social effects, such as resistance to the opening of new mills or factories.
- Consider the trades and industries traditionally associated with your geographic area as a basis of research.
- Log your discoveries and plot the key dates on your timeline.

Mill Lane sign in Dunster

33 THE POOR LAW

In most communities today, we are probably aware that some of the inhabitants have to survive on social security benefits. However, the idea of the state providing for the poor is a relatively recent affair and, in the past, there was often little organised support for the less well-off members of society.

The Church provided a small amount of money for the destitute. But throughout your village's history many people would have simply died of starvation, taken to crime as a way out, or, from the seventeenth century onwards, faced the prospect of the poor house.

BELOW *A family suffering in hardship*

BEHIND & ABOVE *An illustration of Betty Higden, from Dickens' 'Our Mutual Friend', who is terrified at the thought of being consigned to the union workhouse*

Throughout every region in every period of history, there have always been some people who were much worse off than others. Until the end of the Second World War, there was no official welfare state as we would know it today and the poorer people relied on handouts, alms or help from local monasteries to help them survive. Following the Dissolution of the Monasteries in the mid-sixteenth century, this key source of traditional aid was no longer available, which would have had a significant impact on the lives of many.

The Poor Relief Act

The Poor Relief Act was introduced in the early seventeenth century to ensure that each parish took care of its own poor, with various amendments and updates over the ensuing years. Those who were unable to work had to apply to the board in charge, which would decide whether or not to give them aid. This drew a lot of criticism, as it was seen as a way for employers to keep wages down, knowing that employees could apply to the board to 'top up' their income. Partly due to this criticism, the Poor Law was amended in 1834. Aid would only be given out in exceptional circumstances; the alternative was to enter the workhouse.

Having to go into a poor or workhouse was considered a last option for anybody. Families were separated, with men, women and children being sent to different areas for different jobs. Even the youngest of children would be put to work with tasks such as 'oakum picking' – a painstaking job cited in *Oliver Twist*, which involved pulling apart old tarred ropes back to the individual threads so the material could be reused, often in shipbuilding. Adults were given monotonous jobs such as laundry or stone crushing for road building, which they did for over 12 hours a day.

ABOVE *The inside of St James Workhouse, on Poland Street, London (1810)*

ABOVE *Picked oakum*

Life was not pleasant in a workhouse and once you were in there was little opportunity to leave. It's ironic that many at the time considered the poor house to be an improvement for those who ended up there.

Poor relief in Dunster

Dunster had its own workhouse, which was established at the end of the seventeenth century. However, by the mid-1700s there were reports that it was poorly maintained and funded, with inhabitants resorting to stealing grain in order to eat. A public meeting was called, where it was decided that the poor would receive their money every Friday at the parish church. This was so they would be seen to be receiving it and anyone who did not collect it in person would forfeit their money.

There is a further record in 1751 of a lady called 'Widow Helman' who was contracted to look after the poor in the workhouse for the princely sum of 1s 6d per week. She was later succeeded by Sarah Reed who was paid the same amount. In 1766, there were 16 old people and 14 children, all housed in Dunster's workhouse.

Remaining evidence of workhouses

Many examples of workhouses are still standing across the country, whether now converted into homes or offices, or preserved as museums, such as the Victorian Workhouse Museum in Ripon. Larger workhouses were typically purpose-built, sometimes in elaborate designs, such as the imposing Watling Street Road Workhouse in Preston.

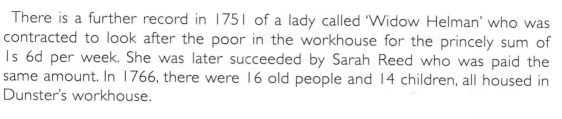

BELOW & RIGHT *The famous workhouse scene in Oliver Twist when Oliver dares to ask for more food*

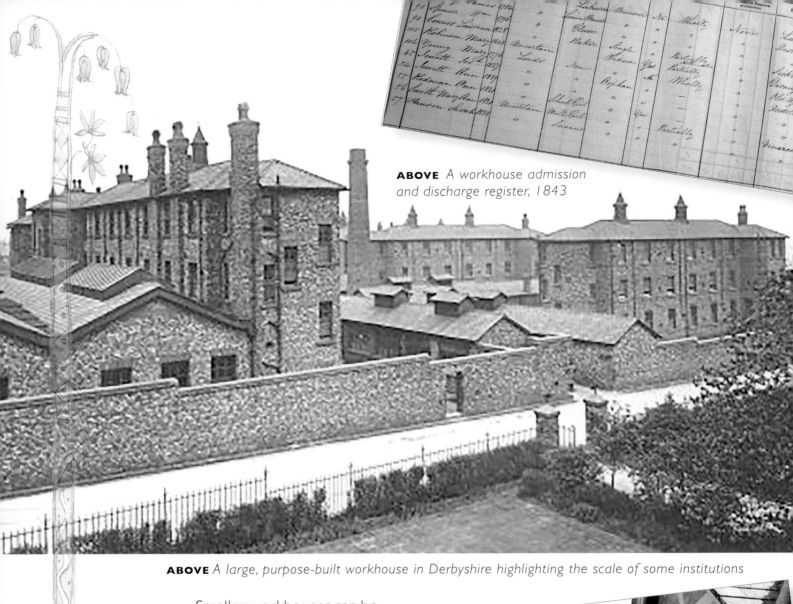

ABOVE *A workhouse admission and discharge register, 1843*

ABOVE *A large, purpose-built workhouse in Derbyshire highlighting the scale of some institutions*

Smaller workhouses can be more difficult to locate and local records or newspaper archives are often the best source for finding one in your area. Dunster's former workhouse, for instance, which stands at the junction of West Street and Mill Lane, is now a bed and breakfast. However, it is only by looking through archives that we can identify its location.

RIGHT *A Victorian almshouse, another way of supporting the poor, tucked away in Padstow, Cornwall, which has since been converted for residential use*

ABOVE *Children at Crumpsall Workhouse, Manchester (1895)*

Workhouses kept a range of registers, including those for admissions and discharge, creed, birth, baptism and death, as well as staff appointments. Many of these still survive in local archives, and they are an invaluable resource for tracing particular individuals. They also provide an enlightening snapshot of life in these grim institutions, where families were separated, young children were put to laborious task and life expectancy could be short. A very useful website providing insights and links to various archives is: ***www.workhouses.org.uk***

A workhouse gate sign

THINGS TO DO

- Search the local records and newspaper archives for evidence of a workhouse in the surrounding area. If you're lucky the admissions and discharge registers may still exist.
- Establish whether the original building still stands, perhaps now converted into apartments or offices.
- Old court records might also include entries of people who were admitted to the workhouse. See if you can find some examples.
- Log your discoveries and plot the key dates on your timeline.

34 EMIGRATION & IMMIGRATION

The British Isles have experienced millennia of immigration, with hordes of tribes, from Vikings to Angles, Saxons and Jutes, crossing the seas from the continent in search of a better life. In later centuries, with the expansion of the British Empire, people from as far as Asia and the West Indies have settled here. More recently, the country has witnesseds greater immigration from Eastern Europe. However, Britain has seen lots of emigration too, with many people leaving to settle elsewhere – whether to flee hardship or try their luck in gaining riches abroad. Modern emigration has largely coincided with the discovery and colonisation of new lands – and the birth of new countries, such as America, Canada and Australia – often promising fortune or freedom from persecution. However, Britain's colonial expansion often directly led to the persecution and subjugation of those who were displaced or brought under British rule.

Changing circumstances

There are countless reasons why people have chosen to relocate over the centuries. Typically, it has arisen from a change in circumstances, and in several notable instances, it has been forced upon people against their will. A rather brutal example was the clearance of the Scottish Highlands over the eighteenth and nineteenth centuries as part of the Enclosure Acts (Category 30). Landowners evicted entire communities in order to overhaul farming practices, and many highlanders were forced to relocate, either to the Scottish coast, or to emigrate to what we now call America, Canada and Australia. Many shipping lines kept records of emigrants and it's possible to trace specific names from your village.

A notable example of involuntary expatriation, the process of leaving the country to settle elsewhere, was the relocation of criminals by transportation. Many people were sent to settle in penal colonies around the world, sometimes for relatively minor crimes. Over 160,000 convicts were sent to Australia from 1788 to 1868. The British Transportation Registers that cover this period have been digitised and some websites allow you to search by surname, year of transportation and ship name.

Others have emigrated for religious reasons, including the Puritans who left England in the early seventeenth century to avoid persecution for their beliefs and start a 'New Jerusalem' in the Americas.

ABOVE *'The Last of England', by Ford Madox Brown (1855), depicting emigrants leaving for the New World*

The first fleet entering Port Jackson (1788), from 'A Voyage to New South Wales' by William Bradley

237

ABOVE & RIGHT *Prospectors hoping to make their fortunes in the Californian 'gold rush' (circa 1850)*

New prospects

Emigration could hold the prospect of a new life and owning your own land if this wasn't possible at home. Thousands were enticed by the nineteenth century 'gold rush' to move to new lands such as California, South Africa and Australia in search of gold and other precious minerals. A few lucky ones did indeed make fortunes.

But there were risks involved too. Many emigrants quickly died in their adopted country, whether through exposure to new diseases, malnutrition, unfamiliarity with the new climate, or through skirmishes with native populations. In the American settlement, this process of acclimatisation to the new environment was known as seasoning.

International counterparts

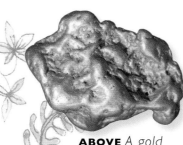

ABOVE *A gold nugget*

Often, emigrants to the New World would name the new settlement after their original hometown and the United States teems with examples deriving from ancient English towns and cities. Boston, Massachusetts has become such a recognised symbol of America, it's easy to forget its origins in the small Lincolnshire town. Winchester (Virginia), Salisbury (Maryland), Stratford (New Jersey) and Macclesfield (North Carolina) are just a few other examples. In Australia, you might discover Ipswich in Queensland or Chipping Norton in New South Wales!

It applies on a local level too. The village of Amberley, Ohio, is named after a small village thousands of miles away in the West Sussex South Downs. Wouldn't it be wonderful to discover a village on another continent named after your own? Perhaps you might even be able to trace some common descendants! Why not set up an exchange with your overseas namesake and help to establish an international Dig Village community?

Equally, the settlement may have been named after the benefactor of the original expedition or another notable contemporary figure. This might create an interesting line of research, by linking an overseas settlement to a prominent figure in your own village's history. The Brisbane suburb of Oxley, for instance, is named after Yorkshireman John Oxley, born near the village of Westow, Ryedale, who explored and surveyed Australia in the nineteenth century.

Drakes Bay, just north of San Francisco, California, gets its name from Sir Francis Drake, who claimed the territory for the English Crown in 1579, during his circumnavigation of the globe. Hundreds of sherds of pottery and other archaeological finds have helped to confirm the original landing point of his ship, the *Golden Hind*.

ABOVE *Drake's Bay plaque*

The villages of Austerfield (Yorkshire), Scrooby and Sturton le Steeple (both in Nottinghamshire) have strong links with the original 'Pilgrim Fathers' who travelled to America aboard the *Mayflower* in 1620. Several US landmarks and settlements are named after the passenger and colony elder William Brewster. Likewise, Mayflower Marina in Plymouth and the Mayflower Theatre in Southampton are just some of the many UK landmarks named after the iconic ship.

ABOVE *Brewster Gardens, Plymouth, Massachusetts, named after 'Pilgrim Father', William Brewster*

The map text reads:

These are the emblems of the principal provinces which form the Dominion of Canada. Most of the emblems are included in the Dominion flag, given on the map below. These three flags form the Union Jack, the national flag of Britain.

BRITISH COLUMBIA | MANITOBA | ONTARIO | QUEBEC | NEW BRUNSWICK | NOVA SCOTIA | PRINCE EDWARD ISLAND | ENGLAND St George's Cross | SCOTLAND St Andrew's Cross | IRELAND St Patrick's Cross | ISLE OF MAN | CHANNEL ISLES Oldest Possessions

These are the emblems of most of the West India colonies, which cannot be shown in their proper places on the map.

There are the emblems of the separate colonies forming the Commonwealth of Australia. They fly over a whole continent, stamped on the Union Jack.

St LUCIA | St VINCENT | CAICOS AND TURKS ISLANDS | WINDWARD ISLANDS | LEEWARD ISLANDS | ORANGE RIVER COLONY | QUEENSLAND | NEW SOUTH WALES | VICTORIA | SOUTH AUSTRALIA | WEST AUSTRALIA | TASMANIA

THE FLAGS OF A FREE EMPIRE, SHOWING THE EMBLEMS OF BRITISH POWER THROUGHOUT THE WORLD

This picture helps us to understand the wonderful way in which the British Empire is established throughout the world. But it helps us to realise something more. The flag that flies over the British Isles is the Union Jack, under which no slave can breathe; and it is a fine thing, of which we may be rightly proud, that the sun never sets upon the Union Jack. But the flags that wave over other parts of the empire have all another sign stamped on the Union Jack, which means generally that these places, though they are loyal to the British flag, have a nationality or government of their own. Great Britain has built up a great empire, because, wherever her influence has gone, she has planted the seeds of freedom, and because, as soon as a British colony is able to govern itself, the power to govern is given to it. So that the separate flags mean that the places over which they fly are separate colonies, under the protection of the British flag. It is not possible to show all parts of the empire or all the flags in their proper places, and it should be carefully noted that the actual empire, marked red, is represented on this map by the flag-staff and not by the flag itself. The flags have their staffs fixed into the places to which they belong, so that it is the place where the flag-staff is fixed that belongs to the British Empire. Many small places have flags that are not shown in this map, and in the cases of Canada and Australia only the federal flags are shown, the flags of the separate parts being along the top and bottom. In many other cases, also, where flags cannot be put in their proper position in such a small space as this, the flags are shown along the borders of the map. The colours of the emblems are not given here, and some of the emblems are shown much larger on the flag than they really are. Some of them are explained briefly in notes appearing on page 1118.

ABOVE *A map highlighting the extent of the British Empire in 1910*

The ugly side of colonialism

While overseas expansion promised wealth, adventure and a new start for many, it brought great upheaval and suffering to those on the receiving end. At the height of the British Empire, up to a third of the world fell under the rule of its monarch.

To many people across the world, the idea of empire represents subjugation, suppression and slavery. Millions of Africans were transported to the West Indies to work the plantations in abhorrent conditions. In Series 6 of Time Team in 1999, we explored British colonial influence on the island of Nevis in the Caribbean, by excavating the remains of plantation houses at Jamestown.

Throughout the book, we discuss how landmarks and locations are often named after a prominent figure in society. Invariably throughout the Georgian and Victorian eras those figures had some connection with colonialism. There's a rising international debate over how these associations should be acknowledged today.

ABOVE *Phil Harding talking with a Nevis resident near the site of a former plantation in the West Indies, during Time Team filming in 1999*

The fortunes of many burgeoning new cities of the Industrial Revolution – particularly key ports like Bristol and Liverpool – were tied to the slave trade. Penny Lane in Liverpool attracts thousands of visitors every year thanks to the whimsical song by The Beatles. But, like many streets in the city, it's actually named after a local slave ship owner and avid defender of the trade – one James Penny.

Bristol is currently facing up to its links with the prominent seventeenth century MP, philanthropist and slave owner Edward Colston, whose name lives on in various locations, monuments and institutions across the city.

The Legacy of British Slavery database lists almost 4,000 addresses in the UK with some historic link to slavery, highlighting the density of regions that played a greater role in the industry. This could be an interesting line of research for your project, particularly if your village is close to a major port or if the wider region has other associations with the machinery of colonialism. This might include factories where sugar was processed, local estates owned by tobacco magnates, or shipyards where boats were built and repaired.

ABOVE *Colston Tower, one of many landmarks in Bristol named after the philanthropist and slave owner, Edward Colston*

The impact of emigration

When assessing the impact of emigration locally, it helps to establish the factors behind it. Was it a 'push' or 'pull' effect that led people to depart? In other words, were people pushed into leaving due to the dire situation at home or even forced relocation, or were they pulled by the allure of the fortunes that awaited them elsewhere? Often, of course, it was a combination of both.

Perhaps your area was denied the opportunity to keep up with new technology. Brewood in Staffordshire, for example, was overlooked for a rail link, which seriously impacted its potential for development. Look for evidence of people moving to the bigger towns and cities in search of work. Comparing available census records reveals the spread of surnames traditionally associated with a certain region over time – this helps give a sense of greater mobility across the country in later years. Workers with a particular skill, such as mining and engineering, may have been enticed by the New World.

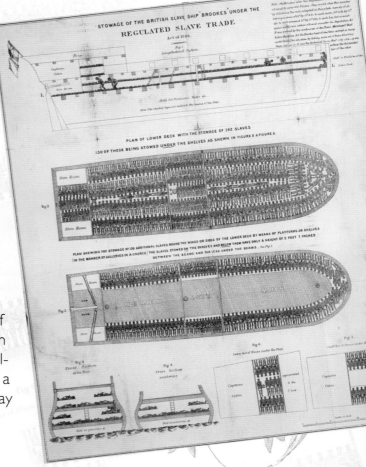

RIGHT *A diagram starkly illustrating the abhorrent conditions aboard a slave ship (1788)*

On the other hand, maybe your village has thrived through the years, developing new ideas to keep up with the changing times. Ask older residents about their memories of notable developments that might have made the village flourish or encourage people to move elsewhere. Wartime evacuation is one more recent example (Category 35).

Relocation within the country

As well as emigration overseas, much internal movement has occurred across the country, notably the movement from the countryside to towns and cities during the Industrial Revolution (Category 32). This will have had an impact on local communities.

People have moved in and around Dunster and the wider Somerset area for thousands of years. Dunster originally had a harbour enabling boats to come right up to the town. Harbours are a good traditional source of revenue, creating industry through trade, ship maintenance and other industry. Over time, Dunster's harbour silted up, leading boats to dock at neighbouring Minehead instead, taking their trade with them. The industrialisation of the wool trade also led to a downturn for a period in the town's fortunes. The stalls used for the weekly market were demolished and the population fell as people moved to find work elsewhere.

BELOW *Minehead harbour picked up additional trade after nearby Dunster's harbour silted up*

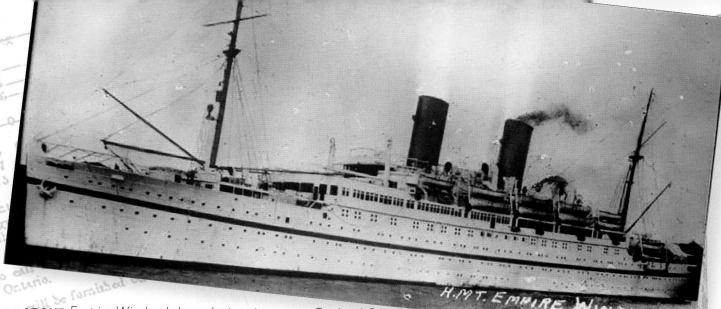

ABOVE *Empire Windrush brought immigrants to England from the West Indies in 1948, sometimes called the 'Windrush generation'*

Immigration

There can be a tendency to think of immigration as a modern phenomenon, but as the examples throughout this book remind us, Britain's history is built upon movement of people, ideas and goods in and out of the isles across thousands of years. Recent DNA analysis of human remains from the *Mary Rose* has revealed people of African origin among the retinue, shedding new light on the diversity of Tudor England.

As well as the arrival of new communities, innovations like farming and Christianity were imported from overseas, eventually becoming woven into the country's fabric and entering local tradition. Our language and tastes for food, clothes and other commodities have long been influenced by various cultures, from French Saintonge ware, as discovered at Dunster Priory (Category 12), to more recent appetites for wearing pyjamas or drinking Prosecco! Likewise, the influence of the 'Windrush generation' has led to new traditions and events including the Notting Hill Carnival becoming staples of the British calendar.

THINGS TO DO

- Look at and compare census records, searching by name with any regionally distinctive surnames typically associated with your area.
- Check passenger lists and the British Transportation Register for names connected with your village.
- Research local records and newspaper archives for any events would have caused people to move (whether a local 'push' or a wider 'pull').
- Do an online search to see if there are towns or villages in other countries named after or otherwise connected to your own. Make contact with local history societies and see if there is common ground in your research.
- Talk to older generations about their experiences of people moving out of (or indeed into) your area.
- Log your discoveries and plot the key dates on your timeline.

Shop fronts in Southall, London's vibrant Indian community

35 THE WORLD WARS

The First World War was dubbed 'the war to end all wars' due to the huge global devastation it caused. Yet, within a generation the world was at war again, with millions more lives lost and further destruction on a scale never seen before. Aside from the casualties, one of the most fundamental impacts of the wars on village life in rural communities was to remove labour from the land. In the First World War this included horses as well. Generations of agricultural skill disappeared with the young men into the trenches, never to return. In both World Wars, the vital role of agriculture was recognised and an army of 'Land Girls' and other available labour cared for the land. Very few villages escaped the wars' clutches and the countless memorials scattered across Britain represent a list of individuals who were a generation lost to families and the land forever. One of the most moving Time Team episodes was in Series 7, when we investigated a Spitfire crash site in Northern France – the rare occasion of a dig concerning events in living memory.

Soldiers marching on the Western Front during World War I

Both World Wars had a colossal impact on communities. In World War I, huge numbers of young men from the same villages were killed in action, almost wiping out an entire generation. Approximately 1.7% of the total population of the UK was killed, some 700,000 men. Villages that didn't lose any men became known as 'Thankful Villages' and it's estimated that there were no more than 32 in the whole country that this applied to.

Evacuation

As well as the thousands of casualties, another consequence was the movement of people through evacuation. During World War II huge numbers of people, mostly children, were evacuated from towns and cities into villages in safer areas. Although teachers and volunteers from the WRVS (Women's Royal Voluntary Service) were drafted in to help, the sudden population increase caused issues for many communities. Another side effect on some communities was the appearance of prisoner of war camps. Prisoners in these camps were well looked after and had to be fed, putting further strain on scant resources. When the war ended, many chose to stay in the communities by which they had been surrounded.

ABOVE *Children being evacuated from Southend during World War II*

ABOVE *A half-buried pill box off the coast of Somerset at Porlock Bay*

Dunster and the wars

Many soldiers from Somerset were killed in World War I. During World War II, Somerset was used as a training area for the 1944 D-Day landings. The pill boxes can still be seen along the seafront at Dunster and the surrounding coast, and some can be accessed, with care, and permission, where required. A memorial plaque was installed in Dunster by the Women's Institute in 1950.

The local impact

As the World Wars are still within living memory, getting a sense of the impact they had on your village should be fairly straightforward. Start by visiting the village memorial to those lost during the conflicts. There may be families still in the village who are willing to share memories, which can be recorded for future generations. You can also research the effect that the wars and resulting movement of people had in your community – for example, use of land for campaigns such as Dig for Victory, where all spare pieces of land were dug up and used for planting fruit and vegetables, which would be rationed. Some of these areas never returned to their original use after the war.

Look for evidence of temporary wartime barracks, training areas or airfields nearby your village. Most villages have examples of concrete air raid shelters dotted about, sometimes on private land.

Coastal communities might also have remains of sea defences, anti-aircraft guns or slipways created for the embarkation of D-Day. The coastline surrounding the Solent, in Hampshire, for instance, has many remains from this period.

ABOVE *A Dig for Victory poster*
RIGHT *Dunster's war memorial*

LEFT *A sign indicating a military training area on Salisbury Plain*

THE THUNDERBOX ROOM

This is where the signatures of past outdoor staff were discovered in 1990. Under one column of names was the date, August 1914. Some of these names were later found on local war memorials. Though exposure to light over the past quarter of a century has faded their marks here now, we honour these men and boys who gave their lives for King and Country...

CHARLES BALL · JOHN GEORGE BARRON · PERCY CARHART · CHARLES IVEY · WILLIAM ROBINS GUY · ALBERT HENRY ROWE · LEONARD WARNE

There are others too, without evidence here, but reported in the Heligan Estate Labour Books, who served and fell...

WILLIAM SAMUEL HUNKIN · WILLIAM GEORGE PERRY

In total 9 lost, more than one third of the whole outdoor team. We also honour those Heligan men who served their country and returned...

FRED PAYNTER, stone mason · ARCHIBALD SMALDON, carpenter
JOHN VAREY, gardener

In 2013 the Imperial War Museum recorded this Thunderbox Room as a 'Living Memorial' to the Gardeners of Heligan in its new National Inventory of War Memorials, ref 63622.

Perhaps some local buildings were damaged or destroyed by bombing during the war. Unexploded shells are still occasionally found in the landscape and rivers including the Thames.

American soldiers were often housed in seaside villages in the build up to D-Day. Many larger country homes were requisitioned for the respective war efforts, and often repurposed as hospitals, intelligence headquarters or barracks. The house at Heligan in Cornwall, for example, was used as a convalescence hospital for officers from 1916 to 1919, and then as a base for American troops during the Second World War. Over this period, trees were felled to help the effort, while the wider estate fell into disrepair with no labour to work the land, only to be rediscovered in 1990. Examples such as this are fairly typical and perhaps a local house near you shared a similar fate in the early twentieth century.

ABOVE *A memorial to the gardeners of Heligan House*

ABOVE *An unexploded shell*

THINGS TO DO

- Document local war memorials. These often list the names of the fallen, giving a sense of the scale of local casualties, as well as men in the same families who died.
- Record the recollections of contemporaries from your village who were alive during World War II.
- Look for evidence of prisoner of war camps in your area. Many useful books have been published on this topic and list of all the camps in England during World War II can be found online.
- Research local estates, manor houses and large country houses to see if they were requisitioned to help the respective war efforts.
- Search for evidence of local land being put to use as military training areas or airfields.
- Look for air raid shelters and defences, particularly on the coast.
- Log your discoveries and plot the key dates on your timeline.

Dunster, High Street and Shambles

V.

Life Within a Settlement

In many respects, life in the typical village from the Medieval period until very recently would have appeared alien to our own. Much of the basic amenities and services that we now take for granted – justice, healthcare, time for recreation and even wine – would have been out of reach of the average villager. In other ways, lots of the features encountered in life would be fairly familiar to us. In this part, we get closer to life within the settlement before the modern age, by taking a look at work, rest and play, and the evidence that these elements might have left in your village or town today.

36 LAW &
THE COURTS

It seems that many of us have a fairly colourful set of images when we think of the process of law and order in the past. What often comes to mind is some of the more gruesome forms of punishment involving trial by fire or water, or individuals on the receiving end of the rack or other horrific forms of torture. But where did the process of law and punishment originate?

ABOVE *Trial by water (1513)*

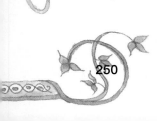

It's always interesting to think about the imperatives that existed to make people feel less inclined to do wrong and more inclined to do right. It's likely that the first set of laws that defined this originated in the Old Testament and usually began with "Thou shalt not... kill, steal", and so on. In Christian communities, the ever-present threat of Purgatory – an intermediate state between Heaven and Hell – must have had a restraining force on those inclined to wrongdoing. The more sins you committed, the longer you would spend in Purgatory. Many churches in the Medieval period contained wall paintings and other decorative features depicting the fires of hell and the suffering that awaited those who broke the law.

The Anglo-Saxons formalised the idea that all members of the village or town were responsible for each other's behaviour, and bringing wrongdoers to a court. Frankpledge, as it became to be known, must have had a considerable influence on the way legal justice was viewed by the community.

RIGHT *Ludovico Carracci's depiction of Purgatory (circa 1610)* **ABOVE & BEHIND** *Trial by fire*

Tithings and Frankpledge

When we think of law and order today, we are used to a legal system of judges and jails, police and law courts in a vast infrastructure. However, in a Medieval village, the question of law and order was much more of a local matter, deriving a lot of its strength from a system of collective responsibility.

This important aspect of Medieval law was introduced in Anglo-Saxon times. Villages were divided into an informal group of ten households, known as a **tithing** (not to be confused with the tax – see Category 17), who were responsible for each other's behaviour. In this system, known as **Frankpledge**, the group was expected to bring justice to everyone in the tithing, ensuring that their members attended the **court leet**, if necessary. The court leet was a manorial court, where local justice was meted out, and repeated unattendance resulted in fines. Some of the first law officers were known as **beadles**, from the old English, *bydel*, meaning 'messenger or herald', whose job it was to summon householders to the court.

ABOVE *A beadle*

BELOW *Anglo-Saxon open farming*

In the early Medieval period, the open field farming system required a group of local people to oversee and manage the work that was done. Making sure people didn't steal each other's land, avoid being present at the time of harvest, or avoid paying their tithe to the lord or Church, needed a local system that could be enforced.

The Laws of Ine

Some of the earliest English written laws we have, the Laws of Ine, from circa AD 694, specifically refer to the legal penalties for those breaking the law in relation to the open field system. Ine was an Anglo-Saxon King of Wessex and the reason we know about his set of laws is that when King Alfred developed his legal system, they were included as a postscript.

The Anglo-Saxons were probably the first people to put a price on an illegal act. Anglo-Saxon laws, developed in the sixth and seventh centuries, often read

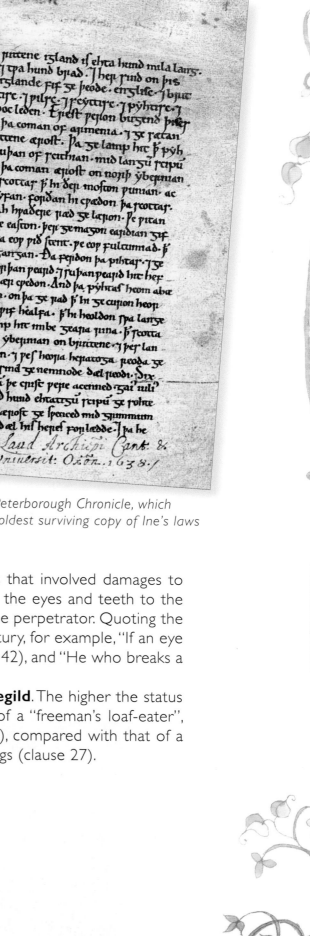

ABOVE *The Peterborough Chronicle, which contains the oldest surviving copy of Ine's laws*

like a shopping list of costs and penalties for crimes that involved damages to the person or property. Each part of the body, from the eyes and teeth to the legs, was given a value, which had to be paid for by the perpetrator. Quoting the Law of Ethelbert of Kent, from the early seventh century, for example, "If an eye becomes gouged out, let him pay 50 shillings" (clause 42), and "He who breaks a jawbone, let him pay with 20 shillings" (clause 47).

Each person had a value, which was called the **weregild**. The higher the status of the person, the higher his or her value. The life of a "freeman's loaf-eater", for instance, was only valued at 6 shillings (clause 26), compared with that of a "freeman of the first rank" whose value was 80 shillings (clause 27).

ABOVE *A hanging noose*

Laws of the Forest

Similarly, the Laws of the Forest contain a list determining what punishments were considered acceptable for various crimes, with the penalty often being mutilation. This must have acted as a considerable deterrent to potential poachers. It's hard to imagine in this day and age exactly what this process would have involved, but it was a relatively frequent occurrence. Some of these laws, which covered crimes such as trespass or poaching in the royal forest, were severely punished. Peasants caught in the act of stealing one of the Crown's deer or trapping rabbits for his family could face being hanged.

Another important part of Anglo-Saxon justice was that someone had to find enough oath takers to confirm his or her innocence. The higher status of the oath taker, the more weight it gave the defendant's case. This was obviously a system that favoured the rich and powerful.

Developments under the Normans

By the time of Henry II, in the twelfth century, the system of **hundreds** was in place, binding each village to produce so many men who were on oath to tell the sheriff if any man or woman had committed a crime. The sheriff was the lord's right hand man on the manor (Category 13), a position that gave him huge power, which was often exploited. Often people become interested in their local sheriff because of folk memories of the Sheriff of Nottingham and Robin Hood.

It's around this time that the idea of a 'gaol' or jail was introduced. The term 'gaol' derives from the Latin, *cavea*, meaning cage. Juries were called upon to settle property disputes from as early as the eleventh century, but the idea of a group of local people reporting on local crimes eventually developed into a more formal jury system and gradually it evolved into a series of travelling judges who represented the king or queen and to whom the local men would report.

ABOVE *The Sheriff of Nottingham*

BELOW *A Medieval painting of travelling judges reporting to their monarch*

254

ABOVE *Trial by fire, with a woman treading on hot irons*

Punishment

Punishment was a brutal business for most of the Medieval period. Up to Elizabethan times, it was believed that unless tortured, no-one told the truth. Hanging, mutilation, and trial by fire, in which a person had to carry, or walk on, a red-hot iron for a length of time, were common place. Trial by ordeal, which was officially supported by the Roman Catholic Church until 1215, was often a foregone conclusion of guilt. A person suffering trial by water would be tied up and thrown into a river or lake. If they floated it was considered proof of their sin, because it was believed that, on God's command, the water refused to accept them; sinking implied innocence, but whether or not they were retrieved before they drowned was open to question. One of the big advantages for the monarch was that the property of someone who was found guilty passed to the state.

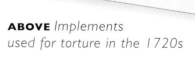

ABOVE *Implements used for torture in the 1720s*

Many villages have an authentic or reproduction pillory or stocks on display. Although this may seem a quaint reminder of the past, being put in the stocks was actually a very serious punishment. In many cases not only vegetables but stones were hurled, and injury or even death was a real possibility.

Justice in Dunster

The average person had very little redress when faced with the lord's courts. Often communities were ruled under the simple idea that 'might was right' and the lord's word was final. In fourteenth century Dunster, one of the Mohun family, in a way typical of the time, took justice into his own hands, when a local landowner tried to resist his lord's demands. Lord de Mohun famously rode to court fully armoured, kidnapped the plaintiff and was only restrained by the Star Chamber and the king threatening to forfeit his land.

ABOVE *Stocks at Belstone village Dartmoor*

Maxwell Lyte's history of Dunster provides some interesting accounts of how justice in the fourteenth century was administered more generally. There were two main courts a year for serious matters and, for managing local and domestic justice, there were courts virtually every month. At these, the lord would be represented by his steward, and the accused would face a jury of twelve free men. In addition, the town had two constables of the peace, and two people each responsible for the standard of bread and ale being produced. This could be seen as an early form of trading standards.

In Dunster, it was the responsibility of the constables to report all "breaches of the peace." Those guilty were referred to as being 'amerced', which indicated that a fine would be imposed, and they were at the mercy of the court. Here are two extracts, the first from the Court Rolls of 1411:

"John Speare Chaplin drew a knife against John Loty contrary to the peace. Therefore he is in mercy 6d and John Loty drew a dagger – forfeited to the lord against John Speare Chaplin, therefore he is in mercy 6d."

RIGHT *A Medieval parrying dagger, perhaps similar to that used by John Speare Chaplin*

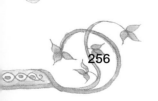

ABOVE *A king overseeing a court, from an illustrated manuscript of legal code (circa 1290–1310)*

Many smaller crimes were dealt with, including petty thieves, who were given the name 'holcrop', as highlighted in this colourful entry from 1408:

"Ellen Watkyns is a common holcroppe of divers things and a common scold and disturber of the peace, therefore she is in mercy 4d. Geoffrey Taillour is a common night walker and disturber of the peace, therefore he is in mercy half a mark."
(Source: Lyte, p.308)

ABOVE *An 1875 depiction of King John signing the Magna Carta*
RIGHT *The Magna Carta memorial at Runnymede*

The Magna Carta

For most of the Medieval period, justice was meted out in French or Latin. It was only when communities developed burgess courts that they became places where some justice could be found. The arrival of lawyers and other legal intermediaries between the ordinary people and the legal system was relatively late, from around the late twelfth century onwards.

Some Medieval monarchs did make attempts to balance justice in greater favour of the common person, albeit often only reluctantly and under great pressure. The most significant example is the drafting of the Magna Carta, which King John begrudgingly agreed to sign in 1215. One of the key statements reads:

"No free man shall be arrested, or imprisoned, or disseised [have their property confiscated], or outlawed, or exiled, or in any way destroyed, nor will we go against him, nor will we send against him, save by the lawful judgement of his peers or by the law of the land."

This essentially meant that every free man had the right to a trial, setting a significant precedent and laying the foundations for modern justice. Whether or not it was always a fair trial, however, is another matter.

The courts

The courts were often a way of controlling the feudal system, and they dealt with any criminal who had broken the lord's law or had failed to perform their duties. Courts were often roving, known as the **courts of assize**, held four or five times a year, and they would be the only place where justice could be obtained. As we have seen in the earlier Dunster example, many small towns had their own court, whose job was to ensure that two of the most basic commodities of life, bread and ale, were sold at a good quality and at a fair price. Today, Ashburton in Devon still holds a celebration of this community service. The key person responsible for this duty was called the **portreeve**.

Many judgements were eventually written down, initially in Latin and then in French, and by the fifteenth century, in English. As a result, the legal system can contain a fascinating amount of detail about life in the past.

It's an interesting piece of research to find out where your local court was held. It was often in the lord's castle, but as time progressed locations away from the seat of power were used. Some of these areas were known as the **court fields**.

The Monmouth Rebellion

As late as the Monmouth uprising, in 1685, three men from Somerset, one of whom was from Dunster, were hanged on a hill overlooking the town. Their crime was protesting against changes in the way religion was practised and they fell foul of the notorious 'hanging judge', Judge Jeffreys.

It was the responsibility of a group of the townspeople to find these men and bring them to their execution. This act, which in itself must have been horrific, was a continuation of the idea of the tithing, reflecting the community's relationship with the law. Yet for the ordinary Medieval person, this kind of punishment must have been a depressingly regular event.

RIGHT *George Jeffreys, 1st Baron Jeffreys of Wem (circa 1685)*

ABOVE *An ancient dungeon pit was discovered in Dunster Castle*

During excavations at Dunster Castle in the early 1700s, a skeleton of a seven-foot tall man was said to have been recovered at the bottom of an **oubliette**, a deep pit where prisoners were left to starve to death. Today, we would find this degree of sadism abhorrent.

Victorian punishment

It would be nice to feel that, as we became more civilised, the process of law and order became more humane. But when you look at crime and punishment in the Victorian period, you realise this wasn't the case. The business of incarcerating someone in a Victorian jail, for example, and putting them on a diet of bread and water, was in itself a form of punishment. It created severe constipation, which was equally brutal. Systematic physical torture was also still commonplace, as highlighted in the notorious case of Oscar Wilde, who was broken on the treadmill at Pentonville Prison in 1895. The treadmill was a severe form of hard labour, in which prisoners were placed on a large moving wheel and forced to walk or run

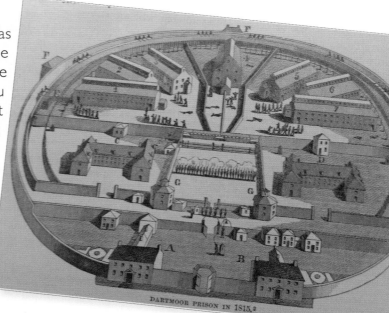

DARTMOOR PRISON IN 1815.

ABOVE *A drawing of Dartmoor Prison*

continuously at a steady pace – sometimes for up to six hours a day with only short breaks. If the prisoner fell over, the wheel continued, causing them considerable injuries. As well as the obvious physical damage, it was designed to break their spirit and resolve.

On Series 10 of Time Team, we did some excavations at Appleby Prison in Cumbria, and one of the researchers volunteered to spend a day and night in a Victorian prison regime. It made us all aware that the effects, while not perhaps physically damaging, had implicit elements of mental cruelty and torture.

ABOVE *Inmates on a treadmill in a Victorian prison (1864)*

THINGS TO DO

- Find out where your local court was held. TIP: It may originally have been in the lord's castle or manor house, before moving elsewhere. Look out for references to the local 'court fields' and 'assizes'.
- Try a search of the local court records for more information on trials in your village or area.
- Log your discoveries and plot the key dates on your timeline.

RIGHT *A Medieval torture chair*

37 TRADES

We live in an era where if something breaks we tend to just buy another one! Make do and mend is a fairly archaic concept, but in the villages and towns of Medieval Britain there was a whole host of trades people whose job involved making and mending many of the essentials of everyday life. Self-sufficiency was the order of the day. Carpenters and smiths were among the most common trades and they would be accompanied by coopers to make barrels, glaziers (for the lucky few that had windows!), weavers, potters, tailors, cobblers and glove makers. To provide for those with money and status, there were goldsmiths and silversmiths. If you visit Shakespeare's birthplace in Stratford-upon-Avon, you can see the evidence of his father's trade as a glove maker.

A woodcut showing cobblers at work (1568)

ABOVE *'The Syndics of the Amsterdam Drapers' Guild', by Rembrandt (1662)*

In this category, we look at trades related to non-food activities. Many of these were a way for ordinary people to raise a little bit of money. It's always difficult to estimate wages and the cost of basic foods but if you imagine that an average wage was between 2p and 6p a day in the fourteenth century, a loaf would have cost a penny and smaller items like cheese would have cost 0.10 to 0.15 of a penny. Mick often made the point that markets must have involved a lot of exchange and barter, or people buying a lot of items at one time, as a penny was the smallest unit of coinage. Learning a trade could significantly improve one's lot. A carpenter, for example, would earn approximately 25 to 30 shillings (12 pence to a shilling) per annum, working 120 days a year.

Guilds

For those skills that required a long apprenticeship and training, many trades in the Middle Ages would form themselves into **guilds**, which would become a powerful force, particularly in towns. The skilled trades people were very protective of their rights. It's from this period that we see the early form of trade associations, which in the eighteenth and nineteenth century were the basis for unions. At the head would be the master, underneath them the journeymen, and at a lower level the apprentices, who were generally unpaid labour, desperate to learn a skill.

RIGHT *Dunster's historic Yarn Market, built to service the town's thriving textile industry*

263

Eventually the guilds would find their way into many aspects of life including finding and taking part in **mystery plays**, which often had a religious Christian theme. This aspect of Medieval life is depicted in Shakespeare's *A Midsummer Night's Dream*, when a play is performed by a group of craftsmen including the weaver, Bottom.

ABOVE *A boiled leather box from the fifteenth century*

Many Medieval crafts people were itinerant tradesmen or women who journeyed from town to town. We still use the word 'tinker' for those who travel from place to place mending pots and pans, and many people spent their lives on the road including masons, thatchers and tilers.

ABOVE *Tanner's Brook in Southampton*

From the thirteenth century onwards, strict laws generally referred to as labour laws were imposed to dictate the level of pay various craftsmen could receive. This acted to restrict the ability of certain wealthy lords to advantageously attract labour to their settlement by offering higher rates, or by offering other inducements like extra food.

Evidence of local historic trades

The court rolls refer to many cases brought against craftsmen and women who were alleged to have been over paid. Often cases were brought for ulterior motives but the list of charges being made helps to give us an idea of the various different trades that existed at the time. In Dunster, where the cloth trade became a successful small industry, the list of occupations that appear in the court rolls and probate records includes webbers, weavers, tuckers and dyers. Elsewhere across the country, we can find cases against tailors, cobblers, tanners, and thatchers, amongst others.

LEFT *Dunster's cloth trade advert in 'The Tailor and Cutter' 1938 still famous for its flannel, called 'Dunsters'*

BEHIND *An archive engraving of Dunster High Street and Yarn Market in foreground*

Another place to look for occupations and trade names in your area is to refer to location and road names. Old Smithy Way, Weavers Close, Carpenter Street can be found in many settlements. Tanner Street is another commonplace name, often located on the outskirts of a settlement due to the unbearable smell of processing leather, which could involve both urine and faeces. Tanners needed a good supply of running water, so you're most likely to find evidence of one near a water source, typically downstream, to take the by-products away from the village. Tanner's Brook, for instance, is a river that runs through a Southampton suburb on the site of a nineteenth century tannery.

Occasionally, we can still see the wooden or metalwork signs hanging above shop fronts, that various trades used to advertise their services. Most Medieval people were illiterate and so a visual representation of a trade was useful. Some wonderful examples have been preserved on Winchester's High Street, including a splendid boot, to indicate a cobbler, and a teapot.

Should you ever find yourself having to make a nail from scratch, create a sharp knife, or attempt to produce your own pair of shoes or gloves, you will get a sense of how valuable these trades people were to the average village.

ABOVE *A locksmith's sign still in use in a European city*

ABOVE *A traditional wrought-iron guild sign for a glazier*

THINGS TO DO

- Research local historic road names and surnames for reference to specific trades (such as Smith, Miller, Tanner and Mason).
- Visit the Ordnance Survey website to download the Open Names survey, a database of all the road names in the country, which is useful in revealing insights into the names found in your area.
- Search for clues in the building themselves, such as historic signs above shopfronts that denote particular trades.
- Search the court rolls and probate records for reference to specific trades in operation.
- Log your discoveries and plot the key dates on your timeline.

RIGHT *A nail found in Dunster during a dig, probably made by a local blacksmith*

A typical smithy

38 INDUSTRIAL ACTIVITY

There's usually a good reason for people deciding to plant roots in a particular area. Other than some form of strategic advantage, it's often an abundance of natural resources making it an attractive proposition. The presence of precious minerals and metals has proved to be a powerful incentive for settlement across history. It's these that confirm the basis for industrial activity, when production is increased to a scale beyond the purely local or to supply a market beyond that for personal use.

Many early settlements developed around the mining of materials useful to the community, including coal, slate, iron ore, lead and silver. Eventually these evolved into villages, towns and, in some cases, cities centred on a specific industry. There are several notable examples of organised mining activity in prehistory, such as the flint mines of Grime's Graves, as mentioned elsewhere. Charterhouse in Somerset has a history of tin and lead mining, from prehistoric times up to more recent generations. The presence at Stonehenge of bluestone megaliths from the Preseli Hills of Pembrokeshire (some 160 miles away) highlights a degree of industrial organisation during the Neolithic period. The logistics of this considerable feat, alone, have baffled historians and archaeologists for years.

BELOW *The historic Towanroath Engine House at Wheal Coates, a tin mine near St Agnes, Cornwall*
OPPOSITE *The preserved Geevor Tin Mine, Cornwall*

The Romans

Arguably it was the Romans who first exploited natural resources on a truly industrial scale in Britain – notably tin and silver, but extending to a wide range of minerals and resources integral to sustaining the trappings of empire. In the centuries that followed the Romano-British period, a wide range of quarrying continued across the country. Entire communities and local economies have been built upon mining in areas such as Cornwall, Wales and northern England, but sadly many of these have now become places of unemployment and decline.

Salt production

Before modern refrigeration, salt was one of the main ways to preserve food. By the Anglo-Saxon period, salt production had become a major industry, with around 1200 salt making sites recorded in Domesday, some of Roman origin. The town of Northwich, Cheshire, for example, owes its existence to the Romans who extracted salt from brine springs. From the late seventeenth century onwards, rock salt was mined from the ground locally, creating a significant regional industry. In coastal communities, sea salt was produced by guiding sea water into purpose-made shallow beds or saltpans. The water would then evaporate to leave a crystalline brine, which could be processed to produce sea salt. Many new routes throughout the country were created as a byproduct of the salt trade. Droitwich in the West Midlands was another town to make its fortunes through salt production, owing to its natural abundance of brine.

ABOVE *An historic manmade salt pan on Dorset's Jurassic Coast*
LEFT *An abandoned coal mine in Wales*

ABOVE *Rievaulx Abbey in North Yorkshire was a hive of industrial activity*

Monastic industrial activity

In Medieval England before the Dissolution, monasteries were traditional hubs of industry. Medieval iron works, for example, could be vast enterprises and there are references to the Cistercians engaged in this industry at Rievaulx Abbey in North Yorkshire.

The Industrial Revolution

The Industrial Revolution and the advent of steam power, from the mid-eighteenth century onwards, dramatically increased the demand for fuel and raw materials. New towns were built to exploit iron ore, local forests and water power. Communities across Britain were transformed into the workshops of the world.

As noted in Category 32, industrial activity demanded a distribution network, and accelerated the development of road links, canals and ports for the export and import of materials. Harbour towns such as Fowey on Cornwall's south coast became major ports for the export of china clay. The harbour at nearby Charlestown was developed in the eighteenth century for the export of copper, which was mined locally. This network provided village communities with the opportunity to exchange precious minerals for their products.

BEHIND *An illustration of a Medieval blast furnace, used to produce iron from ore (1556)*

ABOVE *Fowey in Cornwall became an important harbour for the export of china clay*

kaoline clay (china clay)

Stannary towns

The development of the mining industry led to designated locations where the minerals could be **assayed** – or tested for their quality and composition, to assess their value and purity. Several towns in the West Country evolved surrounding the administration and taxation of refined tin to provide an income for the Duchy of Cornwall. These **stannary towns** (from the late Latin, *stannum*, meaning tin) include Ashburton and Tavistock, in Devon, and Bodmin and Lostwithiel in Cornwall, among others.

A 'Lord Warden of the Stannaries' was first appointed at the tail end of the twelfth century. This prestigious post of office was once held by Sir Walter Raleigh. For the researcher, there are several archives covering stannary town administration across distinct time periods. The Vicewarden's Court of the Stannaries of Devon and Cornwall, held at the Cornwall Record Office, for instance, is a useful record of activities in the mid-nineteenth century.

ABOVE *Sir Walter Raleigh was appointed a Lord Warden of the Stanneries*

Industry in Dunster

In the case of Dunster, as referred to in Category 32, the process of weaving, dying, and distributing cloth increased to the point where Dunster cloth was a recognised 'brand' in the late Medieval period.

Searching for recent activity

The traces of later industrial activity can be difficult to find, often as a result of demoli-

The Pepperpot

ABOVE *Engine houses of tin and copper mines perched above the sea*

tion and redevelopment. The significance of historic buildings has often been overlooked in former generations, with many torn down to make way for modern replacements. In these cases, where a building no longer exists, you can instead look for its 'footprints' as well as any byproducts left behind from that industry. Again, historic maps can be a useful source for locating former industrial sites. It may be that these maps refer to audits, slag heaps (from the production of iron) or other remnants of industrial activity.

THINGS TO DO

tin ore

- As a starting point, base your initial research on known industrial activity traditionally associated with your region. If you live in the South West, for example, you may be situated near a stannary town. Search the archives for relevant information.
- Look for references to industrial activity on local maps, such as audits and slag heaps (industrial waste). Check mineral deposit maps from the British Geological Survey (Category 4).
- Remember you are looking for activity that extends beyond the personal and supplies a market outside the village or town. It probably involves the large scale introduction of new equipment.
- Log your discoveries and plot the key dates on your timeline.

coal

LEFT *Chagford, Dartmoor, showing the Market House or 'Pepper Pot', built on the site of the Stannary Court that met twice yearly to assay the tin and levy the tax*

39 PUBS, INNS & BREWING

We have got so used to the idea that every small village and town has its pub that it tends to make us think they are an institution going way back in time. In fact, the village pub as we know it is a fairly recent phenomenon. Up to the seventeenth century, ale was largely brewed and consumed at home, usually produced by women who were often referred to as alewives. In earlier centuries, a familiar sight in the typical village or town would have been the coaching inn, usually straddling a main thoroughfare. These rest points provided much needed food and accommodation for travellers, as well as facilities for their horses.

The Luttrell Arms, Dunster

ABOVE *The legendary coaching inn, Jamaica Inn, immortalised in Daphne Du Maurier's novel about Cornish smugglers*

Public houses, or taverns, owe their origin to the *tabernae* introduced by the Romans – shops selling wine, strategically situated by the roadside to capture the passing trade. Over time, they evolved into the alehouses and taverns of later centuries. As well as serving messengers riding long distances cross-country, they were particularly useful for pilgrims travelling to and from religious shrines. Generally, inns provided rooms, taverns provided food and drink, whilst alehouses sold beer.

Pub names

Pub names can be revealing of their origins. The Navigation, for instance, is typically situated near a canal. You'll find The Railway Inn near a train line, and The Woolpack on a site traditionally associated with the transport of wool.

BELOW *Many pubs across Britain are called the Railway Inn, even if the original train line has since disappeared*

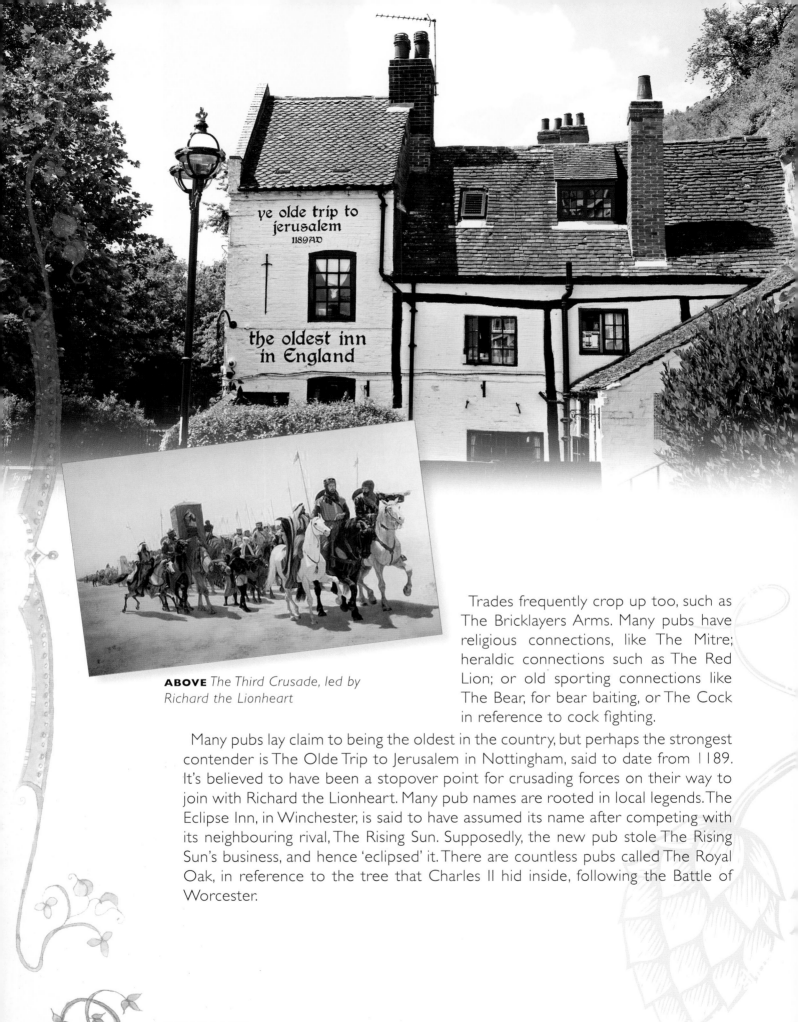

ABOVE *The Third Crusade, led by Richard the Lionheart*

Trades frequently crop up too, such as The Bricklayers Arms. Many pubs have religious connections, like The Mitre; heraldic connections such as The Red Lion; or old sporting connections like The Bear, for bear baiting, or The Cock in reference to cock fighting.

Many pubs lay claim to being the oldest in the country, but perhaps the strongest contender is The Olde Trip to Jerusalem in Nottingham, said to date from 1189. It's believed to have been a stopover point for crusading forces on their way to join with Richard the Lionheart. Many pub names are rooted in local legends. The Eclipse Inn, in Winchester, is said to have assumed its name after competing with its neighbouring rival, The Rising Sun. Supposedly, the new pub stole The Rising Sun's business, and hence 'eclipsed' it. There are countless pubs called The Royal Oak, in reference to the tree that Charles II hid inside, following the Battle of Worcester.

Pubs in Dunster

Today, there are several pubs in Dunster: The Stags Head, The Foresters Arms and The Luttrell Arms. However, records reveal that at one point in the 1700s, there were a further seven alehouses in the town. Dating from the fifteenth century, The Luttrell Arms was originally three separate houses, and served as a guest house for abbots visiting nearby Cleeve Abbey. Consequently, it has many fascinating architectural features, which help to reveal its story over the years. It's common to discover that a pub evolved from another, probably domestic, building.

Equally, many pubs have changed names over the years, reflecting new ownership, change in allegiance, or to capitalise on a recent event or local legend. Again, this is highlighted by The Luttrell Arms, which was known during the English Civil War as The Ship Inn (Category 29) before taking the name of the prominent Dunster family. Of course, this can complicate your research. By the same token, once you've discovered a name change, it might open up new avenues, hopefully enabling you to trace its origins further back.

Research

Why not begin your research with a trip to the pub itself? Talk to the landlord or landlady, and other locals, who will no doubt have many interesting stories to share of its history. Pubs are classic hubs of the oral tradition! Inns and taverns were often places of ill-repute and many historic legal cases centred upon the consequences of over consumption of beer. Many pubs are full of interesting artefacts too.

See if you can discover the approximate age of the building itself, and when it started being used as a pub. Does the name give you a clue to its origins or why it was built, such as The Coach and Horses? It would be interesting to establish if your village was once on an important route for pilgrimage or the stage coach, perhaps linking two major towns or cities.

RIGHT *'The Ale-House Door', by Henry Singleton (circa 1790)*

ABOVE *The Bucket of Blood, Hayle, has an interesting origin story*
LEFT *Medieval brewers at work*

Pubs were also named after important battles, royalty or local heroes. One peculiarly named pub in Cornwall may have a rather gruesome past. Some say that The Bucket of Blood in Hayle is named after an incident that took place 200 years ago, when the pub landlord pulled a pail of water from the well to find a bloodied mutilated body of a smuggler inside! However, some attribute the reddened water to runoff from the old tin mines found locally.

Find out if there were any other pubs in the village that have since closed or even been demolished. In recent years, faced with rising running costs and dwindling customers, many pubs have been forced to close their doors. However, recognising their role as a community hub, some have been kept open by dedicated villagers, often as co-op or community ventures.

The brewing process

While some pubs have sadly called last orders, there has been a sharp rise in microbreweries, craft ale and homebrewing. This revives the old tradition of small-scale brewing at home, which for centuries was a vital source of sustenance.

Throughout history, many water sources were ridden with disease and unpleasant to drink. As a result, ale was essential to communities as the production process made water safe and more palatable to consume. Hence the main drink in the Medieval village would have been a weak ale, consumed by both adults and children. It was often part of a worker's rights during harvest or other physical activities to receive a plentiful supply of ale, provided by the lord. At events like the beating of the bounds there were regular interruptions for 'much drinking' and it's perhaps possible to imagine that in the average Medieval village a reasonable number of the population were mildly intoxicated most of the time!

RIGHT *A Trappist monk brewing beer*

During much of the Medieval period, beer and ale managed to escape taxation by the lord. Female brewers known as brewsters or alewives were common in most villages. Indeed, the surnames Baxter, Brewster and Brewer, denote an ancestral link to the brewing process.

Ale was usually made from barley and oats, which were cheaper than wheat, mixed with hot water and brewed with yeast. Hops were a later addition, probably arriving in the early fifteenth century via Flanders, in what is now Belgium, to create a more bitter drink called beer. Darker ales such as porter were developed in the eighteenth century, using roasted grains for a more full-bodied flavour.

The Church also played a key role in brewing, continuing a tradition that began in the monasteries, pre-Reformation. Church ales were a useful source of income. In Medieval times, an ale-conner or aletaster was appointed to test the quality of ale sold in taverns and inns. There was a penalty for watering down ale, and court records are full of numerous cases.

Eventually, with the onset of industrialised processes, beer was produced on a commercial scale. Purpose-built breweries began to produce large quantities of beer. Many communities across the UK have been built around the local brewing industry.

THINGS TO DO

- Find out about the origins and history of your local pub. Pubs themselves are often mini museums, containing many fascinating artefacts from the village's history, including vintage photographs, crockery and agricultural equipment. (It is also a great place to find a local with a lot to say!)
- Discover whether your village pub's name is linked to any historic events or legends – perhaps the Civil War or famous visitors.
- Since the late sixteenth century, a licence has been needed to sell ale. There are many records and registers of landlords, landladies and licence holders. For more useful information, visit: **www.pubhistorysociety.co.uk**
- Old court records or newspaper archives can be great sources of information on historic disturbances or disputes in pubs.
- Determine whether your local area is traditionally associated with any breweries. Find out if the tradition of home brewing is being kept alive today. Have many microbreweries cropped up in the area in recent years?
- Log your discoveries and plot the key dates on your timeline.

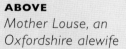

ABOVE
Mother Louse, an Oxfordshire alewife

40 SPORT & RECREATION

Our current obsession with sport and our idea of exhausting ourselves playing any number of different games would appear ridiculous to the average person in a Medieval village! The vast majority of the population would be too tired to consider wasting energy on pointless activities and the idea of leisure time would be a concept that few could ever hope for. There were moments however when activities, often related to military skills, could involve many people in the village. The widespread appearance of the names like 'the Butts' is a memory of the time when it was required that every man regularly practised archery. On feast days and holidays impromptu games of a cross between rugby and football took place. Some of the activities that could be called a game would be frowned upon by the authorities and could be closer to a riot than a sport!

ABOVE *A Medieval carving showing men enjoying a ball game (circa 1350)*

ABOVE *Many Medieval sports had a military emphasis; archery for the average villager and jousting for those of high social status*

The upper echelons of society would have enjoyed pursuits centered upon chivalric values, such as horse training, jousting and hunting. Participation implied wealth and status, due to the social exclusivity and crippling cost of warhorses and armour. Another exclusively high status sport was 'real tennis', a game more akin to modern squash, played inside an enclosed, walled court. It was introduced by Henry V, and Henry VIII was a keen player in his youth.

While recreation time for the wider population was rare, many sports were played in the towns and villages, aside from the required archery practice. Bowls and skittles have some history in antiquity. In England, skittles were mainly played in pubs and alehouses, with bowls played on the village green.

One of the oldest bowling greens is in Southampton, which has been in use since 1299. Legend has it that the sixteenth century seafarer Sir Francis Drake refused to face the approaching Spanish Armada off Plymouth Hoe until he had completed his game: "We have time to finish the game and beat the Spaniards, too!"

ABOVE *Gentlemen enjoying 'real tennis'*

40. SPORT & RECREATION

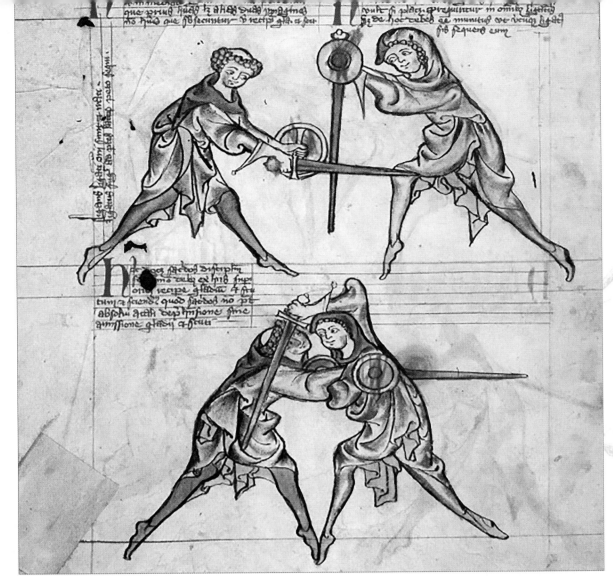

ABOVE *Fencing was a popular sport with a military emphasis among the noble classes*

A military emphasis

Pastimes that received official approval from the authorities were those with a practical purpose. Much like the chivalric activities of the nobility, many popular village sporting tournaments had a military emphasis, preparing the men for battle. Fencing, for instance, would have been widespread in Medieval England, The compulsory regular archery practice proved instrumental on the battlefield in compelling victories at Crecy and Agincourt, when English and Welsh archers overpowered a larger French force. 'Tug of war' has a long and colourful history, often deployed in rituals and the settling of disputes. The Vikings supposedly practised it to build their strength and train for war, while seafarers have long used it in preparation for hauling lines at sea.

BELOW *Tug of war was supposedly played by Vikings to build their strength*

Ball games

Other sporting activities, as we have said, were typically met with scorn from the authorities. Ball games, in particular, were seen as frivolous or encouraging belligerence. As Coulton has noted in *The Medieval Village*, ball games were stamped down in the fourteenth century under royal prohibition, as a distraction from archery practice. As countless records show, these games often took on a bawdy and riotous nature. Football was popular, with potentially a hundred or more villagers chasing after an inflated pig's bladder. Initially, there were very few actual rules, with no designated pitch or goals. Sometimes, rival villages would play against each other, the objective being to kick the ball into the neighbouring village's church entrance! Many of today's football grounds owe their origins to sites where cock fighting and bear bating took place. Tottenham Hotspur's name and crest, for example, reflect the club's association with fourteenth century knight Sir Harry Hotspur and cock fighting.

Games were traditionally partaken on a Sunday after church on the village green – perhaps the early genesis of Sunday football leagues. Seventeenth century Puritans took great offence at such unruly activities being performed on the Sabbath. As rules gradually became more formalised, sports eventually evolved into those that we would now recognise.

ABOVE *A typical English village green*

Indeed, many of the biggest sports played and watched around the world today started out (in their modern forms) on village greens. A Guildford court record from 1597, for example, notes that "hee and diverse of his fellows did runne and play there at creckett and other plaies". Modern football, rugby, hockey, cricket and golf were later exported across the British Empire, cementing their global appeal.

Festivals and regional variations

Religious festivals prompted a range of sporting activities around the country (Category 45). Royal Shrovetide Football is

ABOVE *'The Young Cricketer' by Francis Cotes (1768)*

still played in Ashbourne, Derbyshire, while dancing around the maypole remains popular in some parts, on May Day or Pentecost. Hopscotch, and its regional variations, still frequently played in school playgrounds today, was played in Britain from at least the late seventeenth century, but may even have Roman origins.

There would have been regional preferences for certain sports. Rugby, for example, was supposedly invented in the Warwickshire town of the same name, when a school boy, William Webb Ellis picked up the ball and ran with it. Modern cricket rules were formalised in the village of Hambledon, Hampshire, in the mid-eighteenth century. The Bat & Ball pub is still situated next to the original cricket ground and its then landlord was the team's captain. Modern golf was popularised in Scotland and club houses across the country can be great source of historical information.

Young girls dancing the maypole at Ashover Carnival, Derbyshire

Perhaps your village is in an area historically associated with a specific sport. There is a strong Gaelic sporting tradition, kept alive in the Highland Games, for instance. Sometimes, references to recreation can be found in a location name, such as Playing Place, near Feock in Cornwall, or fields colloquially known as 'the Wrestling Fields'. Of course, many individual villages developed their own traditions, occasionally involving the rolling of something edible!

ABOVE *Tossing the caber, a traditional Scottish sport*

Sport in Dunster

Dunster has a long tradition of sport. Various references can be found in historic archives, from an alleged illicit tennis court in someone's house in 1584 to residents fighting whilst playing 'squarills' in 1606. Perhaps the modern equivalent of chivalric pursuits, polo was played on the castle lawns from 1910 until World War II. Today, the town has a thriving cricket club and football club, with regularly fundraising activity for improving disabled access and maintenance of the buildings and grounds. Meanwhile, the Packhorse playground was created for the younger community. These projects provide social interaction and space, as well as community cohesion. Just as in Medieval times, village greens, playing fields and small parks where people can meet and socialise, continue to play an important role in strengthening and extending community ties.

THINGS TO DO

- Contact your local sports clubs and find out when they were first established. Often the clubhouse contains fascinating artefacts and vintage photography of the teams and sports being played. TIP: Local pubs can also be a great source of artefacts relating to recreational activity (such as the Bat and Ball Inn, Hambledon).

- Search the Victoria County History online for insights on social history in your area. The Dunster record is particularly revealing.

- Find out what you can about your local village green – the traditional social hub of the community, which may have hosted ball games and sporting tournaments for hundreds of years. Walking around the locale may reveal other clearings traditionally used for sports.

- Search court rolls and other local archives for references to disturbances of the peace brought about by games.

- Planning records might contain information on the setting up of local sports facilities.

- Look at maps for references and local place names, such as 'Playing Place' or 'Butts Lane', where archery practice was carried out.

- Log your discoveries and plot the key dates on your timeline.

41 APOTHECARIES & HEALTHCARE

Being ill in a Medieval village must have been a frightening business. It was not until the late nineteenth century that the medical profession began to understand the connection between germs, bacteria and disease. Until then, people would have had no idea how the great epidemics of the Black Death, smallpox, and cholera killed millions. The cause of death was effectively invisible. Many believed that illness was a punishment from God and typically healthcare, such as it was in the Medieval period, was often supplied by the Church.

nettle   dandelion   spearmint   French thyme   apple mint   rosemary   oreg

Medieval villagers relied on a range of herbal remedies produced at home or provided by an apothecary or wise woman

When Time Team excavated the area around St Leonard's Hospital in York, we saw the site of an establishment where the ill could be treated by the monks and nuns. In his reconstruction, Victor captured the arrival in the city of three desperate cases in need of treatment (see overleaf). You may recognise them! Because understanding of illness was so limited, what awaited them was largely ineffective and unpleasant. In such hospitals, patients generally slept three to a bed, and could look forward to a regime of purgatives and enemas, followed by bloodletting and prayer. The ordeal was perhaps alleviated by the diet of a gallon of ale a day, and helpings of fatty mutton! The only anaesthetic generally available was alcohol mixed with herbs, and small amounts of opium. Any wound would be roughly covered using recycled dressings, and the only preventative medicine for infection was yet more prayer.

thyme marjoram lavender thyme sage tarragon basil tarragon camomile

Access to healthcare

In most villages and towns of Medieval Britain, the presence of a physician was rare. While religious houses were traditional providers of care, the level of service varied greatly between establishments and petered out with the Dissolution of the Monasteries (Categories 12 and 28).

For many centuries, 'professional' provision was typically the preserve of the rich, yet this was no guarantee of welfare. Ironically, even for those who could afford it, medical care often did more harm than good. Failure to wash hands and sterilise medical implements, for instance, caused many deaths through the spread of infection.

A village wise woman might be on hand to assist at childbirth and provide healing. But with no standardised health service, the majority had to rely on home remedies, using traditional herbs supplemented with more exotic materials supplied by an **apothecary** (from the Latin, *apotheca*, meaning 'a place where things are stored').

Some herbal remedies were effective; camomile was a well-proved sedative, as was valerian, used since Roman times. Many herbs carry the title *officinalis*, used by the Romans to denote medically useful herbs. Willow bark was known to relieve pain, and its content was synthesised in modern times to produce aspirin. However, lack of scientific knowledge and very little regulation compared with today's pharmacies meant that the true value of remedies could vary greatly.

ABOVE Victor's illustration of three Medieval patients that you may recognise!

LEFT A list of herbal recipes to cure various ailments

286

The barber surgeon

The local barber acted as a part time surgeon and dentist. The traditional barber pole was perhaps an alarming warning to those lining up for treatment. The red stripe represents blood, the white stripe bandages, and the pole something to grip to alleviate the pain. The barber would also help in the process of bloodletting, often guided by an astrological chart to locate the specific vein to open according to the astrological cycle. Hitting an artery instead of a vein was likely to have severe consequences and many patients died as a result.

Bloodletting was considered an answer to the build up of pressure in the various humours of the body –

ABOVE *A fifteenth century apothecary*

blood, phlegm, black bile and yellow bile. This theory originated in antiquity and was particularly advocated by the Greek physician Galen. If cutting open veins didn't appeal, there would always be a handy jar of leeches, and they became so heavily utilised as a cure that by the end of the eighteenth century they nearly became extinct.

Acts of God and the Devil's work

The barber would be of little use when faced by the many contagious diseases that regularly swept through the population. Epidemics across the Middle Ages killed millions and were seen as acts of God. The Black Death occasionally killed off entire villages (Category 27). Diseases like leprosy were feared and led to the existence of many leprosy hospitals, in some cases called lazar houses, located outside the main towns and cities.

Little was understood about the disease, but its horrendous symptoms, in which facial tissue was severely damaged, spread a kind of horror that gripped many villages and towns. Victor's reconstruction of a victim shows the effect. In Series 4, Time Team excavated a **lazar house** in Launceston, Cornwall and many of the burials showed distinct signs of the disease. Many local churches have special windows called squints, to allow the infected to observe services from outside.

Often serious maladies were denounced as the work of the devil, particularly when it came to mental health. Even until relatively recently, many of the conditions we now understand better such as epilepsy, schizophrenia, dementia and various neurological disorders were put down to possession by evil spirits or sorcery.

Giving birth

Before the advent of modern maternity wards, the delivery of babies was an extremely risky business. Poor women who couldn't get into a workhouse infirmary would give birth at home assisted by older women who doubled as midwives. Herbal remedies offered little pain relief. Many women died during and after childbirth, whether through blood loss, infection or complications that can often now be addressed in a hospital.

A caesarean operation was a possible solution to a difficult birth. The procedure was carried out in Roman times, and there is much evidence of it taking place throughout the Medieval period. However, it was a last resort as the mother wasn't expected to survive the ordeal. Child mortality rate was incredibly high, and so wives were expected to produce many offspring to increase the odds of producing a surviving heir. The mortality age in an average Medieval village meant that if you lived to 40 you were doing incredibly well.

Modern medical knowledge

It seems astonishing to us now, but for the duration of the Medieval period, little was known about the true causes of disease. Most of the major discoveries that form the basis of modern medicine occurred from the late eighteenth century onwards.

BELOW *A fourteenth century depiction of man having teeth removed*

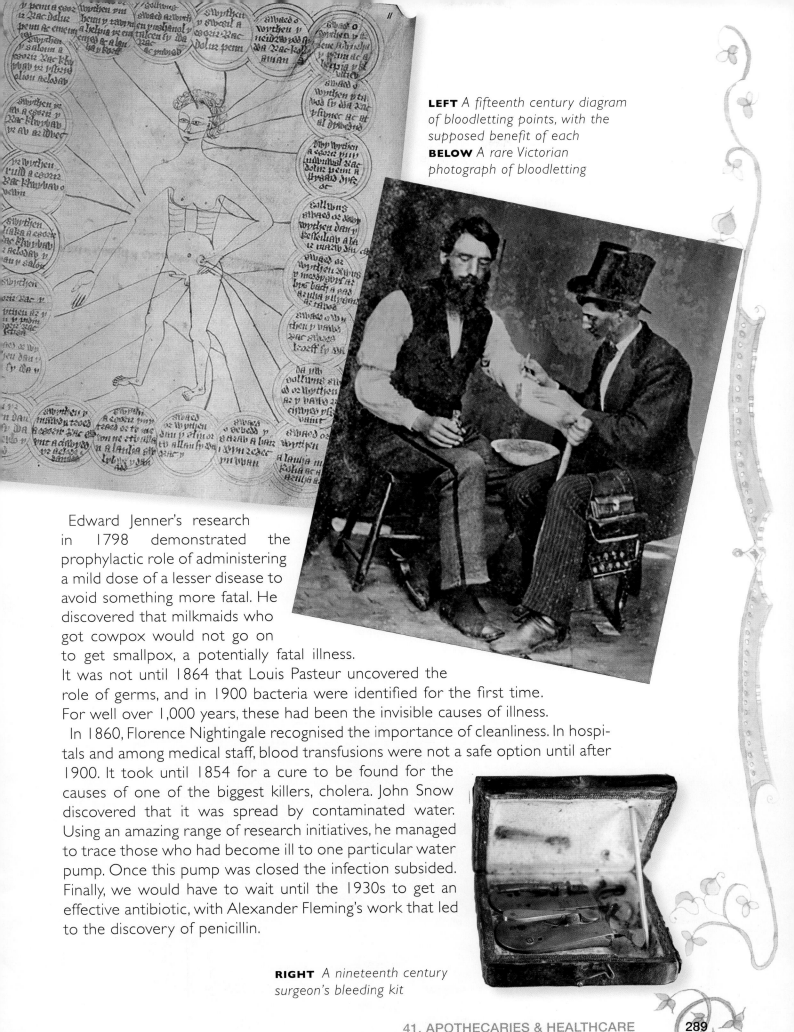

Edward Jenner's research in 1798 demonstrated the prophylactic role of administering a mild dose of a lesser disease to avoid something more fatal. He discovered that milkmaids who got cowpox would not go on to get smallpox, a potentially fatal illness. It was not until 1864 that Louis Pasteur uncovered the role of germs, and in 1900 bacteria were identified for the first time. For well over 1,000 years, these had been the invisible causes of illness.

In 1860, Florence Nightingale recognised the importance of cleanliness. In hospitals and among medical staff, blood transfusions were not a safe option until after 1900. It took until 1854 for a cure to be found for the causes of one of the biggest killers, cholera. John Snow discovered that it was spread by contaminated water. Using an amazing range of research initiatives, he managed to trace those who had become ill to one particular water pump. Once this pump was closed the infection subsided. Finally, we would have to wait until the 1930s to get an effective antibiotic, with Alexander Fleming's work that led to the discovery of penicillin.

RIGHT A nineteenth century surgeon's bleeding kit

It's amazing to think that many of the villages that began life in the Medieval period would have had a population assaulted by a wide arrange of illnesses. It seems rather wonderful that any of them have managed to survive at all!

Hospitals

As society became more informed and educated, hospitals were funded by public and private funds. By the late nineteenth century, many villages and towns had access to small cottage hospitals.

Dunster had its own cottage hospital on West Street, which opened in 1867 and was partly funded by the entrance fee of 6d charged to go into the castle grounds. It initially had provision for nine patients and had its own matron. However, according to the records, by 1899 there was concern about the absence of a trained nurse permanently on site. Several prominent members of the community contributed to employ such a nurse.

By the late nineteenth century, the cottage hospital was oversubscribed and unable to deal with the number of patients admitted, despite the addition of a second ward and an operating theatre. As a result, the decision was made to merge with a hospital in Minehead.

Dunster's hospital building still stands and is now a private residence known as Grabbist House. We also know of at least one apothecary's shop in Dunster, which was situated east of the High Street.

Researching historic healthcare

The relative scarcity of medical facilities can make it difficult to trace evidence of the healthcare system in your village's past. The graveyard records can record the sudden increase in death rate brought about by epidemics like the Black Death. It's worth remembering that the plague reappeared sporadically for hundreds of years and made late appearances in towns including Dunster in the seventeenth century.

Grabbist House

Grabbist House in Dunster, originally the cottage hospital

ABOVE *Passmore Edwards Cottage Hospital, Acton, built circa 1900*

Probate inventories are an invaluable source of information, particularly regarding people's professions, and they are typically kept with wills at the local records office. They list every item of furniture, stock and equipment owned. If there was a physician, surgeon or apothecary in your village, you might be able to find a trace of his profession in the items left in his will. We managed to find a reference to a Giles Poyntez who was listed in public records as a surgeon and apothecary in Dunster in December 1732. This is confirmed by the large amount of glass medical implements left after death.

THINGS TO DO

- Search the records and historic maps for references to a cottage hospital. See if you can find the location and whether the building still stands, perhaps now a private house or put to other commercial use.
- Check probate records for reference to doctors or apothecaries.
- Log your discoveries and plot the key dates on your timeline.

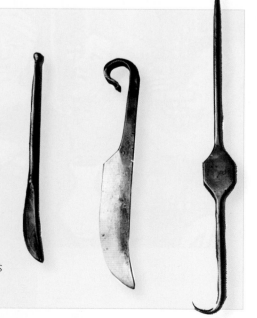

RIGHT *Various surgical instruments*

42 FOOD & DRINK

Today, in many parts of the world, food is readily available in abundance. We can walk into our supermarkets and buy any fruit, vegetables and meat we wish all year round. In fact, with so much food at our disposal, there is a growing concern about the rise of obesity in Britain! In Medieval Britain, the case was very different. People were dependent upon the local produce that was in season and had to plan ahead carefully for the winter months. For the average villager, malnutrition and starvation would have been an ever present danger, and one bad harvest could have dire consequences.

Peasants breaking bread together

turnips

carrots

peas

LEFT *Staple vegetables eaten by peasants*

The Medieval diet

Food in the typical Medieval village was basic. Items we now take for granted such as spices and sugar would have been considered as luxuries, reserved for the very rich, along with meats such as venison and boar. Many of the fruits and vegetables that have become integral to our diets were imported later from the New World. Today's staples such as tomatoes, potatoes, peppers and orange juice, for example, would have been unheard of.

Villagers would have grown their own vegetables native to Britain, such as peas, cabbage, turnips and herbs. At this point, native carrots were purple and not particularly edible! A typical villager's diet consisted large-ly of bread, ale and 'pottage' – a kind of porridge or stew made from boiling grains and vegetables, which had the advantage of making people feel full. Occasionally, meat such as beef, pork or fish would be added when available. The main grain for the poor was barley, the wheat being reserved for making bread.

As noted in Category 14, villagers had to pay the miller for the privilege of grinding their grain, under the strict jurisdiction of the lord of the manor. But the local lord often controlled the baking of bread too, with villagers forced to use the 'lord's oven' – at a price, of course.

In *Life in a Medieval Village*, Frances and Joseph Gies note several examples of fourteenth century villagers being fined for baking without license. As a result, pottage was a more efficient use of scant resources – the grain went further, it didn't rely on the miller's honesty or the local baker, and there was less natural waste in the process of making it.

RIGHT *'Esau and the Mess of Pottage' by Jan Victors (1653)*

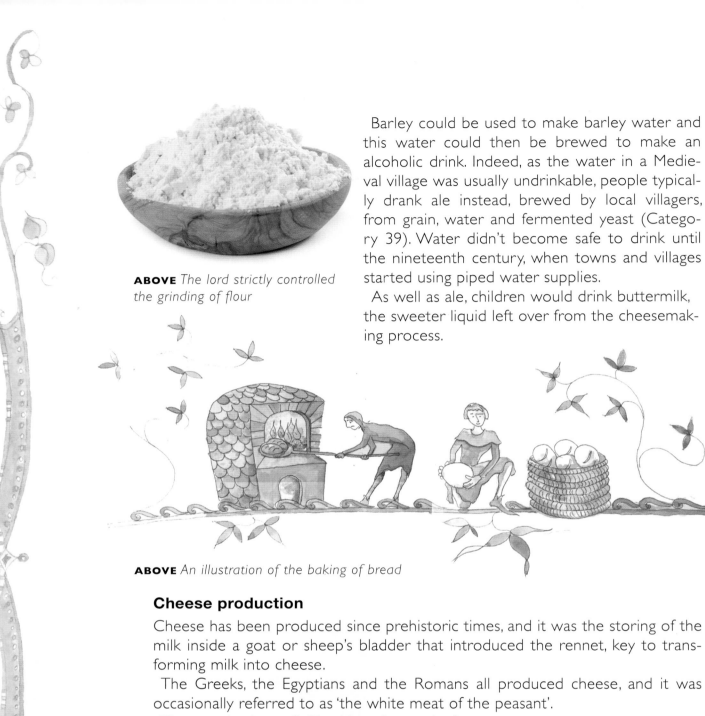

ABOVE *The lord strictly controlled the grinding of flour*

Barley could be used to make barley water and this water could then be brewed to make an alcoholic drink. Indeed, as the water in a Medieval village was usually undrinkable, people typically drank ale instead, brewed by local villagers, from grain, water and fermented yeast (Category 39). Water didn't become safe to drink until the nineteenth century, when towns and villages started using piped water supplies.

As well as ale, children would drink buttermilk, the sweeter liquid left over from the cheesemaking process.

ABOVE *An illustration of the baking of bread*

Cheese production

Cheese has been produced since prehistoric times, and it was the storing of the milk inside a goat or sheep's bladder that introduced the rennet, key to transforming milk into cheese.

The Greeks, the Egyptians and the Romans all produced cheese, and it was occasionally referred to as 'the white meat of the peasant'.

The production of Cheddar cheese is first recorded in the sixteenth century and takes its name from the Somerset village of the same name. Likewise, many other villages and regions across Britain have given their name to a particular variety, including Caerphilly and Wensleydale. Perhaps a village in your area can make a similar claim!

These homemade products were essential for day-to-day life and self-sufficiency was key to survival – every village needed to be able to provide the basics for its inhabitants.

ABOVE *A Medieval scene showing a man eating cheese*

Fast and feast days

Eggs would have played an important part of the village diet. Most households would have had access to a chicken, while both duck and goose eggs were eaten too. It was a tradition to eat eggs at Easter, which were forbidden during Lent, a custom historically associated with spring. Indeed, on village fast days, dictated by the Church, meat, cheese and eggs were some of the foods that were not permitted.

Typically, if villagers had access to fish, this would form the main part of the diet. When you think that a fast period, like Lent, could last up to 40 days, it was often very difficult for the poor to find

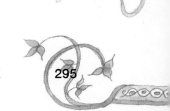

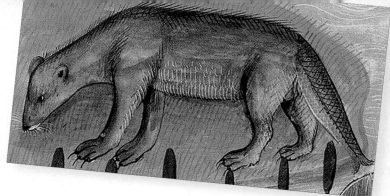

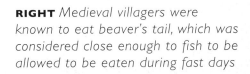

substitute food. In an area like Dunster close to the sea and rivers, there was a wide range of fish including herring, bream, carp, perch, pike, trout, crayfish, eel and occasionally porpoise, as well as a wide range of shellfish.

Benedictine monks were forbidden to eat meat on a Friday. There are accounts of monks eating puffin, under the pretence that it was actually a type of fish!

Evidence of food production, preservation and storage

How did your village sustain itself in earlier generations? Other than mills and pubs, which both played roles in providing sustenance, there are several other types of buildings and landmarks that you can look out for. For example, it's likely that old manors or villages had a dairy and a place to store cheese while maturing. Older farmhouses may still have evidence of these today.

Brueghel the Elder's 'Great Fish Market' (1603)

ABOVE *Before refrigeration, fish and other meats were often smoked for preservation*

Equally, there was no refrigeration in the modern sense until the mid-nineteenth century. Before this time, preservatives such as salt for curing meats and vinegar for producing pickles were essential to store food and help it keep for longer. Again, older properties may contain rooms or outbuildings used to prepare or store produce.

Ice houses were introduced in Britain in the late seventeenth century in wealthier households. The local manor house or stately home may still contain a small stone outbuilding in the grounds. These were often cone-shaped and partially underground to aid insulation, and were packed with ice imported from Scandinavia. Also keep an eye out for evidence of smokehouses, used to preserve fish and meat. Both ice houses and smokehouses might be referenced on historic maps.

Sometimes, the original village bakery survived for many years and there might still be older residents who can tell you where it was. Search local archives for surviving photos from the last 200 years that might reveal where some of these places were located. Sometimes old cottages still have the original bread oven embedded into the kitchen wall. Look out for clues in property names such as the 'Old Bakery'.

ABOVE *A traditional bread oven*

Regional delicacies

Cornish pasty

Perhaps your area has as an association with a particular type of food, such as the Cornish pasty, the Eccles cake, the Yorkshire pudding or Islay Whiskey. For coastal communities, fishing has traditionally been a fundamental part of the local economy. Often the harbour is lined with old buildings such as the 'cellars' in Cornwall where pilchards were cured and stored.

As we highlight throughout the book, traditional surnames often denote a person's trade, so look out for older families with the surname Baker, Butcher, Salter, Whitbread or Fisher.

Fish cellars at Port Gaverne

298

ABOVE *The Old Bakery at Lacock, Wiltshire*

THINGS TO DO

- Try to locate old buildings in the village associated with the production or storage of food, such as a dairy, bakery or ice house. Clues may appear in names still in use, or references on historic maps.
- Research foods typically associated with your area.
- Search for old families with surnames associated with food production, such as Baker or Butcher.
- Log your discoveries and plot the key dates on your timeline.

Eccles cake

43 WORKING ANIMALS

If you wandered into the average village today, you would be lucky to see an animal! In a Medieval village, the streets would have been full of horses, some waiting to be shod at the smithy or being readied to pull carts, oxen heading off to the fields, pigs wandering about and any number of dogs! Throughout history we have relied on animals for our survival. Before the advent of steam power and the use of waterwheels, the muscle strength of animals was the only power source we had. Oxen pulled the plough, horses hauled timber or turned grinding stones and donkeys or mules carried goods.

In addition to providing an essential source of food, we have used various parts of their bodies to make tools and other useful items. From sheep and pigs to goats and cattle – whether nomadic or domesticated – we have long lived with animals for our benefit and continue to do so.

In terms of archaeological finds, it's often the vast number of bones recovered that allow us to identify the type of animals most typically put to use in a village.

ABOVE & RIGHT *Deers' antlers have often been used to create knife handles*

Nothing wasted

Resourcefulness has been a virtue across history and nothing would be wasted when the need came to kill an animal. Almost every part from bone to tissue – and even its waste – would be put to good use in producing everyday household items. Leather, furs and wool have long been used in clothing, shoes and equine accessories. Since prehistoric times, antlers have been used as tools. Horns have been repurposed for cups and vessels, and bones as handles and needles. From the mid-eighteenth century onwards, ground bone ash has been used to make fine bone china.

LEFT *A horse-powered threshing machine*

Bone could also be boiled to extract the marrow for eating, while bone and other tissue could be processed to make gelatin or glue from the collagen. Guts wouldn't be wasted either. Offal is a key ingredient of faggots and, similarly, stomach and intestinal lining have been used to create sausages and Scotland's national dish, haggis. Pigs' bladders could even be inflated to make footballs or balloons!

Since the advent of farming, manure has proved to be an effective fertiliser. Even animal urine has enjoyed a surprisingly diverse array of uses – mostly due to its concentration of ammonia — including gunpowder and leather production, cleaning products and possibly even Roman mouthwash!

ABOVE *A haggis, traditionally made using sheep's offal and stomach; and a cow's 'powder horn' for storing gunpowder*

Domestication

Once we had domesticated animals, it became much easier to get access to these products. In early Medieval Britain, animals would often sleep in the same buildings as people. They were prized possessions that needed safeguarding and they also provided much-needed warmth. Farming became an important way of life for rural communities.

Aside from food and goods, over the centuries we've relied on the taming of beasts as working animals. As we've noted, animal strength has been critical in easing our workload. One remnant of this dependence, that can still be found in some villages and towns, is a circular structure with a central post. This is a mill wheel that would originally have been driven by a donkey, or perhaps a horse,

ABOVE *Dogs pulling machine gun carts for the Belgian Carabiniers,
during the Battle of the Frontiers in 1914*

to provide the power in the grinding of corn, pumping water and in smithies
(Category 14). It is no coincidence then that horsepower is still used today as a
measurement of power in machinery and vehicles.

Horses have a long history in transport, pulling coaches and canal boats, in
addition to their use in military endeavours and more leisurely pursuits such as
hunting. Dogs too have long been our companions. As well as being pets, they
have been put to use in hunting as well as guarding premises.

Animal husbandry and breeding

Over the generations, largely through trial and error, there have been many
significant developments in animal husbandry. Much like the evolution of crops,
humans have learnt how to breed certain traits and characteristics in animals
depending on their required use. Powerful warhorses were bred for battle,
shire horses for working farm machinery, and hounds and retrievers for hunting.
Equally, cattle and sheep stocks have been carefully controlled to produce a
higher yield of meat, milk or wool.

LEFT *A Medieval bas-relief sculpture showing a horse
being used to power the machinery in a mill*

Dunster showground

ABOVE *Breeds of sheep being judged at a county show*

Dunster's wool trade

Throughout the book, we've discussed Dunster's wool trade. The town is still extremely proud of its farming heritage and every year holds a show in the grounds of the castle. The wool trade necessitated a supply of water for the mills which helped to turn the wool into cloth, providing both work and a valuable source of income.

There would have been much larger enclosures for the raising of the town's important source of income – the sheep. Following the Enclosure Acts (Category 30), the local field system has changed largely from a Medieval 'strip' system into the larger, more open field systems we know today.

Local farming and regional breeds

Perhaps your area is associated with a particular type of farming or production otherwise related to animals. Staffordshire, for example, is famed for its bone china potteries, which would have relied upon a large supply of bones, possibly originating from local farms. Indeed, early innovator Thomas Frye of East London made use of his local slaughterhouses and cattle markets in Essex.

Equally, several regions are known for certain breeds of cattle, such as Highland and Hereford cattle and English Longhorn (sometimes known as Lancashire cattle).

Likewise, many dog breeds have a regional association, such as the Norwich and Norfolk terriers of East Anglia. Is there a particular dog breed associated with your region?

Research the local farms near your village or town and determine whether there is any correlation between individual farms and the specific animals they have reared. Often the local topography lends itself to a certain type of farming. Alternatively, these farms may have acted out of necessity by responding to the demand for a particular raw material. Perhaps local farmers have taken to breeding more unusual stock, such as alpacas cherished for their characteristic, high-quality wool. Another avenue of research is to look for clues in the type of goods traditionally been sold at the local market.

BELOW *Distinctive Highland cattle, reared for its meat*

English Herefordshire cattle

English Longhorn

THINGS TO DO

- Find out whether your local area is associated with a specific type of farming or production that relies on a certain animal product. The local archives and old maps might reveal useful information.

- Speak to local farmers, breeders and traders at the local farmers' market, who might be able to provide useful information on the area's traditional links with animal husbandry.

- Log your discoveries and plot the key dates on your timeline.

 44 MARKETS
& FAIRS

The modern shopping experience has, for many, been reduced to wandering around neon lit superstores in a daze, dumping products into a metal trolley, paid for at an automated checkout with little human interaction. Nothing could be further from this than the average Medieval market. The weekly market day would have been a vibrant, bustling encounter for most villages and towns. It was a real social event – the occasion when locals got together, traded their wares, sold any surplus supplies they had, and purchased essential goods that they were unable to grow or make themselves. Occasionally, there may have been visiting traders from other villages or regions, selling more exotic goods from further afield, such as spices and wines.

ABOVE *A Medieval market scene*

ABOVE *The popular Goose Fair in Nottingham dates back to the twelfth century*

The word market originally derives from the Latin, *mercari*, meaning 'to buy or trade', which also gives us the root of 'merchant'. Alongside weekly markets selling the usual wares, there were also seasonal events, sometimes centred upon one specific commodity. Some of these markets continue today, such as the Goose Fair in Nottingham and the Sloe Fair in Chichester. The earliest record of the Sloe Fair, traditionally held at the end of October, is in 1107 when the rights were granted on the condition that the fair was held annually. During World War II, a caravan was parked on the site declaring itself to be the 'fair', ensuring that the right to hold it didn't lapse!

The Goose Fair in Nottingham is believed to be first mentioned in 1164 and was held at the end of September, the culmination of the harvest season. It was an opportunity for farm labourers to make themselves available for further work, as well as selling produce.

ABOVE *A typical Medieval market scene*

ABOVE *A Medieval market scene by Beuckelaer (circa 1560)*

The lord's control of the marketplace

Whilst markets provided an invaluable service to the community, they held other great benefits from the lord's perspective. Crucially, a market was another means of exercising power over the local population – and to extract money from them. Just as the lord controlled the growing and making of produce, he also controlled the marketplace in which it was bought and sold. Markets could be particularly profitable for the local lord. By providing a space for the market to be held, he was then entitled to charge for the pitches, too.

ABOVE *The pannier market in Barnstaple*

In turn, the lord would have had to pay the crown for this right. Indeed, for much of the Medieval period, holding a market required royal permission through the issuing of a charter (Category 19). As a result, the right to hold a market was jealously guarded and carefully managed. In order to protect the market's sovereignty, there were very strict rules that merchants couldn't sell products on their way to the market or outside the designated market area.

The Court of Piepowders

Supervision was usually carried out by the lord's steward and a court, which met in a place called the toll booth or in the upper story of the market hall. In some areas, this administration was known as the Court of Piepowders, a corruption of the French, *Pieds Poudreux*, in reference to visitors' dusty feet! It was here that the rents and tolls were collected, under the watchful eye of the steward. The court also settled disputes that arose within the market's jurisdiction.

As markets prospered, they often evolved into a series of semi-permanent buildings to house the traders. Larger towns may have had a market hall. Sometimes, the upper story also served as the administration centre for the Court of Piepowders. Particularly in Devon, many towns still have a pannier market (from the French for 'basket'), an indoor market building with individual stalls selling fruit, vegetables and various wares.

Dunster's markets

As we discuss throughout the book, Dunster is well known for its distinctive octagonal Yarn Market building, dating from the seventeenth century. Dunster cloth was woven in mills in the area and the covered market enabled people to trade regardless of the weather.

Other physical landmarks may denote a market's location, such as a market cross. Hidden away in Dunster, just outside the town, are the remnants of a stone cross known as a 'butter cross'. Butter crosses were erected to declare the authority of the market, and there is a particularly beautiful example on Winchester High Street, dating from the early fifteenth century. When an eighteenth century local landowner tried to remove it to install as a garden feature, a small riot ensued, ensuring the ancient monument remains preserved for everyone to enjoy to this day!

The Butter Cross at Dunster, hidden away just outside the town

Artisan markets

Many communities still hold traditional annual markets or fairs, although they are no longer the necessity of old. Both Nottingham's Goose Fair and Chichester's Sloe Fair are now more popular for their rides than their traditional roles! Find out what you can about the regular or annual markets held near you. There has been a resurgence in markets in recent years, owing to the growing popularity in local, artisan goods and produce. Research whether the local craft or farmers' markets are more recent additions, or if they have a heritage that stretches further back. It might be that they have evolved over the years to meet the demands of the day. Perhaps, like the Sloe Fair, the tradition was briefly interrupted by the World Wars.

Market charters

With a bit of digging through the records, you should hopefully be able to discover when your local area first gained the right to hold a market. There may even be a copy of the original charter held in a local archive (Category 19). These were often beautiful documents, sometimes offering revealing insights on the region and prominent residents. The greatest number of charters were created in the thirteenth century. It has been estimated that almost 5,000 charters were granted between the thirteenth and fourteenth centuries. The earliest markets may even have had a prehistoric origin, possibly held in Neolithic enclosures. During the Romano-British period, a market place was common in every main town, where the forum was located. If your area has Roman origins, this could be an interesting avenue of research.

Borough Market, Southwark, continues to thrive, helped by the public's growing desire from quality, locally-sourced artisan produce

LEFT *Crediton Farmers' Market in the Market Square*

Next, you can establish where the market was located. Of course, this may be obvious as the central point of the village and is probably still in use today. However, if there is not a natural 'square' or centre point, the market may have been located where the shape of the street widens out. Equally, the original market may have been located elsewhere, before later development. There are many place names associated with markets, other than the self-evident Market Street and Market Square. Variations on 'Cheape Street' and the word 'chipping', for example, derived from the Old English for market (which is also the root of our modern terms 'shop' and 'shopping'). The word 'shambles' can also appear in street names, marking the place where butchers and others plied their trade.

THINGS TO DO

- Establish when the community was first issued with a charter to hold a market. The charter document often provides revealing insights into prominent characters of the time, such as the local lord.
- Look for physical clues in the community, such as a market square, hall or cross. Historic maps may also contain references to where markets were held.
- Log your discoveries and plot the key dates on your timeline.

RIGHT *The Market Square in Wymondham, Norfolk*

45 FESTIVALS, PLAYS & EVENTS

Britain has a rich culture of traditional festivals and events celebrated across the country, both on a local level and more broadly. One of the most famous of these is Guy Fawkes Night, every 5th November. As we all know from the popular rhyme, the fireworks displays and burning of the 'Guy' on the bonfire commemorate the foiling of the 'Gunpowder Plot' to blow up the Houses of Parliament in 1605. In more recent years, this celebration has become increasingly eclipsed by another traditional event, Halloween, at the end of October. While this ancient European festival on the Eve of All Hallows (or All Saints' Eve), can be traced back for centuries, ironically its modern popularity owes more to customs re-imported from North America!

Seasonal rituals

Throughout history, for both hunter-gatherers and agricultural communities living off the land, the annual cycle has played an integral part in people's livelihoods. The seasons provided natural punctuation, dictating the course of events – when to hunt for certain game, when to sow or harvest crops, when to store food and wood for the cold months ahead, and so on. Equally, the monthly full moon provided light to hunt under. As a result, many occasions had a seasonal focus, symbolically marking the changing of the season, the high and low points of the year, and movements of the stars. Harvest Festival and the summer and winter solstices are just a few examples that have probably been celebrated from prehistory onwards.

OPPOSITE *Fireworks over the Houses of Parliament to mark Guy Fawkes Night*
ABOVE *The moon has been associated with rituals for thousands of years and also served a practical purpose in providing some light while hunting at night*

Pre-Christian origins

Traditional festivals commonly began with a religious nature, often involving some form of offering or sacrifice to the gods. Many supposedly Christian festivals are in fact much earlier in origin. Typically, these ancient festivals would be absorbed and integrated into the new religion – providing a comforting continuity with the old ways, while showing Christianity's dominance over them. Easter, for example, which is usually associated with rebirth and regeneration, may well have its origins in a Germanic fertility goddess, Eostre, possibly derived from a Middle Eastern goddess, Ishtar.

May Day is the focus of numerous regional events – sometimes of a wonderfully eccentric English nature, such as the annual cheese rolling event at Coopers Hill in Gloucester. This curious event is believed to stem from the pagan practice of rolling a burning object down the hill after winter, to represent the birth of a new year. Padstow in Cornwall, meanwhile, has its 'Obby 'Oss festival, possibly originating from the ancient Gaelic festival of Beltane. As we highlight in the myths and legends discussion (Category 57), local traditions are often a variation on a theme played out more generally across the country.

ABOVE *The 'Wheel of the Year' at the Museum of Witchcraft and Magic, Boscastle, highlighting seasonal festivities*
BEHIND *Engraving depicting Ostara, the goddess of Easterseum, Bosa*

The 'Obby Oss festival in Padstow

ABOVE *'Clooties' at Sancreed Well in West Cornwall*

Well dressing is another historic practice that's probably pre-Christian in origin. It's mostly associated with areas such as the Peak District, where wells are elaborately dressed with flower blossom and foliage in thanks for the provision of water (see also Category 5). The modern practice gained popularity in the eighteenth century.

Offerings at wells more generally have spanned the length of the British Isles for millennia. Clootie wells can be found from the Black Isle in the Scottish Highlands to Sancreed Well in far West Cornwall. These wells are characterised by strips of cloth (or 'clooties') hung from the surrounding trees.

Countless other traditional rituals and events are still recognised and celebrated today across the country, often unique to a particular area. Ashbourne in Derbyshire, for instance, holds a football match every Shrove Tuesday (Category 40). Teams of 100 players play for around eight hours, following a tradition that has continued since the twelfth century.

LEFT *A fifteenth century carving of an entertainer by Erasmus Grasser*

ABOVE *A Medieval mystery play being performed in Chester*

Plays and pageantry

Pageantry and festivals were a huge part of life in Medieval villages and towns, bringing the whole community together in the rare breaks from toiling in the field. Music and theatrical performances played a role in merrymaking, with morality, miracle and mystery plays central to celebrations. These plays evolved from religious services originally written by monks, with biblical stories delivered in Latin and embellished by actors who recreated the scene.

After the Pope banned the clergy from performing on stage in the early thirteenth century, they were instead organised by craft guilds (Category 37). From this point onwards the plays were performed in English, often with secular and comical elements added to the production. Many English play 'cycles' were written over the Medieval period, and could take several days to perform.

Re-enactments

Today, re-enactments commemorating significant events (typically battles) keep local stories and characters alive, from the Roman period right up to World War II. We've discussed Dunster's involvement in the English Civil War, with the castle's owner Francis Luttrell commanding the local militia (Category 29). The Taunton Garrison camping in the grounds of Dunster Castle is one of many living history events across the country that entertain visitors with battle re-enactments and weapons demonstrations. These regular fixtures ensure that significant events and people from local history are not forgotten.

OPPOSITE *A re-enactment of the Battle of Hastings, 1066*

No doubt you're already aware of existing local traditions and events. Attempting to piece together their real-life origins can be an intriguing and fruitful focus for your research. These customs may not be as well-known as cheese rolling or well dressing but can be equally fascinating, sometimes throwing up unexpected stories.

As is often the case with research, you may not know exactly what you're looking for until you find it! Historic records and personal accounts may contain references to archaic festivities that were taking place at the time. If you're lucky, you may stumble upon an obscure reference to a long-lost tradition that could be revived or commemorated in your annual calendar of events.

ABOVE *An illustration of Bolster Festival held in St Agnes, Cornwall*

THINGS TO DO

- Research the origins of known local traditions and events.
- In your wider research, keep an eye out for references to historic celebrations that have since died out. Perhaps you may be able to revive these in some form. TIP: If you are researching local crafts guilds, for example, you might find references to mystery plays and other performances.
- Log your discoveries and plot the key dates on your timeline.

ABOVE *Master of the cheese rolling ceremony*

317

46 FOOTPATHS

In Medieval Britain, the average villager would have relied upon a network of local footpaths in the carrying out of their daily tasks: trekking into the village centre on market day; heading to and from church on Sunday; to get to the fields to tend to their crops or pasture their livestock; or filling their pails at the nearest water source. Many of these routes would have sprung up organically, trodden down and established over time, as people figured out the most appropriate route to and from their destination. Some skirted around fields or other geographic features, perhaps following the line of the coast.

Pilgrims' Way near Westwell, Kent

ABOVE *A Roman footpath in France*

Footpaths

Paths solely for foot traffic were useful in avoiding the muddy, cartwheel-rutted roads, typically taking a more rural route through fields or woodland. It was the Romans who first made the distinction between designated footpaths and bridle-ways. Indeed, in 2016, a small hoard of coins was found at the side of a footpath just outside the town of Totnes in Devon, helping to confirm that this route has been followed since Roman times.

Other paths

Throughout history, a wide range of other types of path have been created for designated functions: salt paths, mass paths, pilgrimage routes and even corpse roads for carrying the dead! In Anglo-Saxon times, the herepath was an important route taken by soldiers on the way to protect the coastline (Category 25).

ABOVE *Caligae were heavy-duty, thick-soled open work boots worn by Roman cavalrymen and foot soldiers*

As we note in Category 18, a path was often established circuiting the parish boundary. The act of walking the boundary and 'beating the bounds' was an ancient ritual, that was later Christianised into the 'Rogation' ceremony. Meanwhile, routes up to 'common land' for pannage, the feeding of pigs, typically in woodland, and collecting wood would have become established over time.

In Dunster, there is a wonderful route up to the ancient spring of St Leonard's Well. This was probably the route trodden by many villagers collecting water over the centuries. A Medieval stone structure, perhaps dating from the fourteenth century, still stands and is believed to have once supplied water to the town's priory.

Sailors' routes

'The Sailor's Path' in Suffolk is a route historically used by seamen, supposedly when their boats became stranded in mud at low tide. Meanwhile, the 'Mariner's Way' is a route made up of various ancient pathways, linking Bideford in north Devon to Dartmouth on the south coast, via Dartmoor. Allegedly, this land route through Devon meant that sailors could spend an extra day on land rather than sailing around Cornwall via Land's End. They could disembark their ship on one side of coast, then board another (or the same) ship on the opposite coast. However, whilst the various pathways do indeed exist, whether or not this was ever an established route regularly used by sailors for this purpose remains open to debate.

BELOW *Mariner's Way, Devon, an ancient route supposedly used by sailors connecting Bideford on the north coast to Dartmouth on the south coast*

DIG VILLAGE

ABOVE *Pilgrims walking the Camino de Santiago, Navarra, Spain*
LEFT *St James' Cathedral, Santiago*
BELOW *The scallop shell is a traditional symbol of St James*

Pilgrimage

Pilgrimage was a significant part of life in Medieval Europe, with a large, sophisticated network of paths stretching across the continent, and much commercial activity popping up to support it. The 'Camino de Santiago' (or Way of St James), for instance, was established by the ninth century, a European network leading to the Cathedral of St James in Northern Spain. Traders would offer lodgings and sell souvenir trinkets en route, such as the scallop shell associated with the saint.

The Saints' Way

There are many ancient pilgrimage routes across Britain. The Saints' Way, for example, stretches 27 miles from Fowey on the south coast of Cornwall, through Bodmin, to Padstow on the north coast. This route was used by monks from Wales and Ireland on their way to Brittany. Perhaps the most famous is the Pilgrims' Way, which leads from Winchester through the North Downs to Thomas a Becket's shrine in Canterbury. Of course, many revealing insights can be gleaned from Chaucer's *Canterbury Tales*, which recounts the journey of a band of pilgrims from London to Canterbury in the late fourteenth century.

There may well be local points of pilgrimage nearby your area. When conducting your research, it's useful to look into the various trades and industry that would have sprung up around these routes. You may be able to establish, for instance, whether your village emerged in order to capitalise on this trade.

Disputes and rights of way

Another avenue of research is the fact that land and property rights are often at the centre of local disputes. Throughout history, there has often been a tension between those using a footpath (perhaps asserting their right of way through private land) and the local farmer or landowner, obliged to keep the path open. You might find examples of disputes of this nature by looking through local court records.

The western branch of the Saints' Way footpath, with views out to St Austell

We've already discussed the eighteenth century Enclosure Acts, which forced people off land that they had traditionally farmed for generations (Category 30). It's likely, too, that this trend affected some traditional rights of way and footpaths. Compare local Ordnance Survey maps pre and post enclosure to determine whether any historic pathways disappeared as a direct result of this redefining of borders (or at other times throughout history).

ABOVE *A stone stile in the Yorkshire Dales*

Take a walk

Of course, one of the most enlightening ways to learn about local footpaths is to walk them yourself! As well as the paths, you'll discover various features associated with them. Gates and stiles, for example, can vary greatly in design and materials throughout the country. The regional variation of vernacular styles of stiles is a particular wonder of the UK. If you're lucky, there might be ancient stone examples in your area. The word 'stile' stems from the Old English, *stigel*, meaning 'to climb'.

To have the freedom to wander through and around your village or small town and discover small alleyways (or guinnels, or ginnels, as they are known in the north – from the Old English, *ginn*, meaning 'an opening') is one of the pleasures of finding your way around the village.

LEFT *A 'ginnel' in Barrowford, Lancashire*

THINGS TO DO

- Compare historic maps from different periods to see how paths have appeared, evolved or even disappeared. TIP: Pay close attention to maps pre and post enclosure.
- Study court records for any disputes surrounding rights of way over private land.
- Determine whether your village lies on an important route that would have necessitated traffic (such as an ancient pilgrimage route).
- Walk the local paths yourself and enjoy some fresh air! Look out for markers, stiles, crosses and other trappings associated with paths.
- Log your discoveries and plot the key dates on your timeline.

47 PARKS & HUNTING GROUNDS

Whenever we visit Dunster, it's always quite a sight to witness the deer grazing amongst the ancient oaks in the parkland opposite the castle. This area today represents a tiny fragment of the land that was once set aside for the lord and his guests to hunt. All over the country vast amounts of land was commandeered for this purpose and the hunting rights of monarchs, lords and ladies were fiercely protected by law.

You will see from the map in Category 8 just how much land was set aside for the royal pursuit of hunting. After the Norman invasion, William the Conqueror created new areas exclusively for the royal hunt. The New Forest, which would eventually extend to over 90,000 acres, was his creation. It was here that two of his sons would be killed whilst hunting, Richard within the first decade of the

In Medieval times, vast swathes of the countryside were set aside as royal forests, for the Crown and his or her retinue to hunt deer and other game

ABOVE *The king and his lords hunting with hawks*
BEHIND *The Rufus Stone in the New Forest*

Conquest, and William Rufus, many years later in 1100 during his own reign as king. A monument to his death, the Rufus Stone, can still be seen in the forest.

To create these vast hunting areas, many villages were forcibly abandoned, and communities uprooted. Monarchs such as Henry II carried on the tradition of hunting with obsessive dedication.

BELOW *The deer park of Dunster castle*

Parks and forests

The word 'forest' derives from the Latin, *foris*, meaning 'outside' and its original meaning wasn't limited exclusively to an area covered in trees. Some parts of the forest called 'parks' were enclosed to trap deer or other game. The word 'park' comes from the Old English, *pearroc*, itself from the Latin, *parricus*, meaning 'an enclosed area'.

It has been estimated that over 1500 deer parks were created in the Middle Ages, mainly during the twelfth and thirteenth centuries. The deer species were mainly 'red', 'roe' and 'fallow' deer, and provided not only sport but a supply of venison for the lord's table.

BELOW *A Medieval depiction of an enclosed hunting park, from 'The Master of Game'*

Other animals hunted included wild boar. Hawking was also popular and there are many Medieval tapestries and paintings showing ladies carrying hawks to hunt for rabbit, pigeon and other wild birds.

Poaching and the forest laws

The forest laws were some of the most draconian imposed by the Crown, but despite this the theft of deer was relatively common and it can be traced through county records as severe punishment was handed out. The *Anglo-Saxon Chronicle* records that the penalty for killing a deer would be that the person "should be made blind". Yet for many poor families, poaching was the only means of sourcing protein.

Poachers became important figures in folklore, and many were transported overseas. Folk songs often contain dire warnings to those who were tempted. For the origins of folk songs in your areas there is an excellent archive created by Cecil Sharpe House. This kind of material can provide a useful source of information about elements of village life lost in time. The traditional ballad 'Geordie' is a classic example:

> Ah, my Geordie will be hanged
> in a golden chain,
> 'Tis not the chain of many.
> Stole sixteen of the king's royal deer,
> And he sold them in Bohenny.

ABOVE *Ancient arrowheads*

Tracing royal parks

We are familiar with some of the great royal parks like Windsor and Richmond but, as noted, these are just a small fraction of the many thousands that once dominated much of the country. It is an interesting line of research to try to locate them and trace their boundaries, some of which may still be discoverable as earthworks.

Parks, the enclosed parts of the forest, were surrounded by ditches and banks topped with fences – usually called pales, which is where we get the phrase 'beyond the pale', meaning to be outside the formal area. Some of these banks were substantial and metres wide, leaving very visible signs even today. The ditches tend to be less visible but were equally important. Take a walk in the local woods or parkland and see if you can spot the signs.

BEHIND *A typical Medieval hunting scene*
BELOW *A group of beautiful deer in Richmond Park*

Some of the largest hunting forests turn up in areas that today we associate with urban areas. Sutton Coldfield is part of the West Midlands transformed in the Industrial Revolution, but in the Anglo-Saxon period it was the royal forest of Sutton and later a Medieval deer park of vast size. Forest boundaries can sometimes be traced on historic maps, and they were recorded in 'perambulations' as well as other estate documents.

Over the years, many of the great parks have diminished in size or disappeared completely under modern developments like London. The parks of Windsor and Richmond have survived and continue to provide grazing for considerable herds of deer.

Dunster's original hunting forests became more formalised and by the eighteenth century had been included in a formalised landscape. The large scale remodelling of estates by figures such as 'Capability' Brown in the Georgian period saw many of the old hunting parks changed into a more picturesque landscape. Follies, temples, artificial lakes and decorative bridges began to fill the estates where once lords and their retinue had hunted.

Coneygarths

Rabbit warrens, or **coneygarths**, were areas of land set aside specifically for the breeding of rabbits, kept for both their meat and fur. They can be spotted in the landscape by the traces of 'pillow mounds' surrounded by a ditch to ensure the warrens stayed warm and dry. These mounds can be up to 40 metres long and are usually cigar shaped.

A bridge at Blenheim Palace, landscaped by 'Capability' Brown

328

ABOVE *Conygar Tower, an eighteenth century folly built on the site of a Medieval rabbit warren*

Conygar Tower is a circular stone tower, built in 1775, that sits perched on the hillside opposite Dunster Castle. Its placing is interesting, firstly as a classic example of an eighteenth century folly, erected purely for decorative purposes. Secondly, its name suggests it was built on the site of an earlier rabbit warren on the estate, highlighting the changing use of the land over the centuries.

THINGS TO DO

- Look on a 6-inch Ordnance Survey map for farm or field names that include the word 'Park' or 'Kingswood'. If you're lucky, the map may even include the original boundary.
- Scour the local woodland or landscape for ditches and banks, which may be part of the park's original boundary, created to prevent deer from escaping the park and to keep poachers out.
- Look out for 'pillow mounds', artificial warrens for breeding rabbits for fur and meat, which were typically cigar shaped and could be up to 40m long.

A pillow mound

LEFT *A tile depicting a stag, found in Ludlow*

An aerial view of Dunster looking out towards the sea

VI.
Organisation &
Development

Every project lives and dies by the effectiveness of its organisation. If you want to turn a casual interest in local history into a lasting project that engages the wider community and produces valuable results, you'll need to be well organised. Here, we provide advice on assembling your group, forming goals, advancing to active fieldwork, and raising the necessary funds to keep the project going. We then look closer at additional techniques and research frameworks in order to sharpen the project's focus.

48 FORMING A GROUP

Mick always advised people wishing to set up a local history and archaeology group to find their 'first lieutenants' at an early stage. They are the small group of individuals who you can rely on to keep the project going and have enough enthusiasm, energy and local contacts to make it happen. It's important to remember that each new member who joins the project will have a very individual set of motivations and interests. It's part of the leader's job to nurture these and remember that every member is there to find enjoyment and satisfaction in what they do.

Identify people with an interest in the project and a range of skills

ABOVE *Begin in an informal setting to create a relaxed atmosphere and get the conversation flowing*

An initial get together in a local tea room or pub might help to create the right atmosphere. Ask people to bring old photographs of the village or other curiosities, as this may help to attract villagers. Curious souls tend to be more likely to pop along to an open venue than a more official location. A casual environment with plenty of tea and biscuits (or real ale) will help attendees to relax and get the conversation flowing!

The benefits of teamwork

Setting out to find out about the history of your village can be a daunting task on your own. Forming a group will help to bring the project together and give the research a focus. Time Team benefitted from the combined knowledge and experience of our various experts across a range of fields. In an effective team, everyone brings their own unique attributes, and it's through combining this broad range of perspectives that you can make some real breakthroughs. On another note, it's also great simply to share a passion for history and archaeology among like-minded individuals! Much of your own project's success will likely hinge upon forming a group to pool ideas, as well as finding people with the drive and determination to steer it forwards.

Forming a group in Dunster

In Dunster, we've been lucky to enjoy a warm welcome, with many residents who were ready to help. They have been the eyes and ears of the project and clearly knew more about the nooks and crannies of their town than we did! We were often alerted to specific buildings to explore because a local painter or builder had noticed some old beams inside the attic of a roof.

It was decided at an early stage that a local archaeology group should be formed. Called the Dunster Museum Archaeology Group, they began looking into working with other groups and were able to get access to some geophysics equipment. They surveyed an area near Dunster beach, which had come to light after one of Dig Village's friends had noticed Roman pottery eroding out of the cliffs.

We were delighted to see that, after two or three years of working with Dig Village, the group had the confidence to create its own lines of research.

Team organisation

It's often amazing to find out the range of unexpected skills hidden inside a group of enthusiasts. One person may have studied a bit of Latin at school, one might be a retired surveyor and another might have photographic skills. It's surprising how a bit of enthusiasm can convert your volunteers' shyly expressed interests into a useful contribution to the project!

You will gradually accumulate a vital list of names, contact addresses and emails, and hopefully four or five individuals will emerge from this group as key members. Once your core team has established a key set of aims and goals for research, you'll be able to attract other people to help out.

As the project develops, some people will have the organisational skills to take a lead role. Leadership is an important element. If you're lucky enough to have a professional archaeologist or historian to advise you, this will be a useful initial stimulus. However, the main organisational role can be taken up by a non-professional, who has the essential skills needed. Over time a number of leaders will emerge and it's good to share this burden, as after an intensive period of research fatigue can set in!

RIGHT *Find people with the skills and drive to lead others and push the project forwards*

ABOVE *Establishing a steering group will help to maintain the focus of the project*

Your local council may have a community officer (or similar) who can help facilitate setting up a group – they may be able to provide a meeting space or have contacts, ideas and suggestions to help bring the group together. As the group grows, it may be time to appoint a chairperson and set up a committee.

As with all matters to do with villages and small towns, it's important to have a degree of democratic sensitivity and to make sure everyone knows what is happening. The parish newsletter, local paper and social media are all useful outlets for keeping people informed and attracting a wide demographic. It's always beneficial to have a regular meeting with the general public invited, where you explain your goals (see Category 59 on outreach).

Establishing a steering group

Before you get too far, it's a good idea to establish a **steering group**, to help maintain the focus, and keep the group informed of related projects, wider research and other issues. A steering group is separate from the main group and is typically made up of a mixture of group members and other interested representatives, who meet three or four times a year.

It would be particularly useful to get the county archaeologist or a representative from the Historic Environment Record on board. It's important that any work that develops out of the project maintains a high set of standards in both the recording and processing of results. In this respect, regular contact with a supportive professional archaeologist or historian would be invaluable.

Others to consider for your steering group might be a local museum representative, a county records office archivist, a parish council representative, and members of other local groups with coinciding interests. For example, a local group might be undertaking an insect and bird survey, which overlaps with your hedgerow survey.

Collaborating with other groups

Indeed, it's well worth contacting existing clubs and looking for common ground. Local walking associations, gardening societies, art and photography groups, book clubs and so on are likely to have members who are interested in the project. These groups might even incorporate some of your aims into their own programmes. An art class, for example, could create village reconstructions (Category 64); a photography group might record finds and sites; and a walking group may help to study the local topography (Category 52).

Better together

There are many different things to think about when setting up a group. How will the project be funded? Where will meetings be held and how often? Who will be in charge of what? But don't let the details overwhelm you! Many of these answers will become apparent over time.

Begin informally, getting the ball rolling with some basic 'roles and goals', bearing in mind that these are likely to evolve. Finally, reach out to other Dig Village enthusiasts across the country to exchange tips and insights on how they've gone have gone about it.

Ultimately, it's a rewarding experience to bring together a group of people with an interest in their community, ensuring that your discoveries are shared with a wider audience for years to come.

ABOVE *Share ideas on assembling a local group with other Dig Village enthusiasts across the country*

THINGS TO DO

- Start informally, perhaps at a local pub or cafe to assemble your 'lieutenants'. Gradually formalise the group as it grows and roles and goals are established.
- Advertise locally for members to join the group.
- Think about how the project will be funded (Category 51).
- Identify the group's aims and individuals' skills that could be put to good use in the project.
- Set up a steering group, incorporating professional representatives, such as a local councillor, archaeologist or someone from the county records office.
- Look for common ground and shared goals among other groups in the area.
- Reach out to other Dig Village enthusiasts across the country and share insights.

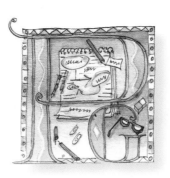

49 PROJECT GOALS: STAGE 1

I t's important to keep your goals in mind, otherwise your research can proliferate and you might end up becoming overwhelmed with information! In Dunster, we were lucky to have an idea of our key goals set by Mick in his overview of the town, 'Historic Towns in Somerset' (1977), written with Roger Leech. Always take time to review your goals as the project develops. It will be an important guide to what you have achieved and where you need to head in the future.

Goal: Determine the oldest tree in the village. Was this once part of a larger woodland area?

Notes from Mick

Can we establish the date of monastery's boundary?

Any evidence of Medieval suburbs?

Find earliest settlement...

ABOVE *Going through the main project goals in Dunster*

Once you've done your initial research on historic maps (Category 1) and then assembled some of the documents and information discussed in the ensuing categories, you may get an idea of the main questions you would like answered, as well as how you might go about answering them. Ask yourself or your group (if you have one):

- Which areas, subjects or topics would be most useful in unlocking the story of the village's history?
- Is there a best way of approaching and framing your research in order to get the answers? Take a closer look at Mick's goals for Dunster in the box overleaf as an example.

The second stage of the project is the refinement of your goals. In the case of Dunster, we wanted to concentrate on areas of the town where more Medieval evidence was being found. You may decide to concentrate your research on specific areas, too. For example, was there an Anglo-Saxon land survey? Was there an area of land that came under the control or ownership of an abbey or priory?

Goal: Find the oldest building in the village. When was it built?

Goal: Check Portable Antiquities Scheme database to establish what finds have been discovered.

ABOVE *Dunster's Gallox Bridge, an area of research set out in our goals*

EXAMPLE OF PROJECT GOALS

Mick had set goals for Dunster, both in documents and verbally.
These included:

- Date the monastic boundary.
- Look for evidence of Medieval suburbs around the
  St Thomas and Gallox Bridge area.
- See if we could find concentrations
  of earlier settlement within the village.

Bringing valuable people on board

In Dunster, we knew Glastonbury Abbey had been the dominant power and therefore we decided to do more research into the records for Dunster. We also had a general goal to look at areas we had not yet investigated, including the castle. As this is a National Trust property, this would involve establishing a good relationship with the National Trust archaeologist and managers of the castle, bringing them along with any potential goals we might have.

Another goal you might have would be establishing a history group or society in the village (Category 48). Locals established the Dunster Museum Archaeology Group and, building on the Dig Village project, they began to develop their own possible goals for the future.

It's important that your project has a good focus on some short-term, achievable goals, as well as those for the longer term. This is also a good time to look at your outreach strategy (Category 59). Make sure you are communicating what your project has achieved to the wider local community. A useful part of this strategy might be the creation of an interim report which outlines what has been achieved so far (Category 65).

Liaison with local professional archaeologists, the local county archaeologist and others with a professional interest in the area, can also provide useful hints and help to point you in the right direction for possible areas of further research (Category 60). An organisation like the British Association for Local History (BALH) is a good resource.

THINGS TO DO

- Look at all your assembled research and bring it together. What have you found out so far?
- Are there any surprising, interesting and intriguing bits of information you have come across that you would like to find out more about?
- Arrange a meeting with your local county archaeologist who might be able to suggest further areas of study or help guide you in your next steps of research by helping you set out your project goals.
- Consider your outreach strategy, by communicating your findings so far and future goals with the wider community.
- If there isn't one already, you could set up a local history or archaeology group.

Project goals...
-Set up a group
-Discuss ideas with other members
-Speak to a local archaeologist?

ABOVE *Local history society website homepages*

50 PROJECT GOALS: STAGE 2

Let's imagine that you've unearthed many interesting facts about your village or small town from the archives. Perhaps you have found a reference to the settlement in Domesday. You've dated the church building, walked the landscape and photographed interesting features. You might have studied old maps and aerial photography to see how boundaries and the street plan have developed over time. Maybe you've investigated local legends and also identified a few heroes and villains along the way too. If you have managed to successfully engage your community in the various aspects we've covered in this book, then first of all, well done! Now, you might reach a stage when you ask, what do we do next? It's at this point that you need to have a few things in place...

RIGHT *Rob Hedge, our professional archaeologist, keeping an eye on a test pit*

An historic building of potential interest to our project in Dunster

RIGHT *The Dig Village team working on a test pit*

Taking stock of your discoveries

Firstly, you should have a general understanding of your settlement based on the materials that you've read about in this book. This is a good opportunity to step back and take stock of what you've discovered and what this tells you about your village. This may help to pinpoint any gaps in its story that you have been unable to fill through research alone. It's worth noting that this stage of the project should not be rushed and may take up to a year or more to complete.

By now, hopefully, you will also have developed a relationship with your local archaeologists and other professionals who will be critical in the next stage of the project (Category 60). This may involve fieldwork, field walking and test pitting. However, bear in mind that this should not be undertaken lightly.

Professional support

Don't forget, archaeology that involves any form of excavation or field walking should only be carried out with professional support. This includes a system in place to analyse and process finds, and a way of recording what you have discovered (Category 53). You have to be aware that you will be working with a finite resource, a unique record of the past, that can easily be damaged by inadequately supervised work. Slap dash work methods won't help your relationship with the professional archaeologists on whom the project depends!

So, with the blessing of the professionals, and once you are confident that you have everything necessary in place, you can begin to consider Stage 2.

BEHIND *A detailed drawing by Richard Parker, buildings specialist*

ABOVE *Stewart analysing his finds*
RIGHT *A Dig Village gathering to discuss objectives before the day ahead*

Progressing to Stage 2

Writing an interim report, detailing what you have achieved in Stage 1, will help you to define your goals for the next stage (Category 65). For example, research carried out so far may have identified the potential earliest parts of the village, earthworks that need further survey, or specific buildings that could be researched in greater detail.

As well as consulting a professional archaeologist, you'll need to take into account the natural interests and enthusiasms of your group for specific lines of research. It's much easier to keep people onside if they have a vested interest in the outcomes of the project. In other words, it will help dramatically if your goals align with existing interests within the community, or otherwise add neighbourhood value. Of course, one of the main tenets of Dig Village is that coming together to discover more about local history is beneficial to all and contributes considerably to community wellbeing.

Practical considerations

When creating a project design, it's important to consider financial restraints (see Category 51 on fundraising) and the amount of time and other resources you will have to play with. Be realistic about what can be achieved within these limitations, to ensure the project remains manageable. There's no need to rush things. Take your time and enjoy the project!

  When it comes to active or intrusive fieldwork, there are other logistical considerations too. For instance, do you have express permission from the landowner to survey or field walk the site? Arranging a small-scale test pit dig in someone's back garden has the benefit of being self-contained and relatively easy to organise. This can also be a good way to demonstrate techniques in a controlled environment under professional guidance. However, unless there is some strategic archaeological reason for digging in that specific location, the information it reaps may not be directly relevant to your research.

A back garden being test pitted in Dunster

345

ABOVE *Langport in Somerset, one of many historic towns investigated by Mick Aston*

For more information on progressing a project to its next stage, as we have said, it's well worth reading Mick's *Historic Towns in Somerset*. At the end of each survey, he highlights opportunities for future research in general. In Section 36, he provides an overview of elements of a settlement offering the potential for more detailed work. This will give you a useful pointer to how a professional archaeologist approaches a site. Also take a look at 'Section 3.1: Research Aims' in Dig Village's interim report, *Unearthing Dunster,* to see how we organised our own research.

RIGHT *Our research aims from Dig Village's official 'Unearthing Dunster' report*

The assessment undertaken by Clare Gathercole had already highlighted a number of research topics which would significantly increase the understanding of medieval Dunster. These topics were:

* *Definition of the constituent elements of the town and its full extent*
* *Extent of the precinct of the Benedictine Priory of St George*
* *Location of the harbour(s)*
* *Early history of the castle and its relationship to any earlier activity on the tor and nearby pre-Conquest settlement*
* *Sequence of mills along a leat below the tor*

Using these topics as a guide, a series of research aims were defined in consultation with Rob Wilson-North, Head of Conservation and Access at the Exmoor National Park Authority. Because the intended structure of the project was to be confined to one or two weekends each year, and with a focus on local volunteer engagement and training within the Time Team Academy framework, it was decided to concentrate on the first two topics. Firstly, defining the constituent elements of the town and its extent (thus increasing knowledge of its development in the medieval period), and secondly, the survival and extent of the priory. For the latter, it was felt that investigation of the size and layout of the cloister and its ranges was of prime importance in both informing the understanding of other areas within the precinct (and thus its likely extent), as well as quantifying how much may still survive below ground. However, it was clear that these two identified research topics were not separate themes, as they were interlinked parts of the town. Their physical layout, evolution, and survival were intrinsically inseparable throughout the medieval period, even though the priory was essentially a religious enclave, nestled within the closely protected boundaries of its precinct. Focussing the Dig Village project on these two topics simultaneously was thought to be the most appropriate strategy to adopt. These aims were considered to be achievable within the constraints of both what were to be essentially weekend events and available resources. Small test-pits were adjudged to be the most appropriate archaeological excavation technique, as this was essentially a sampling exercise. It was also clear that throughout the course of the project, potential new insights would be gained which would also contribute to other research aims identified by Mick Aston and Roger Leech, and Clare Gathercole.

To some extent the first Dig Village event in 2012 acted as a feasibility exercise for the project overall. That session had a limited set of aims and very much focussed on the area of the priory. In addition to research, the practicalities of Time Team Academy volunteers working with local volunteers could be explored and resource implications evaluated. The first interim report from the 2012 session, *Dunster Priory, Dunster, Somerset—Dig Village Evaluations*, was produced by Tim Darch (Darch 2014). Some of the results of that session are included in this current report. Following that initial exercise, a seasonal, longer-term project was defined, and the following Dig Village project research aims were formulated:

Figure 4: Medieval Dunster (Aston and Leech 1977)

study was relatively rapid, and had limited aims, it did however provide an understanding of the medieval town that had not been available before. As a result, the platform was provided for further exploration of those ideas in the future.

That exploration began in 2012, when a decision was made by Time Team Digital to undertake an archaeological research project in Dunster after consultation with Mick Aston. The methodology to be adopted was to include a number of techniques, not just excavation. It had been shown successfully at Shapwick in Somerset, that test-pits dug by volunteers under supervision, and combined with other, largely non-invasive activities, was a productive methodology for integrating the work of communities and specialists (Gerrard with Aston 2007). It was clear that similar work at Dunster could repay dividends.

3.1 Research Aims

The primary aim of the Dig Village project was to undertake an archaeological research project directed at investigating the origins and development of the medieval town of Dunster. To this end it was proposed that a series of research questions would be formulated, and a range of archaeological and architectural techniques would be employed to answer those questions.

In order to identify priorities for the project, and to ensure that the results of the research could also be adopted into wider research frameworks, it was necessary to define its aims tightly.

Today: test pitting in Dunster

RIGHT *Stewart overseeing the digging of a test pit*

Every project is unique and what is appropriate for one village may not be for another. A traditional fishing village in Devon is likely to have very different goals compared to a small town from the industrial heartland, with an economy built on textiles. Hopefully, through your initial research in Stage 1, future goals and lines of enquiry will begin to present themselves naturally. Ultimately, wherever your own research takes you, it pays to have a clear plan and set of objectives to drive it forwards and a good system in place to ensure that anything you find can be adequately processed and recorded.

THINGS TO DO

- Consult with a local archaeologist to ensure you are ready to progress to the next stage of active fieldwork.
- Bear in mind the natural interests of your group and how they will inform future research. Do your objectives tie in with existing aims of the wider community?
- Consider the budget you'll need to allow for, as well as time and other limits to your resources.
- Visit the website for useful links.

FURTHER READING

- Michael Aston and Roger Leech, *Historic Towns in Somerset* (1977)
- Section 3.1: Research Aims, *Unearthing Dunster* (2019), pp.8-9

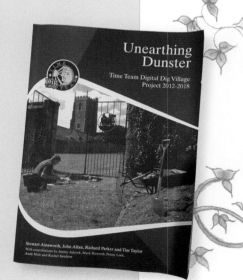

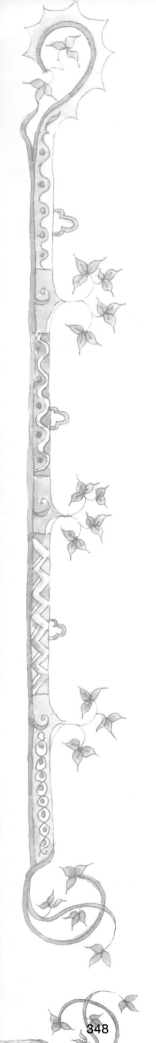

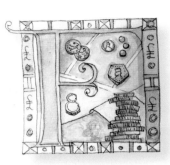

51 RAISING FUNDS

Raising funds for your project is a useful exercise that goes beyond the sole question of hard cash. Working as a group to see how many sources of funding you can access will involve a number of skills that can prove very useful. The first of these is being able to give an account to potential funders of what your project is about and why you are doing it. You will also need to develop some organisational skills in identifying who in your community has the necessary financial acumen to help with this side of the project. There are a surprising number of charitable funds that can be accessed. These can sometimes come from surprising sources, such as money provided by local supermarkets or other commercial organisations as part of their corporate community outreach programme.

Sources of funding

In the case of Dunster, the local community project has managed to secure funds from a wide range of sources. These include a development project based around a new power station; the Exmoor National Park Authority (ENPA); a Tesco community fund; and Somerset County Council. The ENPA, for example, awards small grants up to the value of £2,500 to projects that align with its interests and conservation of the park. So, it's well worth researching similar funds in your area to see if your project might qualify. Ultimately, you may decide that you have done enough work to put an application in to the Heritage Lottery Fund. Of course, completing funding applications can be a laborious task, to say the least. So, when assembling your project dream team (Category 48), look out for someone capable of filling in the endless forms while maintaining some level of sanity!

BELOW *Local events, like Dunster's Apple Day, can be used to raise money for the project*

ABOVE *Brewing ale was a traditional way of raising money for the Church and the poor in Medieval times*

Britain has a long and colourful history of village community fundraising. In Medieval times, money for the Church and associations relating to individual saints, as well the poor, was often raised by **church ales**, when vast amounts of beer and cider were brewed and sold for a small profit. Unfortunately, the Inland Revenue takes a rather dim view of this today!

Nowadays, most villages will have experienced fundraising for the local church or school, by running 'bring and buy' stalls, summer fetes and other small-scale events. Again, these activities can have more value than simply the cash raised, particularly in galvanising the community. Local businesses are often willing to sponsor a community project in exchange for the positive publicity they receive. You might also be able to persuade some of the wealthier members of the community to sponsor a particular aspect of your project, such as a display cabinet or report.

Nominating a treasurer

As the project becomes more formalised, it will be useful to nominate a treasurer to oversee the accounts. Hopefully you can find a professional accountant willing to take on the task, or at least someone who is good with figures and has a keen eye for detail. At some point, it might make sense to set up a community interest company, or other more formal organisation to handle the finances, if necessary. As with any venture that involves money, it's important to be above board and very clear about how the funds are going to be managed and spent!

Church fetes present a great opportunity to both raise money and bring the community together

ABOVE *Jam and wares sold at a village 'bring and buy' sale*

Setting achievable targets

Needless to say, before seeking to raise any money, you should have a fairly clear idea of how much you need, and what it will be used for. Learning to be economical with the limited resources you have is an important part of managing any project. It might be useful to break down your fundraising goals into achievable, 'stepped' levels. Establish 'best' and 'worst' case scenarios, highlighting what could be achieved depending on how much you are able to raise. For example, "raising a relatively small sum will enable the funding of this initial aspect. However, raising an extra amount over and above this, will also enable a more ambitious target to be reached", and so on. This will have the added benefit of sharpening your project's focus and helping to prioritise your goals. Having clear community objectives with an achievable goal to aim towards will be helpful in getting other parties onside. This includes the local press, whose support will be invaluable in spreading the message.

Crowdfunding

An increasingly popular way to raise capital these days is through crowdfunding. Many popular online services have cropped up in recent years, including Kickstarter, Indiegogo and Go Fund Me, each with its own criteria. However, not every platform will be appropriate for this kind of project, so you'll need to establish the one that best fits your needs. Also bear in mind that a localised project is unlikely to attract much global attention. That said, some services such as Crowdfunder specialise in local community-based projects, and can access funds that serve a social purpose. Visit the Crowdfunder website to see the range of projects the organisation has helped to raise money for. Ultimately, for any crowdfunding campaign to be successful, the project needs to have enough momentum. It often hinges on a strong social media presence, so consider carefully whether this is the right approach for your project.

Whatever methods you ultimately decide to use for

INDIEGOGO for Entrepreneurs   How it Works ▾   Resources ▾   About Us ▾   T A CAMPAIGN   Sign U

FEATURED

Webinar: Prototyping 101 - Keys to Success

On average, campaigns with working prototypes raise 186% more than campaigns that don't. Join our webinar with Arrow to learn how to make one.

REGISTER FOR WEBINAR >

‹   ›   1/6

Get the Crowdfunding F Guide

Indiegogo is a launchpad for entrepreneurial ideas. Not sure how to be handy guide walks you through every step of a successful project.

DOWNLOAD GUIDE

Project by project, we're changing the way new ideas come to life.

OPPOSITE & ABOVE *Crowdfunding and social media platforms are fantastic tools for raising funds and spreading the message of your project*

Explore projects   Stories   How it works

✳ Crowdfunder

◯ **Download stunning images** to promote your Crowdfunder project on social media →

For projects that matter this is the best place to crowdfund

So, what are you crowdfunding for?

I'm an individual and I need to quickly raise some money for a personal or charitable cause

0% fee   Get started ❯

My group or I have an idea for a project and it needs some money to make it happen

3% fee   Get started ❯

I want to make a big impact in my community and need £50,000 or more

3% fee   Get started ❯

fundraising, you may find that these activities are the perfect catalyst for getting people excited about the project and bringing new members into the team. As we have said, raising funds can be hard work, but it can also bring the community together and, most importantly, make you learn the skills of presenting your project to the audience that might be able to fund you.

THINGS TO DO

- Firstly, establish how much money you would ideally need to raise, divided into stepped levels for various scenarios.
- Research the various funds and grants that your project is potentially eligible for, on both a local and national level. TIP: Consider supermarkets, national park authorities, local council grants, and the Heritage Lottery Fund.
- Approach local businesses and residents who may wish to become sponsors or patrons of the project.
- You may wish to consider a type of crowdfunding.
- Identify people in your group who are good with accounts or filling out funding applications.

52 LANDSCAPE SURVEY

A key objective of Dig Village is to encourage people to get outside and explore the local landscape. Throughout the book, we've discussed how a simple walk around a field or common land can reveal fascinating insights into local history – if only you know what to look out for. By looking carefully, it can be fairly easy to identify a feature that appears unnatural or at odds with the surrounding topography. Of course, some artificial or manmade features are more immediately identifiable than others, such as barrows and hillforts. Yet, quite often, there are other unexplained ridges and ditches. With the right knowledge and a bit of detective work, you can pick out features you hadn't realised were there. Who knows, for years you might have been walking the dog over a feature of great historic significance!

Look out for irregular lumps in the landscape that warrant further investigation

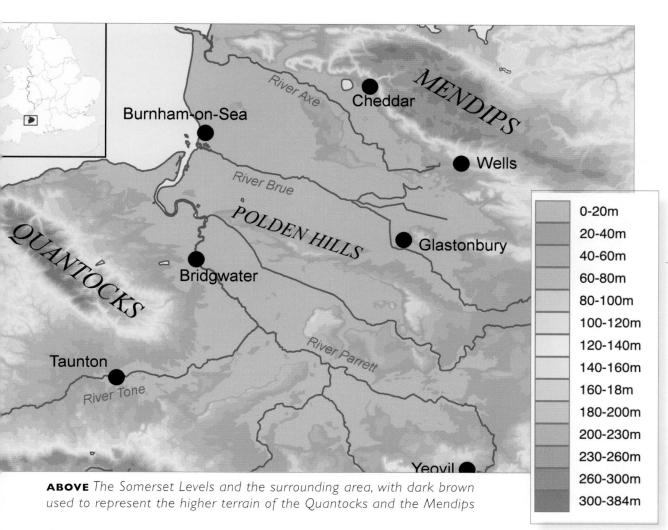

	0-20m
	20-40m
	40-60m
	60-80m
	80-100m
	100-120m
	120-140m
	140-160m
	160-18m
	180-200m
	200-230m
	230-260m
	260-300m
	300-384m

ABOVE *The Somerset Levels and the surrounding area, with dark brown used to represent the higher terrain of the Quantocks and the Mendips*

Topography

A good starting point is to work out the topography of your area, imagining what it would have looked like without the buildings and woodland (Category 4). Which slopes face south? Which areas are liable to flooding? Which features could provide a natural defendable site? It's very useful to be able to convert basic Ordnance Survey data   into a drawing that enables you to estimate the slope of the various hills and valleys around you. The OS website and its various handbooks are excellent resources for interpreting maps and provide information on how you can do this (see also Category 1).

Even in the flattest areas of Britain, small changes in topography can be important. In parts of Somerset or Norfolk prone to flooding, the local population is often only too aware of how critical a small rise in land level can be. Mick particularly enjoyed drawing maps of the areas that interested him. There's nothing like trying to illustrate the local topography on a piece of paper to give you an idea of the key features.

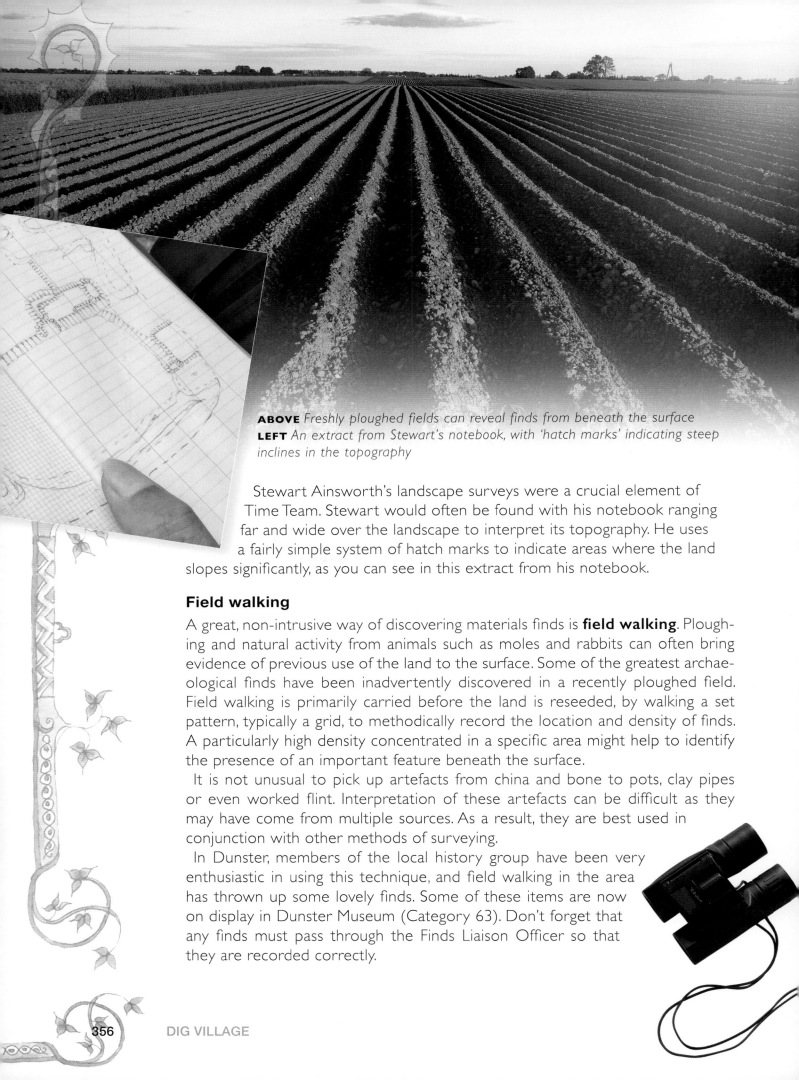

ABOVE *Freshly ploughed fields can reveal finds from beneath the surface*
LEFT *An extract from Stewart's notebook, with 'hatch marks' indicating steep inclines in the topography*

Stewart Ainsworth's landscape surveys were a crucial element of Time Team. Stewart would often be found with his notebook ranging far and wide over the landscape to interpret its topography. He uses a fairly simple system of hatch marks to indicate areas where the land slopes significantly, as you can see in this extract from his notebook.

Field walking

A great, non-intrusive way of discovering materials finds is **field walking**. Ploughing and natural activity from animals such as moles and rabbits can often bring evidence of previous use of the land to the surface. Some of the greatest archaeological finds have been inadvertently discovered in a recently ploughed field. Field walking is primarily carried before the land is reseeded, by walking a set pattern, typically a grid, to methodically record the location and density of finds. A particularly high density concentrated in a specific area might help to identify the presence of an important feature beneath the surface.

It is not unusual to pick up artefacts from china and bone to pots, clay pipes or even worked flint. Interpretation of these artefacts can be difficult as they may have come from multiple sources. As a result, they are best used in conjunction with other methods of surveying.

In Dunster, members of the local history group have been very enthusiastic in using this technique, and field walking in the area has thrown up some lovely finds. Some of these items are now on display in Dunster Museum (Category 63). Don't forget that any finds must pass through the Finds Liaison Officer so that they are recorded correctly.

HOW TO: IDENTIFY SPECIFIC FEATURES IN THE LANDSCAPE

Naturally this can only be a general guide, but there are certain shapes and attributes within the landscape that might help you to correctly identify a specific feature. Also bear in mind that historic features have often been modified for another use by a later settlement. The Romans, for example, have been known to repurpose henges as amphitheatres, while prehistoric barrows have been reused as Medieval rabbit warrens.

1. Barrow: These come in various shapes and sizes, but are often identified by an artificially regular domed mound protruding from the landscape, which may cover a burial.

2. Henge: A circular enclosure on a relatively flat piece of land, which in the past may have had standing stones. Look out for banks on the outside of ditches, as well as entrances.

3. Hillfort: Built on a high, easily defendable site, a hillfort often has a series of banks and ditches that give the effect of terracing.

4. Deerpark: Look in parkland and woodland for embankments and ditches enclosing a large area. Once there would have been a wooden 'pale' fence at the top of the bank.

5. Boundary division: A long, raised embankment, often accompanied by a ditch, as illustrated by Offa's Dyke, Shropshire.

5. Ridges and furrows: These look very different from most other earthworks, with straight parallel lines from ancient ploughing and farming.

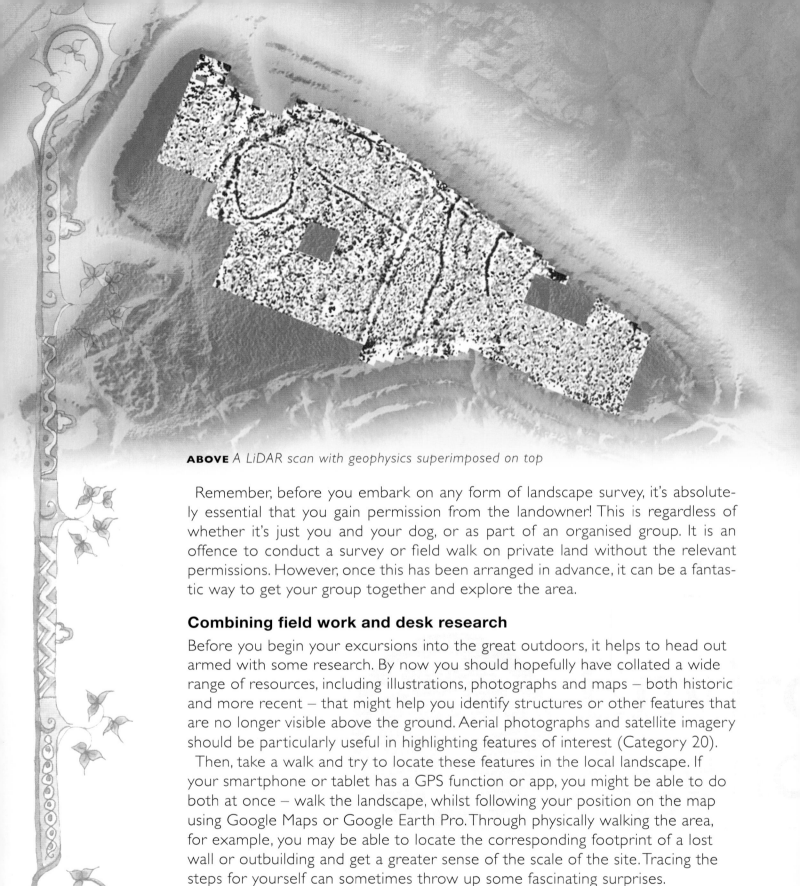

ABOVE *A LiDAR scan with geophysics superimposed on top*

Remember, before you embark on any form of landscape survey, it's absolutely essential that you gain permission from the landowner! This is regardless of whether it's just you and your dog, or as part of an organised group. It is an offence to conduct a survey or field walk on private land without the relevant permissions. However, once this has been arranged in advance, it can be a fantastic way to get your group together and explore the area.

Combining field work and desk research

Before you begin your excursions into the great outdoors, it helps to head out armed with some research. By now you should hopefully have collated a wide range of resources, including illustrations, photographs and maps – both historic and more recent – that might help you identify structures or other features that are no longer visible above the ground. Aerial photographs and satellite imagery should be particularly useful in highlighting features of interest (Category 20).

Then, take a walk and try to locate these features in the local landscape. If your smartphone or tablet has a GPS function or app, you might be able to do both at once – walk the landscape, whilst following your position on the map using Google Maps or Google Earth Pro. Through physically walking the area, for example, you may be able to locate the corresponding footprint of a lost wall or outbuilding and get a greater sense of the scale of the site. Tracing the steps for yourself can sometimes throw up some fascinating surprises.

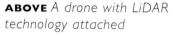

LiDAR scans

In Dunster, we have taken advantage of Stewart's access to LiDAR scans provided by the Environment Agency. LiDAR (light, detection and ranging) is a relatively new tool for surveying sites, using a form of laser scanning to cut through surface features such as trees to create a 3D model of the site.

ABOVE *A drone with LiDAR technology attached*

New forms of the technology can now be mounted on drones, providing a relatively low-cost way of scanning the topography accurately. Much of Great Britain has been has scanned by the Environment Agency using LiDAR, with some data available through the website: ***https://data.gov.uk/publisher/environment-agency***

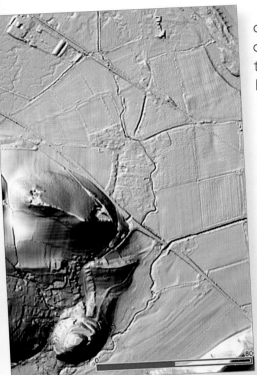

Physical modelling

Plymouth University has recently carried out a project working with schools using a variety of physical media to recreate models of local landscapes. This proved to be a very engaging and illuminating way of understanding local topography. You may wish to embark on a similar project of your own, perhaps liaising with the local school (Category 61).

LEFT *A LiDAR scan showing topography with surface features removed*

THINGS TO DO

- Organise a local field walk, using aerial and historic photography to help inform your search.
TIP: If possible, use GPS to locate your exact position on the map.
- Don't forget to get the permission of the landowner in advance and to report any finds to the local Finds Liaison Officer (Category 60).
- See if you can get hold of LiDAR scans of the area through the Environment Agency.
- Log your discoveries and plot the key dates on your timeline.

53 TEST PITTING

Assuming that your group has done all the initial research and work referred to in the earlier categories, you may find yourself in a position to consider test pitting. This is not something to be undertaken lightly and should not be done without support from professional archaeologists. You will have to prove that you can do the work, as well as process and record anything found responsibly. Nothing can be more damaging to the project than unsupervised, randomly dug test pits.

A test pit in Dunster, dug under the supervision of Dig Village's professional archaeologists

ABOVE *Test pits are dug in 10cm layers, with each layer photographed*

Ultimately, archaeology is the destruction of a site. Once a location has been dug for the first time, it cannot simply be backfilled to provide the same information again. Although further insights can be learned from revisiting the site, that initial dig is the most crucial. As a result, it's essential that each dig is approached methodically and overseen by professional archaeologists, with finds handled carefully and recorded accurately. Many important sites across the globe have been harmed by often well-meaning but over-eager individuals who failed to approach the dig systematically, destroying invaluable information forever! That said, nothing can be more exciting than digging that first test pit and seeing what the earth reveals. When it's done right, its insights are invaluable. Test pitting deserves a whole book on its own, but I hope this will give you an idea of the possibilities!

The value of physical investigation

You can discover a huge amount from archival research, comparing maps and satellite imagery, using advanced scanning technology and unobtrusive observations of the landscape. But there are some questions that cannot be answered without some active digging by a trained professional. A map or satellite image might, for example, identify a potential earthwork or footprint of a building.

But only through digging a portion of the site can this be confirmed and dated to a particular period.

Obviously, it is often hugely impractical to dig an entire site. And, nevertheless, you would want to test a sample area first, perhaps to identify the correct location of a feature such as the foundations of a wall. Hence, archaeologists often first dig a **test pit**, or a series of them, in order to make initial observations, before proceeding with further digging if necessary. Testing a small section also has the benefit of quickly providing insights with minimal intrusion.

A test pit revealing foundations

ABOVE & RIGHT *Carefully sieving the soil for potential finds*

A variety of factors might determine where to site a test pit, or group of them. Typically, the general area will already have been identified as being of interest, perhaps through study of maps or the topography. There are other practical considerations too, such as how easy a site is to access, and whether you have permission to dig in that specific location.

A test pit, typically of a square metre, is dug and record- ed methodically, layer by layer, every 10cm down. This is to ensure the correct sequence of finds is documented within the **stratigraphy** (**strata** being the individual layers of rock and earth). Think of each layer as a distinct chapter in the narrative of the site. These need to be evaluated in the right order to appreciate how the site has evolved over time. Another way to look at it is imagining it's a crime scene – piecing together clues and events in chronological order will help you understand what happened, who did it, and when. Mix up the order and you'll probably reach a completely different conclusion!

A way of collecting samples

various tools
and finds

Test pitting is fundamentally a way of taking samples of materials across a site. In their work at Shapwick, Professor Mick Aston and Teresa Hall supervised nearly 500 test pits, over a period of around ten years! The vast amount of material this generated can proba- bly be imagined, but that material is only as good as the skilled processing

and interpretation that followed it. Fairly subtle differences in dates of pottery can alert you to the fact that a particular area of the village may have had the earliest settlement. Equally, a few fragments of high-status pottery might indicate a connection with a priory or manor house that could afford expensive imports. The analysis of any test pitting depends on having an expert who can look across many seasons of such activity and draw some general conclusions.

In Dunster we dug over 50 test pits, and that was really only scratching the surface. There was always an archaeologist on site to oversee the process, alongside members of the Time Team Academy. Having been provided with training themselves, they proved an invaluable resource in ensuring the integrity of a site.

If you would like to get some firsthand experience, there are services that offer places on training digs. Visit the websites of the Council for British Archaeology and *Current Archaeology* magazine for more information.

ABOVE *Stewart Ainsworth, on hand to oversee the process*

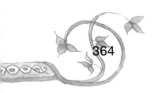

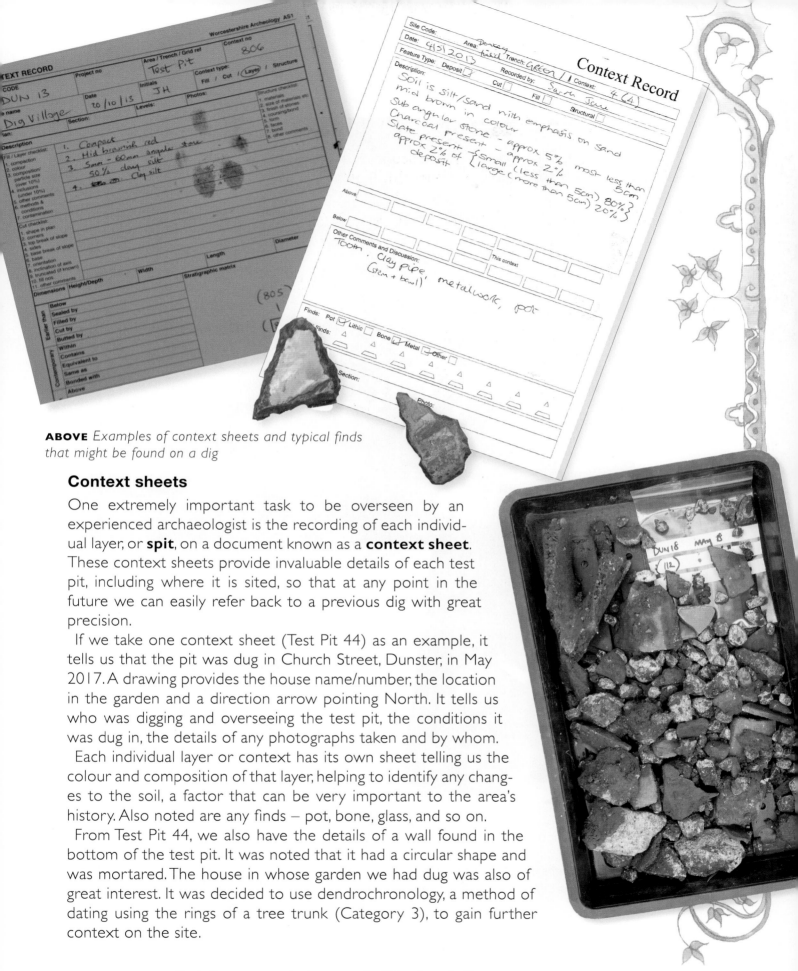

ABOVE *Examples of context sheets and typical finds that might be found on a dig*

Context sheets

One extremely important task to be overseen by an experienced archaeologist is the recording of each individual layer, or **spit**, on a document known as a **context sheet**. These context sheets provide invaluable details of each test pit, including where it is sited, so that at any point in the future we can easily refer back to a previous dig with great precision.

If we take one context sheet (Test Pit 44) as an example, it tells us that the pit was dug in Church Street, Dunster, in May 2017. A drawing provides the house name/number, the location in the garden and a direction arrow pointing North. It tells us who was digging and overseeing the test pit, the conditions it was dug in, the details of any photographs taken and by whom.

Each individual layer or context has its own sheet telling us the colour and composition of that layer, helping to identify any changes to the soil, a factor that can be very important to the area's history. Also noted are any finds – pot, bone, glass, and so on.

From Test Pit 44, we also have the details of a wall found in the bottom of the test pit. It was noted that it had a circular shape and was mortared. The house in whose garden we had dug was also of great interest. It was decided to use dendrochronology, a method of dating using the rings of a tree trunk (Category 3), to gain further context on the site.

RIGHT & OPPOSITE *Finds from a test pit dug near the Tithe Barn in Dunster*

TOP *The locations of individual test pits dug across Dunster*
ABOVE *Members of the Dig Village preparing to dig some test pits*

"I'm a big fan of test pits... If you want to learn something about a place, it needs to be done systematically and be systematically recorded."
Mick Aston

Reporting your findings

There will come a point in any archaeological investigation when an interim report or full report will need releasing (Category 65). Any report is only as good as the original sources it draws upon. So, it's vital that all the context sheets are accurate, down to recording the smallest pieces of pottery, to help prevent misinterpretation of the site.

When it came to compiling the interim report for Dunster (published in January 2019), a wide range of information from the surrounding area was collated and examined. This allowed us to consider each test pit within the wider context, while categorising them into specific areas.

Test Pit 44 fell in to the area '5D', the outer court of the priory precinct. The information taken from this test pit and others in the vicinity helped us to interpret the development of the buildings in the wider precinct, as well as what they were used for. As we've demonstrated from this one example, the information a context sheet contains is invaluable in evaluating an area.

Anyone can dig a hole in their own back garden and find things, from pieces of pottery and clay pipes to glass. But unless these 'test pits' are dug and recorded appropriately, any information found is essentially useless!

ABOVE *Making sure the edges are straight and recording and photographing each layer – note the use of a scale*

THINGS TO DO

- Carry out test pit digging only under the strict supervision of professional archaeologists, and once you have established appropriate locations.
- Remember that irresponsible archaeology is essentially vandalism! It's vital that any intrusive work is carried out appropriately, with the necessary information recorded for posterity.
  - Visit the website to see examples of context sheets. TIP: for further information on Dunster and all its test pits, look for the *Unearthing Dunster* report (published January 2019).

LEFT *A piece of flint*

54 DESERTED MEDIEVAL VILLAGES (DMVS)

It has been estimated that there are over 8,000 deserted Medieval villages in Britain. Once thriving villages and towns, perhaps a bit like the one you currently live in, have gradually disappeared. There has always been something fascinating about rediscovering these lost settlements and it is a subject that has remained close to the hearts of amateur enthusiasts and academics alike. We looked at many examples on Time Team with Mick, and soon discovered that the investigation revealed more than simply the buildings themselves. A search for what has been lost can help to develop an awareness of the various elements that make up a village. It also makes one more aware of the generations of people who have contributed to the growth of

BELOW *Today, lumps and bumps in the landscape are all that remains of Gainsthorpe*

the village. It is sobering to consider that all those years of occupation can disappear over a relatively short period, leaving only faint traces. Hunting for those traces is one of the great detective games for local history enthusiasts.

DMV 'lumps and bumps' at Nether Adber, Somerset

Medieval abandonment

A significant number of villages appear to have been abandoned during the Medieval period. These sites are typically known as '**deserted Medieval villages**' or DMVs. Given that many of the structures in a Medieval village were made of natural materials like cob, clay, wood and thatch, once abandoned it's almost as if they have melted back into the landscape.

Some of the well-known sites, such as Wharram Percy in Yorkshire and Gainsthorpe in Lincolnshire, are now under the protection of English Heritage. Both sites have been scientifically excavated and this enables us to see the relationship between the archaeological evidence and the scars that remain visible above ground. By looking at the research and findings from these sites you will get a much clearer sense of the features to look out for.

BELOW *The ghostly remains of the church at Wharram Percy*

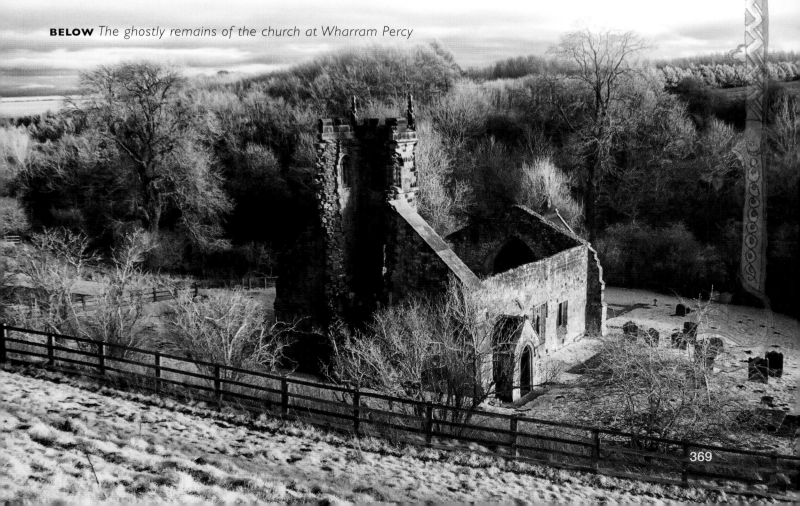

Whilst the buildings may have long since disappeared from sight, the underlying lumps and bumps visible at ground level are a good indicator of what once may have existed there. You can often get the best perspective from above. Aerial photographs or scans from drones and even Google, can reveal the distinct outline of manor houses, smaller dwellings, outbuildings, and sometimes even streets and roads. Archaeologists often use the term 'ladder settlements' to describe the distinctive shape of villages with a set of crofts or small buildings behind which are rectilinear strips of land called **tofts**.

Reasons for abandonment

In the absence of written records or other evidence, it can be difficult to know the exact reason why a particular village was abandoned. However, there's no doubt that a significant cause would be needed. After all, it takes a considerable investment of time and resources to establish a settlement. A number of causes could be responsible for desertion, but likely candidates might include persistent plague, repeated famine or the long-term failure of crops to thrive.

The Black Death (Category 27) from 1348 onwards is often considered to be one of the main causes for desertion. The plague killed up to half of the country's population, and one notable consequence was a diminished and more mobile supply of labour. As a result, villagers who were previously tied to their village or manor found themselves in a position to barter for better wages or move on elsewhere.

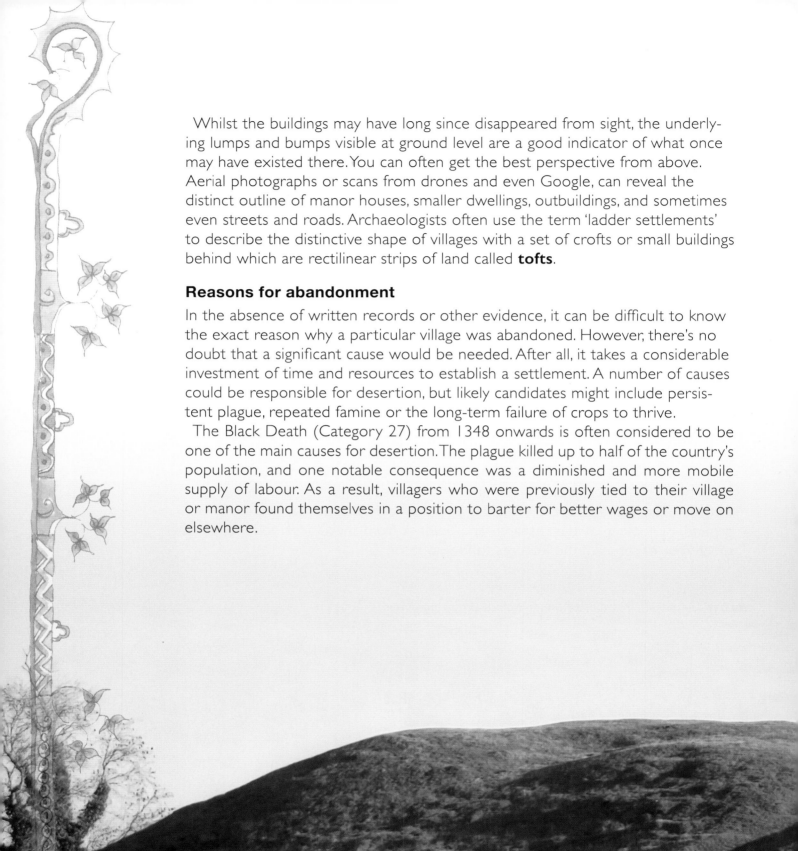

The remains of Yielden Castle, a motte and bailey in Bedfordshire

ABOVE *The Black Death may have contributed to some villages being abandoned*

Faced with rising labour costs, many manorial lords decided to change how they farmed. Large areas of fields were enclosed in order to farm sheep, which could be more profitable than crops. As this approach only required shepherds, everyone else would simply have had to move and find work elsewhere, which in some cases depopulated villages.

It is probably unwise to blame an outbreak of the plague for every village abandoned from the mid-fourteenth century onwards. Of course, entire communities were wiped out by the plague, in some cases in a single summer. However people could have relocated due to a whole combination of factors. A good historian or archaeologist will always look at all the available evidence before arriving at a conclusion! There are other environmental factors to consider that might have led to gradual change in the landscape, rather than a single event causing a sudden 'flight'. Throughout the book we have highlighted the strategic benefits of choosing to settle in a particular location. These include topographic or geological advantages, such as proximity to a water source or the abundance of useful raw materials, like wood or coal. By the same token, communities might have been tempted or even forced to relocate if these advantages had ceased for whatever reason. Natural phenomena like coastal erosion or a river's course naturally shifting away from the village, or manmade issues created by the villagers, perhaps overuse of the natural resources, might be accountable. Today, we are increasingly becoming aware of the long-term effects of deforestation on climate and fertility of soil. A once thriving habitat can become barren in just a few generations.

DMVs near Dunster

Whilst Dunster itself has thrived over the centuries, we don't have to look too far to find some deserted Medieval villages. Badgworthy, on Exmoor, for example, was a small settlement consisting of 14 structures and a field system that are still visible today in aerial photos. The last written reference of Badgworthy comes from 1430, when the village was described as 'run down'. Today all that remains is a few lumps and bumps in the fields. Whilst researching the area around Dunster, it was great to find a reference that Mick Aston had made to a series of strip fields that might have been evidence of a larger settlement that once existed.

Lumps and bumps

DMVs can be found all over the country and there are many still waiting to be discovered. Maybe while walking around the local landscape you have noticed a series of unexplained ridges or lumps and bumps. There may be many explanations, such as a prehistoric site or something relatively modern, but you might just have evidence of a DMV. Firstly, have a look in the local records office to see if there is any reference to them, or if the site has been investigated previously. You will need to take the map reference with you (Category 1). In addition, the names of any fields, if you have them, may be a useful indicator of an earlier lost settlement. Looking at aerial photographs or satellite imagery might reveal hints of a possible village or settlement. Finding the exact location on Google Earth is a relatively easy way to get started. If you do find references to a DMV, establish if the settlement had a name. This name might still be used locally as the name of a field, feature, or otherwise have another connection to the area. As always, it helps to connect with other Dig Village enthusiasts who are carrying out similar research and exchange ideas with them.

ABOVE *A field showing a Medieval ridge and furrow system*

This category allows us to refer to two of the great heroes of local history, Maurice Beresford and John Hurst, whose book, *Deserted Medieval Villages*, is a must read for anybody interested in the subject. It gives numerous examples and in the back is a gazetteer, which provides references by county to DMVs with map references. Today, a Deserted Medieval Village Research Group carries on the work of Beresford and Hurst.

LEFT *John Hurst and Maurice Beresford in Wharram Percy in 1989, taken by Mick Aston!*

THINGS TO DO

- Search the local landscape for lumps and bumps that might be evidence of a deserted Medieval village.
- Look at aerial photography or satellite imagery (Google Earth can be a very useful tool). Perhaps someone you know has a drone that can be used to survey local fields. Please check that you have the appropriate permission from landowners and are aware of any restrictions in your area.
- Visit the local records office to find information on any known DMVs in the region.
- Log your discoveries and plot the key dates on your timeline.

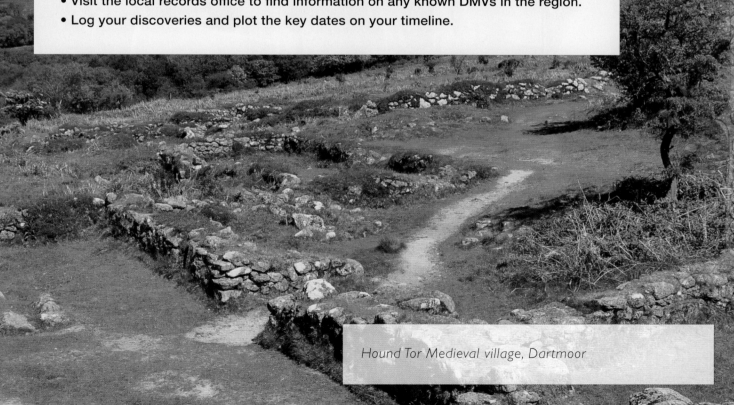

Hound Tor Medieval village, Dartmoor

55 OLDEST FAMILIES

The past decade has witnessed a huge upsurge in people taking an interest in their family history. Ever more online services have become available, enabling us to trace our family histories through census and parish records online with relative ease. Often, a visit to the parish archives in person will allow you to access records that go even further back than those currently held online. With some digging and a bit of patience, you may be able trace the family name back several hundred years.

ABOVE *A collection of old family photos*

Tracing a family back in time

Researching family history is known as **genealogical research**, and it can incorporate a mixture of historical records, memories from living relatives and genetic analysis. How do we go about tracing the oldest families that originate from a particular village or town?

Dunster is blessed with particularly good written records of its more prominent historic residents, the de Mohuns and the Luttrells. As we highlight in Category 16, the de Mohuns first entered the record in Domesday, following the Norman invasion, almost a thousand years ago.

The de Mohun family's coat of Arms

Following the old adage that 'history is written by the winners', it's perhaps no surprise that the families of higher social status typically have a greater wealth of written records. For the ruling classes, proclaiming the family's pedigree and links to great leaders or dominant families has long been a means of asserting their authority and legitimacy to rule over others. Showing a clear lineage over generations set a precedent and reinforced the idea that their place in the social order was ingrained in history.

BELOW *Proud displays of pedigree have helped families to assert their power and legitimacy, as highlighted by this wonderful sixteenth century example of Ludwig Herzog von Württemberg's family tree*

Tracing the lesser known families far back into history may require a little more perseverance. Most average Medieval villagers would have been illiterate, and so unlikely to leave many of their own written records behind. What's more, their lives were perhaps not regarded as particularly noteworthy by contemporary chroniclers. In fact, much of the information we do have of specific individuals from the wider population throughout history comes from attempts by those of higher social status to either tax them or prosecute them for some minor misdemeanour in the courts!

Set a starting point and work backwards

As a general rule, genealogists begin with the present and work backwards. So start by looking at some of the surnames of current village residents. Find a name that appears to be relatively common, and preferably another that is less widespread. In theory, an individual family with a more unusual surname should be easier to trace back further in time, without getting them confused with unrelated individuals with the same surname. Just looking at the telephone directory can be a useful starting point.

In the case of Dunster, we found three families with the surname 'Sully'. This sparked our interest because we knew from our existing research that one of the men hanged following the Monmouth Rebellion was called William Sully. Was this just a coincidence? This knowledge immediately gave our search historical relevance and a potential family connection to the area going back over 300 years.

ABOVE *A burial list from St John's Church, Fort William (1843)*

LEFT *The Sully family name recorded on a plaque outside Dunster Memorial Hall, which now houses the museum* **BELOW** *Genealogy websites*

Once you have chosen a family, collect all the family documents you can and question any relatives. Older members of the family may know about letters, diaries, papers and photographs. They may be able to estimate dates and locations, even if they cannot give exact details. Even vague remarks may prove to be unexpectedly useful at a later stage. Make a list of all the family names, including maiden names, as far back as the eldest generation can remember. This list will create the foundation for your future documentary research.

Birth, death and marriage

Three of the key events in life – certainly as far as the state has traditionally been concerned – are birth, death and marriage. For the genealogical researcher, they can perhaps be seen as the Holy Trinity! It was Thomas Cromwell who ordered that burials, marriages and baptisms be recorded from 1538 onwards, owing largely to the monetary value of the death tax. Both Henry VIII and Cromwell were ever alert to the possibilities of extracting money on whatever pretence!

ABOVE *Thomas Cromwell, by Holbein (circa 1532)*

Most historic Church of England parish records have been deposited in local records offices, although a few remain within parish churches, and access to the original registers is mostly free. Some have been transferred online and can be found at either **www.familysearch.org** or the National Archives website. You'll also find more information for your area in the National Index of Parish Registers.

Since July 1837, births, marriages, and deaths have been officially recorded by the General Register Office (GRO). Check the GRO website to find out where certificates are available (**www.gro.gov.uk**). Some commercial organisations such as **www.findmypast.co.uk** and **www.ancestry.co.uk** have launched digital databases of these certificates that can be viewed on a pay per view or subscription basis.

RIGHT *Baptism register for St Stephen's Church, Norwich, showing entries between July 1796 and January 1797*

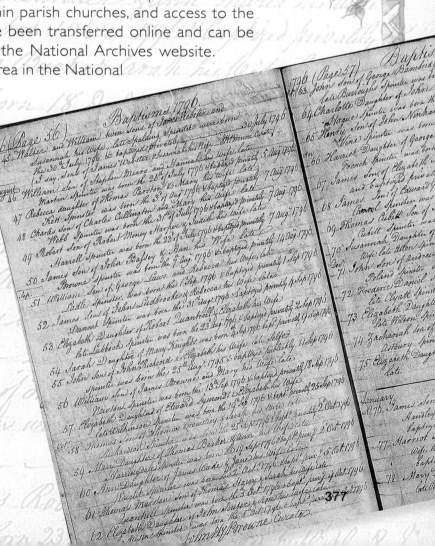

377

Death and taxes

Death creates a lot of paperwork! Much valuable information can be gained from probate records, wills and administrations. You can search online for records of wills from 1858 (*https://probatesearch.service.gov.uk*). Wills before 1858 fell under the jurisdiction of the Church court and are mostly likely to be found in local archives.

Inquisitions Post Mortem Records, which can be viewed at the National Archives, are another useful source for tracing families. These mainly apply to landowners and prominent individuals with a degree of wealth. That said, it can be surprising to discover that some of the poorest individuals were required to leave a statement of their goods and chattels. In the case of Dunster, we have a will for one Gilbert Scut, dated 1369, which revealed such details as his bequest to his family of:

> *"one velvet gown… one sword with its sheath…*
> *one bow with its arrows.*
> *To John my Son, my bed and my plough.*
> *To Alice my younger daughter,*
> *one bed and one new brazen pot."*

In this example, we discover the names of Gilbert's children, which might spur additional research, while the objects he bequeathed give an idea of his wealth and status.

In your research into this area, you might find references to the escheator, the officer responsible for administrating the property of the deceased. It's from this that we get the modern word executor.

Next, take a look at the burial index for your local church. With a bit of luck, it will already have been digitised, but if not you should hopefully find it at your local records office. The National Burial Index (NBI) contains over 18 million entries from registers across England and Wales.

RIGHT *William Shakespeare's will (1616)*

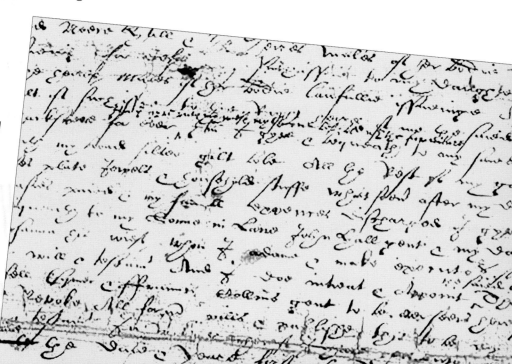

ABOVE *A census taker visits a Romani family, Netherlands (1925)*

Local census records

Another good place to start is the local census records, which are recorded by address. Focussing on your village, or even a specific street, you can go back to the 1700s in general without too much effort online. County directories and street directories can also be useful tools for historic research, as they often give the names of owners or occupiers. From then on, it is a case of again visiting your local records, or diocesan office to look at the parish records.

A **dioceses** is an area under the pastoral care of a bishop of the Christian church, the word being derived from the Greek, *dioikesis*, meaning 'administration'. You will probably need to make an appointment to access either of these resources, but it is worth doing as records can often go back to the fifteenth century and earlier.

Official census returns are incredibly useful documents because they provide a snapshot of a family on a particular night. The first official nationwide census occurred in 1801, which was then updated every 10 years. The first few were largely just statistics. However, from 1841 onwards they include important details such as each member of the household, their relationship to the head of the family, ages, occupations and birthplaces. A nationwide set of census returns is held at the National Archives in Kew, London. However, many local records offices will hold copies of the records relating to your surrounding area, so it is worth checking there first.

Howard 1952

Your grandfather Newman on the left

ABOVE *Look out for dates and other useful details written on the back of old family photos*

Other avenues to explore

Of course, there are countless other historic documents that record the names of local inhabitants. As well as Domesday, you mind find references to individuals or families you are researching in other taxation records, court rolls, receipts for goods and services, paperwork relating to membership of guilds, apprenticeship documents, minutes from meetings, newspaper articles and even personal diaries or letters to be found in various collections, whether public or private. These all might prove valuable in your research and sometimes it helps to try a different approach once you've exhausted traditional avenues.

When searching for a particular name or date, be aware of both human error and the fact that levels of literacy varied greatly throughout the ages. There are often several alternative spellings (or abbreviations) for the name of the same person. Even William Shakespeare's name was spelt in various ways throughout his own lifetime and in later centuries. Documents have been

"Nobody could spell, it was all phonetic. Often what's on the grave slabs is totally different to what's in the burial register. There's usually quite a discrepancy."

Mick Aston

ABOVE *Stinchcombe Hill in Gloucestershire gives rise to the toponymic surname*

found referring to him as Shaggespear, Shakespole and Shaksper! So, if you aren't having much luck with Taylor, for example, then try searching similar variations, like Tailor, Tayler, Taylour, even Tyler, and so on. Equally with dates, it helps to search around the specific date of interest, bearing in mind that the day on which an event was actually recorded may be very different to the day when it happened.

As we note in Category 9, many surnames are 'toponymic', which means they derive from geographical features in the landscape. If you're lucky, you might be able to trace that surname to one precise location, such as Stinchcombe in Gloucestershire.

Field research

Don't just limit your research to the archives, when you can embark on some field research. A walk around the local graveyard, for example, is a simple but effective way of identifying some of the local prominent families. See if you can find the oldest marked grave in the village. Of course, there would have been many who didn't have the luxury of a marked grave. However, more prosperous families would have had larger gravestones or even more elaborate monuments. Equally, there might be further clues inside the church building itself. Wealthy patrons may have had chapels or crypts dedicated to them. If anything, this may provide a starting point for further research.

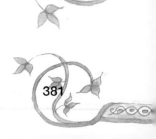

We note in Category 35 that World War memorials are useful sources of surnames of local inhabitants. See if any of these more recent names correspond to the older gravestones in the churchyard. In Dunster, for example, we found references to the Sully family mentioned earlier.

Final thoughts

Finally, remember to keep a record of every document that you look at and the information you have gained from it. As well as proving invaluable to your own research, you can also enter the data onto online genealogical software, which will help others with their research. Most of the major genealogy software packages can be downloaded free of charge as trial versions. Try several until you find one that suits you.

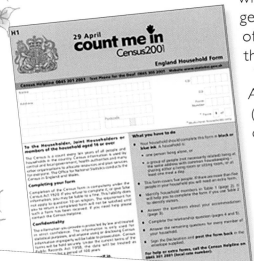

Two key websites when searching online are Access to Archives (**www.A2A.org.uk**) and the National Archives (**www.nationalarchives.gov.uk**). Although online databases are good catalogues, they will rarely contain all of the information within a particular document, so make sure you go and examine the records yourself.

LEFT *The National Census form of 2001*
BELOW *An example of a family tree website home page*

The Society of Genealogists in London is well worth visiting. It has a remarkable library that collects research notes from other genealogists as well as published family histories and biographies, and special collections of genealogical research.

One area that has been growing in popularity in recent years is genetic analysis. Many over the counter DNA testing kits are now available. These kits provide revealing insights into people's heritage, such as whether they have Viking or Norman genes, for example. Sometimes they throw up some unexpected results!

Perhaps village residents have already looked into their own lineage. It's worth asking whether interested parties are willing to share this research with the wider community.

ABOVE *The Society of Genealogists, London with their logo*

THINGS TO DO

- Look at local census records throughout the years, as well as the local burial index and probate records.
- Other local records such as court roles, administrative accounts and so on will provide names of former inhabitants or people associated with the community.
- Look at the names in the local graveyard and inside the church, as well as local memorials dedicated to former inhabitants, such as war memorials. You might find some correlation between prevalent surnames of the area.
- Ask whether any local inhabitants have conducted their own research into family trees that can be incorporated into your research.
- Visit the Dig Village website for weblinks on genealogy and tracing families, including information on producing your own family tree.
- Log your discoveries and plot the key dates on your timeline.

56 HEROES & VILLAINS

All the best stories throughout history have a hero or villain at their centre. It's likely there will have been some of these in your own community over the centuries. It can be very useful to uncover these kinds of people, who may have made a significant contribution to your settlement's story. Equally, it may just be a bit of fun! These individuals and their escapades bring colour to the past, putting flesh on the bare bones of the story. If you imagine a timeline featuring a selection of these characters, your village history will instantly become more exciting and enticing. The idea of heroes and villains is a simple but effective way to frame your research, a hook to pull others in who might not have previously shared an interest in the past.

RIGHT & ABOVE *Tom Cobley, famed for riding his old horse to Widecombe Fair, collecting various villagers en route, until the horse collapsed and died*

Dunster's heroes and villains

Ask yourself a question: who would you consider to be a hero or villain of your village? In the case of Dunster, the Royalist army that occupied the castle during the Civil War in November 1645, managed to survive a siege lasting around six months.

The Parliamentary troops were so impressed that, when the castle finally surrendered, the governor Colonel Francis Wyndham was allowed to lead his men out with flags flying and drums beating. His heroism was considered so exceptional that a number of pubs in the West Country are named after him.

Another candidate for a group of heroes are the townspeople of Dunster who, in protest against the overweening power of the Church during Henry VII's reign, took down the ropes in the church tower to silence the bells (Category 12). We know their names, and it's right that they should be celebrated as heroes. They included Sir William Harries, Thomas Upcote, Thomas Codogan, John Wyther, Adam Wilkyns, William Crasse, Symond Pers, John Gryme, John Philippis, John Paynter, John Morgan, and Martyn Glover. A brass in the floor of Dunster's church still commemorates one of the perpetrators.

As a villain, we might have chosen Judge Jeffreys, the seventeenth century 'hanging judge' who sentenced three local men to be hanged on the gallows for their part in the Monmouth Rebellion (Category 36).

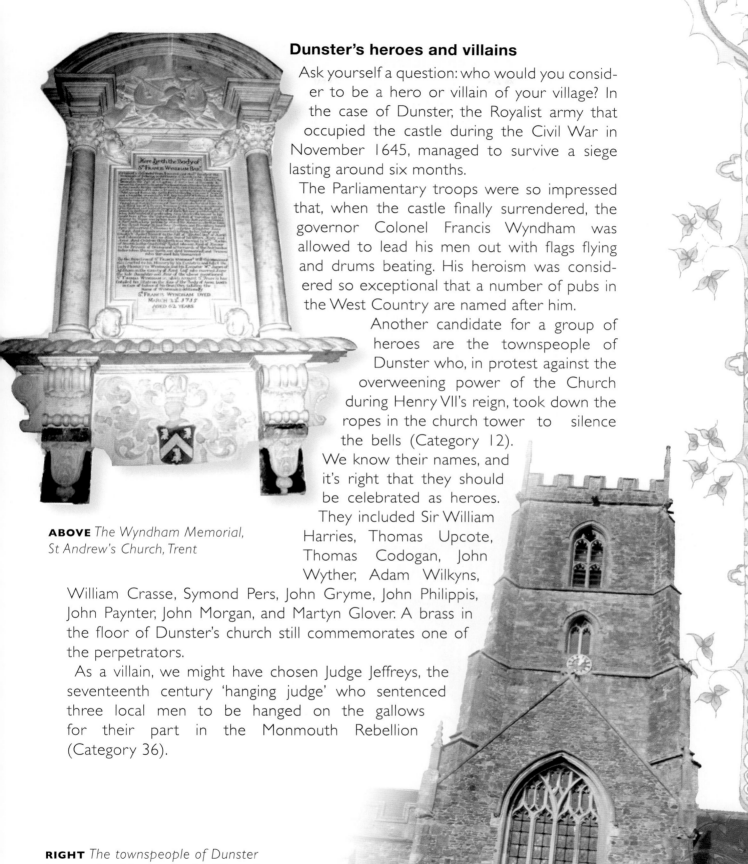

ABOVE *The Wyndham Memorial, St Andrew's Church, Trent*

RIGHT *The townspeople of Dunster became local heroes in the fifteenth century, when they cut the ropes of the bells in protest against the power of the Church*

Identifying the key characters

But how do you go about finding heroes and villains? There's no right or wrong approach and you'll probably stumble upon a few without really looking. As your research progresses, certain characters will emerge who have shaped the history of your village, for better or worse. Court rolls can be extremely revealing of grizzly details. Newspaper archives are a fantastic source for identifying the everyday people who have achieved amazing feats, often against the odds. Maybe someone saved another from drowning, harboured a political or religious fugitive, or fought against developers to preserve the character of their village.

ABOVE *An eighteenth century depiction of Robert Kett who became a folk hero for leading a rebellion in 1549 against the enclosure of land*

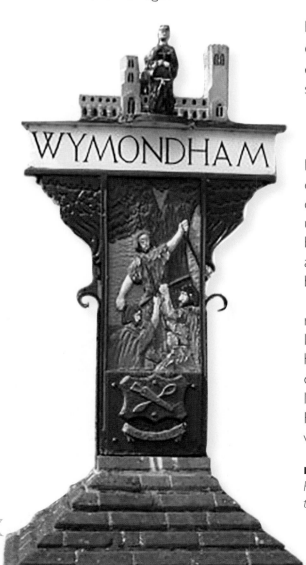

Hero or troublemaker?

Of course, someone's hero may be another person's villain, depending on which side of the fence, or social divide, they are standing on. Throughout history, landowners have traditionally played the role of baddies. There are countless records of local lords encroaching on the livelihoods of their tenants, whether through enclosing common land or otherwise treating them unfairly. At the same time, individuals who have been vilified as troublemakers by the authorities have been regarded as heroes by their fellow villagers for making a stand.

Robert Kett, who led a sixteenth century rebellion against landowners for enclosing land, is a good example. Kett, who ironically had fenced in land himself, was originally one of the rebels' targets. Yet he offered to lead their revolt and became a folk hero. His efforts would cost him his life, and he was hanged by the authorities for treason.

LEFT *A monument commemorating Kett's Rebellion in Wymondham, Norfolk, where the uprising began*

War heroes

The World Wars made reluctant heroes of millions of men and women the world over. Your village no doubt had its share of men who sacrificed their lives in the trenches of the Somme or over the skies of Berlin. But perhaps some made contributions that directly affected your community closer to home.

These might be 'land girls', members of auxiliary units, families who took in evacuees from the city, or a brave individual who helped others during a bombing raid. Countless civilian heroes played a significant contribution to the respective war efforts, often without reward.

Alternatively, there might have been a traitor in the midst, feeding information to the enemy.

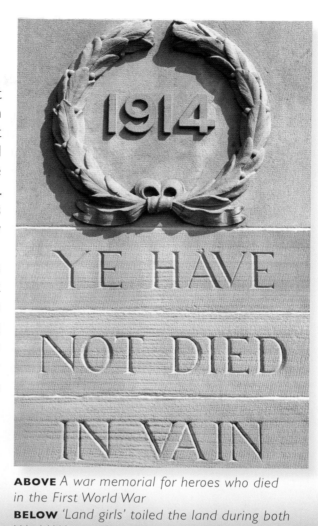

ABOVE *A war memorial for heroes who died in the First World War*
BELOW *'Land girls' toiled the land during both World Wars to keep the nation fed*

387

Focussing on a particular event or period, such as this, can be a good way of identifying the heroes and villains. Revisit some of the key events throughout the nation's history: the Industrial Revolution, the English Civil War, the Reformation, the coming of the Spanish Armada or, more recently, the Women's Suffragette movement. When faced with a particular challenge, opportunity or threat, how did people respond? Keep an eye out for references to mill breakers or machine wreckers whose livelihoods were threatened by the opening of a new mill or factory; a local militia raised to fend off Parliamentary attack; a farmer who incited rebellion; a martyr who denounced the new prayer book; or a local who joined the Navy to fight the Spanish.

Engaging a wider audience

Of course, it's all too easy to oversimplify a complex situation into black and white or right and wrong. Ultimately everyone has their own circumstances that cause them to take a particular stance or spur them into action. Some have argued that even Judge Jeffreys was simply following legal protocol of the time in sentenc-

Time Team's Victor Ambrus, illustrating historic heroes and villains

ing death for treason. But highlighting the supposed 'goodies and baddies' of your community is a handy and often revealing way to spark debate and get others interested in the project. Identifying villains can help to give us a greater appreciation of the harsh realities of former times.

On a more positive note, everyone loves a good story of the underdog defeating the oppressive 'powers that be'! When you come to consider community outreach (Category 59) and museum displays (Category 63), having a few 'headlines' and gripping or inspiring stories about individuals will be invaluable in attracting a wider audience for your finds.

ABOVE & BEHIND *Hereward the Wake fighting Normans (1865)*

THINGS TO DO

- As your research progresses, make note of the characters who stand out for taking a particular stance, perhaps saving the village from a specific threat.
- See how individuals responded to particular situations or key events in the Dig Village timeline.
- Perhaps use your findings as a framework in your community outreach or museum displays, to grab the attention of a wider audience.
- Log your discoveries and plot the key dates on your timeline.

RIGHT *Victor Ambrus's illustration of hangings*

57 MYTHS & LEGENDS

Every village has its own unique local legends and stories that have been passed down from generation to generation. Of course, some have a greater grounding in fact than others. These colourful tales tend to take on a life of their own, as they become increasingly embellished with each retelling. Their narratives can be viewed as part of a wider, ancient folk oral tradition. Whilst there is invariably a regional twist, often there are stark similarities and recurrent themes in tales from different parts of the country. Whether fact or fiction, these tales reveal fascinating insights into the superstitions, world views and environments of the people at the time of their inception.

Men-an-Tol in Penwith, West Cornwall, possibly dates back to the late Neolithic and is steeped in myth and legend

OPPOSITE *An illustration of Molly Leigh's cottage*

Real-life origins of folk traditions

While the authenticity of these gripping yarns should be taken with a pinch of salt, we can trace the real-life origins of some folk traditions. For instance, the churchyard in Burslem, Stoke-on-Trent, contains the eighteenth century grave of Molly Leigh. There's nothing particularly unusual in that, except that the grave was turned after Molly's burial from east-west to north-south.

Molly lived a reclusive, isolated existence, her only companion being a blackbird often perched on her shoulder. She rarely attended church after being shunned by most of the villagers. As a result of her unconventional lifestyle and allegations of sorcery around the village, including turning beer sour, she was accused by the local parson of being a witch.

Molly died in 1746 before being brought to trial. However, after her burial the blackbird is said to have become a nuisance, so the priest and others visited Molly's cottage to try to capture the bird. Upon arrival, they supposedly discovered Molly sitting in her rocking chair by the fire knitting. The men all fled. They re-opened Molly's grave the next day and buried the captured blackbird in the coffin with her, turning the whole grave from Christian east-west to north-south. The legend prevails today, with children being told that if they sing "Molly Leigh, Molly Leigh, chase me round the apple tree" while running around the grave, then Molly's spirit will appear!

Legends of Dunster Castle

The English Civil War proved fertile ground for legends, and Dunster Castle's involvement in the conflict gave rise to an enduring folk tale. As we note in Category 29, a hole in the woodwork of the Yarn Market is said to have been caused by a cannonball fired during this period. When Dig Village first arrived in Dunster, the team were regaled with the legend that the cannon that fired the shot may be still buried somewhere in the town. Unfortunately, despite our concerted efforts using geophys equipment over the last few years, we have so far been unable to locate it. The legend lives on!

Another of Dunster's mysteries is the seven foot tall skeleton found in an ancient dungeon beneath the gatehouse, as recounted in Category 36. No-one knows how the giant ended up there, but tales of haunting wails and sightings of other ghostly apparitions around the castle continue.

ABOVE *Goram the Giant, Bristol*

A frequently recurring theme across Britain is that of the 'grey lady', with practically every region laying claim to its own local variation. Dunster Castle is no exception!

A reflection of the times

Dunster's tales highlight how legends often stemmed from a specific event or wider concerns of the time. The New Forest has its own legend of Dame Alice Lisle, who was beheaded in Winchester for sheltering fugitives following the Monmouth Rebellion in 1685. Her ghost is still said to haunt her home of Moyles Court, near Ringwood, and the Eclipse Inn, where she spent her final night.

LEFT & RIGHT *Alice Lisle stayed at the Eclipse Inn, Winchester, the night before her beheading*

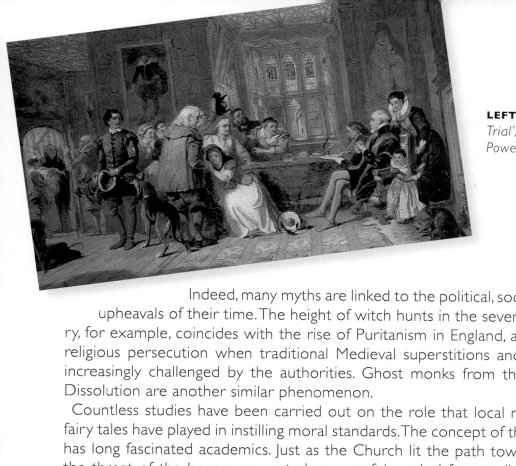

Indeed, many myths are linked to the political, social or religious upheavals of their time. The height of witch hunts in the seventeenth century, for example, coincides with the rise of Puritanism in England, a time of great religious persecution when traditional Medieval superstitions and beliefs were increasingly challenged by the authorities. Ghost monks from the time of the Dissolution are another similar phenomenon.

Countless studies have been carried out on the role that local mythology and fairy tales have played in instilling moral standards. The concept of the 'bogey man' has long fascinated academics. Just as the Church lit the path towards salvation, the threat of the bogey man acted as a useful symbol for warding villagers off evil. This beast crops up in various guises throughout the country, often sharing certain common characteristics, yet taking a form that reflects regional considerations, whether local traditions or, as we shall see, features of the landscape itself. Mawnan Smith in Cornwall, for instance, is famed for the 'owl man' that guards the churchyard, while many regions are said to home to a giant, like Goram of Bristol and Cormoran of West Cornwall.

Geographic features

In the cases of these giants, the legends are linked to a local natural geographic feature: the 'Giant's Footprint' at Henbury Gorge and St Michael's Mount, respectively. Another famous example is the Giant's Causeway, Northern Island.

RIGHT *The Giant's Causeway, Northern Ireland*

Equally, other topographic features like lochs and coastal regions give rise to accounts of mythical sea beasts, from Morgowr in Cornwall to Nessie of Loch Ness. Open countryside and moorland can also provide the perfect setting for legends to manifest. Perhaps a modern incarnation of the historic 'black dog' apparition, a recent phenomenon is that of 'phantom big cats'. These allusive animals, notably the Beast of Bodmin Moor, have been reported to roam the countryside and ravage livestock. Are they ancient beasts, animals that have escaped from zoos or private collections, elaborate hoaxes, or simply the product of deluded minds? On more than one occasion, emergency services have been called to challenge what has turned out to be an oversized cuddly toy!

Megalithic monuments often assume supernatural legends and supposed magical powers over the centuries too, from Stonehenge to Men-an-Tol. Sometimes these tales centre around the idea of individuals who have been turned to stone, perhaps as punishment for dancing on the Sabbath.

An interesting framework for presenting research

But why do these myths still matter today? Other than the historic social insights they provide, many myths have a very real impact on the local tourist trade. Ghouls and ghosts are great for business! An entire industry has sprung up around the legend of King Arthur, in communities such as Glastonbury

ABOVE *The legend of King Arthur is big business in the village of Tintagel, supposedly the site of his birth*

Nessie of Loch Ness, one of Britain's most popular and enduring legends

394

and Tintagel, for example. Most historic towns and cities offer a ghost tour.

What's more, similar to the idea of heroes and villains discussed in Category 56, the notion of myths and legends can be a valuable and fun way of framing your research. The more engaging you can make your findings the better!

Find out what you can about legends from your area. These tales might recount anything from witch burnings and famous visitors to buried treasure, smugglers or the sounds of bells in the wind where a chapel once stood. Look into these stories to see if there is any foundation for them. Determine if they are historic or more recent, and if they can be linked to a specific event or period, whether locally or nationally. Court records may reveal interesting facts about local disputes or why people were put to death (such as the case of Alice Lisle).

Compare the local legends with stories from other villages to identify potential common themes. As we have noted, when some of these stories are looked into, it's surprising just how similar they are across the country.

ABOVE *The Three Crowns in Chagford is said to be haunted by a ghost from the Civil War*

THINGS TO DO

- Ask residents about any local myths and legends that they are aware of. Next try to determine any real-life people or events that they are founded on.

TIP: Court records and newspaper archives may be helpful. Look for gravestones of genuine residents.

- The area's links to major events (such as the Civil War or the Dissolution of the Monasteries) is a good place to begin your research. Known prehistoric monuments often have their own set of legends attached, too.
- Log your discoveries and plot the key dates on your timeline.

58 QUESTIONS & ANSWERS

As you're reading this book now, you no doubt have many questions about your village. Often, the more you discover, the more questions arise as a result! Many of the answers you seek should be found somewhere within these pages. If not, then at the very least we'll hopefully have pointed you in the right direction to find them. In reality, though, there's not always one simple answer, particularly when trying to piece together and make sense of scattered fragments from the past. So, helping to solve those really tricky challenges is where the Dig Village community comes into its own. As well as our experts, the other member villages are a wealth of information to tap into – our biggest asset is you! Together, we can share our collective experience and expertise, and put the pieces of the puzzle together. So, what would you like to know?

Archives

Questions come in many forms. If you are trying to find out a specific piece of information relating to your village — say, the date of an event or the name of a noted individual — then the answer, if it exists, is most likely to be found in a recorded archive somewhere.

Throughout the book, we've highlighted various archives that are particularly helpful when researching a specific category. One of the most useful archives across most categories is your local public records office. You might soon become a regular face, so the more you understand what you're looking for, the more likely you'll be received with sympathy. In general, you'll be talking to people who are endlessly busy, answering questions. So, make certain you've done your homework before you arrive! (See Category 60 for advice on liaison with archaeologists and other professionals.)

With increasing digitisation of various archives, many of the answers you'll need can be found online without leaving your armchair. Make use of our official website, which contains list of archives and links to useful online sources. As we highlight in Category 21, the Victoria County History and the Historic Environment Record Archive are incredibly useful resources too, with lots of information now available online.

ABOVE & OPPOSITE *Libraries, your local records office and online archives will be some of your best friends throughout your project*

The Dig Village community

If you're still stuck, then the next step is to talk to enthusiasts from other villages who are carrying out their own research. It's very likely that others across the country have been asking similar questions and finding their own ways to answer them – sometimes through trial and error, or with a little good fortune!

Perhaps, for example, someone has discovered a unique way of locating the earliest doctor, pharmacist, nurse or wise woman. Use our social media channels to start a new discussion asking the community how they have resolved these challenges. Likewise, if you have stumbled upon an interesting research insight, why not post a thread sharing it, so others can learn from it too?

One of the key tenets of Dig Village is building a community; a network of like-minded people, sharing finds, discoveries and insights for the benefit of all. Why do all the hard work independently, when others are doing the same thing? Think of Dig Village as the hub that brings everyone together – the Mumsnet for amateur historians and archaeologists, if you will!

Ask the experts

Of course, every now and then, there will be a really tough question that needs the input of an expert. Over the years, Time Team and Dig Village have worked with countless experts across the country and further field. Some of them are available to answer your questions. Typically, their expertise will be most valuable in answering questions relating to strategy. It's probably not a good idea to ask them something you could easily find out yourself with a quick Google search! So, once you've explored other avenues, try the 'ask the expert' function on the Dig Village website. We can't guarantee that we'll be able to help every enquiry, but we'll certainly endeavour to get back to you as soon as possible.

Framing your questions

In all of your research, bear in mind that the kind of questions you ask may dictate the response you get. Having a rough framework for your research is essential (Category 49). While your goals

ABOVE *A tooth and a piece of turquoise pottery, both found in Dunster*

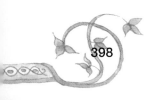

Child waiting to go on a dig at Dunster

are likely to evolve as the project gathers momentum and new information comes to light, it will help to have a clear idea of what your objectives are early on. This will help considerably when it comes to stage 2 of your project goals (Category 50).

Organise a group creative thinking session to figure out the kind of questions you'd like answered. How do we identify the oldest building? How do we find the earliest part of the village? What is the oldest object ever discovered locally? Questions such as these make a good basis for discussion. Collate a list and establish which of them you can answer with you own resources. The typical village has a wonderful mix of skills and interests to draw upon, so make sure you fully harness this resource. You are also probably going to have to prioritise what are the most important questions to answer.

THINGS TO DO

- Organise a group session to establish your goals and the key questions you want answered.
- Identify strengths and skills in the team that are best suited to answering specific questions.
- Visit our website for a suggested list of links and resources.
- Before visiting an archive, find out as much as you can in advance and come armed with a plan.
- Don't forget to make use of one of your biggest resources – the Dig Village community! Reach out to fellow enthusiasts across our social media channels, pick their brains, and share your own insights.

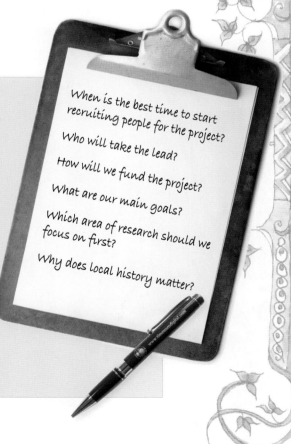

When is the best time to start recruiting people for the project?

Who will take the lead?

How will we fund the project?

What are our main goals?

Which area of research should we focus on first?

Why does local history matter?

An aerial view of Dunster Castle looking towards the Tithe Barn and church

VII.
Outreach & Presentation

This final part of the book addresses outreach strategy and the presentation of findings in greater detail. There's no point getting stuck into research if it can't be shared with a wider audience. Likewise, if you are conducting active fieldwork, you'll need to be able to present your results both in a responsible manner to professionals and in an accessible format for the general public. But engaging the community shouldn't just be left to the conclusion of the project. Outreach is a continuous process that you'll need to consider from the very start of your journey onwards.

59 OUTREACH

The real joy of making discoveries is sharing them with others. As Mick once said, "More than any other aspect, the community needs to be carried with the project." Alongside his books and articles, Mick produced a number of small pamphlets, which are an invaluable guide for local groups. His Avon Local History and Archaeology booklet from 2012 is an excellent example. Many of the activities you might organise during the project, like field walking, test pit digging and pot washing, are brilliant ways of including local groups. As we note in Category 61, working with school children is especially important in engaging and enthusing the next generation about the past. The final step is bringing together all your findings in an accessible and exciting way.

Villagers pot washing following a dig in Dunster

ABOVE *Dunster's residents have been invaluable throughout Dig Village's time in the town*

Sharing with the community

Learning about the history of your area is a fun and worthwhile pastime. But don't keep it all to yourself! You might be surprised at just how many people will be interested to hear about your research, both from the professional world and the wider public. This category provides ideas for reaching out to the local community. Presenting your findings to professionals and academics requires a very different approach (see Category 65).

Sharing information with others is not just a great opportunity for them to learn more about their community. It may help to inspire new projects, encourage others to undertake research, and build community spirit through a greater collective understanding of the area.

Outreach Ideas

There are various ways to reach out to the public, and bear in mind that different activities will attract different audiences. Some people will enjoy an evening talk in the village hall, followed by drinks and nibbles. Those with young families may prefer an informal open morning, with displays to view and activities to keep the children entertained. A 'drop in' at the local pub or church coffee morning will also help to spread the word. You could arrange presentations to other local groups, putting out a press release summarising the 'exciting bits'.

In Dunster, Dig Village organised a community event in the Tithe Barn. The night included a few fun archaeological presentations and some historical stories told by a professional storyteller.

When to begin your outreach?

Outreach starts from Day One! These days, one of the best tools we have for directly approaching individuals is social media. If you're not too familiar with it, find someone who is and bring them on board! Category 48 provides more tips for assembling your team. Create an email newsletter that locals can subscribe to, and keep them regularly informed of developments.

Having engaged the community throughout the project, you'll already have a captive audience for presenting your findings. But don't let the momentum fade as the project reaches its conclusion. The hope is that Dig Village is simply the start of an ongoing journey, laying the foundations for a continued interest in our heritage!

Continuation of the project

The project can continue with regular lectures, teaching sessions, pottery organising and finds surgeries, where residents bring finds from their back gardens to be identified by experts. Why not organise a stall at the village fete or fair? Write an article for your local magazine, or publish it online. It's also a good idea to create a shorter, easily accessible version of your final report (Category 65), with a greater focus on the findings and interpretation sections. As always, include as many pictures as you can.

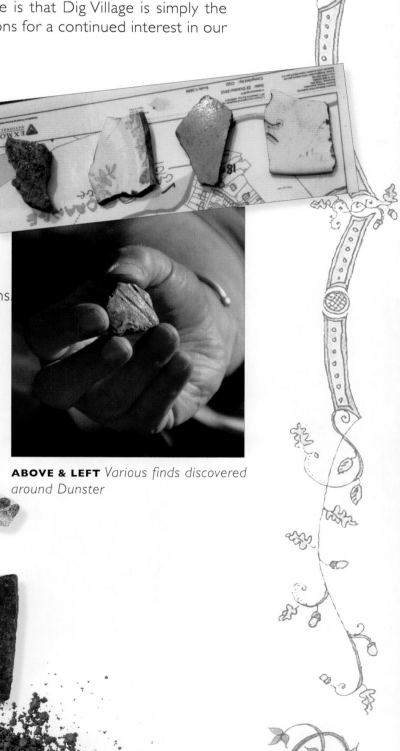

ABOVE & LEFT *Various finds discovered around Dunster*

Promoting accessibility

Archaeology is not just a subject that stays within the realm of professionals and academics, so it's really important that your project is available to anyone who is interested, in a language and form that is accessible.

Many of the ideas we've suggested, such as producing a timeline, creating a reconstruction, researching myths and legends and identifying heroes and villains will bring real colour to the project, highlighting just how exciting history can be. Any activities you can organise that involve direct participation will be likely to get the best response. Invite the community to be part of an experience, not simply spectators. For children, this might include dressing up in period costume, performing scenes from historic plays or playing games once enjoyed at Medieval fairs.

Collaborating with the local museum, or setting one up where it doesn't already exist, is another fantastic way to enhance your public outreach. Finding a permanent home for your discoveries would be a fitting tribute to all the hard work you've carried out (Category 63).

BELOW *Find ways to engage the public with your project, like events that involve re-enactment in period costume*

Dig Village

ABOVE *We hope that Dig Village will become a community of likeminded enthusiasts across the country and further afield who share their insights with one another*

The wider Dig Village community

Of course, as well as your local community, there will be people from other villages who are conducting similar research. This is where the Dig Village online community comes into its own. By regularly updating your timeline with your latest finds (Category 62) and keeping us informed of discoveries on our social media channels, you'll be extending your outreach on a global level. You could set up a 'exchange programme' with Dig Village enthusiasts from other parts of the country – or the world! Give presentations to each other, swap your local experts for the day, and share insights on the areas of research you've focused on. The possibilities really are endless!

THINGS TO DO

- From the start of the project, bring the community on board. Don't wait until the research is complete to reach out to the public.
- Bear in mind that different activities will appeal to different groups, so adapt your approach accordingly.
- Use our social media channels to share your discoveries with the wider world, perhaps setting up an 'exchange programme' with other enthusiasts to share insights and expertise.

RIGHT *A musket ball found in Dunster*

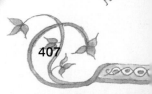

60 LIAISON WITH ARCHAEOLOGISTS & OTHER PROFESSIONALS

At the start of the Dunster project, we spent a lot of time liaising with the archaeologists from the Exmoor National Park and researching the evidence available to us from the Historic Environment Record. These contacts have proved to be invaluable as the project progressed. Making contact with the key local archaeologists will be vital to your project's success. There will usually be a county archaeologist based in a department at 'County Hall' or its equivalent. Many counties have also set up records offices and heritage research centres, where you can ask for advice and contacts.

From the beginning, it's important to let your local county archaeologist know about the research you intend to do. The county archaeologist is usually based at the local council offices within the Historic Environment Record (HER) and is a very useful person to get onside. They will be able to advise on research already undertaken, and show you how to access relevant information at the

Exmoor National Park, Somerset

HER (Category 21). They may also share interesting insights and ideas for particular areas of research.

If you are lucky enough to live near a National Park (such as Dartmoor, the Lake District or Snowdonia) you'll find it valuable to contact the park's archaeologist. Like HERs, National Parks hold archaeological records about the area. The National Trust has an archaeologist for various areas around Britain and again they may be able to provide useful pointers. In addition, the National Trust has its own HER, with more detailed information about specific sites.

Another extremely useful contact is the local authority conservation officer, as it's likely that they will be the most knowledgeable about the listed buildings and conservation areas in your region. They will also know which villages have a conservation area management plan.

ABOVE *Rob Hedge, Paul Blinkhorn, Dr Richard Parker, Dani Wootton and Stewart Ainsworth, working on Dig Village*

ABOVE *A tray of finds from a test pit*

The importance of expert evaluation

To the untrained eye, it can be very difficult to assess the significance of a small sherd of pottery. Is it a trivial fragment of a mass-produced IKEA mug or an ancient Roman wine jug? At Dunster, we have been lucky to enjoy the support of John Allan who has spent a lifetime distinguishing between minor variations in pottery, and such expertise is vital. We have also been fortunate having Dani Wootton to help identify our small finds, and she is one of Dig Village's experts who have helped to create this book.

Your local **Finds Liaison Officer (FLO)** is an expert in recording and identifying archaeological finds, particularly small metal objects and finds of a personal nature. If the FLO can't identify a find personally, they can usually recommend a specialist in that area. Even if you don't yet have any finds to report, introduce yourself and share your plans. Please bear in mind, however, that these people are extremely busy and will usually be drowning under the weight of enquiries from a range of sites!

BELOW *Experts Dani Wootton and John Allan looking at finds from a test pit at Dunster's Tithe Barn*

Recording finds

FLOs add information about finds onto the national Portable Antiquities Scheme database (*www.finds.org.uk*). As well as providing contact details for your local FLO, this is a fantastic resource for learning about existing finds discovered in your area (Category 21).

Perhaps several musket balls have been found in a field, for example, suggesting evidence of a Civil War skirmish or battle near your village. Search your village by entering its name into the database and see what has already been discovered.

Other heritage professionals such as an archivist at your local county records office can advise on helpful documents such as historic maps. It is also worth contacting your local museum curator (Category 63).

ABOVE *A Medieval thimble, found in North Yorkshire and recorded by the PAS*

Professional support

Getting the support of local professionals at the start of your adventure will help to focus your research, avoid fruitless tangents, and ensure the academic integrity of the project. As we note throughout the book, any intrusive field work must be carried out under strict supervision and with permission of the landowner. So, a professional archaeologist's advice is invaluable in promoting responsible archaeology and sharing insights from their experience of the area.

THINGS TO DO

- Make contact with your local county archaeologist and Finds Liaison Officer to introduce yourself and keep them in the loop with your wider plans. TIP: Remember that every find must be reported to the FLO, to ensure it is correctly identified and recorded.
- Search the Portable Antiquities Scheme database for existing finds in your area.
- Contact other professionals, such as the local record office, local authority conservation officer (for advice on listed buildings and conservation areas), the museum curator and librarian. TIP: They will be useful people to have aboard your steering group (Category 48)

LEFT *A piece of clay pipe and a sherd of pottery, both found during digs at Dunster*

61 LIAISON WITH SCHOOLS

It's essential to engage the next generation in archaeology and history, and getting your local school involved is a fantastic way to do this. On a recent test pit dig in Dunster, we were delighted to be joined by a group of school children with their parents, grandparents and guardians. Their enthusiasm and excitement was incredibly encouraging! One of my early memories of Mick is of him captivating a group of school children at Ribchester as he described the importance of some small finds. He noted how even the smallest, unglamorous find

School children getting involved in a dig in Dunster

ABOVE *School children from former generations*
BELOW RIGHT *An ivory toothbrush, perhaps similar to the one discovered by Mick*

can tell us something about the past. Despite being on a Roman site, we had discovered a Victorian ivory toothbrush from later occupation! Mick spoke in a fascinating way about where that ivory might have come from, what it said about personal hygiene and how a simple object like this can reveal a great deal. For many children, the process of discovering any find from the past can be thrilling and lead into a wider understanding of local history and archaeology. We've been lucky at Dunster to have a school that is keen and engaged with the project.

Engaging children

The current curriculum for primary school children encourages engagement with local history. There is also a growing appetite for projects that span multiple subject areas at once. Study of history can often be expanded to include other subjects like maths, science and geography, adding further context to the children's studies.

ABOVE *Dunster First School*

There are a number of simple ways for school children to learn more about their village or town. The possibilities really are endless. They could, for instance, start by studying local street names, as we have done, to see what this might reveal about their historic origins. Equally, it can be a fun task to search for popular local surnames associated with trades, such as Miller, Baker, Hooper and Fletcher.

Hands-on activities that bring the sights, sounds and smells of the past to life are a wonderful way to get youngsters engaged. This might mean playing traditional games, singing historic songs, dressing up in period costume, or even preparing meals that would have been popular in centuries gone by.

Learning about history helps to fuel the imagination

114

ABOVE *Time Team looking for a Tudor palace in Northwood Preparatory School's playing field*

ABOVE *A close-up of Dunster's tithe map where the school is now located*

Many historic maps are now readily available online, and these make a great starting point for discussing an area's history and later development. Looking at a map from the eighteenth century, you may be able to show that the site where the school is now situated was once a farmer's field or in the grounds of an ancient manor house. Indeed, in Series 20 of Time Team, we visited the site of Northwood, a grand palace once said to rival Hampton Court. Today it's home to a school playing field!

Another place to begin is by looking at the history of the school itself. Even if the current building is modern, it may have replaced another smaller Victorian school that still stands somewhere in the village.

The search for people's ancestors can lead children on an amazing journey into the past. With ever more people taking an interest in their family histories, there are now many local societies, with resources available for projects involving the younger members of the community.

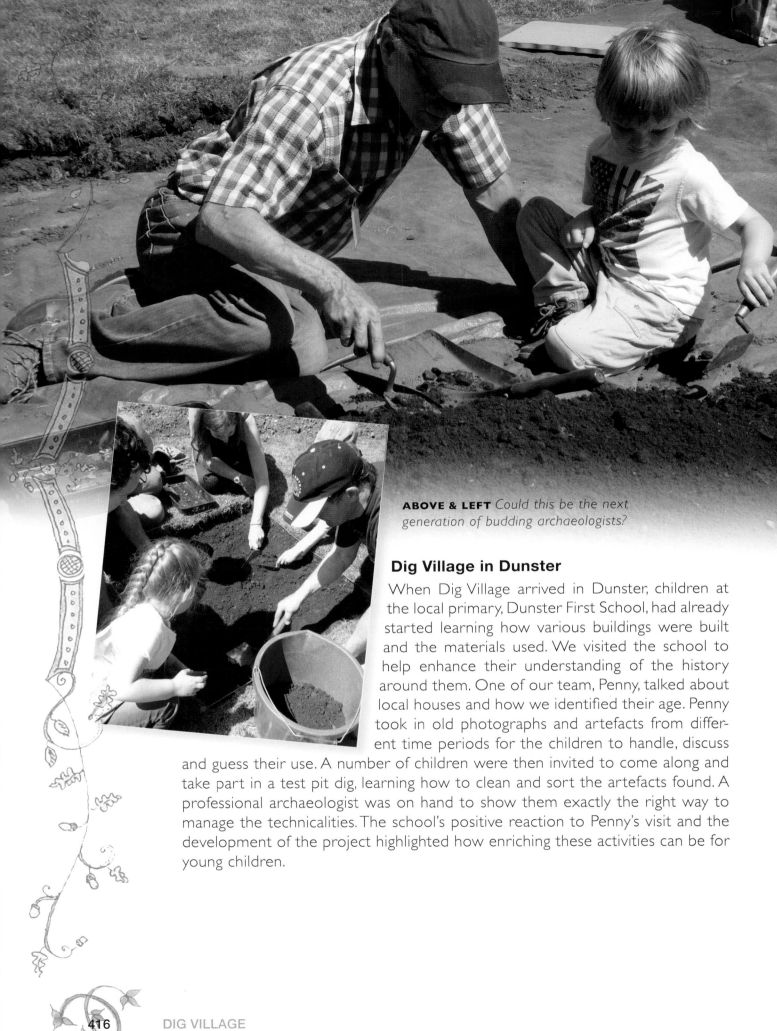

ABOVE & LEFT *Could this be the next generation of budding archaeologists?*

Dig Village in Dunster

When Dig Village arrived in Dunster, children at the local primary, Dunster First School, had already started learning how various buildings were built and the materials used. We visited the school to help enhance their understanding of the history around them. One of our team, Penny, talked about local houses and how we identified their age. Penny took in old photographs and artefacts from different time periods for the children to handle, discuss and guess their use. A number of children were then invited to come along and take part in a test pit dig, learning how to clean and sort the artefacts found. A professional archaeologist was on hand to show them exactly the right way to manage the technicalities. The school's positive reaction to Penny's visit and the development of the project highlighted how enriching these activities can be for young children.

Working with local organisations

While the Dig Village team sadly can't visit every community, as much as we'd love to, you may be able to organise similar experiences with local archaeologists or historians. Often museums have an educational outreach programme, so it's worth speaking to the curator about ways to work together.

ABOVE *Time Team presents an award to a YAC member at the British Museum*

What's more, any children who express a further interest can be pointed towards the Young Archaeologists' Club (YAC). This wonderful organisation, which we are proud to support, has many branches around the country, helping children to engage in national projects and providing invaluable experience of archaeology. The Historical Association is another fantastic resource for all levels of education.

Important considerations

When trying to engage younger people in the community, ask yourself what you are trying to achieve. Do you simply wish to spark their interest and engage with different age groups within the community, or are you looking to create a lasting legacy for the future? Will your activities be coordinated through a local school or more generally as part of the whole community? When interacting with children, it's essential that you are aware of the surrounding rules and regulations, such as risk assessments, safe-guarding and DBS checks.

If you would like the local school to be part of your project, make an appointment to visit the head to discuss ideas, always remembering that teachers have a heavy workload and can't always respond immediately. Who knows, you might even unearth tomorrow's young Indiana Jones or Lara Croft!

THINGS TO DO

- Contact the headteachers of your local schools to see how you might be able to work together on educational projects.
- Don't forget to be aware of administrative and safe-guarding issues, including risk assessments and DBS checks.
- There are many ways to engage children with local history. Many of the activities in this book can be adapted for younger members of the community.
- Visit the Historical Association's website for ideas, resources and information on teaching history at all levels, from primary to university: *www.history.org.uk*
- Young members of the community might wish to join the wonderful Young Archaeologists' Club: *www.yac-uk.org*

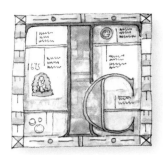

62 TIMELINE & CHRONOLOGY

Many years ago, we produced a book, 'The Time Team Guide to What Happened When', which attempted to lay out a timeline of most of the key events in British History. Having an approximate idea of what happened when provides an essential context within which to place the notable buildings, events and people of your village. As you begin to make discoveries about your village or town, it's very useful to see where in history they can be placed. What else was going on at the time elsewhere in the country? To take an example, you might know that your

BELOW *An abstract from Time Team's 'What Happened When' time wheel*

church font dates to 1278. You can then find out which king or queen was on the throne at that time, which important battles or wars were being fought and other national or global historic events.

Types of timelines

Timelines come in all shapes and formats. You may remember the classic wooden rulers often for sale in museum giftshops, listing the nation's kings and queens in order of reign. Timelines also crop up as mugs, posters, playing cards and in various other novel forms. It's always useful to have a timeline attached to an object that's easily visible as a handy reference.

Timelines come in a broad range of scales, from the events of a single day, or an entire life, from the history of a village, to the story of a complete historic period. Perhaps the Bayeux Tapestry could be considered an early form of a timeline. It depicts a series of events, in chronological order from left to right and has a unique visual and artistic style that helps to distinguish each notable piece of action.

ABOVE *Even mugs can make good timelines!*

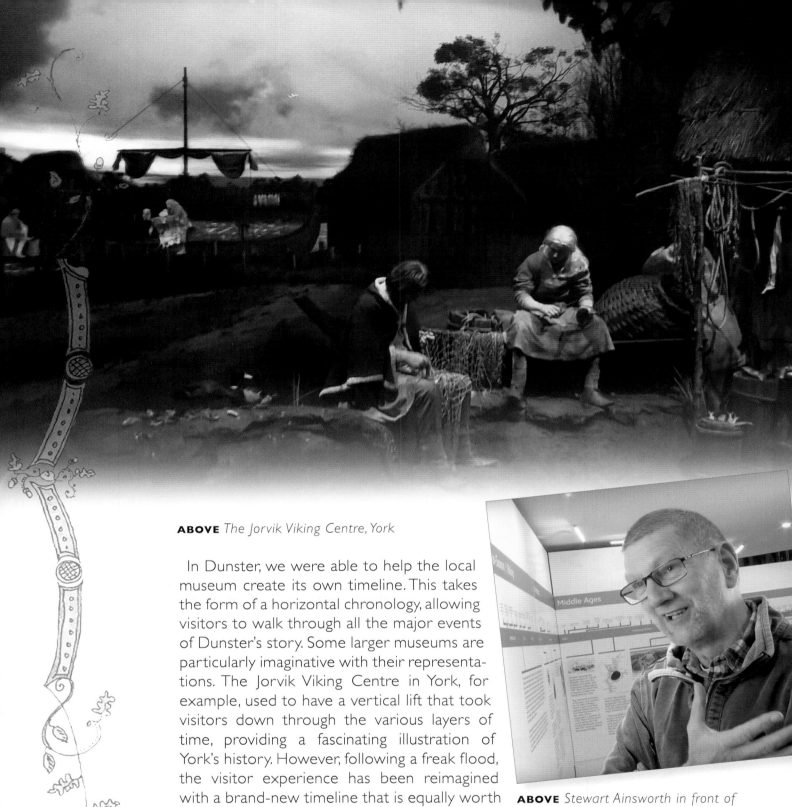

In Dunster, we were able to help the local museum create its own timeline. This takes the form of a horizontal chronology, allowing visitors to walk through all the major events of Dunster's story. Some larger museums are particularly imaginative with their representations. The Jorvik Viking Centre in York, for example, used to have a vertical lift that took visitors down through the various layers of time, providing a fascinating illustration of York's history. However, following a freak flood, the visitor experience has been reimagined with a brand-new timeline that is equally worth a visit.

You too can create your very own timeline and a physical representation would make a fantastic addition to your local museum, or as a display board in the local school, church or village hall (Category 63).

ABOVE *Stewart Ainsworth in front of the new timeline at Dunster Museum*

Virtual timelines

You can easily create a virtual timeline, using a range of software packages and online tools. Our favourite of these is 'Tiki-Toki' – a wonderful tool that produces very visual chronologies of events, both on a local and wider scale, and presents them in 3D! We heartily recommend that you set up your own timeline on Tiki-Toki.

Using Tiki-Toki, we have created a universal Dig Village timeline of 25 key periods or events in British history. It was a huge challenge narrowing it down, but we selected some of the core dates likely to have had the biggest impact on village life across the nation.

We have also produced an extended timeline, providing further context via other key dates throughout history. Links to these can be found on the official Dig Village website.

It's an extremely useful thing for each village to get a sense of its own chronology and a fantastic way of helping bring the past back to life in an accessible, visually enticing format.

ABOVE *Visitors enjoying Dunster Museum's timeline*

LEFT & BELOW
A timeline of Dunster's history, created by Exmoor National Park using the online tool, Tiki-Toki

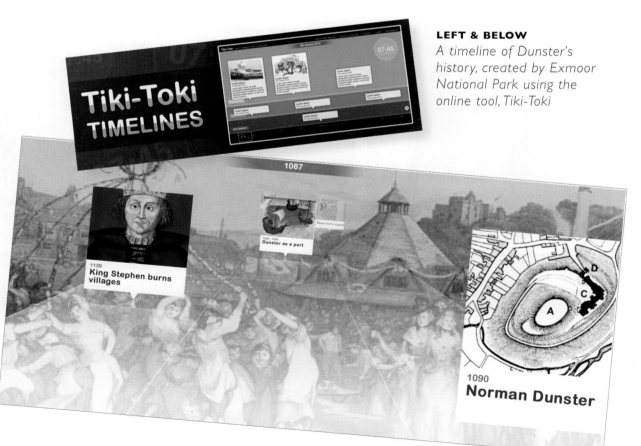

Populating your timeline

Once registered, you can upload the key events and finds that illustrate your village's settlement story onto your timeline. You might, for example, start with a reference in the Domesday Book, or the earliest known record of human activity in the area, such as prehistoric flint discoveries. As you make new discoveries and populate Tiki-Toki, the narrative will gradually take shape. Have you discovered when the church was first built or later extended? Did a battle or skirmish occur nearby on a particular date? Did the village suffer bomb damage during World War II? Not only will you build a picture of your community's history, you'll also see how these events fit within the wider narrative.

As we have noted, one of the most important things a timeline does is to create context for events. You might be aware of a big increase in deaths in your village around 1350. However, being able to link this to an outbreak of plague (which was spreading across the country at the time) can be invaluable and set your local event in a national context. While Medieval village life was relative-

ABOVE *Tiki-Toki is a wonderful tool for visually representing key events and discoveries on a timeline*
BEHIND *Rural life at the medieval village, ink drawing*

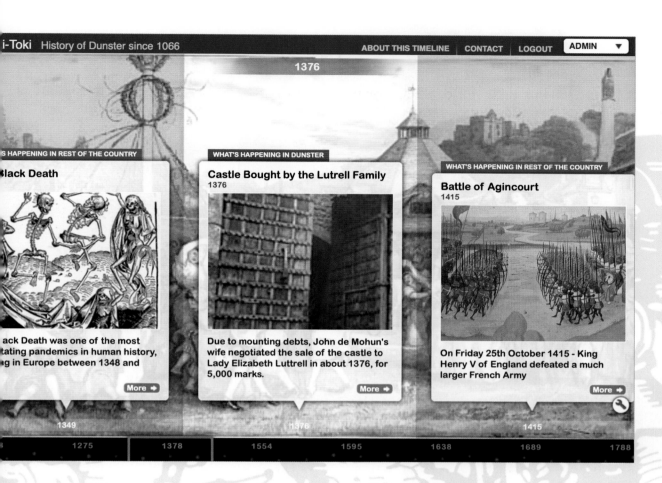

1376

WHAT'S HAPPENING IN REST OF THE COUNTRY

Black Death

Black Death was one of the most devastating pandemics in human history, ...ng in Europe between 1348 and

More ➡

WHAT'S HAPPENING IN DUNSTER

Castle Bought by the Lutrell Family
1376

Due to mounting debts, John de Mohun's wife negotiated the sale of the castle to Lady Elizabeth Luttrell in about 1376, for 5,000 marks.

More ➡

WHAT'S HAPPENING IN REST OF THE COUNTRY

Battle of Agincourt
1415

On Friday 25th October 1415 - King Henry V of England defeated a much larger French Army

More ➡

1349   1376   1415

1275   1378   1554   1595   1638   1689   1788

...ly self-contained, the impact of major events, both across the British Isles and further afield, would have been felt to some degree. Civil war, a king's desire to increase taxes to fund a French campaign, or a sudden increase in the wool prices paid on continental markets, could all have a notable impact on local livelihoods. A timeline provides an indispensable overview, enabling greater perspective of what might have seemed an isolated local event on the wider stage of history.

THINGS TO DO

- Research existing timelines in various formats, to get a feel for how they contextualise events in history.
- Look at the Dig Village 25 key dates and extended timeline on the Dig Village website.
- Set up your own virtual village timeline and begin to populate it with your findings.
- Consider creating a physical timeline as part of your local museum display. (See Category 64 on reconstructions)

Tiki-Toki
TIMELINES

63 MUSEUMS & FINDS

Showing people what you have found is an important aspect of any community project. It encourages them to be more aware of the archaeological past beneath their feet and can provide a real stimulus to their interest. It also makes those involved work out the important elements of the story they are trying to tell. In the case of Dunster, we were able to help the local museum reimagine the space that had previously been given over to one of the country's largest displays of dolls. In the past, a visit to the museum was always accompanied by the rather uncomfortable sensation of being watched by hundreds of tiny eyeballs! Now, half of the space is being used to display a timeline of Dunster's history.

ABOVE *The collection of dolls previously displayed at the museum*
LEFT *Dunster Museum*

ABOVE *Finding a permanent home for your discoveries will be a fitting tribute to your project, perhaps inspiring the next generation*
LEFT *Historic photographs provide a wonderful snapshot of village life in times gone by*

Museums and history

Museums play a fundamental role in making history accessible. Seeing physical objects with your own eyes helps to develop a greater understanding of the people who created them. Likewise, the rise in interactive exhibits allows visitors to step back in time and immerse themselves in an era. If there is a museum local to you, then a visit would be a fantastic way to kickstart your own Dig Village project. It's a great place to experience a snapshot of local life in times gone by, and perhaps also find likeminded individuals to join the team. Very often there are small regional museums, some run by volunteers, holding local finds and archives that will be of great interest to your research.

Many museums hold a wide range of artefacts and records, aside from physical finds. As well as vintage photographs and curiosities, they might include audio and film recordings. It can be enlightening listening to elderly farmers talking about life on the farms decades ago, and you might discover useful historic footage of ancient buildings now lost under modern developments.

ABOVE *Villagers gathering for a talk given by Tim Taylor about Dunster's Dig Village project*

Dunster Dig Village Team return to share their latest findings

Saturday 26th January

1pm - 4pm
Dunster Museum
Open drop in - meet the building and dendro-dating experts with a talk and presentation at 2pm.
Wine and nibbles

7.30pm til late
Room above Rohan Shop
Open Dig Village Event.
Wine and nibbles (first drink free)

ABOVE *A leaflet advertising a community 'findings' talk by our Dig Village team*

Community outreach

Some museums offer a community outreach service. Experts might be able to visit your group to give a talk, perhaps on a specific area or time period. These can be extremely useful evenings, opening up discussion among interested villagers. Bear in mind that many museums struggle with funding, so there may be a nominal charge for some services. However, it might be that your own Dig Village project develops a more formalised partnership with the local museum, pooling resources towards a shared goal.

As we've noted, Dunster has its own small community museum and members have formed the Dunster Museum Archaeological Group. The group continues to investigate the history of the town using some of the methods developed with Dig Village.

Starting a museum

If there isn't a museum nearby, perhaps your Dig Village project might form the basis of one. Every collection starts somewhere! What better culmination of your group's collective efforts than to collate the finds and research into an exhibition for everyone to experience? Your own display may begin with a simple online photo gallery, or a small display case of finds in the church or village hall.

However, there is an important step you will have to take first. You'll need to decide which objects and other evidence would be most effective in telling the story of your village or small town.

Imagine that the shelves of the Time Team archives are crammed with endless boxes of finds and other objects. From these we should be able to select the key finds that enable us to tell the story of a particular site. This is what you must do.

ABOVE *Various finds from Dunster during the Dig Village project*

We have come a long way from the idea that a museum or exhibition of archaeological evidence has to centre upon a sea of glass-fronted cases! Virtual museums, digital displays and pop-up exhibitions are just a few creative ways of giving people access to your discoveries. Ultimately, the more interactive, immersive and accessible you can make the presentation of your findings, the more likely that people will engage with them!

THINGS TO DO

- Visit your local museum at the beginning of your Dig Village venture. You might end up forging an important partnership of collaboration in the months ahead.
- Bring the experts along on your journey. If the museum has an outreach service, perhaps an expert might give a talk to your group.
- As the project progresses, the local museum might be a natural base for collating your finds. If there isn't a museum nearby, perhaps you could start one, beginning with a simple display cabinet of discoveries in a local community space.

ABOVE & RIGHT *Pottery sherds found in Dunster*

64 WHAT IT LOOKED LIKE
(RECONSTRUCTIONS)

Most visitors to a Time Team site couldn't wait to see the reconstructions of what it looked like in the past, courtesy of our brilliant historic illustrator Victor Ambrus. Seeing your village or town as it may once have looked – in say the Roman or Medieval period – can be a highly satisfactory conclusion to a long spell of research. Once completed, such illustrations can form the backdrop to museum displays or act as a focus for work by local school children. Dunster was lucky enough to have a reconstruction of what the town looked like on a busy market day in the Medieval period (see page 434).

Visualising the past

What does a reconstruction do? It can bring the past to life, and it can serve as a place to record the information you have found about each period. A good set of reconstructions will record the changes in architecture, transport, technology and even fashion. If you know that your village was active at a certain period in history, it's possible to look at reconstructions of buildings of that era from

RIGHT *Victor Ambrus's reconstruction of a Medieval market*

other sources as a reference. Victor's book, *Drawing on History,* is an excellent place to start. These drawings, taken from many historical periods, are the result of Mick, Victor, and some of the specialists on the team, working together to create a picture that summarises all the evidence we were able to find on the dig. The whole process was helped by Victor's encyclopedic knowledge of what buildings looked like in the past.

429

Living models

Wonderful as they can be, reconstructions don't have to be limited to static images. They can take the form of an entire living model, illustrating what the buildings and village life were like in a certain period. A good example is St Fagans National Museum of History in South Wales, where many periods have been reconstructed. It is one of Europe's leading open-air museums and features a working farm with re-enactors in historical costume.

One of the useful things about these kinds of museums is that they research the technology and lifestyle from a given period. In doing so, they shed light on the technical reality of how these activities worked and the sort of archaeological traces they may have left behind. When Time Team worked in America at St Mary's City, we were able to experience the living museum of the village, which featured re-enactors dressed in Medieval clothing and speaking in a version of Tudor English. As well as St Fagans, there are several living museums across Britain, such as the Black Country Museum near Birmingham, which demonstrates the living and working conditions of those who lived there during the Industrial Revolution.

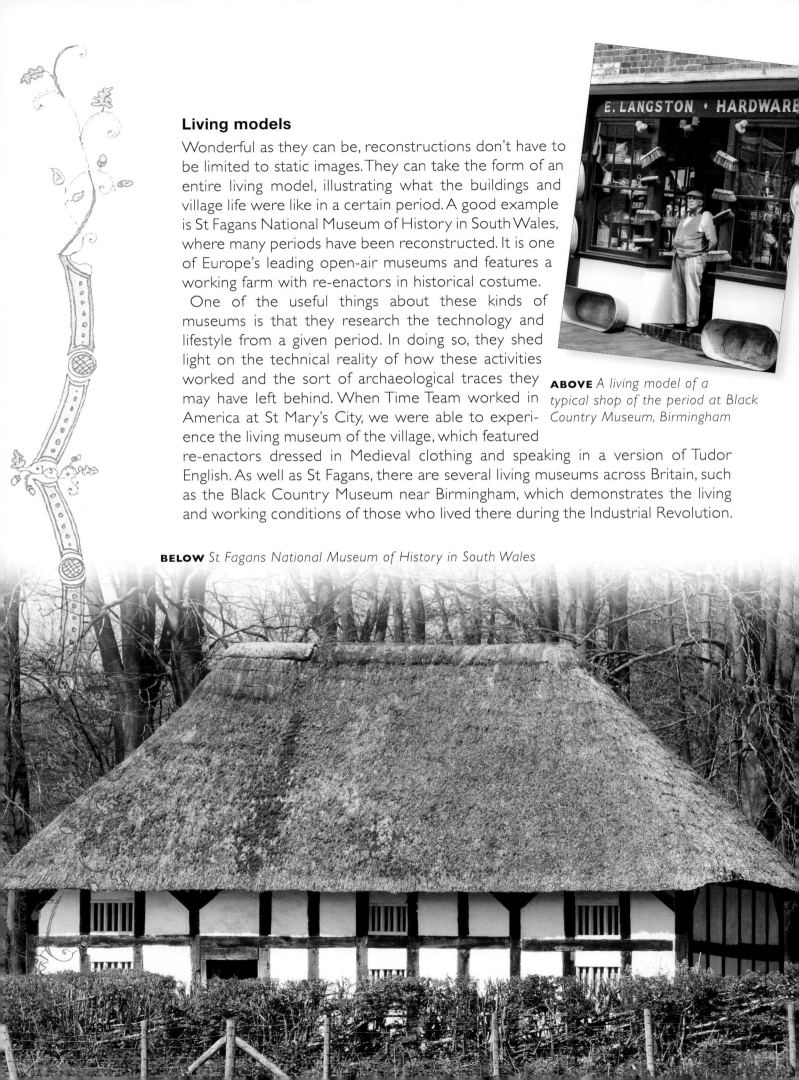

ABOVE *A living model of a typical shop of the period at Black Country Museum, Birmingham*

BELOW *St Fagans National Museum of History in South Wales*

ABOVE *Weald and Downland Living Museum in West Sussex*

The Weald and Downland Living Museum in West Sussex has saved many old buildings and reconstructed them on one site, allowing you to see how they were used over a period of 950 years. The Jorvik Viking Centre in York provides a wonderful immersive participation of the past, including the chance to experience the smells of a Medieval cesspit! Particularly for school children, this kind of experience can be very memorable and a great way of introducing the past. Given enough smoke from a fire or misty weather conditions, there can be moments when a partly glimpsed vision of re-enactors can create quite a frisson!

Ladies dressed as peasants

Celebrating Dunster's history

Dunster has a thriving community that's keen to keep its history alive. The castle, the working mill and the recently restored Tithe Barn are three of the locations that celebrate its history. Preservation of ancient buildings plays a role in allowing us some sense of how these places might have looked in the past.

A pig sty at Weald and Downland

Planning your own reconstructions

So how do you decide which specific period to reconstruct? A good place to start is to identify the key phases or developments in your location's history. You should already have a fairly good idea of this if you have attempted to create a timeline of your village's history (Category 62). Are there any historic highlights – in terms of

A reconstruction of a smithy

trade, industry or prosperity — that particularly stand out on the timeline?

Obviously, the objective of a reconstruction is to provide a window into another world. So, for contrast, you might want to choose a period when the village looked radically different — perhaps, for instance, before Second World War bomb damage destroyed the ancient street plan, or a Medieval square made way for a new phase of development.

You could focus on one specific building and show its development through time. In the case of Dunster, we have a good set of reconstruction pictures that show how the castle developed from the Norman period to the eighteenth century. As the church may be one of the oldest buildings in your village, it might be worthwhile to do a set of reconstructions showing its evolution. This could document the changes to various chapels, vestries, towers or spires over the centuries.

Other approaches to reconstruction

Reconstructions can take various forms, and you might be in a position to utilise more sophisticated 3D modelling software, such as that used by architects, animators and gaming developers, for a virtual simulation. Perhaps the local college, university or a technology start-up company has the skills and

BELOW *Time Team's illustrator Victor Ambrus at work*

facilities to help create a village reconstruction. You might be able to persuade students to incorporate the project into their own studies. (See Categories 59 and 61 for details on community and educational outreach.)

In 2000, we produced a Time Team book, *Timechester*, which illustrates the development of an imaginary town, using Victor's reconstructions to show what it looked like at various phases, from prehistory to the present day. The popularity of these sorts of books, including *A Street Through Time* by Steve Noon and Dr Anne Millard and *A Farm Through Time* by Eric Thomas and Angela Wilkes, illustrates the pleasure people get from visualising the past.

THINGS TO DO

- Collate a mood board (either physical or virtual) bringing together visual sources to inform your reconstruction, from old maps to photographs.
- Identify a specific period or several phases that you would like to reconstruct. TIP: For greatest effect and insight, choose a period that was notably different to today, or when the community was 'thriving' through a specific trade.
- Decide the form that your reconstruction will take: illustration, 3D modelling, physical reconstruction, or a combination of these. TIP: Look for people in the community with the skills to help realise your reconstruction, whether artists, modellists, architects, gaming developers or local tradespeople. The local college or university may have students who can help.

RIGHT *Historic postcards of Dunster*

An artist's impression of Dunster market in the Medieval period

434

459

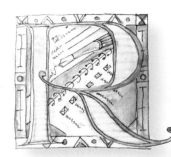

65 REPORT WRITING

Mick used to say that whenever you do archaeology, it's important to write a report about the work you have done. He used to describe this as not 'messing up' your nest! Put another way, by the great archaeologist, W.G. Hoskins, doing archaeology without writing it up is little better than vandalism. On Time Team, report writing was a vital element of each dig that didn't often appear on camera. Obviously, it may not seem that exciting from a viewer's perspective, but every archaeologist has a duty to approach and record a dig appropriately. Once the cameras have left, the archaeological report lasts forever, so it's important the process has been documented correctly.

During the dig, something crucial may have been discovered that could provide the vital clue to a question that other archaeologists are trying to solve. By communicating what has been done, it allows other academics to benefit from your work. In the past, reports would be published in local learned journals, but the tendency now is for everything to be published online.

Unearthing Dunster

Time Team Digital Dig Village
Project 2012-2018

Stewart Ainsworth, John Allan, Richard Parker and Tim Taylor
With contributions by Jimmy Adcock, Mark Haworth, Penny Lock,
Andy Moir and Rachel Swallow

Professional integrity

As well as reaching out to the wider community, it's essential that you engage with the professional archaeology world too. By the report writing stage, you'll no doubt have already forged strong links with some professional archaeologists. Perhaps you've managed to enlist one or two into your steering group (Category 48). Particularly with intrusive research, it's crucial to seek professional help in the initial gathering and recording of information to ensure its academic integrity (Category 53). In the case of Dunster, we asked our pottery expert, John Allan, and our buildings expert, Richard Parker, to contribute pieces to our interim report. This sort of expert input needs to be budgeted for.

Creating a report

Remember, clarity is key! Begin with a title page, listing the name of your village, its exact location, the names of the report's authors and the date. List your acknowledgements on the following page, including the names of all the landowners of your sites, volunteers and anyone who helped during your project. Next, provide a brief introduction to your village, which only needs to be a page or so long. Include a concise outline of the historical evidence you've looked at, and any previous archaeological work conducted on the site.

ABOVE *Buildings expert, Richard Parker (top), and pottery expert, John Allan*
OPPOSITE & BELOW *Dig Village's official 'Unearthing Dunster' report*

ABOVE *Extracts from our 'Unearthing Dunster' report*

Follow this with a section about your aims, objectives and limitations. Now you can present any map work, elevation drawings, floor plans, landscape surveys, genealogical work or information on relevant buildings collated or carried out for the project. Any additional research, such as dendrochronology should be included. The dating of buildings can provide revealing insights on how the area has expanded and developed over time.

In Dunster, for example, our property in Church Street (Category 3) was dendro-dated to around 1307, a fantastically early date. That said, the oldest property we have found in the town so far is the west wing of the old priory, dated to around 1286.

Test pits

If after careful consideration, and with professional archaeological support, you have undertaken some test pits, these will need to be recorded in a very specific manner (see Category 53 and the *Unearthing Dunster* report). Include a map outlining all the locations of your test pits and their individual numbers. This will make it much clearer for readers to follow. Explain why you chose to dig in the specific locations. Perhaps, for example, it was due to an interesting feature in the ground, or because an historic map suggested there was once a building in that location.

Next, explain your methodology, or approach to conducting the archaeology. For example, you may have dug down in ten-centimetre spits. Note whether you dug a single test pit at a time, or had many people working across the village at once. Record who dug each test pit, the equipment used and any problems encountered. Then describe exactly what you found especially interesting, detailing anything examined by a local expert and the information relevant to these finds.

Remember to make note of any features that couldn't be excavated. These might include ditches or walls and should all be listed on your context sheets. Even if you came across a modern feature, such as an electricity cable, you should mention it, as features like this can affect any further interpretations of the site. Discuss how you washed your finds once the excavation was completed and state how they will be preserved and stored or displayed.

Interpretation

Finally, write up your own interpretations of the site. These can be simple, for example, "the excavation of Anglo-Saxon material suggests the existence of a settlement in the area during that period", or much more complex. Just remember, that your interpretation should be backed up by the advice of professional archaeologists. By including your own analysis, you may spark discussion with other archaeologists, historians or interested members of the community.

ABOVE *A sherd of pottery*
BELOW *Pot washing in Dunster*

Don't be put off by the idea that this final report has to be too formal in your choice of language. You are aiming for clarity rather than an artificial archaeological scientific tone. A useful model for what your report should look like is Time Team's Dig Village interim report, *Unearthing Dunster* (2019). Many more examples can be found online with a quick Google search.

If you need any additional help, ask your local county archaeologist to view a draft. The report should be submitted in a timely fashion while everything is still fresh in your memory. While digital publishing is becoming more prevalent, there's still great value in producing a printed version of the report.

ABOVE *A selection of archaeological reports*

Existing reports based on previous research can be invaluable resources for today's archaeologists

Writing up details will be the basis for good reports in the future

As archaeology is basically a 'destructive' science, it's essential that your report is as thorough as possible. You are now creating a record that may be used by future generations to reinterpret the site. It might be that further assessments are needed. So, note down everything, even if it doesn't seem important at the time. Finally, it's always a good idea to include lots of pictures with your report, such as the trenches, artefacts and surrounding landscape.

Producing a report may seem a daunting prospect, but equally there's a wonderful sense of achievement in bringing together all the hard work and research you have completed, perhaps over a period of years, into one handy document. In creating this report you will be adding to the wider understanding of your village or town for future generations. What a fantastic accomplishment!

THINGS TO DO

- Read through some existing examples of reports, to get a feel for how they are presented. TIP: Visit the Dig Village website for links to existing reports.
- Write up your report, providing as much detail as possible, including any details that may seem irrelevant.
- If you need more guidance, speak to your local archaeologist and share ideas on our social media channels.

ABOVE A selection of finds from Dunster

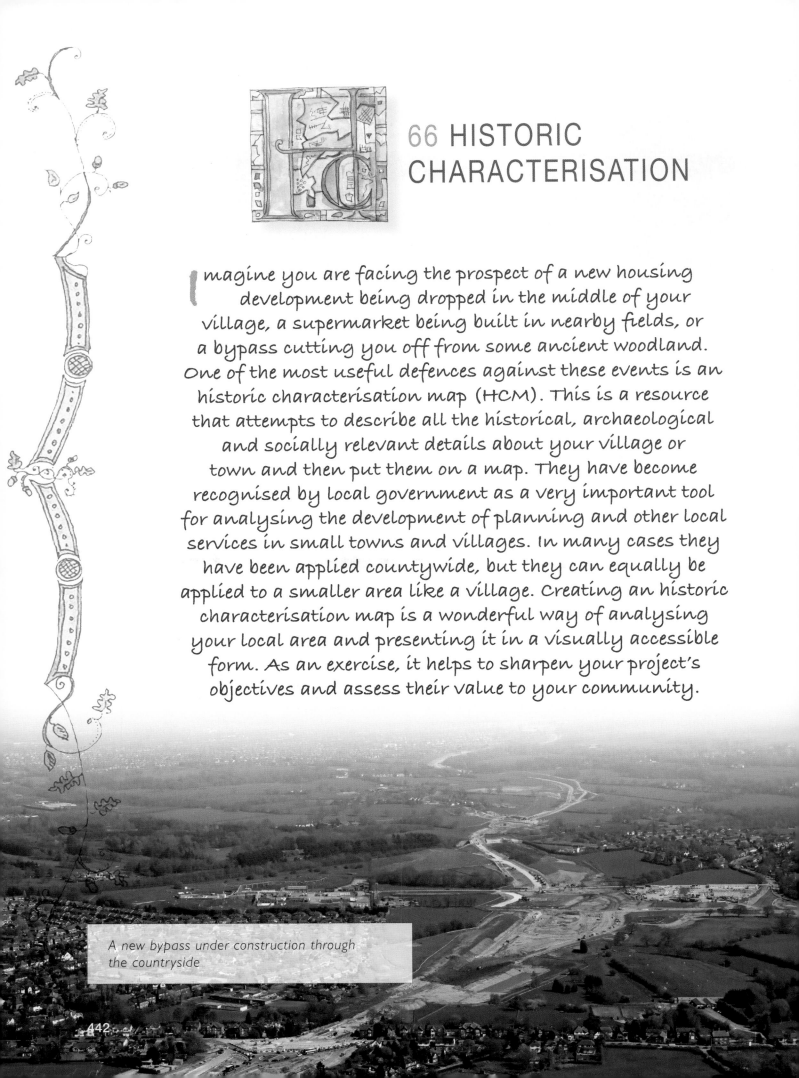

66 HISTORIC CHARACTERISATION

Imagine you are facing the prospect of a new housing development being dropped in the middle of your village, a supermarket being built in nearby fields, or a bypass cutting you off from some ancient woodland. One of the most useful defences against these events is an historic characterisation map (HCM). This is a resource that attempts to describe all the historical, archaeological and socially relevant details about your village or town and then put them on a map. They have become recognised by local government as a very important tool for analysing the development of planning and other local services in small towns and villages. In many cases they have been applied countywide, but they can equally be applied to a smaller area like a village. Creating an historic characterisation map is a wonderful way of analysing your local area and presenting it in a visually accessible form. As an exercise, it helps to sharpen your project's objectives and assess their value to your community.

A new bypass under construction through the countryside

442

ABOVE *Redruth, once a prosperous Cornish mining town, has been the subject of an historic characterisation*

If there's one key theme running throughout this book it's that every settlement develops, fluctuates, and sometimes even declines over the course of time. Many historic high streets are a mixture of architectural styles and materials, representing the various periods in which individual structures were built. An historic characterisation map helps to record the current state of play before it is lost under new development or architectural 'improvements'.

The mid-twentieth century saw many beautiful older buildings of merit pulled down to make way for modern counterparts that are often unsympathetic to the historic vernacular architecture. Fortunately, many 'grander' buildings have been saved from the wrecking ball over the years. Yet the fate of surrounding structures, such as stable blocks or workshops, has not always been so positive. Perhaps once viewed as peripheral or inconsequential, they might today be regarded as important aspects of a community's narrative that should be preserved in some form.

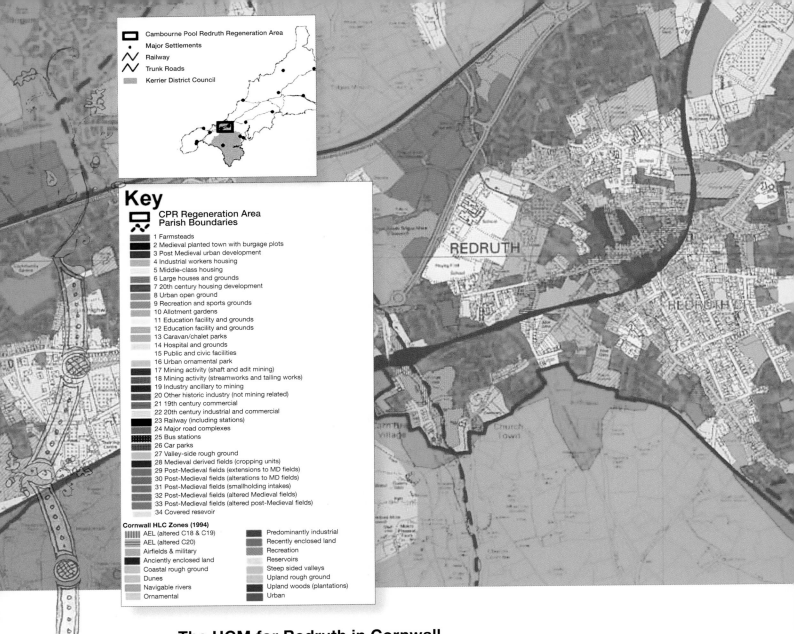

Key

CPR Regeneration Area
Parish Boundaries

1 Farmsteads
2 Medieval planted town with burgage plots
3 Post Medieval urban development
4 Industrial workers housing
5 Middle-class housing
6 Large houses and grounds
7 20th century housing development
8 Urban open ground
9 Recreation and sports grounds
10 Allotment gardens
11 Education facility and grounds
12 Education facility and grounds
13 Caravan/chalet parks
14 Hospital and grounds
15 Public and civic facilities
16 Urban ornamental park
17 Mining activity (shaft and adit mining)
18 Mining activity (streamworks and tailing works)
19 Industry ancillary to mining
20 Other historic industry (not mining related)
21 19th century commercial
22 20th century industrial and commercial
23 Railway (including stations)
24 Major road complexes
25 Bus stations
26 Car parks
27 Valley-side rough ground
28 Medieval derived fields (cropping units)
29 Post-Medieval fields (extensions to MD fields)
30 Post-Medieval fields (alterations to MD fields)
31 Post-Medieval fields (smallholding intakes)
32 Post-Medieval fields (altered Medieval fields)
33 Post-Medieval fields (altered post-Medieval fields)
34 Covered resevoir

Cornwall HLC Zones (1994)

AEL (altered C18 & C19)
AEL (altered C20)
Airfields & military
Anciently enclosed land
Coastal rough ground
Dunes
Navigable rivers
Ornamental

Predominantly industrial
Recently enclosed land
Recreation
Reservoirs
Steep sided valleys
Upland rough ground
Upland woods (plantations)
Urban

The HCM for Redruth in Cornwall

To illustrate how HCMs work, let's take a closer look at an example produced on behalf of Cornwall Council for the town of Redruth, in the former mining heartland of Cornwall. What you see above is the HCM of Redruth and its surrounding area. The map indicates important areas of historic interest and other key elements of the landscape like woodland, playing fields and former mining areas. The key highlights the various elements and, if you imagine applying this list to your village or town, you will be able to see how much detailed information can be located on a single map.

Zooming in to a specific area can be particularly revealing. If we look at the town centre, for example, we can see how the original burgage plots have been designated in a dark maroon colour. This would be an important piece of information in any future planning application.

RIGHT *The centre of Redruth, with its burgage plots marked in dark maroon*

444   DIG VILLAGE

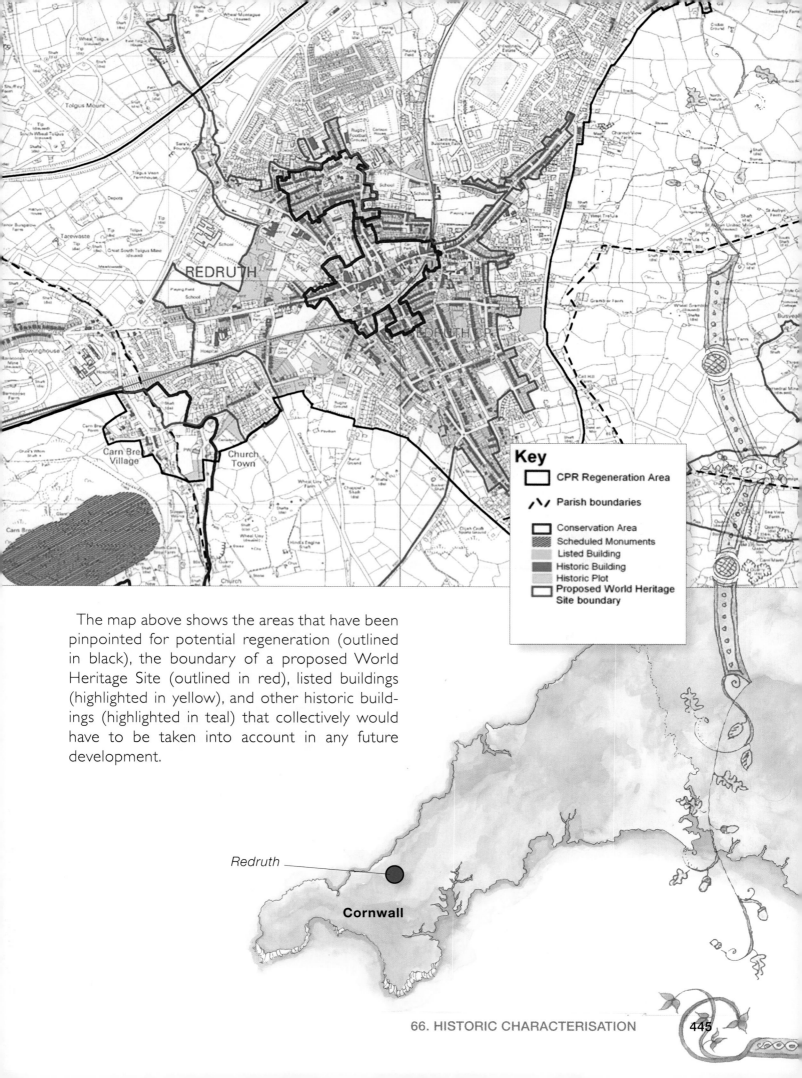

The map above shows the areas that have been pinpointed for potential regeneration (outlined in black), the boundary of a proposed World Heritage Site (outlined in red), listed buildings (highlighted in yellow), and other historic buildings (highlighted in teal) that collectively would have to be taken into account in any future development.

Key

- CPR Regeneration Area
- Parish boundaries
- Conservation Area
- Scheduled Monuments
- Listed Building
- Historic Building
- Historic Plot
- Proposed World Heritage Site boundary

Redruth

Cornwall

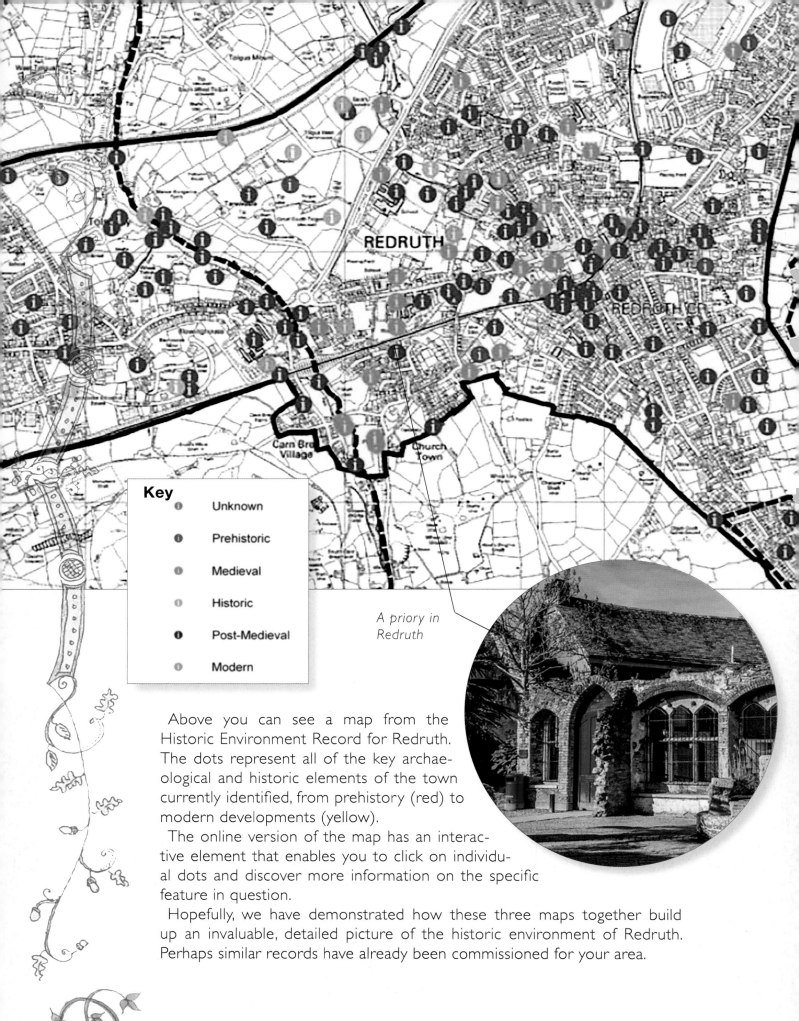

Key

◐	Unknown
◐	Prehistoric
◐	Medieval
◐	Historic
◐	Post-Medieval
◐	Modern

A priory in Redruth

Above you can see a map from the Historic Environment Record for Redruth. The dots represent all of the key archaeological and historic elements of the town currently identified, from prehistory (red) to modern developments (yellow).

The online version of the map has an interactive element that enables you to click on individual dots and discover more information on the specific feature in question.

Hopefully, we have demonstrated how these three maps together build up an invaluable, detailed picture of the historic environment of Redruth. Perhaps similar records have already been commissioned for your area.

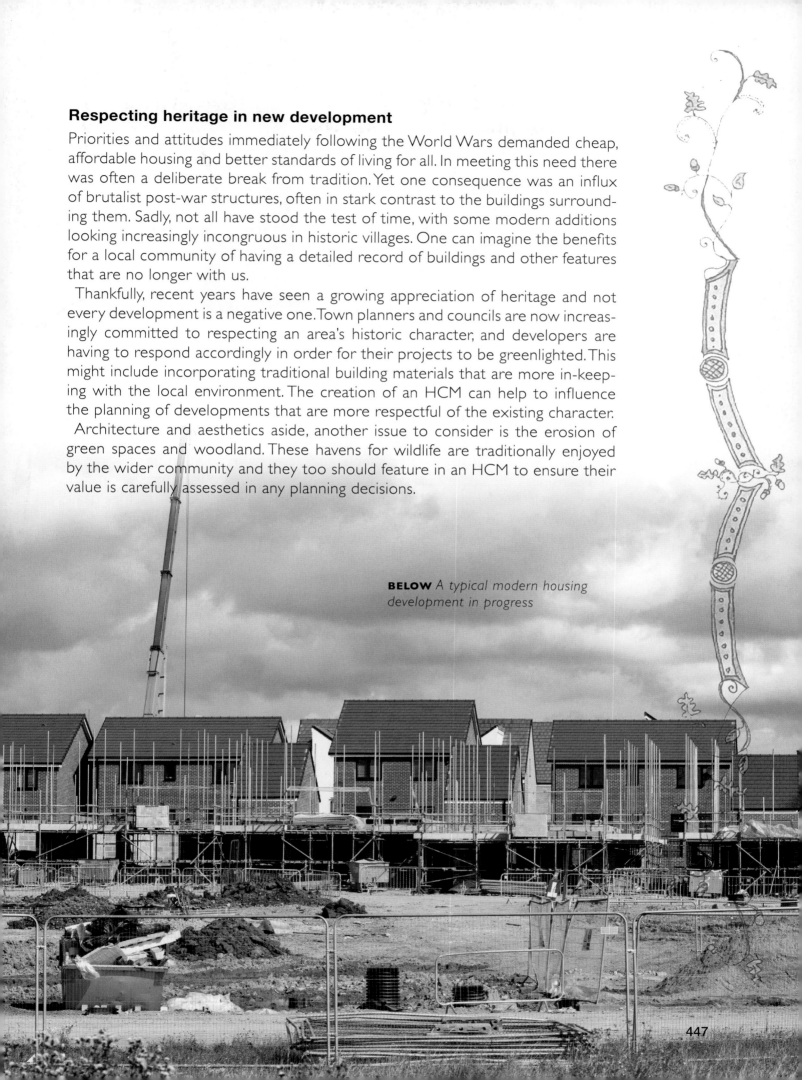

Respecting heritage in new development

Priorities and attitudes immediately following the World Wars demanded cheap, affordable housing and better standards of living for all. In meeting this need there was often a deliberate break from tradition. Yet one consequence was an influx of brutalist post-war structures, often in stark contrast to the buildings surrounding them. Sadly, not all have stood the test of time, with some modern additions looking increasingly incongruous in historic villages. One can imagine the benefits for a local community of having a detailed record of buildings and other features that are no longer with us.

Thankfully, recent years have seen a growing appreciation of heritage and not every development is a negative one. Town planners and councils are now increasingly committed to respecting an area's historic character, and developers are having to respond accordingly in order for their projects to be greenlighted. This might include incorporating traditional building materials that are more in-keeping with the local environment. The creation of an HCM can help to influence the planning of developments that are more respectful of the existing character.

Architecture and aesthetics aside, another issue to consider is the erosion of green spaces and woodland. These havens for wildlife are traditionally enjoyed by the wider community and they too should feature in an HCM to ensure their value is carefully assessed in any planning decisions.

BELOW *A typical modern housing development in progress*

447

Putting together an historic characterisation brings all of the above concerns into a single, easily accessible document that has huge value in planning decisions. There are examples of potentially damaging developments being blocked as a result of the production of an historic characterisation.

Often, when an undesirable development is imminent, it's already too late to develop your own HCM. In many cases it ends in a battle between a developer and a village. One current case rather sadly involves East Coker, the Somerset village immortilised in T.S. Eliot's poetry, whose residents are objecting to a new set of buildings on the edge of the village.

ABOVE *A stunning floor mosaic from a Roman villa discovered in East Coker in the eighteenth century*

Creating your own historic characterisation

As we have highlighted with the example of Redruth, an historic characterisation takes a wide range of components into account. In addition to buildings, it also considers the wider tapestry of field systems, hedgerows, borders – in fact, everything in the landscape, whether manmade or natural, which together paint a picture of its heritage. In many ways, an historic characterisation is the culmination of all the hard work, research and investigations carried out during your Dig Village project.

Paraphrasing the great W.G. Hoskins, it's essentially a recognition that the landscape itself is an invaluable historical record, which reveals the development of settlements over a great period of time. The Council for British Archaeology notes that its function is to find the 'essential qualities and character' beneath the surface. The methodology is employed by various bodies, sometimes using different terminology, but Historic Landscape Characterisation (HLC) is the name used by English Heritage.

The results can be presented in a range of forms, and often they are collated into a formal, detailed report (Category 65). However, as we emphasise in the report writing section, the more accessible you can make your findings, the more

ABOVE & OPPOSITE *The existing character and heritage of a village should be considered carefully with every new development*

effective they will be. It is also worth considering the specific audience you are reaching out to, in order to tailor the approach appropriately. The great benefit of a map is that it's a very visual medium, providing an immediate snapshot of a situation that's easy to understand.

It's always a good idea to look at existing examples to get a sense of the various formats and settle upon an approach that will hopefully achieve the greatest impact. We have provided links to some historic characterisation maps and reports on the Dig Village website.

Regeneration is a wonderful thing and well thought out developments are essential in helping to rejuvenate communities. News reports often remind us of the need for new housing in many parts of the country. Historic characterisation reports are a fantastic tool in helping to ensure that the existing heritage and character of the area are carefully considered in the process.

THINGS TO DO

• Visit the Dig Village website for links to existing historic characterisation maps and reports.

INDEX

Page numbers in italic denote photographs or illustrations.

F

fallow years 52, 219
farming 50–9, 218–23, 225, 252–3, 304–5
fast days 295
fencing 280
fennel 67
festivals 312–7
feudal system 52, 139, 190–5, 197
field names *54*, 80, 183
field walking 356
Field Work in Local History (Hoskins) 80, 116, 118
fields 50–9
  see also crop rotation; feudal system; field names;
  field walking; harvesting; ploughing
Finds Liaison Officers 410–1
'first lieutenants' 332
First World War (World War I) 71, 244–5, 246,
  247, 387
fish 295–6, *297*, 298
Fishbourne Roman Palace 182
FitzAlan, John (Earl of Arundel) *200*, 201
Fleming, Alexander 289
flint 175
floor tiles 93, *96*, *112*, 182
folklore 174, 327
fonts *94*, 95, 97
food 292–9
football 281, 282, 283, 315
footpaths 19, 318–23
fords 18–9
Forest of Arden 76
Forest of Dean 74
forest fruits 74
forests 70–7
forts 100–5, 154
  see also hillforts
Fosse Way 15, *181*
fossils 38, 40
Fountains Abbey 109, *202–3*
Fowey 269
fracking 40
Frankpledge 251–2
Frith Common *151*
Frye, Thomas 304
fulling mills 122, 226
functional place names 83
fundraising 345, 348–53
fundraising goals 351
furlongs 51

G

Gainsthorpe *368*, 369
Gallox Bridge 14, 19, 157, *340*
Gallox Street (Park Street) 49, *80*, 81
gaols 254
'gate', place name 153
Gater, John 104
Geevor Tin Mine 267
geld 136
genealogical research 375–83
General Register Office 377
geographical features, place names 83, 84
geology 36–41
Giant's Causeway 393
ginnels *323*
Glastonbury Abbey 47, 108, 340
glebe terriers 131
Glenfinnan Viaduct *226*
gold rush 238
golf 282
Google (Google Earth) 8, 84, 158, 162, 174, 199,
  372, 398
Goose Fair 307, 310
Goram the Giant *392*, 393
Goring Gap *41*, 42
Gough Map 16
Grabbist House 290
Grand Union Canal *229*
granite 36, 37, *39*, 40, 41
graphic timelines 418–9
graveyard surveys 93, 98, 290, 381–2
great halls 185
'green man' myth ('Green Man' celebrations) 76
Grim Reaper *196*, 201
Grimes Graves *170*, 267
Grimspound *174*, *178*
gristmills 122, 226
ground elder 67
group organisation 332–7, 344
gryphaea *38*
guilds 263–4, *265*, 316, 380
gunpowder mills 122
Guy Fawkes Night 312

H

haggis 302
Hailles shrine 18
Hall, Teresa 363
Halloween 312
'ham', place name 80
Hambledon 282
Hands Well 46
Hangar Close *80*, 82, 83
Harbours 242, 269
Harding, Phil xi, 70, *240*
Harold Godwinson (Harold II) 102, 136, *191*
harvest feasts (festivals) 59, 313
harvesting 50–2, 140, 220, 222
Hastings Castle 102
hatch marks 356
Hawkesly, Thomas 49
hawking 326
hawthorn tree 64, 67
hay ricks 53
hazel trees 63, 76

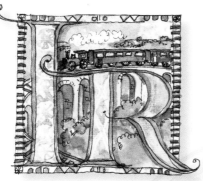

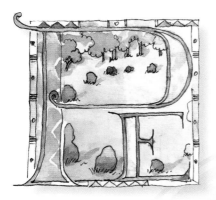

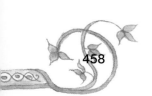

ACKNOWLEDGMENTS

This book would not have been possible without the help and support of many people. It has been a big enterprise and we hope those mentioned below will think that all their efforts have been worth it! We have, as always, tried to ensure that there are no errors or omissions. However, if anything has slipped through the net, that will be the sole responsibility of the author!

We would like to thank the following:

For contributing additional material, research and development: Dani Wootton, Penny Lock, Jo Howell, and Dr Richard Parker.
For editorial support and project organisation: Felix Rowe and Frances Barr.

For overall advice and guidance during the Dunster project: Professor Stewart Ainsworth, Rob Hedge for archaeological input, John Allan and Paul Blinkhorn our pottery experts and Dr Andy Moir our dendrochronologist.

The Time Team Academy, who not only supported the Time Team Dig Village project in Dunster over several years but have acted as readers of the text, giving us feedback and advice: Mark Haworth, Sheila Bliss, Ivan Clowsley, Simon Fuller, Stuart Coomber and Penny Lock.

The readers groups, including Nick Johnson MBE, Lynn Robertson, Roxana Howkins, Susan Ford, Liz Palmer and Fern Wetzel-Harrison for her support and encouragement throughout the project.

Throughout the Dunster project we have been grateful for the support of Rob Wilson North and his staff at Exmoor National Park.

Finally, to all our good friends in Dunster who made us welcome from the start, including Biddy and Martin Bale, Carole and Arthur Ell, Phil and Ruth Webber, Jane Forshaw, Jeni Fender and the Dunster Museum Archaeology Group, Grahame Lamacraft and the late Martin Harborne.

BIBLIOGRAPHY

Ainsworth, Stuart; Allan, John; Parker, Richard and Taylor, Tim, *Unearthing Dunster: Time Team Digital Dig Village Project 2012-2018* (2019, Time Team Digital)

Ambrus, Victor, *Drawing on Archaeology: Bringing History to Life* (2006, Tempus)

Aston, Michael, *Shapwick & Winscombe: Contrasting Communities in the Somerset Landscape* (2012, Avon Local History & Archaeology)

Aston, Michael and Leech, Roger, *Historic Towns in Somerset* (1977, Littlehampton)

Aston, Mick and Gerrard, Chris, *Interpreting the English Village: Landscape and Community at Shapwick, Somerset* (2013, Windgather Press)

Aston, Mick, *Interpreting the Landscape: Landscape Archaeology in Local Studies* (1985, B.T. Batsford)

Beresford, Maurice and Hurst, John G., *Deserted Medieval Villages* (1971, Lutterworth)

Beresford, Maurice, *The Lost Villages of England* (1983, Sutton)

Bradley, Simon, *Churches: An Architectural Guide – Pevsner Architectural Guides* (2018, Yale)

Chaucer, Geoffrey, *The Canterbury Tales* (2003, Penguin Classics)

Coulton, G.G., *The Medieval Village* (1989, Dover Publications)

Cram, David and Forgeng, Jeffrey L., *Francis Willughby's Book of Games: A Seventeenth-Century Treatise on Sports, Games and Pastimes* (2017, Routledge)

Crawford, O.G.S., *Air Photography for Archaeologists* (1929, His Majesty's Stationery Office)

Gies, Joseph and Gies, Frances, *Life in a Medieval Village* (2016, Harper Perennial)

Greeves, Tom, *The Archaeology of Dartmoor from the Air* (1985, Devon Books)

Hall, Linda, *Period House Fixtures and Fittings 1300-1900* (2005, Countryside Books)

Henderson, Charles and Coates, Henry, *Old Cornish Bridges and Streams* (1928, Simpkin Marshall)

Hoskins, W.G., *Field Work in Local History* (1967, Faber & Faber)

Hoskins, W.G., *Local History in England* (1984, Routledge)

Jackson, Sophie, *Churchill's Unexpected Guests: Prisoners of War in Britain in World War II* (2010, The History Press)

Lyte, Henry Churchill Maxwell, *A History of Dunster and of the Families of Mohun & Luttrell* (1909, Andesite)

Mills, A.D., *Dictionary of British Place Names* (2011, OUP)

Morris, Marc, *Castle: A History of the Buildings That Shaped Medieval Britain* (2012, Windmill)

Mortimer, Ian, *The Time Traveller's Guide to Medieval England: A Handbook for Visitors to the Fourteenth Century* (2009, Vintage)

Muir, Richard, *The Lost Villages of Britain* (1985, Book Club Associates)

Newberry, Christopher and Graham, Rodney, *Look Up! Winchester* (2010, Look Up! Publications)

Noon, Steve and Millard, Anne, *A Street Through Time: A 12,000-Year Walk Through History* (2012, DK)

Padel, O.J., *Cornish Place-Name Elements* (1985, English Place-Name Society)

Quinn, Robin, *Hitler's Last Army: German POWs in Britain* (2015, The History Press)

Reaney and Wilson, *Oxford Dictionary of English Surnames* 3rd Edition (2005, OUP)

Renfrew, Colin, *Archaeology & Language: The Puzzle of Indo-European Origins* (1998, Pimlico)

Robertson, A.J., *Anglo-Saxon Charters* (2009, CUP)

Robinson, Stephen, *Somerset Place Names* (1992, The Dovecote Press)

Sharpe, Geoffrey R., *Historic English Churches: A Guide to Their Construction, Design and Features* (2011, IB Taurus)

Taylor, Tim; Lewis, Carenza; Harding, Phil and Aston, Mick, *Time Team's Timechester: A Companion to Archaeology* (2000, Channel 4)

Taylor, Tim, *The Time Team Guide to What Happened When* (2006, Channel 4)

Thomas, Eric and Wilkes, Angela, *A Farm Through Time: The History of a Farm From Medieval Times to the Present Day* (2002, DK)

Yorke, Trevor, *How To Date Buildings: An Easy Reference Guide* (2017, Countryside Books)

CREDITS

The publishers would like to thank the owners of all third party material reproduced in this book. Every effort has been made to contact the relevant rightsholders where applicable. However, if any acknowledgements have been inadvertently missed, please let the publishers know and we will be very happy to amend this in any future reprint or edition.

IMAGES

All new illustrations by Sara Nunan. Dunster drone images by Steve Shearn. Stock library images provided by Shutterstock, Alamy, Pexels and Pixabay. Ordnance Survey maps reproduced with kind permission of Ordnance Survey. With thanks to Victor and Glenys Ambrus for use of Victor's timeless illustrations: p286, p386, p389, p429. Unless where stated below, all other images and photographs from the Time Team / Dig Village archive.

p15 (FM) Ellis Martin, Ordnance Survey 1919 (map cover); p15 (FM) Ordnance Survey 1902 (map cover); p16 (FM) Ellis Martin, Ordnance Survey 1918 (map cover); p4 Ellis Martin, Ordnance Survey 1936 (map cover); p5 Ellis Martin, Ordnance Survey 1933 (map cover); p12 Ellis Martin, Ordnance Survey 1922 (map cover); p16 Bodleian Libraries (Gough Map); p17 Gillian Spraggs, 2007, www.outlawsandhighwaymen.com (highwayman); p18 John Lord, CC BY-SA 2.0 (Gallox Bridge); p23 Nilfanion CC BY-SA 3.0 (Dunster lodge); p24-25, 31 Richard Parker (abbey refectory); p45 Hchc2009, CC BY-SA 4.0 (Sulis); p46 Dennis Thorley, CC BY-SA 2.0 (Hands Well Tissington 2006); p47 Rbe2057, CC BY-SA 4.0 (Chalice Well); p49 Francois de Dijon (lavabo); p52 Nilfanion, CC BY-SA 3.0 (Dunster Tithe Barn); p55 Tony Atkin, CC BY-SA 2.0 (Dartmoor ruin); p73 British Library (Forest Charter); p76 Naturenet, CC BY-SA 3.0 (coppice stool); p90 Robert Willis, The Architectural History of Canterbury Cathedral, 1845 (cathedral plan); p99 Jonathan Wilkins, CC BY-SA 2.0 (St Peter's Church); p104 Virgil Master, Koninklijke Bibliotheek (Edward III); p105 Library of Congress (Rothesay Castle); p106 MortimerCat, CC BY-SA 3.0 (Cleeve Abbey); p110 The National Archives (Valor Ecclesiasticus); p112 Crown Copyright, A. Hamilton Thompson, Ministry of Works Official Guidebook 1952 (Netley Abbey); p113 I Quilley, 1814 (Kilburn Priory); p113 Andreas F. Borchert, CC BY-SA 3.0 (stonework); p116 Cothay Manor, CC BY-SA 2.0 (manor); p117 William R. Shepherd, Historical Atlas, 1923 (hypothetical Medieval manor); p121 Basher Eyre, CC BY-SA 2.0 (Dunster Mill wheel and exterior polaroid); p121 Ashley Dace, CC BY-SA 2.0 (Dunster Mill internal machinery); p122 Derek Harper, CC BY-SA 2.0 (powder mill); p123 Martin Bodman (waterwheel); p127 Stuart Shepherd, CC BY-SA 2.0 (Fornham); p129 Nikki Mahadevan, CC BY-SA 2.0 (St Margaret's Chapel); p130 J Thomas, CC BY-SA 2.0 (St Jude's); p130 Rept0n1x, CC BY-SA 3.0 (Christ Church); p137 Anna Powell-Smith, Professor John Palmer, George Slater and opendomesday.org, CC BY-SA (Open Domesday); p147 Andrew Gray, CC BY SA 2.0 (beating the bounds); p153 Kim Traynor from the 1690 Gordon of Rothiemay Map of Edinburgh; p154 Hel-hama, CC BY-SA 3.0 (Anglo-Saxon burhs map); p155 William Ashton (Caernarfon map); p160 Dr John Wells / West Lothian Archaeology / Archeoscan (aerial photo); p161 Keble College, Oxford (OGS Crawford); p161 Royal Air Force (RAF Wrexham); p162 J. Dassie, CC BY-SA 3.0 (aerial photo); p166 Portable Antiquities Scheme (PAS), Find ID: 662681. The PAS is a voluntary programme run by the United Kingdom government to record the increasing numbers of small finds of archaeological interest found by members of the public. The scheme started in 1997 and now covers most of England and Wales. Finds are published at https://finds.org.uk, CC BY SA 2.0 (Philip and Mary Tudor coin); p170 Michael Allen, CC BY-SA 2.0 (Arbor Low); p174 Vince Hogg, CC BY-SA 3.0 (Grimspound); p178 Herby, CC BY-SA 4.0 (Grimspound roundhouse); p178 Portable Antiquities Scheme (PAS), Find ID: 252312, CC BY-SA 2.0 (bead); p178 Dave Price, CC BY-SA 2.0 (Castell Mawr); p181 Dave Spicer, CC BY-SA 2.0 (Stane Street); p181 Stephen Jones, CC BY-SA 2.0 (Wroxeter baths); p182 Charlesdrakew (mosaic); p181 Immanuel Giel (model); p184-185 British Museum, CC BY-SA 4.0 (brooch); p185 Geni, CC BY-SA 4.0 (helmet); p188 Dave Price, CC BY-SA 2.0 (Castell Mawr); p200 Lampman, CC BY-SA 3.0 (tomb); p201 Jack1956, CC BY-SA 1.0 (inscription); p206 Jim Sweeney (Mottisfont cellarium); p206 Andrew Mathewson, CC BY-SA 2.0 (Mottisfont Abbey); p212 National Archives (death warrant); p215 British Library (illumination); p220 Queensland Museum, CC BY-SA 3.0 (bushel); p225 Pit-yacker, CC BY-SA 3.0 (Manchester mill); p227 Keith Pickering, CC BY-SA 3.0 (coalfields map); p228 Kelvin Davies, CC BY-SA 2.0 (Micheldever); p235 Jean Perry (Crumpsall); p236-237 State Library of New South Wales (Port Jackson); p237 Birmingham Museum and Art Gallery (emigrants); p239 Pcvjamaica, CC BY-SA 4.0 (Drakes Bay); p239 New York Public Library (Brewster Gardens); p240 Arthur Mee (map); p241 Rodw (Colston Tower); p242 Catherine Edwards, CC BY-SA 2.0 (Minehead); p243 Royal Navy (Empire Windrush); p246 Steve Rigg, CC BY-SA 2.0 (pill box); p251 Pinacoteca Vaticana (Purgatory); p256 Ethan Doyle White, CC BY-SA 4.0 (stocks); p259 Sotheby's (George Jeffreys); p263 Rijksmuseum (Rembrandt); p264 Geni, CC BY-SA 4.0 (Tanner's Brook); p264 Gift of Harry G. Friedman, 1956 (leather box); p273 David Lally, CC BY-SA 2.0 (Railway Inn); p278 Dominic Strange © www.misericords.co.uk, CC BY-SA 3.0 (carving); p287 Warja Lavater (apothecary); p289 National Library of Wales (diagram); p289 Burns Archive (bloodletting photo); p289 Anagoria, CC BY-SA 3.0 (bloodletting kit); p291 HTUK (hospital); p293 Lazinki Palace (painting); p298 Martin Bodman, CC BY-SA 2.0 (fish cellars); p302 Victorgrigas (t3xt), CC BY-SA 1.0 (powder horn); p303 Imperial War Museum (Carabiniers); p304 Lewis Clarke, CC By-SA 2.0 (Devon County Show); p308 National Museum in Warsaw (Beuckelaer); p311 Cmglee, CC BY-SA 4.0 (Wymondham); p314 Midnightblueowl, CC BY-SA 3.0 (wheel); p315 shakko, CC BY-SA 3.0 (entertainer); p317 Warwick University Real Ale Society, CC BY-SA 3.0 (cheese roller); p318 Oliver Dixon, CC BY-SA 2.0 (Pilgrim's Way); p319 Prioryman, CC BY-SA 4.0 (caliga); p322 Tony Atkin, CC BY-SA 2.0 (Saints' Way); p323 Alexander P Kapp, CC BY-SA 2.0 (ginnel); p328 Tedster007, CC-BY SA 4.0 (Lancelot Brown); p329 Bob Embleton, CC BY-SA 2.0 (pillow mound); p329 Hchc2009, CC BY-SA 4.0 (stag tile); p339 Nilfanion, CC BY-SA 3.0 (building); p342 Ellis Martin, Ordnance Survey 1932 (map cover); p342 Richard Parker (building drawing); p345 Ordnance Survey 1913 (Ireland map index); p346 Ken Grainger, CC BY-SA (Langport); p355 Nilfanion using Ordnance Survey OpenData, CC BY-SA 3.0 (map); p357 A Mitchell25, CC BY-SA 3.0 (barrow); p357 David Berry51 (henge); p357 Spoonfrog (hillfort); p357 Aloys5268, CC BY-SA 3.0 (boundary division); p357 Matt Neale, CC BY-SA 2.0 (ridges and furrows); p358 © Environment Agency copyright and/or database right 2015. All rights reserved. Contains public sector information licensed under the Open Government Licence v3.0 (LiDAR scan); p359 Ordnance Survey 1945 (map cover); p368 Richard Croft, CC BY-SA 2.0 (Gainsthorpe); p369 Derek Harper, CC BY-SA 2.0 (Nether Adber DMV); p373 Mick Aston (Hurst and Beresford); p373 Nilfanion, CC BY-SA 4.0 (Hound Tor); p375 Landesmuseum Wurttemberg (family tree); p376 Schwiki (St John's Church); p377 The Frick Collection (Cromwell); p381 Maurice Pullin, CC BY-SA 2.0 (Stinchcombe); p383 Fergusfish, CC0 1.0 (building); p384 Sarah Smith, CC BY-SA 2.0 (memorial); p386 Katy Walters, CC BY-SA 2.0 (Wymondham sign); p392 Bristol Icarus, CC BY-SA 4.0 (Goram); p392 Ptelea, CC BY-SA 4.0 (Eclipse Inn); p411 Portable Antiquities Scheme (PAS), Find ID: 662823, CC BY-SA 2.0 (thimble); p420 Chemical Engineer, CC BY-SA 4.0 (Yorvik); p431 National Museum Wales, CC BY-SA 3.0 (pig sty); p431 Breznay (smithy); p434 Exmoor National Park Authority, exmoor.gov.uk (Dunster reconstruction); p448 Rodw, CC BY-SA 3.0 (mosaic).

TIME TEAM DIGITAL LTD
Glebe House, Farringdon, Exeter, EX5 2HY
A division of Videotext Communications Ltd

Published 2019 by Time Team Digital

Text copyright © Tim Taylor 2019

Illustration copyright © Sara Nunan 2019 under exclusive
licence to Time Team Digital

The right of Tim Taylor to be identified as the author of
this work has been asserted in accordance with sections
77 and 78 of the Copyright, Designs and Patents Act 1988.

A catalogue record for this book is available from the
British Library.

ISBN 9781916278806

Typesets in Gill Sans, Times, Cardinal and Bradley Hand

Editor: Felix Rowe
Designer and illustrator: Sara Nunan
Production coordinator: Frances Barr
Indexer: Sarah Hilton

Printed in the EU by Print Trail – printtrail.com